INSTRUCTIONAL PATTERNS

INSTRUCTIONAL PATTERNS

Strategies for Maximizing Student Learning

Larry C. Holt
Marcella Kysilka
University of Central Florida

SAGE Publications
Thousand Oaks ▪ London ▪ New Delhi

For information:

Sage Publications, Inc.
2455 Teller Road
Thousand Oaks, California 91320
E-mail: order@sagepub.com

Sage Publications Ltd.
1 Oliver's Yard
55 City Road
London EC1Y 1SP
United Kingdom

Sage Publications India Pvt. Ltd.
B-42, Panchsheel Enclave
Post Box 4109
New Delhi 110 017 India

Printed in the United States of America

Library of Congress Cataloging-in-Publication Data

Holt, Larry C.
Instructional patterns : strategies for maximizing student learning / Larry C. Holt and Marcella Kysilka.
         p. cm.
Includes bibliographical references and index.
ISBN 0-7619-2824-3 (pbk.)
   1. Effective teaching. 2. Learning, Psychology of. I. Kysilka, Marcella L. II. Title.
LB1025.3.H65 2006
371.102—dc22

                                                    2005021099

This book is printed on acid-free paper.

06 07 08 09 10 9 8 7 6 5 4 3 2 1

Acquisitions Editor:	Diane McDaniel
Associate Editor:	Katja Werlich Fried
Editorial Assistants:	Erica Carroll, Marta Peimer
Production Editor:	Denise Santoyo
Permissions Editor:	Karen Wiley
Copy Editor:	Deborah Ring
Typesetter:	C&M Digitals (P) Ltd.
Indexer:	Pam Van Huss
Cover Designer:	Michelle Lee Kenny

Brief Table of Contents

Detailed Table of Contents

List of Tables, Exhibits, and Figures

Tables

Exhibits

Figures

Preface

INSTRUCTIONAL PATTERNS: STRATEGIES FOR MAXIMIZING STUDENT LEARNING

Effective instruction has many complex patterns. If you were a fly on the wall, peering in on the thousands of classrooms all over the world, you would find that the one constant, overriding dimension of any classroom is the existence of patterns. Patterns are present in the daily routines of the classroom. Patterns are a way of knowing, a way of organizing and classifying information, and a way of thinking and strategizing. In the classroom, the content is often formed by the pattern suggested in a textbook or by the teacher, who brings to the classroom his or her patterns of thinking about the content and how it needs to be presented to students. The students have developed their own thinking, organization, and learning patterns. The interactions among the teacher, students, and content are highly dependent on the teacher's ability to select instructional patterns that enhance the learning experience and match the needs of the students. As teachers make decisions about how to instruct, the appropriate pattern must be selected by considering how to maximize the potential for learning of each student.

ORGANIZATION OF THE TEXT

This book is divided into six parts representing various instructional patterns. These parts are explained here and illustrated in relation to the patterns that are influenced by the teacher, the student, and the organization of the content.

Learning Tenets are presented that emphasize instruction from the student's point of view. The Learning Tenets presented in Chapters 6–15 explain how to maximize students' potential for learning when using that instructional pattern.

Each of the six parts of this book categorizes a set of instructional patterns. Part I, "Factors That Influence All Instruction," covers learner exceptionalities and the historical, sociological, and psychological factors that influence all instruction. Part II, "Practical Issues of Instruction," discusses the pedagogy of lesson design, behavior management, and classroom assessment. Part III, "Teacher-Centered Patterns," represents instruction when the teacher is on center stage and includes direct instruction and mastery learning. Part IV, "Teacher–Student Interactive Patterns," reflects the instructional patterns of cooperative learning and role play, in which the student and

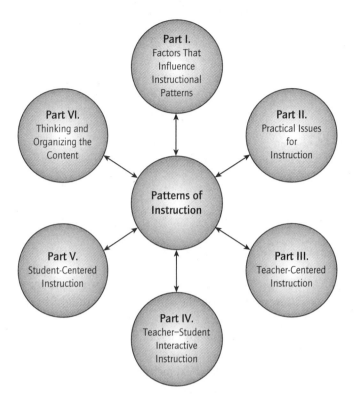

the teacher share ownership of the things to be learned. Part V, "Student-Centered Patterns," includes patterns that represent situations in which the learner is in control, nondirective learning, and self-taught instruction. Part VI, "Thinking and Organizing the Content," represents ways that content can be organized to promote critical thinking, such as thinking patterns, memorization, attaining concepts, and inquiry.

The figure shown here organizes this text graphically and depicts the way instructional patterns can be grouped when considering the influence of control by the teacher, the student, and the content to be learned.

Part I: Factors That Influence Instruction

Instructional patterns are influenced by the statement, "It depends. . . ." In turn, "It depends…" is influenced by the type of organization, the degree of interaction between students and teachers, and the factors that influence instruction. We begin our dialogue by helping you understand that instructional patterns are influenced by forces that shape our practice. Chapter 1 examines where we've been, what we know, and where we're going. This chapter addresses the evolution of teacher-effectiveness research and introduces the Learning Tenets that are repeated in each chapter.

Chapter 2 addresses differentiated instruction and learner demographics that influence choices of instructional patterns. Included are historical, sociological, and psychological factors that must be considered when working with diverse populations. Decisions about how to teach rest on the understanding that students are different—that what works for one student does not necessarily work for all students. The degree of instructional adjustment for diverse learners and the choice of appropriate instructional patterns for them are complex decisions and depend on many different perspectives.

Part II: Practical Issues of Instruction

Part II presents pedagogical information on levels of thinking, lesson plans, management, and assessment. The chapters in this section explain the science and pedagogy of instruction.

Chapter 3 examines unit and daily lesson planning, agencies that influence curriculum plans, Bloom's taxonomy, writing objectives, and methodology.

Chapter 4 is divided into two distinct parts that separate classroom management from discipline models. The first section includes communication, monitoring, delivery of instruction, organization, working with parents, and types of teacher power. The second part of the chapter presents five discipline and behavior-management models: behavior modification, assertive discipline, choice theory, teacher-effectiveness training, and cooperative discipline.

Chapter 5 explores assessment and accountability, including a definition of assessment, forms of assessment, and test-construction strategies such as two-choice response, multiple choice, matching, short answer, constructed response, and essay. Additionally, information is provided about how to grade your students.

Part III: Teacher-Centered Patterns

Teacher-centered instruction occurs when instruction is focused on the actions of the teacher. Does the teacher begin the lesson on time? How many questions does the teacher ask? Does the teacher present the content knowledge? How does the teacher control the classroom? In this type of instruction, teachers have predetermined goals and objectives and plan their instruction in small increments or daily lesson plans that are parts of a larger unit. The actions of the teacher are paramount to the delivery of the lesson. The teacher should proceed in small steps, provide many examples, and provide for continued practice.

In this section, Chapter 6 examines direct instruction and Chapter 7 explores mastery learning. In each of these forms of instruction, the teacher is the purveyor of knowledge. The role of the student is more passive, and these forms of instruction assume that students are auditory learners. We will examine the research, theory, and instructional practices of each in these chapters.

Part IV: Teacher–Student Interactive Patterns

Teacher–student interactive instruction occurs when the ownership of what is to be learned is shared by the teacher and the students. This form of instruction examines more than the behavior of the teacher; it also examines the process of learning. Which forms of interaction are needed to enhance the learner's understanding of the content? If the teacher provides a learning experience for the students, will the things learned be retained more easily? How can the teacher balance the ownership of what is to be learned? Which instructional practices will influence the students' feeling of ownership in relation to the content? The patterns of instruction that best represent the process of learning are included in this section of the book.

Chapter 8 examines cooperative learning and Chapter 9 focuses on role play. Ownership of the content is often shared in these forms of instruction, and these instructional types consider how students can work in groups. The focus is the process rather than a predetermined set of teacher objectives. In these patterns of instruction, student learning outcome objectives are often activities that permit the learner to examine the things to be learned with the teacher.

Part V: Student-Centered Patterns

Student-centered instruction occurs when the learner comes first. The approach is based on psychology as a human science rather than a natural science. Chapter 10 explores nondirective learning and Chapter 11 looks at self-taught instruction. These chapters reflect a pattern of learning that is focused on helping each student "actualize" and become an emotionally healthy person. The rationale is that learners seek knowledge as they need it and make wise personal decisions independently throughout their lifetimes when presented with these patterns of instruction. Teachers are facilitators who may provide a rich array of materials, give emotional support, and clarify dialogue but do not instruct the learner or present a predesigned curriculum. The learners guide their own progress in self-taught instruction.

Nondirective instruction, a model advocated by Carl Rogers, is considered student centered. When learners depend on their own motivation for the completion of an instructional task, then this type of learning is regarded as student centered. Motivation and task independence may exist within other instructional patterns, but when the learner is the primary focus, these instructional patterns are considered student centered.

Part VI: Thinking and Organizing the Content

Examining the content and choosing the best way to approach the organization of the material is the focus of this final type of instruction. How can I best organize the concepts that belong to a subject to enhance the learning process? What do I need to know about the content in relation to the students' perceptions of the things to be learned? This section represents more than just the teacher's knowledge of the content; it is the concepts within the content that determine learning outcomes. What patterns exist between and among the concepts that can be organized to enhance student learning?

Chapter 12 examines thinking patterns, Chapter 13 explores memorization, Chapter 14 looks at attaining concepts, and Chapter 15 investigates inquiry.

FEATURES OF THE TEXT

This book explores the interactive patterns that exist in today's classroom and demonstrates how teachers can facilitate the interactivity of these patterns to match their goals for student learning. *Instructional Patterns: Strategies That Maximize Student Learning* focuses on how to use these patterns to maximize the potential for students to learn. Our thinking about effective instruction has been influenced both by classroom organizational patterns and by research that supports the idea that effective instruction must consider the ways that students learn.

Several features make this book more accessible. At the beginning of each chapter, you will find a graphic organizer that depicts the information presented in the chapter and the relationship of the topics. Chapters 1–5 focus on the pedagogical elements of successful teaching and student learning. Each of these chapters features an *Overview* of the pattern, *Educator Biographies* of the theorists or researchers associated with the instructional pattern, a *Summary*, a *Thought to Action* feature, and appropriate *Tables*.

Chapters 6–15 focus on instructional patterns that can be used to maximize your students' potential for learning. These chapters contain an *Overview* of the pattern, a *Research Anchor* feature, *Educator Biographies* of the theorists or researchers associated with the instructional pattern, one or more *Classroom Scenarios*, *Assessment* and *Technology* suggestions, a discussion of the *Learning Tenets* that support the instructional pattern, a *Summary*, and a *Thought to Action* feature.

The **Overview** introduces the chapter and explains the rationale for the material that follows.

The **Research Anchor** is a synthesis of educational studies that have been conducted in the relevant area, including the findings of researchers and theorists whose work has shaped the outcome of each pattern being investigated. Additionally, this section explains the steps, procedures, and protocol for the instructional patterns.

Educator Biographies are provided to give the reader a sense of the accomplishments of each theorist, author, consultant, or educator who has influenced the field of education. Photos of each theorist are provided in the biography section to help preserve the history of those individuals who have had an impact on the education field.

The **Classroom Scenario** gives readers a glimpse of how the instructional pattern under consideration may look and sound when practiced by classroom teachers. Scenarios focus on real classroom practice and help readers better understand the interaction among the instructional pattern, the classroom teacher, and the student.

The **Assessment** section helps the reader to understand the possible outcomes of each instructional pattern. Instruction is designed with the end in mind. Assessment is a part of every lesson in learning.

Technology is a tool that advances instruction and enhances the way teaching and learning takes place. This section explains the technological tools available to teachers using the various patterns of instruction.

Learning Tenets explain the implications of the instructional pattern from the student's point of view. Past research focused on the impact of teacher behavior on instruction. The Learning Tenets explain the relationship of each instructional pattern to the student's potential to learn. This is a shift from examining teacher behavior within instruction to examining student learning within instruction.

The **Summary** of the chapter recaps the important points covered in the chapter. Each summary also provides a rationale for the placement of each instructional pattern under consideration in the book.

Thought to Action gives readers more detail on each topic under investigation by asking for specific actions that might be performed. This section bridges the gap between theories of instruction and the practice of teaching. Follow-up activities and inquiries are suggested for each instructional pattern.

On Your Own directs readers to the web-based student study site at http://www.sagepub.com/holt where they will find activities and study aids to help them engage with the text.

CD-Based Ancillary Materials for the Instructor. An instructor's manual is available on CD to help instructors plan and teach their courses. It has been designed to help instructors to make the classes interesting and engaging for students.

For each chapter, this supplement includes:

- A **Lecture Outline** to assist instructors in planning their lectures

- **PowerPoint® Slides** that feature tables and figures from the text to be used in class or adapted to supplement lecture

- **Teaching Activities** that will aid students in processing the material

- A **Test Bank** of exam questions (multiple choice, short answer, and essay) for each chapter to use either as tests or adapted to individualized test formats

- **Student Projects** to expand on the ideas presented in the text

In addition, the CD will feature **Sample Syllabi** (in both Semester and Quarter format) to aid instructors in planning the course and **Web Resources** that provide supplemental reading to enhance lecture materials, discussion prompts, and assignments.

A Web-Based Student Study Site is located at http://www.sagepub.com/holt. This site has been designed to help students extend their learning and put into practice the concepts presented in the text. These resources can also be used by the instructor to supplement instruction.

For each chapter, the site offers the following:

- Restatement of **Chapter Objectives** to guide student learning

- Electronic **Flash Cards** of major terms to help students memorize new terminology

- **Standards-Based Student Projects** to help students connect the material from the text to the learning and instructional standards for the particular state in which they will be teaching

The website also features **Links to Standards for U.S. States**, so that students can review the standards that apply to them and use these standards to complete the Standards-Based Student Projects; content-related **Journal Articles** with focus questions to prompt further discussion, introduce students to the professional literature of their discipline, and motivate students to research issues in more depth; and a list of **Web Resources** to provide supplemental reading and up-to-date information for students.

ACKNOWLEDGMENTS

We want to acknowledge all the students and colleagues who have shaped our educational experience and influenced our thinking about teaching and learning. We especially want to thank the graduate students who participated in developing the research and writing for this book: Kimberly Dahl, coauthor of Chapter 15, "Inquiry"; Linda Giar, coauthor of Chapter 10,

"Nondirective Learning"; Janet Rasmussen, who created the graphic organizers; Jeff McCullers, for the classroom scenario in Chapter 6, "Direct Instruction"; and Cheryl Young, coauthor of Chapter 11, "Self-Taught Instruction." We also want to acknowledge the following reviewers of this book:

Barbara Slater Stern, James Madison University

Anna Lowe, Loyola University Chicago

Lynn M. Burlbaw, Texas A&M University

James R. Birch, Kent State University Ashtabula

David Flinders, Indiana University

Margaret M. Ferrara, University of Nevada, Reno

Michael J. Wiebe, Texas Woman's University

Noreen A. Hosier, Medgar Evers College of the City University of New York

Anonymous Reviewer, George Mason University

Norman Dale Norris, Nicholls State University

Patricia J. Wall, University of Portland

Betty Jo Simmons, Longwood University

PART I

Factors That Influence All Instruction

Instructional patterns are influenced by the statement, "It depends. . . . "

In turn, "It depends . . ." is influenced by the type of organization, the degree of interaction between students and teachers, and the factors that influence instruction. We begin our dialogue by helping you understand that instructional patterns are influenced by forces that shape our practice. Chapter 1 examines where we've been, what we know, and where we're going. This chapter addresses the evolution of teacher-effectiveness research. Chapter 2 addresses differentiated instruction and learner demographics that influence choices of instructional patterns. Included are historical, sociological, and psychological factors that must be considered when working with diverse populations. Decisions about how to teach rest on the understanding that students are different—that what works for one student does not necessarily work for all students. The degree of instructional adjustment for diverse learners and the choice of appropriate instructional patterns for them are complex decisions and depend on many different perspectives.

Where We've Been, What We Know, and Where We're Going

TEACHING IS A HIGHLY COMPLEX ACTIVITY THAT IS MADE MORE COMPLEX AS OUR SOCIETY BECOMES more diverse and our technology makes knowledge of all kinds more accessible. This complexity raises a multitude of questions for the teacher, particularly the novice teacher: What should I know about myself, my students, the content, and the methods for teaching? What is the difference between the old model and the new patterns of teaching and learning? How do the school environment and philosophy affect decisions made about my teaching? This chapter will lay the foundation for some of these ideas and explain where we've been, what we know, and where we're going.

WHERE WE'VE BEEN

Factory Model of Teaching

The Industrial Revolution created a way of thinking about learning. Schools were built to follow the successes of the new factories. In the factory model of schooling, knowledge consists of sets of facts, concepts, and principles that are known and must be passed on to students, and man's desire to obtain that knowledge is based on his search for reality. Our grandparents', parents', and, to a large extent, our own school experiences were based on this factory model of teaching and learning. The model presumes that instructional tasks can be standardized and that teachers can pass knowledge on to their students in the form of truths. It assumes that there is a set number of skills for every learner within a curriculum and that this knowledge can be transferred to students when teachers perform certain behaviors. It also assumes that the knowledge of the curriculum can be most effectively measured by students' performance on standardized tests.

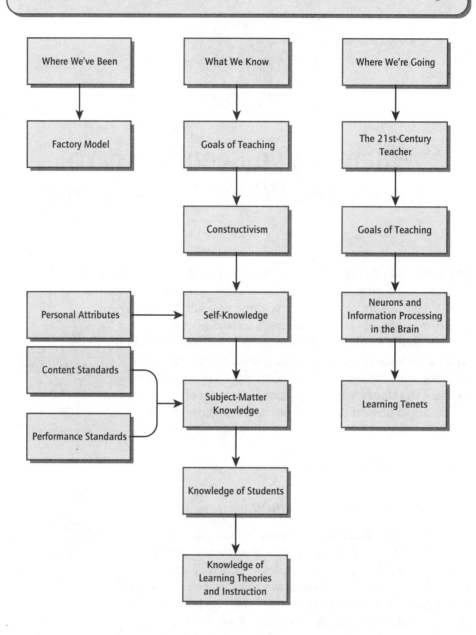

Chapter 1 Where We've Been, What We Know, Where We're Going

Where We've Been

What We Know

Where We're Going

Factory Model

Goals of Teaching

The 21st-Century Teacher

Constructivism

Goals of Teaching

Personal Attributes

Self-Knowledge

Neurons and Information Processing in the Brain

Content Standards

Subject-Matter Knowledge

Learning Tenets

Performance Standards

Knowledge of Students

Knowledge of Learning Theories and Instruction

This way of thinking about school and the curriculum has contributed to the high-stakes testing movement we have been experiencing for the last 20 years. This view of learning assumes the teacher is in control of learning and that the teacher's point of view is *the* valid perspective on how learning should be instructed in the classroom. Standardizing a set of teacher behaviors or "teacher-proofing" the curriculum assumes that the methods chosen will work for all students. However, such beliefs do not reflect what we know about the nature of students and their potential ability to learn. In fact, in this notion of teaching, the needs of the learner are rarely considered. It is time to examine whether this organizational structure is still viable for the teachers of the 21st century. But first, we must ask you to consider the goals of teaching.

WHAT WE KNOW

Goals of Teaching

In U.S. culture, we are encouraged to set goals for ourselves and to establish strategies to reach those goals. Children are taught from an early age that relatively little is beyond their reach, if only they work hard enough to reach their goal. The setting of goals and strategies to reach them also applies to planning for teaching. We, the teachers, think through what we hope to have our students accomplish as we begin to form questions and outcomes for teaching and learning. These are important considerations as we develop our plans.

What are the central goals of teaching? If you were to survey individuals in a school environment, you would discover that not everyone thinks and behaves alike when it comes to teaching. In fact, the school's culture supports many points of view and yet operates in a smooth and organized manner. Often, elementary, middle, and high school teachers have different goals for teaching their students because they think differently about the importance of a learner-centered approach versus a content-specific approach to teaching and learning. These different approaches shape the instructional decisions that teachers make and are grounded in teachers' personal belief systems. Within the educational community, questions about effective teaching and learning have been investigated for years, yet there still is no clear consensus on the beliefs that represent either. Educators have argued that the central goal of teaching is to develop the student's ability to think clearly; to nurture the individual child's unique potential; to diagnose the learner's needs and abilities through appropriate instructional strategies; to transmit to young people basic knowledge, skills, traditions, academic concepts, and values; or to create a future world condition of peace, harmony, equality, and love. Each of these goals is a valuable aim of education, and each represents a different approach to teaching and learning.

Educators have different belief systems that represent different aims in education. Whether they verbalize them or not, they hold deep beliefs about their work, their students, the role of school in society, the curriculum, and, of course, teaching. A teacher's beliefs are often an indicator of how he or she might respond to the decisions and actions of others in the educational environment. We want students to become good problem solvers, we want them to develop critical-thinking skills, and we want them to become self-actualized, knowledgeable adults. Each belief statement can guide instructional decision making. Along with beliefs, a different system for examining how learning is shaped and how it changes based on one's experience is gaining popularity. This theory is called *constructivism*.

Constructivism

The theoretical framework of constructivist theory predates John Dewey but was first iterated by Jerome Bruner (1960). Bruner believed that learning is an active process in which learners construct new ideas or concepts based on their current and past knowledge. The learner selects and transforms information, constructs hypotheses, and makes decisions by relying on a cognitive structure (i.e., schema and mental models). Rather than view knowledge as fully known and fixed, the constructivist perspective is based on the belief that the learner creates new meaning from experience. Learning is a social and cultural activity in which the learner derives meaning from the interaction of prior knowledge and new experiences. Learning is more personal in this way of thinking, and knowledge is shaped by experiences in life.

From an instructional perspective, this theory allows students to discover concepts, principles, laws, and ideas by themselves. The teacher simply provides active dialogue or patterns to facilitate the translation of information to be learned into a format appropriate to the learner's current state of understanding. Although constructivism certainly is not a new idea, it is now the preferred way of thinking about learning and is based on the following factors: (1) The knowledge explosion is so great that schools cannot possibly teach all the facts and concepts that exist; (2) students need to learn how to think, how to solve problems, and how to create new ideas if they are to harness the information age; and (3) higher-order thinking and problem-solving skills are needed to ensure the positive outcomes of 21st-century society.

If teachers are going to be effective facilitators of student learning in the diverse classrooms of the 21st century, they need to develop knowledge in four specific areas: self-knowledge, subject-matter knowledge, knowledge of students, and knowledge of teaching and learning theories. Each contributes to our understanding of a fundamental question of education: What knowledge is of most worth?

Self-Knowledge

To make a difference in the lives of your students, you must begin with an understanding of yourself. Self-knowledge is not fixed; it changes as you grow and as you experience new things. You have the power of choice, and you control the type of attitude you exude. Self-knowledge means having the freedom to choose the way you feel because you understand that you are in charge of your own feelings and experiences. There are those who believe that someone or something else makes them feel sad, angry, or frustrated; they say, "You made me mad" or "You made me angry." These kinds of statements are born out of the notion that someone else is in charge of your feelings and experiences. A teacher who exemplifies self-knowledge will say, "I am angry," "I am frustrated," "I am disappointed," or "I am happy," choosing his or her own feelings based on the situation at hand.

Obviously, you are not going to be in control of every situation that occurs in your classroom or your life; things happen in life that you cannot control. For example, you may find yourself in a traffic jam or a snow storm; you may discover that your classroom has many problem students placed in it, or you may have the "perfect" classroom. Although you cannot control events, you do have the power to control how you respond to them. The essence of your humanity is the power of choice. You choose what to wear in the morning, you choose your friends, your food, and your activities. Your choices are up to you, and that means that you are not a helpless victim. Understanding that you are not a victim means that you are accountable as a teacher and that you know the choices you make lead to results.

Being aware of the human characteristics that you possess when interacting with others is important to self-knowledge. An awareness of your own personal attributes and how these can contribute to your success in the classroom are pivotal aspects of the success that you can have with your students. Your self-understanding and self-acceptance are prerequisites for helping students to know and accept themselves. The following personal attributes are important to teaching:

- Reflective decision making: You show a willingness and ability to reflect on your strengths and weaknesses as they relate to what you do, who you are, and how you think. You reflect on educational issues and the abilities of others working in the profession. You make appropriate decisions about lesson objectives, designs, delivery, and evaluation.

- Professional commitment: You are punctual and responsible, complete work assignments in a timely fashion, and demonstrate pride in self and work. You are intellectually and academically curious and receptive to suggestions for improving your instruction.

- Communication skills: You show an ability to speak and write clearly and demonstrate standard English usage in writing and speaking. You are verbally fluent and good at listening.

- Interpersonal skills: You show an ability to get along with others (e.g., students and colleagues) and establish positive rapport and relationships. You are tolerant, adaptive, open-minded, supportive, and encouraging. You are sensitive to *all* students and committed to teaching all students regardless of ability; socioeconomic, cultural, linguistic, or ethnic background; exceptionality; gender; sexual orientation; religion; or other variables.

- Classroom personality: You are positive, enthusiastic, resourceful, energetic, optimistic, empathetic, encouraging, adaptable, polite, tactful, and attentive, yet you are also businesslike, task oriented, and efficient. You possess acumen.

- Emotional makeup: You are self-controlled yet flexible. You are willing to accept responsibility for your own actions, accept and adapt to change, react appropriately under stress, and express positive and negative feelings in a nondefensive manner.

- Academic integrity: You do not plagiarize or use others' materials in the classroom without permission. You are knowledgeable about the content to be taught and keep up to date with new information, content, methods, and theories. You follow the National Education Association's code of ethics.

As you reflect on who you are and how you think, you will develop such personal attributes as open-mindedness, introspection, and willingness to accept responsibility for your decisions and actions. You will be willing to consider new evidence and to admit to the possibility of error. Moreover, you will be responsible and use ethical as well as educational criteria in examining the consequences of your choices as you implement them (University of Central Florida, 2004).

Subject-Matter Knowledge

As a teacher, you must have a broad-based knowledge of the content and how that content contributes to the overall curriculum of the school. Content knowledge is generally obtained through course preparation in college. When you have knowledge of the subjects you are expected to teach, you are better equipped to help students learn. You understand the ins and outs of the content and are able to link the subject-matter concepts to national, state, or district curriculum standards. When you thoroughly understand your subject, you can modify it to meet the academic and learning needs of your students.

Teaching today means more than knowing your subject matter.

Content is often dictated to teachers by district curriculum guides or state standards. As a novice teacher, you lean on these guides to help you plan your lessons during your early years of teaching. You are consumed with so many aspects of the total classroom environment—meeting your students' needs, communicating with parents, learning your school's culture and grading policies—that you become overly dependent on subject-area books, curriculum guides, and national, state, and district standards.

Because the present educational reform movements emphasize accountability, national, state, and district standards have increased in importance. These standards are often known as *outcome-based* or *performance-based* standards. They are developed by each state and district based on the national standards written for various content areas by professional organizations such as the National Council for Teachers of Mathematics, the National Science Teachers Association, the National Council for Teachers of English, and even the federal government in the Goals 2000: Educate America Act.

There is tension among the national, state, and local governments regarding the ownership of education when it comes to standards. Education, according to our Constitution, is a function of the state, and local districts should be involved in the decision making at the community level. However, much funding for public education is controlled by the federal government, and with that funding comes restrictions on what will be taught and how it will be taught.

Goals 2000 mandated eight education goals that schools across the country were expected to meet. Adoption of the goals created an impetus for the establishment of curriculum standards and assessments to indicate achievement of the goals.

Today, school districts may be implementing and assessing national, state, and local standards or a combination of these. As a teacher, you need to know which standards to focus on for curriculum planning and, ultimately, for the high-stakes tests students need to take to demonstrate their content knowledge. Standards are generally defined as what students need to know (content) and what they are able to do (performance). Consequently, students are faced with a body of knowledge they need to learn, as well as identified strategies by which they can demonstrate their learning.

Knowledge of Students

You must know and understand your students. You must find a match between yourself and the age group with which you prefer to work. Once this match is found, you must really get to know your students. You must understand their interests, aptitudes, learning styles, and what motivates them. You must understand their physical, emotional, intellectual, and social development. You gain this knowledge through formal study, observation, and constant interaction with them. What is considered normal behavior for middle school students is very different from what is expected of elementary or high school students. Jacob Kounin (1970) coined the phrase "withitness" to refer to the teacher's awareness of what is occurring in the classroom.

As a part of the Florida Performance Measurement System (Orange County Public Schools, n.d.), educators adopted this phrase. In other words, teachers have to be "with it" as perceived by the students. Students know that you know. Knowledge of your students is vital to your success.

One reason that teaching is different today than it was in previous decades is that the students are different. Research indicates that the first few years of life are significant in developing motor skills and temperament and customizing a particular lifestyle (Goleman, 1995). Harry Chugani states that the experiences of the first year "can completely change the way a person turns out" (cited in Kotulak, 1996, p. 46). From the day you are born, the brain prunes away unneeded cells and billions of unused connections. The brain is receiving and selecting stimuli in vast amounts. Thus, the talents and abilities of students in school might be directly related to the experiences they had or did not have during the early years of their life (Jensen, 1998). Figure 1.1, adapted from Jensen (1998), represents how children today are different from those of 30 years ago.

Knowledge of Learning Theories

Teachers who have knowledge of educational theories are better equipped to make decisions that inform practice. So theories about learners and learning guide teachers when they make professional judgments about teaching and learning. You should not only have the knowledge of the theory but also understand why it works. The greater your knowledge of learning theories, the greater your options for problem solving and adjusting your strategies to meet the needs of your students.

The research from the 1970s and 1980s—process-product research—measured correlations between teacher behavior and student achievement to identify effective teacher practices. These kinds of practices were organized into a structured set of functions that provided guidelines for effective teaching (Rosenshine, 1983):

Fewer natural foods and
more additives

More children raised in
single-parent households with
fewer resources

More exposure to drugs
and medications

More exposure to passive
babysitters and sedentary
entertainment, such as television

Less early motor stimulation
from swings, see-saws,
merry-go-rounds, and
playground games
because of safety and
liability concerns

Use of car seats and seat belts
restricts movement but is safer

Source: Jensen (1998).

- Review and check the previous day's work.

- Present new content and skills.

- Provide for initial student practice.

- Provide for feedback and correctives.

- Provide for independent student practice.

- Provide weekly and monthly reviews.

Communicate with your students about their potential and be an authentic adult to all students.

Knowledge of research and practices that work can be used as a rule of thumb for teachers. Not every theory works the same with each student or group of students. But having this knowledge allows teachers to apply theoretical knowledge to the practical problems of teaching. The research from the 1960s to the 1980s focused on teacher behaviors that support effective instruction. The assumption was that if the research could identify the characteristics and techniques used by effective teachers, that information could be used in the pre-service and in-service training of teachers to ensure quality teachers in every classroom. Unfortunately, much of this research provided little evidence that could guarantee an effective teacher. Teaching is highly influenced by the nature and needs of the students; what might work in one classroom could be a disaster in another. Teaching is not about what a teacher knows and believes but, more important, how a teacher puts that information into practice when interacting with students. Now that we have entered the 21st century, we are moving away from research that specifically addresses teacher behaviors (i.e., starting class on time, asking higher-order questions, etc.) to research that examines the relationship between teacher behaviors and how students learn.

WHERE WE'RE GOING

The 21st-Century Teacher

To be a successful teacher in the in the 21st century, you must approach the teaching and learning process by recognizing that you will and can make a difference in the lives of your students. Teaching in the 21st century means approaching students from their point of view. If a student is interested in sailing, you may have to relate course instruction to that interest. This means being willing to adjust your approach when students do not understand the material. Does this sound like more work for you as the teacher? Yes! In the beginning, you provide the environment for learning. You bring out the best in all learners. You engage their curiosity about a particular subject. You create support systems and make other resources available to them. You challenge them to discover new worlds. Once students are given the opportunity and accept the responsibility for their learning, they become empowered. They will not become empowered until they take ownership of their learning.

You cannot assume that because you *covered* material the students get it. Most of the time, this is not the case. When you explain cell division to your students and they do not understand, you can take one or more of the following actions: You could assume that the learners are slow in catching on to the new information. You could reteach it the same way, or you could teach it using a different approach. Often, teaching necessitates repackaging material to meet your students' needs. This means that you are constantly reformulating what you do because you realize that the students' learning is a journey you take with them. There is responsibility to be assumed on your part, along with the students' responsibility for learning the material.

If you accept the sole responsibility for your students' learning, you will fail a lot. In a classroom, the students are responsible for their learning; you are responsible for facilitating that learning by finding the right strategies and methods to stimulate the students to learn. When your students fail to learn, both you and your students share in that failure. By reflecting on what you did in the classroom, you can learn. Ask yourself: Did I prepare the students for learning? Did I select appropriate strategies? Did the students have the prerequisite knowledge? Was the environment conducive to learning? If not, why not? What did the students do or not do to contribute to their learning? Did your students understand their responsibility for their learning? What do you need to change in the classroom to ensure that the reteaching will be successful?

Each "failure" in teaching occurs when you do not get the desired results; however, each failure informs you about what does and does not work with your current group of students. When you reflect and restructure, you are teaching. Teaching is just as much about your own learning as it is about your students' learning. Each and every thing that is tried in your classroom eventually builds success. It adds to the knowledge necessary for success and increases the chances that the next event will be more closely aligned with the desired outcomes. In a sense, failure becomes feedback. Mistakes and failures become feedback that you can use to lead to your success. With many types of learners in your classroom, you will need many techniques that require plenty of flexibility. Each failure gets you closer to your outcome—so the greater your flexibility, the greater your chance of a successful outcome. If this belief system becomes a part of your everyday life, imagine the excitement you can generate. With each experience, positive or negative, a new gift can be discovered. What you look for, you will find. If you look for the negative, it will find you. Look for the gift of your mistake and realize that if you do not welcome taking chances, then you are not living to experience all that is possible in your life (Jensen, 1995).

Accepting the fact that you learn from experience means being willing to seek the resources you need when things are not working. Tapping experienced colleagues at your school is essential for your success. Once you ask for their advice or assistance, be willing to be coached. Progress toward effective teaching means being willing to be evaluated by experienced colleagues. Your willingness to allow yourself to be coached can lead to your success.

The best teachers keep a clear focus and communicate the possibilities regarding how they want things to be. Look for the possibilities in every situation. Communicate with your students about their potential instead of complaining to your students about their limitations. Very few of us become empowered out of complaints or limitations. Have conversations with your students about new ideas, breakthroughs, and possibilities for learning. What's the possibility that homework can be a joy and not a punishment? What's the possibility that learning can be fun and not routine? (Jensen, 1995).

Be an authentic adult to your students. Teachers who want to become friends to their students lose their ability to be real. Teaching is about being the responsible adult in the lives of your students. Don't act—be real; be yourself. Although it is true that we all wear different hats in different situations in our lives, we do not treat our parents and grandparents the same way we treat our friends. If you are yourself, you will make mistakes in your classroom—you are, after all, human. When you do, acknowledge your mistakes and go on; students will learn from your actions that when they make mistakes, it's okay. The classroom should be a place where everyone can learn from mistakes. Perfection at all times is unrealistic.

The notion that teaching is a safe, easy-going job is not true. Teaching is a frontline job, and that means taking risks, making mistakes, and being committed to learners. It takes courage to do this job and do it well. Teachers have to face whatever challenges are brought to them by their students and the system, and they have to be willing to face these challenges to do what is best for the students. Teaching is a job requiring six hours of face-to-face engagement with a variety of students while setting an example of caring, integrity, love, and commitment. Once you accept the responsibility of becoming a teacher, you must be there 100%. You must act as if it matters—because it does matter. A great teacher is a work in progress. Teaching is not an event. It is a lifelong learning process that needs to be massaged and reshaped as you go along. One does not become a great teacher; one simply commits to it as a path (Jensen, 1995).

To maximize student potential, we must study how learning occurs. To study how learning occurs, we must study the biology of the brain. As technology has advanced in the medical field, we have been able to get a glimpse of what happens in the brain at the moment when learning occurs. We believe that this knowledge of brain research has implications for the whole process of teaching and learning and increases our ability to understand the learner's point of view.

Technology and the Brain

There has been an explosion of information about the brain in fields such as genetics, physics, neuroscience, and pharmacology. What we learned two years ago is already outdated because of evolving technology that has allowed us to get a glimpse into the function of the brain. The intent of this book is not to cover the scientific operation of the brain but to consider how various fields of science are influencing our thinking about teaching and learning. Educators must be careful not to jump on every bandwagon that comes to town but to demonstrate caution in the way that any new knowledge is interpreted and used to inform practice. Brain-based research does not prove anything. Educators seeking solutions to the problems of the profession who blindly adopt brain-based research may be sorely disappointed in the results. We have experienced many fads in education; veteran teachers often say that if you stay in education long enough, you will see certain practices come and go and then come back again. However, new technologies are providing us with better information that can inform us, particularly our knowledge of the operation and function of the brain.

Eric Jensen has authored more than 22 books, including *Student Success Secrets, Super Teaching, Brain-Based Learning, Learning With the Body in Mind, Different Brains, Different Learners, Brain-Compatible Strategies, The Great Memory Book, Teaching With the Brain in Mind,* and *Arts With the Brain in Mind.* His prolific writing in the area of brain research as it applies to education has provided us with much food for thought as we cope with an increasingly diverse society.

Source: Jensen Learning Corporation, retrieved June 25, 2004, from www.jlcbrain.com/what.html.

Pat Wolfe is a former teacher of kindergarten through 12th grade, county office administrator, and adjunct university professor. Over the past 15 years, as an educational consultant, she has conducted workshops for thousands of administrators, teachers, boards of education, and parents in schools and districts throughout the United States and internationally. Her major area of expertise is the application of brain research to educational practice. Her entertaining and interactive presentation style makes learning about the brain enjoyable as well as practical. She is an author and has appeared on numerous videotape series, satellite broadcasts, radio shows, and television programs. Dr. Wolfe is a native of Missouri. She completed her undergraduate work in Oklahoma and her postgraduate studies in California. She presently resides in Napa, California.

Source: Mind Matters, Inc., retrieved June 25, 2004, from www.patwolfe.com/index.php?pid=99.

There are no conclusive models of how the brain works. It is too soon to empirically state causal relationships from research on the brain and how learning occurs. Furthermore, the knowledge is changing as rapidly as the technology is changing. What we think is true today may be obsolete next month or next year. Many educators who are reading and listening to brain research may say, "What research is not brain based?" or "Brain-based research is being used as a means for marketing new books." These statements may be true. However, technological advances that have been made in the medical field should not be ignored by researchers in the field of education. It is time to put away our doubts about this developing knowledge and examine what we know and what can be learned. The complex neuronetwork of cells called the brain is fascinating, and as new knowledge is obtained, it will influence nearly every aspect of teaching and learning.

Doctors and neurosurgeons are learning more about the brain and its operation through imaging technology. The first imaging machine was the x-ray, developed in 1895. In the early 1970s, a technique was developed to increase the gradations in shades of gray in the normal x-ray from 25 to more than 200. This procedure is called *computerized axial tomography* or CAT scanning (Wolfe, 2001). The use of these pictures of the brain helped doctors to locate and determine the extent of tumors or lesions in the brain and the loss of brain tissue. These devices that provide pictures of the brain are useful, but they do not inform neurosurgeons about the brain and its functions.

The newest technology available to doctors provides insight into the brain's function by monitoring its energy consumption. The brain is responsible for about 20% of the body's energy. This is surprising because the brain composes only 2.5% of our total body weight. Glucose and oxygen are the major sources of energy for the brain, and these levels change as various parts of the brain function. Glucose is a type of carbohydrate. Monitoring the flow of glucose and oxygen is important to neurosurgeons because they realize that these substances can inform us about the consumption of energy in various parts of the brain and provide insight into how various actions occur.

Advances in technology such as positron emission tomography (PET) and magnetic resonance imaging (MRI) measure the emissions given off by oxygen and glucose and tell us how the brain consumes these substances. Functional magnetic resonance imaging (fMRI) technology is one of the newest imaging devices. This device is used to show not only structures of the brain but also neural activity. The subject is asked to engage in an activity such as tapping the toe or listening to sounds. Neurons fired in the brain require energy, and more blood flows to these regions. The fMRI scanner detects and measures these changes in intensity and produces a computer image. By subtracting this image from an image of the brain at rest, the computer produces a detailed picture of the brain activity responsible for tapping your toe or listening to music. The rapid images produced by the scanner make a miniature movie of the brain (Wolfe, 2001).

The electroencephalogram produces readings of the electrical output of the brain. Another procedure, known as magnetoencephalography, uses high-tech sensors containing supercooled liquid helium to locate faint magnetic fields that are generated by the brain's neural networks. Other imaging techniques that combine multimodal imaging are single-photon emission computerized tomography and near-infrared spectroscopy. These forms of multimodal imaging, which combine two or more techniques, are becoming increasingly popular. These patterns help doctors to detect brain-wave patterns and cerebral problems such as seizures or dementia. Additionally, these devices can help doctors track brain activity during problem-solving situations (Wolfe, 2001).

According to Pat Wolfe (2001),

PET scans of a reader show that much more frontal lobe activity occurs when the subject reads silently than when he or she is reading aloud to others. Activity in the frontal lobes often indicates higher-level thinking. On the other hand, the scan of the student reading aloud glows brightly in the motor area of the brain that governs speech, while showing little activity elsewhere. One way to interpret these scans is that there is more comprehension of what is being read when one reads silently. Do these scans prove that students should never read aloud? Of course they don't. Armed with this information, however, teachers are able to make more informed decisions about how to

Robert Sylwester is Emeritus Professor of Education at the University of Oregon who focuses on the educational implications of new developments in science and technology. He has written several books and more than 150 journal articles. His most recent books are *Student Brains, School Issues* (1998) and *A Biological Brain in a Cultural Classroom* (2000). The Education Press Association of America gave him Distinguished Achievement Awards for his 1993 and 1994 syntheses of cognitive science research, which were published in *Educational Leadership*.

Dr. Sylwester has made more than 1,250 conference and in-service presentations about educationally significant developments in brain and stress theory and research. He writes a monthly column for the internet magazine *Brain Connection* (www.brainconnection.com).

Source: "Get Connected—The Joint Iowa ASCD-ITEC Conference," retrieved June 25, 2004, from www.itec-ia.org/confer/speakers/sylwester.htm.

balance silent and oral reading to obtain both diagnostic information on decoding problems and how to enhance comprehension of what is being read. (p. 11)

It is unlikely that neuroscience could prove that a particular classroom strategy works, but the information can provide a more informed basis for the decisions we make in our classrooms and allow us, as teachers, to think of ways to organize learning opportunities that may enhance the learning process.

Neurons and Information Processing in the Brain

Although there are billions of neurons in our brains and they are quite complex, the details inside a neuron are much the same in animals and in humans. *Neuron* means "nerve cell" (Greek for bowstring). Neurons can vary widely in shape, position, and size, but the architecture and functional principles are the same. A neuron is made up of prototypical features. It has an *axon*, a primary output pathway by which the neuron sends information to other neurons. The neuron's *dendrites* are tree-like branches that collect information sent by other neurons. The inputs that arrive at a neuron are called *afferents.* In most cases, the axon of the afferent neuron comes very close to—but does not touch—the dendrite of the receiving neuron. The gaps between neurons are called *synapses*. The chemicals that are released by the afferent neuron are called *neurotransmitters*. The neurotransmitters are picked up in the receiving neuron's dendrites.

A neuron integrates all the information it receives from all its afferents and, in turn, may produce outputs by releasing neurotransmitters from its own axon. Some neurons have an *excitatory effect* on the receiving neuron, meaning that they increase the net activation of the receiving neuron. Other neurotransmitters have an *inhibitory effect*, reducing the net activity of the receiving neuron. The strength of both the inhibitory and excitatory inputs can vary depending on the chemical composition of the neurotransmitters, and the strength or efficacy

As young children explore their world, connections are made as things are learned.

of the synapse itself. Some synapses simply have a greater effect on the overall activity of the receiving cell than others (Gluck & Myers, 2001).

Most neuroscientists now believe that a basic mechanism of learning is the alteration of synaptic strength. This may occur by creating new synapses (and deleting defunct ones) or by adjusting the strength of existing synapses (Gluck & Myers, 2001, p. 45).

Neuroscientists define learning as occurring when two neurons communicate with each other. Neurons have "learned" when one neuron sends a message to another neuron (Hannaford, 1995). A neuron has three basic parts: the cell body, the dendrites, and the axon. The action of neurons talking is electrochemical: The action within the neuron is electrical, but the message becomes chemical as it travels between neurons. The chemicals are the neurotransmitters.

As young children, connections are made as things are learned. The more frequently a neural network is accessed, the stronger it becomes. The connections made can be compared to a path in the woods. At first, it is hard to see the path because the weeds are overgrown. But with use, the path becomes clear and the route is easy to find. In a similar way, the neural networks get more and more efficient and messages travel more swiftly as they are used.

Fitzpatrick (1996) has investigated research regarding *long-term potentiation*. Neurons that fire information across a synapse are encoded exponentially. That means the information is learned multiple times each time it is practiced. The signal changes the potential of the receiving neuron, giving it the potential to learn faster.

During the first two years of life, the brain becomes wired as we learn. It makes neural connections at an enormous rate. Infants make connections for movement, sight, and sound. Additionally, babies are connecting with their primary caretaker. The baby quickly learns which sounds and movement will get him or her the desired attention.

Another type of cells found in the brain are *glial cells*. Glial means "glue." During fetal brain development, glial cells assist in the migration of neurons. Glial cells are the most common cells in the brain, outnumbering neurons 10 to 1. Their fibers act as ropes for the neurons to hold onto as they make their way through the brain. The glial cells work as the housekeepers of the brain, attaching themselves to the neurons to keep them nourished. The more often the brain uses neurons, the more glial cells it needs.

Another coating found in the brain is myelin. Myelin coats the axons of neurons. The coating acts as insulation and allows messages to travel quickly without any loss of transmission. Two theories exist about myelin production and release.

Carla Hannaford (1995), a neurophysiologist, says that myelin is added to the axon with use. As the neuron is called on to fire, a coating of myelin is put down. As networks of neurons are fired on, a coating of myelin is formed. Like the path in the woods that is constantly walked upon, the neural path becomes smoother and faster.

Jane Healy (1994) theorizes that the myelination of neurons is a developmental process that begins at birth. According to this theory, the brain releases myelin in stages, beginning with the lower-brain areas. The portion of the brain in the prefrontal cortex, behind the forehead, is the final area to be myelinated. This is where decision making, planning, and many higher-order thinking skills are located. This area is also associated with short-term memory.

Healy's theory of the release of myelin in the brain corresponds to the four developmental stages proposed by Piaget:

Sensorimotor stage (Birth–2 years): At this stage, the child interacts physically with the environment. A set of ideas about reality and how it works is developed.

Preoperational stage (Ages 2–7): At this stage, the child is not yet able to think abstractly. The child operates in concrete physical situations.

Concrete operations (Ages 7–11): At this stage, the child has accumulated enough experiences to begin to conceptualize and to do some abstract problem solving, though the child still learns best by doing.

Formal operations (Ages 11–15): At this stage, the child's thought processes are beginning to approach those of an adult.

Healy (1994) states that the largest release of myelin may occur during the adolescent years. Once this dose is released, children have an easier time making decisions, planning for the future, and working out problems.

Piaget's formal operational stage occurs between the ages of 11 and 15; however, other research suggests that this final stage varies among individuals. Jensen (1998) states that only

50% of the population ever reaches this stage at all. Short-term memory does not reach capacity until approximately the age of 15. The capacity of short-term memory in a fully developed brain consist of seven chunks of information. At age 3, space exists for only one chunk. In light of the discovery that short-term memory is held in the frontal lobes (LeDoux, 1996), the last area to be myelinated, it makes sense that the frontal lobe's incomplete development because of a lack of myelin would influence short-term memory. Many students today have difficulty with higher-order thinking skills. Although children of every age have some ability to synthesize, abstract, and evaluate, some children have more difficulty than others. Realizing that this difficulty may be the result of a lack of myelin or its delayed release could lessen both children's frustration and that of the adults trying to help them (Sprenger, 1999).

Table 1.1 compares Piaget's stages of development with the theory of myelin release in the brain described by Marilee Sprenger in *Learning and Memory: The Brain in Action* (1999).

Understanding this theory and its implications brings to mind the middle school students whom one of the authors worked with for years. He observed these students in various stages developmentally but did not know at the time that their ability to formalize their thinking may have been the result of the release of myelination in their brain. He attributed the differences to maturation, which is a psychological concept, not a physical one.

In the explanation of myelination provided, we know that the brain is either doing something new for the first time and creating new pathways, or we are repeating things previously learned, thus enhancing existing pathways. If we are repeating something that we have previously learned, we know that the neural pathways will become more and more efficient. Research studies have discovered that there is a difference between how much the brain "lights up" (as indicated on the PET scan) when it encounters something that is new versus something that was previously learned. Newly initiated learning is brighter on the PET scan than previously learned material (Jensen, 1998). Novices use more of their brain, but they are less efficient in how they use it. This quality illustrates how quickly the brain adapts and rewires itself. Knowing this information may help us, as teachers, to understand why some students "get it" faster than others. If they have been previously exposed to information, they may remember it and be able to use it more efficiently than students who have had no or limited exposure to information. Think about this with respect to differences in students resulting from differences in economic or social class.

So far, we have explored the goals of teaching and how these goals are changing for teachers in the 21st century. We have provided a foundational knowledge for classroom teachers, and we have synthesized some of the research from neuroscience and the medical field that has implications for how learning occurs. In the next section, we want to list some tenets that we believe influence how instruction should occur based on the information provided thus far.

| TABLE 1.1 | Piaget's Stages and the Stages of Brain Development |

Piaget's Four Stages of Child Development	*Four Stages of Myelin Release and Brain Growth*
Sensorimotor (Birth–2 years)	Large motor system and visual system
Preoperational (Ages 2–7)	Language acquisition
Concrete operations (Ages 7–11)	Manipulation of thoughts and ideas
Formal operations (Ages 11–15)	Higher-order thinking

Learning Tenets
Where We've Been, What We Know, and Where We're Going

As authors, we realize that we need to make explicit the beliefs that reflect the particular preferences, perceptions, interpretations, and priorities to which we subscribe. These include perceptions about teaching and the learning process that we think shape all instructional patterns. As we mentioned earlier in this chapter, we are moving from the factory model of teaching to an understanding of the relationship of learning to instructional effectiveness. Students become a part of the equation when we teach. Rather than examining just the teacher's behavior in relation to instruction, we need to examine the students in relation to how they learn. If we want to enhance our students' ability to learn, then we need to consider Learning Tenets that are fundamental to any instructional pattern. Each of the following Learning Tenets as it applies to a pattern of instruction is covered in the chapters of this book.

The brain seeks to classify information and the things to be learned.

The brain seeks to organize our world. Our world does not come already organized, so we have to find the pattern that makes sense to us. Patterns are repeated classification systems. Patterns are a way of knowing. They are the facts and concepts of our world. Patterns exist in every part of our world. We use patterns in our spoken and written language. Art and music often follow a pattern. Architectural patterns are evident in buildings, floors, and ceilings. The subjects we teach are full of patterns. Our interactions with each other form patterns and expectations with one another. As we learn, we recognize the patterns that support our way of knowing. This process occurs in much the same way that the brain seeks to organize new information, and the formation of patterns enables us to recall what has been learned. According to Pat Wolfe (2001), when we experience something new, the brain looks for an existing network into which to fit the new information. If the fit is good, what was learned or stored previously gives meaning to the new information, and a positive transfer occurs.

The emotional system drives attention, and attention drives meaning and memory.

Emotions and attention are the principal preliminary processes that the body and brain use in their efforts to survive and thrive. Emotion provides a quick, general assessment of the situation that draws on powerful internal needs and values (survive, eat, nurture, and mate), and attention provides the neural mechanism by which we can focus on the things that seem important while monitoring or ignoring the unimportant (Sylwester, 1995). Music and emotion influence learning in ways that have yet to be explored. Research is now being developed that will help us to unlock the mysteries of what our body likes, dislikes, and avoids. We know that emotional events that have occurred in our lives are things that are remembered. Emotional states bind learning. Peak learning happens in peak states when the brain is in a state of high challenge and low stress. During times of stress or threat, blood moves away from the frontal lobes, thereby reducing the ability to think clearly or recall information. Music, however, evokes emotions that contribute to the overall calm of the body, support positive transfer, and soothe the stress of perceived difficult concepts.

Learning occurs in both conscious and unconscious states.

How much of our learning is conscious? How much is unconscious? A number of studies have demonstrated that humans are immersed in a vast sea of sensorial possibilities. According to Coyner and Wilson (2002), "Unconscious learning is 99% of the process."

Our sense organs can register in the range of 11 million bits of information each second (Davis, Sumara, & Luce-Kapler, 2000). Only a small portion of these sensory possibilities ever reach consciousness. In fact, a typical person is consciously aware of only 10 to 40 bits of information per second—that is, a person consciously notes about one out of every million sensory events.

Try this experiment: Think about a familiar shopping center in your neighborhood. Is there a yogurt shop? Is there a dry cleaner? What about a bookstore? You may have regularly walked past specialty stores without ever noticing them—until of course, you needed one of them.

Try another example: Pause from reading this text and try using another sense, focusing on the sounds in the surroundings that you are in. There is likely to be a broad range of sounds all around you. However, these sounds may go unnoticed for a large portion of your day. The difference here is the distinction between sensation and conscious perception. Sensations—even though they may not impinge on consciousness—still play a profound role in shaping what we think and do.

If consciousness is really so small, why does it seem so much larger? That is, if we humans are capable of perceiving so little information at so slow a pace, why do we feel so aware of so many features of the world? One analogy that has been developed to explain this phenomenon is a comparison of consciousness to a spotlight. Whenever its narrow beam is directed, the world is illuminated. In the same manner, detail is made available to consciousness wherever it is focused. At the same moment, however, previously illuminated details are pushed into conceptual oblivion (Davis et al., 2000, p. 6).

The brain generates our emotions and our motor output. It is the source of cognition, memory, thoughts, and what we call "intelligence." Your ability to understand and speak comes from the brain. Some functions controlled by the brain, such as our heart rate, respiration, breathing, hormone secretion, and immune system, are automatic and unconscious. To understand the process of learning, the relationship between conscious and unconscious learning needs to be explored.

Human beings are constantly doing far more than we are consciously aware of. Even now, you are performing the very complex task of interpreting the marks on this page, and this is happening without consciously having to examine the shape of the letter or sound of each syllable. If you were aware of the complexity of what you were doing, then you would not be able to do it. In fact, in some instances, drawing conscious attention to some interactions can cause them to fall apart.

Think about a basketball player who is getting ready to shoot at the foul line. If the crowd shouts, jeers, and otherwise distracts the player from what he is doing, then he is likely to miss the shot. Consciousness is often too small to accommodate both engagement in an activity and awareness of one's self or one's actions. In fact, it is often reported that exemplary performances and profound engagements correspond to "forgetting" one's self. Related to instruction, if we are to practice the skills that we need to learn, then the tasks may be unconscious and more automatic. It's like hitting the first domino, and then all other dominos follow. Practicing with content, interacting with fellow students, watching a teacher model a skill, or observing a variety of examples are behaviors that result in pattern making. These events may be both conscious and unconscious.

The brain is designed for ups and downs, not constant attention.

Eric Jensen (1998) has made the point that the amount of time learners can attend to information being presented is generally equal to their ages. This means that if you are working with 5-year-olds, you have approximately five minutes for the students to attend to your directions; if you are working with 12-year-olds, you have 12 minutes, 17 minutes with high school students, and so on. The maximum amount of time that adults can attend to one thing is approximately 20 minutes. Taking this into account, instruction should not be presented beyond the time allotment for the age of the learner unless students are extremely interested in what is to be learned. Interest can mediate attention. The brain needs downtime. The brain needs time to reflect and process the content that is to be learned. If we are to ensure that real learning occurs, then the learner needs processing activities that will enhance the concepts to be learned through auditory, visual, and kinesthetic modalities.

Learning occurs through processing and active engagement with visual, auditory, and kinesthetic modalities.

The brain can encode a picture more easily then text. Put another way, seeing is believing. Recent research indicates that 90% of learning is visual. Our eyes register 36,000 visual impressions per hour. The brain is wired for visual processing. Color and movement boost learning (Coyner & Wilson, 2002). Auditory rehearsal of things to be learned can enhance the retention of the concepts. Just as we have indicated that some learning is visual, auditory processing is an important learning modality that can assist the transfer of the things to be learned. Kinesthetic learning, the kind of learning in which students are immersed in getting their hands and bodies into it, can be a preferred modality for some learners.

Learners need to be conscious of their learning modalities so they can maximize the way they receive and share information. For example, musicians may be auditory learners, architects visual learners, and athletes kinesthetic learners. The point is that to successfully encode information, processing strategies must accompany learning lessons. Good teachers will select a variety of processing strategies to reinforce learning from each modality.

Good teaching is about recognizing and selecting instructional patterns that match the context for learning and the students we are teaching.

So finding, recognizing, and using patterns form the basis of our everyday life. Just as our brains seek the organization of new information, educators must seek ways to assist students in their efforts to learn by selecting appropriate instructional patterns to maximize their learning potential. As educators make decisions about how to operate in the classroom, we seek the pattern that is most appropriate to the contextual factors in the learning environment and the learners we are teaching. We realize that introducing the idea of patterns is fundamental to education and the process for understanding instructional decision making. Patterns in instruction are considered from a constructivist view of teaching and learning based on reflection and "meaning making." We also know that modern perspectives on how students learn are changing educators' views of best practices. A number of cognitive and developmental psychologists have found that students learn best by first making connections between what they know and have experienced and the new content. Active construction of knowledge, rather than the solely passive absorption of knowledge, increases the probability that students will go beyond simply knowing to developing understanding (Wilen, Ishler, Hutchison, & Kindsvatter, 2000).

Active knowledge means active classrooms in which students are engaged with the content, the teacher, and each other. Actively engaging in knowledge means understanding how learning occurs. Knowing how learning occurs means knowing how the brain works and how it sends and receives information to various locations for processing. Teachers must then learn which instructional patterns maximize the potential of the students, given the appropriate context and the things to be learned.

Summary

Today, exciting changes in education are evolving as a result of information learned through the study of neuroscience, cognitive science, and brain research. Education as a discipline is gaining recognition and momentum as we examine the transition from how teachers teach to how students learn. This chapter's intent was to lay the foundation for how teaching and learning is changing in the 21st century. To illustrate the evolution of the teaching and learning process, the chapter was divided into three distinct sections: where we've been, what we know, and where we're going. Many of the changes occurring in education are a result of advances in technology in the medical profession that have allowed us to understand how the brain works and how students learn. Considering learning from the student's point of view provides us with a totally different perspective on the teaching–learning process and helps us to develop our thinking about the instructional patterns we can use to maximize learning opportunities for our students. The material presented in this chapter shapes and influences the teaching and learning process. The Learning Tenets introduced in this chapter emphasized the shift from how we teach to how students learn. An explanation of the Learning Tenets will be provided in Chapters 6–15, which address the uniqueness of each tenet to each instructional pattern.

Thought to Action

1. Examine the personal attributes associated with the profession of teaching. Select one and explain how you will demonstrate this characteristic in your everyday life as a teacher.

2. What do you do that stands for your commitment to being a good teacher—one who can be coached? How will you integrate the things to be learned?

3. Survey the book and identify what you think might be your favorite instructional strategy. Why is it your favorite?

4. Explain how new brain-imaging techniques provide us with more information about the brain but do not necessarily prove that certain strategies work.

5. Read a book or article on brain-based learning. How does the information in that material help you to understand your own learning?

ON YOUR OWN

Log on to the web-based student study site at http://www.sagepub.com/holt for access to a Standards-Based Student Project that will help you connect what you have learned in this chapter to your state's standards; study aids, such as electronic flashcards; and research recommendations, including journal article links and other Web resources.

2

Confluent Forces and Differentiated Instructional Practices

SCHOOLS ARE ONE OF THE FEW ENTITIES IN OUR SOCIETY THAT EVERYONE HAS EXPERIENCE WITH and opinions about. Whether you attended a private or a public school, you know what happens within the walls of a school. Some people have positive experiences in school, others have negative experiences; however, the majority of students who matriculate in our schools view the experience as a necessary and mandatory ticket to life after the age of 18. Unfortunately, for approximately 11% of students (nearly four million) in 2001, school was another institution and experience that failed them; they were so unsuccessful that they perceived their only alternative was to drop out (U.S. Department of Education, 2003). The dropout rate in American schools has been systematically tracked as one of the indicators of the effectiveness of public education. The highest rates are found in our inner-city districts and among Hispanic and black students, usually those living at or below the poverty level. In spite of this problem, schools remain a bastion of hope in preserving the democratic principles important to the survival of our country. In 1818, Thomas Jefferson stated, "If the children . . . are untaught, their ignorance and vices will in the future life cost us much dearer in their consequences, than it would have done, in the correction of a good education" (Monticello, 1989).

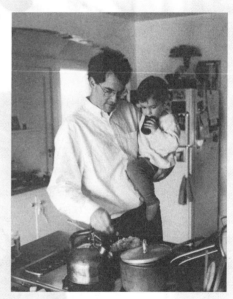

Our forefathers realized the importance of an educated populace to the future of the budding democracy. They perhaps had no way of predicting what the new country would ultimately become: a home to millions of people, many immigrants like themselves, who had neither the need nor desire to build a new society but wanted to merge into an existing society. The growth and change in our country since its inception has created a multitude of challenges for us, especially for those of us engaged in the education of our youth.

Before you can successfully plan for the instruction and assessment of your students, you need to have some knowledge of the factors that affect the way you think about your teaching and, most important, students' learning. Teaching is a very complex endeavor that is influenced by many confluent forces: historical precedents, economic issues, sociological realities,

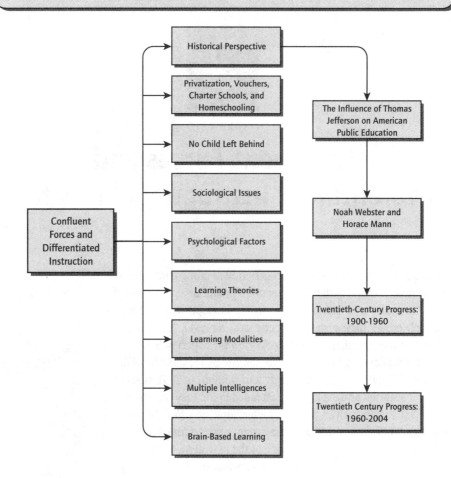

psychological advancements, and legal decisions. Although teachers have much autonomy in their classrooms, they also must live within the rules and regulations imposed on them by federal, state, and local legislation and policy, which are usually generated by the demographics of the greater population of the country and what research tells us about how we learn.

In this chapter, we will explore the confluent forces that teachers must understand to plan effective learning practices for their students in an increasingly complex and diverse society.

HISTORICAL PERSPECTIVE

There is no way that we could provide you with a complete history of the development of schools within the borders of the United States; however, we will try to give you an overview of their development and the important role schools have in ensuring that our democratic way of life is not threatened by the ignorance of the populace, a major concern of our founding fathers. History, thus, is an important confluent force that influences where we are and what we do in today's educational environment.

Our education system is shaped by its history.

The Influence of Thomas Jefferson on American Public Education

Historically, schools have been a means of shaping American society, but as our society has changed, this task has become increasingly more difficult because the original purposes and goals of public education have faded from the historic memory of most educators and politicians. Our public school system has often been referred to as a "great experiment in universal education." Our founding fathers believed that a republic could only survive if its citizens were educated. Thus, in the 1700s, schools were part of the "great plan" for the United States.

One of the strongest supporters of public education for the common good was Thomas Jefferson. In 1818, he stated, "A system of general education, which shall reach every description of our citizens from the richest to the poorest, as it was the earliest, so will it be the latest of all public concern, in which I shall permit myself to take an interest" (Monticello, 1989). He supported local control of schools. He wanted all (male) students to have access to basic education, which would teach them the correct political principles that were the foundation of the republic—how to read, write, and decipher (arithmetic)—and to exercise self-rule of the schools for their children. Jefferson supported three years of public education for girls so they could master the basic literacy skills and become good mothers and wives. He did not address the education of slaves.

Jefferson worked diligently to pass legislation in the Virginia Assembly, but he was defeated many times and lamented the slow process of changing the minds of the community. He continued to advocate his educational plans throughout his political career. Finally, he managed to implement some of his ideas through the establishment of the University of Virginia, where the state would ensure that public education would be available to all males through the secondary level and where postsecondary education would be free to many budding scholars, regardless of their status within the community. Thus, farmers' children had the opportunity to go to college. There is no doubt that Thomas Jefferson was a strong advocate of education for the common good. He once stated, "If a nation expects to be ignorant and free, it expects what never was and never will be" (quoted in Barlett, 2002, p. 359).

Thomas Jefferson's desire for a well-educated populace was evident in the Northwest Ordinance, which he proposed in 1784. This document explained how the United States would expand westward into the territory acquired from Great Britain in the aftermath of the American Revolution. On July 13, 1787, the Confederation Congress passed the ordinance, which made four crucial promises to residents in those territories regarding their prospective statehood:

1. Each would enter the union "on equal footing with the original states."

2. Revenue generated from the sale of the 16th parcel of a 36-parcel township would fund public education (the first instance of federal aid to education).

3. "Neither slavery nor involuntary servitude" were allowed.

4. A good-faith effort would be made to respect the native Indians of the territory.

Eventually, the Northwest Territories became the states of Ohio, Indiana, Illinois, Michigan, Wisconsin, and Minnesota (our current Midwest). The guarantee of public education for the common good was firmly established.

Noah Webster and Horace Mann

While Jefferson worked toward his notion of public education in Virginia, two other leaders were having a major impact on the future of education in the budding democracy: Noah Webster and Horace Mann. Noah Webster, a teacher in Connecticut, was insistent that if the new nation was going to succeed, it must remove itself from the vestiges of England; the first step was the elimination of British textbooks from American classrooms. In 1783, Webster published his own textbook, *A Grammatical Institute of the English Language,* referred to as the "Blue-Backed Speller" because of its color. This book was used to teach students to read in the public schools for nearly 100 years. In 1801, Webster began writing the first American dictionary. He was concerned that students in different parts of the country spelled and used words differently, and he thought that, for the common good of the country, all American citizens should speak and write in the same way. It took him 27 years to complete the dictionary, which included nearly 70,000 words. There is hardly a household today that does not contain a Webster's dictionary. Not only was Webster responsible for Americanizing the English language, he also worked on the first copyright law passed in the United States on May 25, 1790.

Horace Mann, often referred to as the father of American public education, was the first secretary of the Massachusetts Board of Education, serving from 1837 to 1848. Under his leadership, Massachusetts became a leader in public education. He was a strong advocate of public support for education, and as a result of his efforts, teachers wages doubled, supervision of teaching improved, 50 public secondary schools were built, and state aid to education doubled. He established the first Normal School to train teachers and the first free school district libraries.

Mann also published the *Common School Journal* and wrote annual reports that gave much direction to public education. In his *Fifth Annual Report* (1841), he indicated it was in the self-interest of businesses to pay taxes to support public education. In his *Tenth Annual Report*, he asserted that education is a natural right of all children, and thus it is necessary for the state

Thomas Jefferson was the third president of the United States and a revered states-man whose belief in natural rights, equality, individual liberties, and self-govern-ment found its fullest expression in the Declaration of Independence. Jefferson was also a skilled writer noted for his simple yet elegant prose. By clearly and per-suasively articulating the revolutionary political philosophy of an emerging nation, Jefferson profoundly influenced the direction of American politics, inspiring gen-erations of Americans. Yet his stature as a writer is often overshadowed by the variety of his accomplishments: In addition to his pivotal political role, he was an educator, architect, philosopher, scientist, linguist, and inventor.

Source: "Thomas Jefferson," *Dictionary of American Biography Base Set,* American Council of Learned Societies, 1928–1936; reproduced in the History Resource Center (Farmington Hills, MI: Gale Group, 2005).

to provide such an education. In 1852, Massachusetts was the first state to adopt a compulsory attendance law. In his final report, in 1848, he presented a rationale for the support of public edu-cation through taxation and successfully argued that nonsectarian schools should be established by public dollars so that taxpayers would not be beholden to a specific established religion.

In Boston during the 1840s, black children had the opportunity to attend primary school, but these were segregated schools, and only two schools were open to them in the community. In 1846, a group of African Americans petitioned the Boston School Committee to end segre-gation in the Boston schools. Their argument was that separate schools deprived their children of equal opportunities and cost the people more than if the schools were integrated. Although the committee agreed that the conditions of the black schools were not comparable to the white schools, they took no action. In 1855, Massachusetts passed the first state law abolishing seg-regation in public schools. In 1954, nearly 100 years later, the U.S. Supreme Court ruled in *Brown v. Board of Education of Topeka* that the separate-but-equal policy was unconstitutional, and the desegregation of schools spread across the country.

By the end of the 19th century, "the United States was providing more schooling to their children than any other country in the world" (Bernard & Mondale, 2001, p. 58). Not all of America's children were equally served or had access, but millions were receiving a free edu-cation. We still had a long way to go to ensure quality education for all, but the great experiment in universal education was working.

According to Diane Ravitch (2001), the greatest success of public schools in our country was the Americanization of the immigrants who founded and continued to build the country. One of the authors of this text is a second-generation American. Growing up in a large, indus-trial inner-city, she had firsthand experience of how the public schools she attended served to turn the children of immigrant families into highly patriotic American citizens. The families these children came from immigrated to the United States to build a new life, free from oppression, starvation, and poverty. Their loyalty to their new country was unquestioned. America, the land of diverse immigrants, was becoming America, the land of unity and commonality.

Noah Webster (1758–1843) wrote his own textbook, *A Grammatical Institute of the English Language,* in 1783. Most people called it the "Blue-Backed Speller" because of its blue cover. For 100 years, Webster's book taught children how to read, spell, and pronounce words. It was the most popular American book of its time. Benjamin Franklin used the book to teach his granddaughter to read.

At age 43, Webster started writing the first American dictionary. Americans in different parts of the country spelled, pronounced, and used words differently, and he thought that all Americans should speak the same way. He also thought that Americans should not speak and spell like the English.

Webster used American spellings such as *color* instead of the English *colour* and *music* instead of *musick*. He also added American words, such as *skunk* and *squash*, that weren't in English dictionaries. It took him more than 27 years to write his book. When finished in 1828, at the age of 70, Webster's dictionary comprised 70,000 words.

Source: "Noah Webster—A Short Summary of Noah Webster's Life," retrieved June 28, 2004, from www.ctstateu.edu/noahweb/biography.html.

Horace Mann, born in 1796, lived in poverty and suffered many hardships during his youth on the family farm. As a boy, he had formal schooling only three months out of each year, but by age 10, he had mastered the tenets of the orthodox Calvinist faith. Mann's efforts to establish free, public, nonsectarian education for every man and woman stemmed from his Unitarian convictions and a rejection of the Calvinist faith he had learned as a boy.

Mann graduated from Brown University, where he studied law, and was admitted to the bar in 1823. Between 1827 and 1848, Mann had a brilliant career as a state representative and then as a senator in Massachusetts. In 1837, he accepted the position of first secretary of the state board of education in Massachusetts.

Source: University of Central Florida, Biography Resource Center.

20th-Century Progress: 1900–1960

The beginning of the 20th century saw the United States engaged in World War I. Not only was this a significant world event, but also our engagement provided us with the opportunity to assess the quality of the men who were recruited or volunteered for military service. Psychologists used the servicemen to judge intelligence tests, which were developed in France and adapted in the

At the end of WWI, the United States was faced with large numbers of immigrants. This provided a challenge to our nation's schools.

United States. Louis Terman, an American psychologist, developed the intelligence tests that became widely used in American schools to determine the intellectual capacity of children and then to track students into the most appropriate educational programs. This test was also the precursor to other tests such as the SAT and ACT, which were eventually used to determine a student's ability to go to college. Thus, America's love affair with testing of students began.

At the end of World War I, the United States was once again faced with large numbers of immigrants, mostly from eastern and southern Europe. These individuals settled in large cities and placed immense demands on the public schools. Most of these children did not speak English, and thus schools became places where children would learn English. In some communities, because of the large number of immigrants, schools taught the basic subjects in the native language of the majority population. It was not unusual to find German, Russian, Polish, or other Slavic languages used as the instructional language in schools—at least at the elementary level. Faced with educating the new immigrants and having gained knowledge from the intelligence tests, schools introduced vocational programs to prepare these students to become good contributors to the workforce, whereas others (frequently women) maintained a general education that would allow them to succeed in their daily lives or followed a college-preparatory track.

It was during this period that progressive education made inroads into the thinking of educators and politicians. The progressive education movement was an attempt to restructure how children were taught as well as what they were taught. Fueled by ideas from John Dewey, "progressive schools" were found in almost all communities. The emphasis at these schools was students' engagement in their learning, or "learning by doing." Unfortunately, implementers of progressive education veered widely from the basic tenets of the philosophy. Thus, many progressive schools were like ships without a rudder, having neither a defined curriculum nor appropriate teaching methods to meet the needs of the diverse students found in those schools. Further development of progressive education was interrupted by yet another war.

World War II was another crucial turning point for American education. While American troops fought in Europe, Africa, and the Pacific, the education of their children on the home front was put on the back burner. Changes to the curriculum and exploring new and better ways to meet the needs of students were simply put on hold. However, in the large cities, many schools became community centers for air raid drills. Students were asked to plant victory gardens to ease the pressure on food production and the rationing that went on in the cities, and schools in the cities had children collecting tin, paper, and string—all for the war effort. For the first time, large numbers of children went home from school to an empty house as many women went to work in the factories to keep production going while the men were overseas.

During this time, many American children found their lives disrupted because their parents were identified as potential threats to American security. Internment camps and relocation camps were scattered throughout the United States. These camps housed mostly Japanese and German families, but many camps still provided education to the children. Depending on where the camps were located, American children could find themselves attending German, Japanese, or American schools. The curriculum of the schools was determined by the type of school found in the internment or relocation camps (Riley, 2002).

After World War II, U.S. schools were overcrowded with students—the postwar baby boomers. Attention once again turned to what schools should be teaching and what students should be learning to survive in the postwar economy. In parts of the country, however, schools were segregated: separate schools for blacks and whites. This was true in the large cities in the North as well as many communities throughout the South. In 1954, the U.S. Supreme Court ruled in *Brown v. Board of Education of Topeka* that the separate-but-equal policy was unconstitutional. Communities were told to integrate their schools with due speed. This ruling set the stage for many other lawsuits throughout the country as communities struggled to provide quality education for all children.

In 1957, the Russians successfully launched *Sputnik*, and our schools became the center of attention and the scapegoat for America's national embarrassment—the Russians had beaten us into space. National legislation was passed to ensure that federal dollars would be spent to shore up our schools and to tighten the curriculum to include more mathematics and science for all students. A more rigorous curriculum was demanded for the schools; teachers were provided with scholarships from the National Science Foundation to improve their skills as mathematics and science teachers—all at the federal government's expense.

20th-Century Progress: 1960–2004

The 1960s were very tumultuous times in our country. Ten years after the *Brown* decision, schools were still segregated. More and more attention was given to the desegregation of schools. Demonstrations and marches were occurring throughout the country. The federal government dispersed the National Guard to protect black children who were bused to white schools and adults who were trying to integrate the universities. In other parts of the country, desegregation was being done quietly, respectfully, and peacefully.

Bilingual education has been controversial since its inception.

President Lyndon B. Johnson, a former schoolteacher, championed the cause of integrated schools. In 1964, he signed the Civil Rights Act, which banned discrimination based on race in all federally funded programs. By now, public schools were recipients of many federal dollars, and therefore the ban applied to them. If they did not desegregate, they could lose their federal funding. In 1965, the Elementary and Secondary Education Act was passed, which provided $4 billion to aid disadvantaged youth. Now that the federal government was heavily investing in public schools, it also had the authority to impose sanctions on districts that were not in compliance with the law. According to Gary Orfield, a desegregation expert, between the mid-1960s and the early 1970s, "[W]e took a society that was like South Africa, an apartheid society where everything was defined by race, in seventeen of our states and we made it the most integrated part of the United States. That was a huge accomplishment, an accomplishment very few democracies have ever done in peacetime . . . we kind of take that for granted now, but we should never forget what we did in just a few years of serious effort" (cited in Bernard and Mondale, 2001, p. 149).

Although initial efforts to desegregate schools were focused on black and white children, other groups were beginning their efforts to get equal educational opportunities: non-English-speaking children, females, and children with disabilities. In 1968, the Bilingual Education Act was passed, providing guidelines and funding for programs in schools in which children's native language was not English. In 1974, the U.S. Supreme Court ruled in *Lau v. Nichols* that schools had to provide programs for children who did not speak English. In that same year, the federal government provided $68 million for bilingual education programs.

Bilingual education has been controversial since its inception. According to Arthur Schlesinger, Jr. (1998), bilingualism has created limited opportunities for many children. Because Hispanics are the largest portion of the population whose native language is not English, many bilingual programs have maintained children's reliance on Spanish instead of helping them to become fluent in English. Latino parents, Schlesinger contends, want their children to learn in English and view the institutionalization of bilingualism as a door shutter, not a door opener for their children: "Using some language other than English dooms people to second-class citizenship in American society" (1998, p. 113).

The 1990s produced a swell of support to amend the Constitution to designate English as the official language of the United States. In fact, by 1997, 22 states had such statutes. However, Schlesinger points out that such a move is extremely shortsighted on the part of politicians and citizens: "English is not a language in retreat, fighting for its life, requiring drastic measures of defense. It is triumphant around the planet. Four million people spoke English in Shakespeare's time; a billion speak it now. More books are published in English than in any other language. English will be, ironically, the *lingua franca* of the twenty-first century" (1998, pp. 114–115). The problem we face is not to constitutionalize English but to provide sufficient, efficient, and effective programs to teach English to those who need it. The cost in dollars may be high, but the cost to the United States as a democracy is much higher. In 1998, the United Nations ranked the United States 45th in literacy rates; in 1900, we were deemed the most literate nation.

Gender bias has been entrenched in American education since the beginning of our country. Modeled after the Civil Rights Act, Title IX was passed in 1972, prohibiting federal dollars from being distributed to schools or programs that discriminated based on gender. Although most of us recognize Title IX as a law that has benefited the funding of women's athletic programs, particularly at the university level, it was the fear of losing federal funds under this law that supported the inception of coeducational vocational programs, bias-free textbooks, and more educational opportunities for women. Young girls were encouraged to enter fields that were dominated by men: science, mathematics, engineering, law, and medicine. As women began to gain their rights within the educational sector, the focus then became the rights of the disabled.

In 1975, the federal government passed the Education of All Handicapped Children Act. Under this legislation, children who were denied access to public school programs because of their disabilities were now able to attend regular public schools. Schools needed to adjust both their physical facilities and their curriculum to accommodate the children who would be attending the schools. Special classes were initially the means by which many children received their education, but subsequent rulings required schools to provide education to these children in the "least restrictive environment"—thus the beginning of mainstreaming. Funding for children with disabilities was strongly supported by Congress. In 2001, more than $10 billion was spent on the education of handicapped children enrolled in our public schools (U.S. Census Bureau, 2003). Today, "the rights of students with disabilities in many ways are stronger and better enforced than the rights of any other groups" (Jay Heubert, cited in Bernard and Mondale, 2001, p. 163). Part of this is because the parents of these children have been extremely strong advocates for their children.

The last 20 years of public education have brought additional challenges to our schools, teachers, and students. In 1983, the report *A Nation at Risk* was published by the U.S. Commission on Excellence in Education. The report was extremely critical of the quality of American public schools. Fueled by input from the business community regarding its frustration with competing in a global marketplace and the reported mediocre performance of students on national and international tests, *A Nation at Risk* was a wake-up call to the states to "fix" their schools. In 1989, President George H. W. Bush met with the governors of all 50 states at what was called the Education Summit to discuss the state of American education. As a result of that meeting, the National Education Goals were published. Eight goals were established for schools to meet by 2000:

1. All children in America will start school ready to learn.

2. The high school graduation rate will increase to at least 90%.

3. All students will leave Grades 4, 8, and 12 having demonstrated competency over challenging subject matter, including English, mathematics, science, foreign languages, civics and government, economics, arts, history, and geography, and every school in America will ensure that all students learn to use their minds well, so they may be prepared for responsible citizenship, further learning, and productive employment in our nation's modern economy.

4. The nation's teaching force will have access to programs for the continued improvement of their professional skills and the opportunity to acquire the knowledge and skills needed to instruct and prepare all American students for the next century.

5. U.S. students will be first in the world in mathematics and science achievement.

6. Every adult American will be literate and will possess the knowledge and skills necessary to compete in a global economy and exercise the rights and responsibilities of citizenship.

7. Every school in the United States will be free of drugs, violence, and the unauthorized presence of firearms and alcohol and will offer a disciplined environment conducive to learning.

8. Every school will promote partnerships that will increase parental involvement and participation in promoting the social, emotional, and academic growth of children.

Not long after these goals were published, individual states passed their own sets of goals, reinforcing these and adding others. These state goals served as a stimulus for curriculum reform in the schools, assessment strategies to measure student progress, and much more attention to data gathering and documentation to meet the accountability issues raised by Goals 2000 and its corresponding state goals. Many programs that focused on vocational education, particularly in our high schools, were gradually removed from the curriculum. Arts programs were cut from many schools. Tougher academic courses were put into place, and higher standards for graduation were adopted by many school districts. Some communities where schools were not succeeding very well in helping students to progress to graduation turned to the private sector to run their schools.

Privatization, Vouchers, Charter Schools, and Homeschooling

Education Alternatives, Inc., became a major player, agreeing to work in some of the tougher schools in our inner cities. Businesses and industries began to see schools as viable markets for their products. In exchange for allowing companies to place their logos in the schools, schools could earn extra money to be used as they needed. Some districts signed exclusive contracts with corporations, such as Coke or Pepsi, allowing only products from those companies to be sold in the schools, usually through vending machines. Corporations frequently supplied the scoreboards for the football stadium or the basketball arena. Athletes wore Nike or Adidas products.

Channel One television, which is broadcast in 25% of the nation's secondary schools, provided free media equipment for the schools. In exchange for the equipment, schools needed to guarantee that students would watch 12 minutes of news and commercials geared toward young people. Alex Molnar (1996), a harsh critic of the commercialization of the schools, raises the question, does the school or the business control the curriculum and the education the students receive?

Another challenge to public schools has arisen from the poor performance of students in inner-city public schools: vouchers. Public schools have attempted to change the performance indicators by establishing alternative schools and magnet schools. Often, such schools receive additional funding to offer failing students a different approach to learning or to offer better students opportunities to excel in the arts, mathematics, science, technology, or other attractive programs. Jonathan Kozol describes this mentality in the cities as a "lifeboat mentality." Cities assume they cannot reverse the underachievement of city youth; therefore, they establish these small, attractive schools to help the few who want to succeed. However, such alternatives simply sweep the problems under the rug, and the majority of children in the city are neither understood nor properly served (Kozol, quoted in Bernard and Mondale, 2001, p. 192).

When alternative or magnet schools do not work or are not sufficiently available to city youth, parents now have a choice of asking for vouchers to send their children enrolled in failing schools to successful schools. Most of the schools the children go to are private schools, secular or religious. In essence, they take their public dollars to pay for private education. The use of vouchers for religious schools was tested in Cleveland, Ohio, in 1996 and was found not to conflict with the principle of separation of church and state. In 1990, Milwaukee, Wisconsin, was the first major public district to allow the use of vouchers. That year, approximately 400 low-income public school children attended private, secular schools at public expense. In 1998, 1,500 students attended private schools, both secular and religious, at public expense. The loss of students from the public schools has created an increased deficit for the public schools in Milwaukee (Reaves, 2001).

Charter schools are another alternative to the crowding of public schools and the failure of the public schools to provide adequate education for America's children. Charter schools are another form of public education. They are supposed to be open to all children. They usually are designed to appeal to the special needs of students, whether those needs are social, emotional, or academic. The schools must apply to either a district or state to obtain a charter and identify how the school will meet the objectives of the targeted population. Charter schools may be organized by private corporations, former educators, or in some cases, school districts. Several regular public schools have transitioned into charter schools.

Charter schools can offer more flexibility in programs because they are only accountable to the state in which they are organized and are often free of the rules and regulations that apply to regular schools in that state. They are funded by public dollars. The school receives the per-pupil expenditure that is used by the district or state in which it operates. Charter schools do not have to deal with the typical bureaucracy of district schools. Generally, there is no district office, central board of education, or superintendent that they are accountable to. If they do not meet their goals and students do not meet the state achievement goals within three to five years, the schools can lose their charters.

In some states, the chartering of schools is done through district offices, and schools are held accountable to the board of education and the superintendent of the district in which the school is located. However, the schools are still removed from things such as high-stakes testing, standardized tests, district examinations, etc. In 2001, there were 2,100 charter schools in the United States and more than 93,000 regular public schools (U.S. Census Bureau, 2003).

Whether charter schools are good or bad is highly contested in public education, as are vouchers used to send public school children to private schools. The supporters of both programs insist that public schools will improve as a result of the competition they now face and cannot remain complacent about the failure of their students to succeed. On the other hand, those opposed to these plans insist that vouchers and charter schools simply dilute the resources that public schools need to reform and improve. There obviously are some excellent charter schools, excellent private schools, and excellent regular public schools. How these types of schools and the services they provide the young people of our country will fare in the future is a story that is yet to be told.

Homeschooling is another option for parents. In 1999, nearly 2% of the entire school population was homeschooled. Most of these children were in the elementary grades, and parents chose to homeschool their children for religious or safety concerns. In some school districts, homeschooled children are still under the oversight of the public schools. If the children fail to make progress under homeschooling, parents may be required to enroll their children in the public schools, particularly if private schooling is not an option. Failure to enroll children in school is a violation of mandatory attendance requirements established in each state.

No Child Left Behind

In 2001, Congress passed and President George W. Bush signed the No Child Left Behind (NCLB) Act, a renewal of the Elementary and Secondary Education Act. This act may be the most highly debated piece of national education legislation to cross the thresholds of the public school systems. The law requires that children be tested every year using standardized tests. Curricula and teaching practices used in the schools are to be based on "scientific evidence." Schools must report the annual yearly progress (AYP) of each subgroup of children enrolled. If one group of children fails to make its projected AYP, the school may be considered a failing school. Schools on the national failure list for two years may have the faculty and administration removed from that school. Children can get vouchers to attend other schools, and students who fail to pass high-stakes tests in high school could be denied a high school diploma, even though they may have passed all of their subjects.

The stakes for public education are very high under NCLB. States with large minority and non-English-speaking populations are crying foul and demanding that provisions be made to give schools more time to deal with the language challenges of students. Large school districts with majority minority populations are asking for some relief from the deadlines imposed by NCLB.

Although the intent of NCLB is to raise the achievement bar, the reality is that many schools face horrendous challenges to meet the new criteria because of many years of inappropriate funding, growing populations, much more diversity in those populations, increases in school violence and drug abuse, and shortages of well-qualified teachers.

Criticism of public education seems to be a pastime for anyone who has ever attended school. Granted, today, schools face challenges that were never dreamed of by our founding fathers. Yet before we are quick to condemn and deride, we must recognize that American public schools on the whole have been very successful. Our schools educate all children, regardless of economic status, ethnicity, physical, or mental ability. We really do have an open-door policy for our children. In 2001, nearly 59.5 million students were enrolled in public schools, approximately 90% of the total K–12 school population (U.S. Census Bureau, 2003). Of that number, nearly one-fourth were foreign born or had at least one parent who was foreign born, and nearly 10% were students classified by the Census Bureau as handicapped. For more than 200 years, our public schools have been a constant influence that has helped to make us the Americans we are. Are they perfect? No. Are they failing? Not really. Do they need the public's support? Yes. If we want a unified country that operates on the basic principles of democracy, our schools need to be supported by the public. As Thomas Jefferson said, the future of democracy depends on the education of its people.

SOCIOLOGICAL ISSUES

The demographics of the United States have changed dramatically since our country was founded. As the country has grown and as we have had waves of immigration over the years, population figures indicate that our country is becoming much more diverse. According to the U.S. Census Bureau (2003), the population of the United States is projected to increase 50% to 420 million people during the next 50 years. Much of that increase is the result of the current flood of immigrants, 1.5 million people a year. Current immigrants are coming from North America (Canada, Mexico, the Caribbean, and Central America), Asia (Afghanistan, India, China, Korea, and the Middle Eastern countries), and Europe (Poland, Bosnia and Herzegovina, Russia, Ukraine, United Kingdom, and other eastern and western European countries). In 2001, nearly half of the immigrants to the United States were from Europe, one-fourth from North American countries, one-fifth from Asian countries, and the remainder (about 5%) from Africa and South America.

The ethnic profile of the United States is changing from European White, African American, and Hispanic to European, Hispanic, Asian, and African American. But using such large categories to describe the potential mix of Americans overlooks the differences that exist within each of these categories. There are major differences in religion, mores, culture, language, social practices, and economics between and within these categories. Thus, describing the "typical" American will become increasingly difficult as our population changes. Planning an appropriate education for the children who represent this population will become increasingly difficult as schools attempt to honor the diversity while educating the masses.

Shifting Populations

The question before us is not just about the ethnic profile of our country but also where all of these people are going to settle. According to Ted Landphair of Voice of America (2004), the majority of these immigrants are not headed for the wheat fields of our great plains states but for the big cities and the Sun Belt. The population on both coasts is already quite dense, and states such as California, Texas, and Florida are struggling to meet the demands of rapidly growing, diverse populations. Not only are the new immigrants settling in the cities and the Sun Belt, but internal migration is also causing severe economic distress in some states. States such as Florida, Nevada, Texas, Arizona, and the Carolinas are growth states not only because of immigration, but also because retirees like to settle in these states, and families with younger children are choosing to avoid the bad weather and poor economic conditions of our northern states.

	TABLE 2.1	Changing Migration									

	1965–70			1975–80			1985–1990			1995–2000	
Rank	City	Net Gain	City		Net Gain	City		Net Gain	City		Net Gain
1	Los Angeles	55,943	Los Angeles		32,764	Atlanta		74,705	Atlanta		114,478
2	Detroit	54,766	Atlanta		27,111	Washington, DC–Baltimore		29,904	Dallas		39,360
3	Washington, DC–Baltimore	34,365	Houston		24,267	Norfolk– Virginia Beach		27,645	Charlotte		23,313
4	San Francisco	24,699	San Francisco		16,034	Raleigh– Durham		17,611	Orlando		20,222
5	Philadelphia	24,601	San Diego		15,621	Dallas		16,097	Las Vegas		18,912
6	New York	18,792	Dallas		12,460	Orlando		13,368	Norfolk– Virginia Beach		16,660
7	Dallas	16,384	Norfolk– Virginia Beach		10,141	Richmond		12,508	Raleigh– Durham		16,144
8	Houston	16,301	Washington, DC–Baltimore		9,998	San Diego		12,482	Washington, DC–Baltimore		16,139
9	Chicago	14,061	Killeen–Temple		9,959	Minneapolis– St. Paul		11,765	Memphis		12,507
10	Cleveland	10,914	Columbia, SC		9,082	Sacramento		10,848	Columbia, SC		10,899

Source: *Orlando Sentinel*, May 24, 2004, p. A4.

According to the report *The New Great Migration: Black Americans Return to the South, 1965–2000* (Frey, 2004), more African Americans moved into than out of the South during the 1990s, which is a very different pattern from the 1970s and 1980s. Table 2.1 illustrates this changing migration, measured by the net gain of African Americans in 10 cities from 1965 to 2000. As you read the table, note the differences in the locations of the cities and keep in mind that this reflects only a part of the population of our country. Many whites and Asians are following similar migration patterns, whereas Hispanics are focusing on California, Arizona, New Mexico, Texas, and Florida.

With these shifts in population, school districts in areas receiving and losing populations are challenged to meet the needs of their changing environments. Much of this challenge is economic: how to support and build the schools needed for the community. Where population has been lost, schools may face the loss of their tax base and the need to close schools or lay off faculty. Where populations are increasing, school districts are faced with the cost of building new facilities and hiring teachers, frequently with no major increase in funding. Funding often comes after the initial need is demonstrated, so schools in high-growth areas are often overcrowded and understaffed. All of these factors play into the challenges teachers have in working in these environments.

Language and Culture

Looking at the immigration and migration patterns raises another issue for teachers: With ethnic differences rising in communities, there is the real possibility that teachers will be working with students who are not only culturally very different from them but also may not speak English as their native language. Cultural and language differences can create serious communication problems within the classroom unless the teachers are adequately prepared to adjust their teaching to meet the needs of these students. In some states, such as Florida, teachers who are likely to have non-English-speaking students in their classrooms must meet the certification endorsement for ESOL (English for speakers of other languages). ESOL requirements vary by subject matter and grade level, but most K–12 teachers are required to have a minimum of 60 hours of training in ESOL strategies to meet the needs of the students in their classrooms.

Language is not the only problem facing teachers who have culturally diverse classrooms. Selecting curriculum materials that will not be offensive to students and their respective cultures is imperative. Teachers need to examine all curricular materials they are using to ensure that the materials positively and accurately reflect the cultures that are present in their classrooms. Reading selections should include, when possible, the writings of various cultures. Social studies materials should be inclusive and reflective of all cultures. Textbooks need to be examined to ensure that no one culture is deemed "better" than another. These tasks are very difficult when many cultures exist in a classroom, but teachers need to be attentive to these ideas to make the classroom an inviting and friendly place for all students.

Concept of Family

In addition to the ethnic differences that are plentiful within the classroom, other sociological factors are playing out in the classroom that make teaching much more challenging. The changing definition of what constitutes a family is by far the most pertinent. A teacher cannot assume that the students in his or her classroom come from the "typical" family that consists of a mother, father and 2.5 children. Many children come from very complex family configurations. Children may have no parents (raised by their grandparents or other relatives), no father or no mother (raised by a single parent), multiple parents (with parents divorcing and remarrying), foster or adopted families, gay or lesbian parents, or, if the children are older, they may be gay or lesbian themselves. Children's lives may be tumultuous. They may be living in very difficult circumstances. In an inner city, where one of the authors is working, several of the students attending high school are homeless, living in a shelter or on the streets. Some of the students are living in family situations in which they are constantly abused, either physically or verbally, and have no support to remove themselves from the situation. Many of the young ladies (60%) attending this school are teen parents, and 40% of the young men have already been incarcerated.

Statistics like these are common in inner-city school districts, but they may also exist in other more affluent school districts. When students have these types of living situations, it becomes very difficult to engage them in learning. School for many of these students is a place to socialize, not necessarily a place to learn. School may be a safe haven where they can get decent food and some quiet time, which is more important, perhaps, than trying to pass a science test or complete mathematics homework. As a teacher, the most important thing you can do is try to understand the population you will be working with in your school. Having a good understanding of the population will help you to make adjustments to your teaching strategies that will benefit the learning of the students. If you come from a middle-class, intact home environment, recognizing the chaotic lifestyles of some of your students may prove to be difficult, but it is essential if you plan to maximize the potential for learning of these students. You may not be able to change the students' home or family environments, but by understanding their lifestyles, you can adjust assignments and instructional patterns to provide them opportunities for school success and perhaps provide them with some hope for their futures.

Economics and Social Class

Economics also play an important role in determining the types of students a teacher may encounter in the classroom. American class structure, regardless of mobility, has remained fairly stable throughout the 20th century. Table 2.2 reports the current percentage of the population classified as poor, middle class, or upper class and the corresponding income of each group.

Students from the lower and lower-middle classes may come from environments that are very mobile, meaning that families live in rental property and move frequently, particularly if the breadwinners in the family change jobs to improve themselves or cannot hold onto jobs because they do not have the requisite educational skills to keep them. Unemployment rates and incarceration rates are relatively high among the poor, as are juvenile and adult crime patterns. High school dropout rates are higher among the poor: approximately 9% compared to 3.8% among families earning more than $20,000 and 2.3% among families earning more than $40,000 (Jamieson, Curry, & Martinez, 2001). High school dropout rates are highest among Hispanics (34%) and African Americans (16%), whereas 92% of non-Hispanic whites and 90% of Asians and Pacific Islanders complete their high school education. More females complete high school (83%) than males (79%) (Jamieson et al., 2001).

TABLE 2.2	Social Class and Income				
	Poor (Lower class)	Lower Middle Class	True Middle Class	Upper Middle Class	Rich (Upper Class)
Income	Less than $15,000; (Less than $30,000 in big cities)	$15,000–$35,000; (Less than $50,000 in big cities)	$35,000–$75,000; ($50,000–$150,000 in big cities)	More than $75,000; (More than $150,000 in big cities)	More than $1 million
Assets	Less than $10,000	Less than $55,000	Less than $500,000	$368,000 under age 30; $1 million under age 60; otherwise, $5 million	$3 million under age 45; $5 million under age 60; otherwise, $10 million
Percentage of population	20%	29%	33%	17%	1%

Source: www.socialclass.org, retrieved May 23, 2004.

Other Sociological Forces Affecting Schools

So far, we have explored the history of our schools and the changing demographics of our school population to help you to better understand some of the forces that influence what and how you teach. But there are many other factors that impinge on your decision making about your instructional strategies.

In recent years, gender has become a focal point of criticism of the public school curriculum. Thus, teachers need to ask themselves, "Am I presenting a lesson that values one gender over another?" The question has been a major issue in mathematics and science curricula: Boys typically have outnumbered girls in advanced science and mathematics classes in secondary schools. Likewise, these issues are raised in language arts classes, where girls typically outperform boys. According to Ornstein and Hunkins (1998),

> Many feminists [cultural feminists] engaged in scholarship for the advancement of girls' and women's rights want the curricula offered to be redesigned and reconceptualized so that significant aspects of the female experience and female ways of knowing are included in the curriculum . . . . Others, known as liberal feminists . . . argue that the curriculum as it now exists can be presented in a way to that students are not taught to behave in sex-stereotyped ways. (p. 148)

A study conducted by the American Association of University Women, *How Schools Shortchange Girls: The AAUW Report* (1992), indicated that girls in Grades K–12 receive a poorer education than boys. According to the report, girls receive less attention in classrooms than boys; teachers in elementary schools frequently choose classroom activities that appeal more to boys than girls; standard teaching methods are still competitive even though research shows that girls learn better in cooperative groups; curricula ignore or stereotype women; girls do not pursue mathematics and science careers in proportion to boys; standardized tests contain elements of gender bias; girls' reports of sexual harassment by boys are increasing in our schools; and African American girls are more likely than white girls to be ignored by teachers.

Reports such as this one point out inequities in the classroom that teachers have the power to change. Fortunately, more researchers are studying gender issues and publishing their findings, which illuminate the inequities faced by both girls and boys in our public schools. Brain-based research indicates there are structural differences in the brains of boys and girls that may be linked to how they excel in various school subjects. Regardless of what we learn about learning differences in boys and girls, the gender issue will not go away. Being equitable in dealing with these issues is what is important, and we must ensure that both boys and girls have equal access to knowledge and that their contributions to the classroom are equally acknowledged and celebrated. According to Ornstein and Hunkins (1998),

> The challenges for dealing with diversity, with race, class, and gender, are extremely complex. . . . Perhaps the key for educators is the realization that we are all members of particular ethnic groups; . . . class or social groups, and we all have gender. . . . These attributes make us diverse and unique, but they also bespeak of a commonness . . . we all have these attributes. (p. 150)

In the history section, we addressed the passage of the Education of All Handicapped Children Act and its subsequent legislation and mandates. Classroom teachers are expected to meet the needs of the special needs students who are mainstreamed into their classrooms. Some of these students may have very mild disabilities that can be addressed easily. For example, a student with a mild learning disability may be able to use computer programs or extra practice time to overcome that disability. A mildly visually handicapped student could be seated at the front of the room to make reading from the chalkboard or overhead projector easier, and that student could have access to a computer on which the text could be enlarged to accommodate his or her visual problem.

However, when the disabilities are more severe, teachers need to plan how they will accommodate those disabilities. It is imperative for regular classroom teachers to work collaboratively with special education teachers to make appropriate accommodations for disabled students. Teachers cannot ignore students in the classroom who have diagnosed disabilities. In many school districts, teachers must list on their lesson plans the strategies they will use to meet the learning needs of these students.

In addition to working with students whose disabilities are diagnosed, it is essential that teachers constantly observe their students to determine whether students who are underperforming or exhibiting behavior problems have legitimate causes for their actions. Students often reactive negatively in the classroom when they are bored with what they are learning. They may, in fact, need more intellectual challenges. Often students' intellectual abilities are not properly diagnosed, and their classroom behavior is a result of their not being challenged appropriately to meet their intellectual needs. We are much more successful in diagnosing learning disabilities or intellectual deficiencies than we are at identifying giftedness or creativity. The teacher's job is to constantly assess what he or she is seeing and to make recommendations to the proper support staff in their school to ensure that all students are receiving the most appropriate opportunities for successful learning in school.

PSYCHOLOGICAL FACTORS

Teachers today have far more information about how students learn than any other generation of teachers. The field of psychology has provided educators with masses of theories and data that can inform the practice of teaching. The difficult part of all of this information is trying to make sense out of it and applying the information appropriately in the classroom. This section will examine some basic learning theories: the concept of multiple intelligences, emotional intelligence, and brain-based learning principles. Within the boundaries of this text, there is no way that these ideas can be explored in depth, but we hope this information will provide you with sufficient knowledge to explore ideas that resonate with you and that you believe will help you to make good decisions about how to meet the needs of your students.

The field of psychology is relatively new in the academic world. Unlike philosophy, which has existed for centuries and has been the foundation of thinking for many educators, psychology has a rather short life span—it is a 19th-century phenomenon for the most part. Because psychology is the study of the mind and mental and emotional behaviors, there is little doubt as to its application to education, particularly as educators search for better means of meeting the ever-changing needs of students.

Learning Theories

All of us in the field of education have some sense of how we learn. We may not be able to verbalize our understanding of our learning process in scientific terms, but we know when and under what conditions we learn best. We know that some subjects are easier for us to learn than others. We often say things such as "Language is not my forte," "I can get really involved in history," or "My worst subject in school was geometry." All of these statements reflect our perception of our abilities and skills with respect to what and how we learn best. The study of learning theories helps us not only to understand ourselves better but also to make appropriate decisions when we are working with students.

There are numerous learning theories in psychology, and new ones are being discovered all the time. Unfortunately, as teachers, we are not always cognizant of the newest ideas on learning: It usually takes 25 years for psychologists to translate a theory of learning into practical applications for the classroom, and even then the new theory does not necessarily replace existing ideas but merely competes with them (Bigge & Shermis, 1992). In this section, we will summarize the most prevalent theories of learning found in our schools. These theories fall into three broad categories: mental discipline, behaviorism, and cognitive.

Mental discipline theories, which became popular during the 19th century, contend that learning consists of disciplining or training the mind. In a typical classroom, a teacher who believes in the mental discipline concept of learning would use activities that require students to practice specific learning tasks until those tasks become automatic. For instance, the use of flash cards to learn multiplication facts or the spelling of common words requires repetition until the students get it right. Teachers focus on recitation, having students memorize and repeat passages. Drill question-and-answer sessions are a common strategy for those who subscribe to mental discipline theories of learning.

Historically, such strategies were accompanied by the belittling of students who got the answers wrong. The punishment for wrong answers would be more repetition of what was to be learned. Modern-day supporters of mental discipline include writers such as Mortimer Adler, Allan Bloom, and Harry Broudy. These advocates certainly do not subscribe to the punishment or belittling of students or to the excessive punishment of those who do not get the answers right, but they do believe in the intrinsic mental power of individuals and the ability to develop mental power through repetitive exercising of the mind. They support memorization, recitation, and lots of practice.

The concept of the brain as a huge muscle that needs to be trained is basic to the theory of "apperceptive mass" promoted by Johann Herbart (Bigge & Shermis, 1992). Essentially, Herbart believed that learning takes place when ideas are introduced sequentially so that students can "hook" new ideas to existing knowledge. For example, a teacher would teach reading by first getting the students to memorize the letters of the alphabet and their sounds. The teacher would then explain how letters and sounds are put together to make words. He or she would explain the difference between vowels and consonants and how they work. The teacher would teach the students the rules of language. Once the students had this knowledge, the teacher would introduce them to common objects and then show them how the words for those objects are spelled. Everything is done in a systematic pattern.

To teach in this fashion, teachers would have to take every concept or idea they wanted the students to learn and break that down into all the prerequisite knowledge necessary to learn that concept or idea. This in itself can be a tedious task, yet some students, parents, and teachers find this systematic approach to learning helpful. Many textbooks are designed along these lines: Content is sequentially organized with skills repeated from chapter to chapter as new information is introduced. Curriculum guides are often written with these ideas in mind. Many teachers are comfortable teaching in this fashion.

Behavioral theories of learning were popularized during the early part of the 20th century. Behaviorists believe that learning is a change in the observable behavior of the student. This behavioral change is attributed to stimulus-response (S-R) activities. Given a stimulus, the student responds, and that response is positively reinforced (PR). The S-R-PR pattern is repeated until the student responds without the reinforcement—that's when learning has taken place. Ivan Pavlov's experiments with training dogs in Russia to salivate using the S-R-PR pattern were highly influential in the development of U.S. theories of learning. Edward Thorndike, John Watson, and B. F. Skinner were early believers in the stimulus-response theory of learning. Their ideas were popularized not only in the learning of content but also—and more important for some teachers—in the training of students to behave properly in the classroom. There were many classroom management programs designed using behaviorist ideas of learning. These programs are still popular in exceptional education programs and among teachers dealing with particularly difficult children.

During the late 1960s and early 1970s, Robert Mager advocated writing behavioral objectives in precise terms with specified, observable achievement levels for individual students and the class as a whole as a means of organizing a class for maximum learning. Teachers wrote their objectives in observable language and measured students' success by assessing their behavior. For example, a typical behavioral objective would read something like this: "When given 20 two-digit addition problems with regrouping, 90% of the students will answer them with 80% accuracy, with no student scoring less than 70% accuracy." To ensure that students could achieve this objective, the teacher would have the students practice similar problems until he or she was reasonably sure that the students had learned how to do basic two-digit addition with no regrouping. The students knew ahead of time what they needed to accomplish and how they were to be assessed.

The reason that Mager's behavioral objectives became so popular was twofold: Programmed instruction was beginning to become popular in the schools, and specificity of expectations was mandated for self-correction to occur in such a learning environment. Second, the specificity of expectation for students made it easier for teachers to be held accountable for student learning, and schools were being asked to demonstrate that they could successfully teach what they were supposed to be teaching. This was the era of minimum competencies in curricular programs. Schools were expected to have all students meet the minimum competencies designated at every grade level for the core subjects of mathematics, science, social studies, and language arts.

Cognitive theories of learning define learning as a process of human interaction with the environment or with other people to gain or change insights, outlooks, expectations, or thoughts. Much of cognitive theory supports the notion that in order for a person to understand what he or she is learning, that person must be consciously aware of the thinking patterns that are being used and explored (metacognition). Cognitive theorists are concerned with human perception, motivation, and thinking, which all influence how a person processes information that he or she receives. In these theories, the acquisition of knowledge is an active process stimulated by curiosity, interest, and need.

Cognitive psychologists also believe that humans construct much of their knowledge by relating incoming information to acquired knowledge. Each person receives, selects, and transforms information and then constructs and alters hypotheses according to the evidence he or she receives; thus, two people can be exposed to the same information, process it differently, and have different outcomes of learning. Learning is a very active and engaging process but also very personal. Cognitive psychologists have varying perspectives on exactly how learning takes place, but they agree it is an active, thoughtful, engaging, and very personal process. Some of the more widely read cognitive theorists are Jerome Bruner, Albert Bandura, and John Dewey.

This section has tried to provide you with an overview of learning theories that affect how you think about the learning process. No attempt has been made here to delve deeply into each of the theories or to discuss the merits of any of the theories. That is something you can do on your own at another time. What you need to be conscious of is that there are theories that explain our learning. Most of us may be eclectic in how we learn, and as teachers, we certainly are eclectic in how we teach. The need for knowledge about specific learning theories and styles of learning is important when we are confronted with students who do not respond to what we are teaching and how we are teaching it. Then it is time to rethink what we are doing and how best to meet the needs of all of the students we teach.

Learning Modalities

Another area of information related to learning is that of *learning modalities*. Have you ever wondered why some people are adept at working with their hands whereas others cannot figure out how to hang a picture? Have you wondered why some people can listen to a radio broadcast and have a very different perception of the message than you had? Have you marveled at the person who can stand up and make a spontaneous speech that sounds as if it was written by a collection of speechwriters? Have you ever tried to draw a picture about something you are trying to understand?

As you think about these questions, what you are engaging in is the knowledge that different people receive and create information using different physical modalities. Some of us are visual learners: We learn best through access to visual inputs of information. Those inputs might be pictures, words, diagrams, or figures. Many visual learners can sit down, read a book, and learn. We may, if we are having difficulty understanding an idea, draw a picture or diagram to help us figure out the information. We may choose to seek out additional materials to read or locate a video or film that may describe the phenomenon we are trying to grasp. We rely on our eyes to provide the information, which we then must internally process. Some visual learners respond to pictures and diagrams more so than words, but the reality is that we seek information through our visual senses regardless of the form of that information.

The auditory learners among us, on the other hand, rely more on what we hear than what we see. Often, we might find it necessary to close our eyes and simply listen to the speaker or the radio or television to understand what we are hearing. We might even find ourselves reading aloud to help us understand a passage in a book, a theorem, or a chemical equation. We may prefer to hear the teacher lecture rather than read the book. We might choose to do a presentation or demonstration in the classroom rather than write a paper or take a test. We need to "hear ourselves think" in order to learn. We like to work in groups because we can listen to our colleagues and reinforce what we think we know through our conversations.

Learn by doing is the mantra of the kinesthetic learner. We need to explore, feel, touch, taste, and experiment with the content we are trying to learn. We do best if we can become physically engaged somehow in our learning. Sometimes, when we are having a particularly difficult time learning something, we may find ourselves fidgeting or walking around, unable to sit still. We may find it easier to memorize something by setting it to music and dancing about. We may be excellent workers in a laboratory because we get to measure, cut, dissect, pour, or plant.

The majority of us learn equally well through our three modalities, and we call on whichever modality is best suited to the task at hand. Yet many students do not have the flexibility to work in all three modalities and have specific preferences for one or the other. The Swassing-Barbe Modality Index and similar tools can help the teacher to determine whether a student has a preference for one modality or another (Barbe & Swassing, 1979). If a student has a modality preference, the teacher can teach the student through that preference while helping the student to develop skills in the other two modalities. Even if a teacher does not have access to an assessment tool, simple observations can usually uncover a student's modality preference. Teachers can also plan a variety of activities in the classroom to address each of the modalities, thus ensuring that all students have access to the information through their strengths, not their weaknesses.

Multiple Intelligences

In 1993, Howard Gardner published his book *Frames of Mind,* in which he defined seven different types of intelligence, known as the *multiple intelligences theory.* In his book, he indicated that there is both a biological and a cultural basis for multiple intelligences. Different types of learning are found in different areas of the brain; consequently, for an intelligence to be identified, there must be a unique area within the brain where that intelligence can be identified. Different cultures honor different types of intelligence, and the culture motivates and supports the development of that intelligence. In addition, multiple intelligences do not operate separately but frequently work together. His original theory outlined seven types of intelligence:

1. Logical-mathematical intelligence: The ability to detect patterns, reason deductively, and think logically.

2. Verbal-linguistic intelligence: The mastery of language, including the ability to express oneself rhetorically or poetically and to enhance the remembrance of information.

3. Visual-spatial intelligence: The ability to manipulate and create mental images to solve problems.

4. Musical-rhythmic intelligence: The ability to recognize and compose musical pitches, tones, and rhythms.

5. Bodily-kinesthetic intelligence: The ability to use one's mind to coordinate physical ability.

6. Interpersonal intelligence: The ability to work in groups, socialize, get along with different people.

7. Intrapersonal intelligence: The ability to be introspective and understand one's emotions and feelings.

In 1996, Gardner added an eighth intelligence, *naturalistic intelligence*: the ability to observe, understand, and organize patterns in the natural environment. He also has indicated that he is exploring the nature of *existential intelligence*, the intelligence of "big questions" (Gardner, 2003).

All of Gardner's intelligences rely on patterns of behavior that are peculiar to that type of intelligence. Perhaps this is because brain-based research contends that the brain is constantly searching for patterns to make sense of the information it receives.

Gardner cautions educators to know the difference between learning styles, which are preferred ways to receive and process information and multiple intelligences, and ways of thinking and behaving. He also is opposed to describing different racial or ethnic groups in terms of their intelligences (Gardner, 2003). What Gardner does advocate is for teachers to plan lessons and strategies to be inclusive of a broad range of students' talents, skills, and interests.

As we learn more about how the brain functions, we will discover many more forms of intelligence or ways of describing intelligence. Other theories of intelligence include Robert Sternberg's idea of the triarchic mind (1988), David Perkins's "popcorn" theory of intelligence (1995) and Daniel Goleman's theory of emotional intelligence (1995).

Brain-Based Learning

As Chapter 1 indicated, the emphasis throughout this book is what we have learned about how the brain functions and how we can use that information to maximize the potential of all learners in our classrooms. The amount of information we have is often overwhelming as we struggle with decisions about why, when, what, and how we will teach something to our students. What we do know is that students must be the focal point of our thinking about what will ultimately occur in the classroom. We must take into consideration who these students are, what their unique characteristics are, what their lifestyles are, and how these factors may influence how they function in school. We need to consider how to find the best ways to meet their multitude of needs and abilities. We need to recognize how to use new technologies to help us accomplish the job we have ahead of us, whether that technology provides us with information to use in the classroom, gives us tools for assessing our students, or gives students multiple means by which they can learn and practice the information they are expected to know by the time they finish school.

THE NEED FOR DIFFERENTIATED INSTRUCTION

Now that we have explored the confluent forces that influence the thinking and behavior of teachers and students, you should be cognizant of the fact that no two learners are alike, nor is there only one way for them to learn or one way for you to teach. Faced with the increased diversity of students in our schools, increased knowledge of how students learn or think, and a variety of tools and practices you can incorporate into your classrooms, you can better meet the needs of your students through the practice of differentiated instruction.

According to Carol Tomlinson (2005), teachers can differentiate four classroom elements to accommodate the learning needs of students: content, process, products, and learning environment. The *content* is what is taught and how students access the material to be learned. *Process* is the set of activities students engage in to master the content. *Products* are students' culminating projects, which demonstrate what they learned, and the *learning environment* is the way the classroom works and feels.

Tomlinson identifies differentiated instruction as having the following qualities:

- Proactive: Teachers recognize the different learning needs of students and plan a variety of ways to meet those needs.

- Qualitative rather than quantitative: Students are not given more or less work because of their learning needs but appropriate assignments that match their needs.

- Rooted in assessment: A good teacher employs a variety of formal and informal assessment strategies to better understand the learning needs of the students. This assessment is ongoing and focuses on readiness levels, interests, and modes of learning.

- Multiple approaches to content, process, and product.

- Student centered: Teachers find ways to help students become increasingly responsible for their own learning. Because not all students learn the same way, the key to increasing student responsibility is to incorporate a variety of strategies to make learning engaging, relevant, and interesting.

- Blend of whole-class, group, and individual instruction.

- Organic: It is constantly evolving. "Differentiated instruction is dynamic: Teachers monitor the match between learner and learning and make adjustments as warranted" (Tomlinson, 2005, p. 6). Teachers do not follow a recipe to differentiate but combine their own professional instincts and knowledge base to do whatever is needed to reach out to each learner (p. 7).

The remainder of this book is designed to provide you with the necessary professional knowledge to differentiate your instruction, thereby maximizing the potential for learning of all of your students.

Summary

This chapter reviewed the historical, sociological, and psychological factors that influence our thinking about who, what, and how we teach. This knowledge is important because it forms the background against which you will make decisions about how you conduct your classroom. In today's complex and diverse society, it is extremely important that you understand the purpose of education in our country and how the educational process is influenced by the changing nature and culture of our society.

Thought to Action

1. Identify ideas from the history of public education that still influence what happens in school. Why do you believe these ideas have prevailed? How long do you anticipate that they will continue to influence what we do in our public schools?

2. Examine the changing demographics of your community over the last 25 years. Develop a paper or presentation that shows how the demographics have changed and how that change has affected your community. Explain how demographics have affected the development of schools within your community.

3. Look at the census data for your community. How would you describe the community in which you live? Find a longtime resident of the community and interview that person to determine whether your profile of the community is consistent with his or her view. If there has been a change, ask the interviewee how that change has affected his or her perception of the community.

4. President George H. W. Bush adopted Goals 2000 as a means of directing the efforts of public schools. Examine those goals and determine which, if any, schools have accomplished and which, if any, schools have not accomplished. Give plausible reasons as to why schools did or did not reach those goals.

5. Study the Supreme Court's *Brown vs. Board of Education of Topeka* decision. What impact did that court ruling have on the schools in your community? How would you describe the progress toward the integration of schools in your community 50 years later?

6. Check with your local school board to determine whether your community has any charter schools. If there are charter schools in your community, find out the purpose of those schools and determine the impact they have had on the public schools in your community.

7. Investigate the homeschooling movement in your community. What is the primary reason parents in your community choose to homeschool their children? Do you think their choice is valid and realistic for their children? How do parents select the materials they use to homeschool their children? Are those materials equivalent to those used in regular public schools? What are the advantages and disadvantages of homeschooling students? How would you evaluate the effectiveness of the homeschooling movement in your community?

8. Observe a classroom or school for 15–20 hours. Do you see any evidence of gender or racial bias in practice in the classroom or school? If that practice exists, do you think it is deliberate or incidental on the part of the teachers or administrators in the school? What would you do to avoid racial or gender bias when you are teaching?

9. How would you describe how you learn best? What theories of learning influence your description of your learning preferences? How do you think your preference for learning will affect decisions you make about how you organize your classroom to maximize the potential for learning of all your students?

10. Complete the multiple intelligences inventory found at www.ldrc.ca/projects/miinventory/mitest.html. After you complete the inventory, analyze your perceptions of what you found out. Were there any surprises?

ON YOUR OWN

Log on to the web-based student study site at http://www.sagepub.com/holt for access to a Standards-Based Student Project that will help you connect what you have learned in this chapter to your state's standards; study aids, such as electronic flashcards; and research recommendations, including journal article links and other Web resources.

Practical Issues of Instruction

Chapter 3
Developing the Lesson Methodology

Chapter 4
Classroom Organization and Management

Chapter 5
Classroom Assessment and Accountability

P art II presents pedagogical information on levels of thinking, lesson plans, management, and assessment. The chapters in this section explain the science and pedagogy of instruction.

Chapter 3 examines unit and daily lesson planning, agencies that influence curriculum plans, Bloom's taxonomy, writing objectives, and methodology.

Chapter 4 is divided into two distinct parts that separate classroom management from discipline models. The first section includes communication, monitoring, delivery of instruction, organization, working with parents, and types of teacher power. The second part of the chapter presents five discipline and behavior-management models: behavior modification, assertive discipline, choice theory, teacher-effectiveness training, and cooperative discipline.

Chapter 5 explores assessment and accountability and defines assessment, forms of assessment, and test-construction strategies, such as two-choice response, multiple choice, matching, short answer, constructed response, and essay. Additionally, information is provided about how to grade your students.

3

Developing the Lesson Methodology

PART OF BEING A SUCCESSFUL TEACHER IN ANY CLASSROOM IS YOUR ABILITY TO PLAN EFFECTIVE lessons that meet the learning and instructional needs of your students. To do this type of planning, you need to understand the importance of planning, the purposes of planning, your students' needs, as well as your own needs. Planning will help you to achieve that which the state, district, and school expect you to accomplish with your students. These goals for accomplishment are usually determined by national and state standards, subject-matter sequences, required standardized testing, and most important, the needs of your students. Balancing all of these needs becomes tricky at times, but you really do need to understand your role in this planning process, what you have control over, and what you need to implement because it is expected at the grade level and subject field you are teaching.

In this chapter, we will examine factors that influence your decision making about what you will teach and how you will plan your lessons to reflect the pre-active, interactive, and post-active dimensions of your teaching. The chapter will also focus on writing instructional objectives using Bloom's revised taxonomy. Instructions for writing unit and daily lesson plans are also included.

PLANNING THE CURRICULUM

More than 20 years ago, in 1982, Galen Saylor wrote a dynamic little book titled *Who Planned the Curriculum?* In this book, Saylor defined the *curriculum* as a "set of learning opportunities for persons to be educated" (p. 1). He also contended that it is the classroom teacher who is the ultimate curriculum planner because he or she is the one who determines which activities are going to occur, when, and by whom. The teacher's problem is to sort through the multitude of

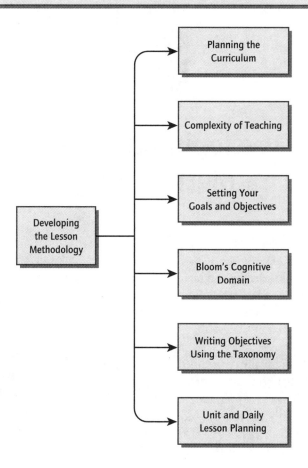

Developing the Lesson Methodology

Planning the Curriculum

Complexity of Teaching

Setting Your Goals and Objectives

Bloom's Cognitive Domain

Writing Objectives Using the Taxonomy

Unit and Daily Lesson Planning

materials and guidelines generally provided to the teacher and to select the materials and methods that will maximize the learning of every student in the classroom. This is in no way a small task. But who exactly establishes these materials and guidelines, which Saylor refers to as the *curriculum plans reservoir*.

Figure 3.1 illustrates the groups and agencies that influence what initially gets put into the curriculum plans reservoir. As you examine the diagram, look at the external agencies and persons who can (and frequently do, with exuberance) provide criteria, ideas, content, and methods for curriculum implementation.

Exactly how do textbook authors and publishers influence what goes into the curriculum plans reservoir? The answer to this question is quite simple: By selecting what goes into the books and supplementary materials, textbook authors and publishers can control much of the decision making of teachers. Textbook publishing is a major, multimillion-dollar business. Publishers spend a lot of time and energy creating textbooks, series of materials,

FIGURE 3.1   Saylor's Model: Curriculum Plans Reservoir

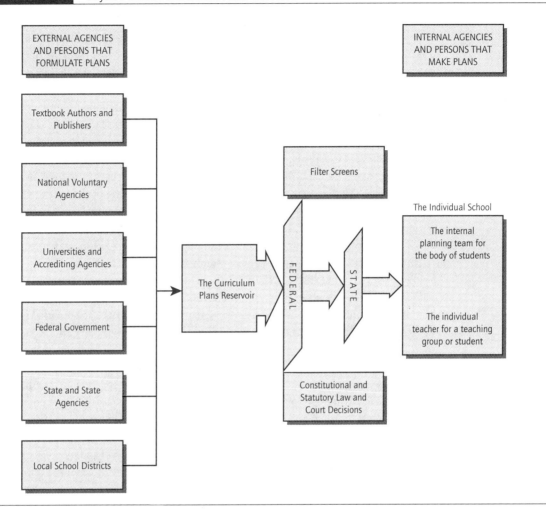

supplemental materials, and assessment instruments that can be used in any given classroom. Teachers rarely teach without a textbook, and they frequently use many of the supplemental materials that accompany the textbooks.

Today, not only do textbook publishers have the books and the written supplemental materials, but more and more frequently, the adoption of a textbook guarantees that teachers will have multimedia materials to use with the book, and they may even receive some in-service training in how to use the materials. These multimedia materials can provide self-instruction for students who need remedial help, enrichment activities for more able students, or self-checking exercises to reduce the time the teacher spends to grade papers, and, more often than not, test banks to make test construction easier for the classroom teacher. Regardless of the amount or kind of supplemental materials that accompany a textbook, teachers, by and large, rely almost exclusively on the textbook itself for instructional purposes.

Given that teachers rely heavily on textbooks, how are the textbooks selected for use in a school? The procedures for textbook use or adoption vary from school to school, district to district, and state to state. In some states, such as Florida, California, and Texas, teachers cannot use textbooks in their classrooms that are not part of the "state-adopted" list of materials. What this means is that public funds will not be used to buy books that are not on the state-approved list. Because many states with large pupil populations are using a state-adopted method for textbook selection, authors and publishers find themselves having to produce materials that will be acceptable in these states, thus in many ways dictating what is taught throughout classrooms in the United States.

State-adoption procedures may affect the content that is included in textbooks, particularly if the content is controversial—for example, evolution. Evolution has been in and out of science books over the years, but it was the efforts of science teachers in states with state adoption, notably California, that eventually got the topic of evolution back into the science textbooks. Why? Because publishers could not afford *not* to be competitive for sales in states such as California, Texas, Florida, and New York.

With the implementation of the No Child Left Behind legislation, and with school districts around the country establishing curriculum standards on which students' progress is being measured, publishers are finding that in order to have their products be viable alternatives for teachers, their products must address the standards. Content and activities must match the minimum expectations addressed in the standards movement. Many school districts will not look at materials that are not matched to the curriculum standards of their state.

Much more can be said about the content of textbooks, their use, the supplementary materials that are available, etc., but what needs to be understood here is that what is in the textbooks is what teachers will use to plan their instruction. What is in the textbooks is now influenced much more by legislation and standards than by academics or subject-matter experts. Historically, textbooks have dealt with more controversial, in-depth, and "meaty" content than is found in many of the books today, which are trying to be politically correct and meet the expectations of all cultures and political positions, as well as legislative mandates. This is not to criticize today's textbooks but rather to inform you of what you, as a teacher, have available for use in your classroom.

The second set of external agencies that influence what you can teach in your classroom are what Saylor refers to as *national voluntary agencies* or, more specifically, professional organizations and learned societies. Particularly during the last 20 years or so, these groups have had a major influence on what is taught in our schools because they are responsible for establishing most of the curriculum standards that have been adopted by states and implemented in textbooks. These groups include such organizations as the National Council for Teachers of Mathematics, the National Council for the Social Studies, the National Council for Teachers of English, the International Reading Association, and the National Science Teachers Association. Every subject area has a professional organization, and some have two or more. There are groups that focus only on elementary or early childhood levels or special education. The point is that these groups, through their professional literature and their professional meetings, can significantly influence what gets taught in classrooms. The Association for Supervision and Curriculum Development is a huge organization that appeals to K–12 principals, superintendents, and other administrators. It has actively become engaged in publishing materials on what to teach and how to teach.

Universities and accrediting groups also have a major impact on the curriculum, particularly in our secondary schools. Universities control the curriculum of high schools by establishing their minimum requirements for entry into the "hallowed halls of academe." For example, foreign languages have been in and out of the curriculum of public high schools based on whether universities require a foreign language as an entry or exit requirement. Physical education and the fine arts are frequently relegated to electives in high school or limited in the number of credits they may offer because universities do not deem these courses to be as relevant as, say, a third or fourth year of science or mathematics or English. Examinations used to determine entrance into college, such as the SAT or ACT, set the minimum requirements for what students need to learn to be successful on these examinations and thus improve their chances for acceptance into college. Because of claims of discrimination and the consistently lower performance of some ethnic groups on these examinations, more and more colleges are looking at a variety of criteria to determine a student's acceptance into the university.

Accreditation of schools, mostly secondary schools, has historically been provided by at least three different groups: colleges and universities, regional associations of colleges and universities, and state departments of education. Colleges and universities control the quality of public secondary schools through their insistence on the use of college entrance exams, their collaboration with publishers, and their consulting work with schools and communities. The regional accreditation groups grew out of a demand to have common standards by which to judge schools. Most colleges will not accept a student for admission who has not graduated from a high school accredited by one of the five regional accreditation groups: The Southern Association of Colleges and Schools, New England Association of Schools and Colleges, Middle States Association of Colleges and Schools, North Central Association of Colleges and Schools, and Western Association of Schools and Colleges. These groups set standards that include the quality and sufficiency of facilities, library books, course work, resources, equipment, faculty, and staff. State departments of education set their own criteria for accreditation, but they are usually similar to that of the regional agencies. The major difference would rely on schools meeting specific state legislative mandates.

Federal and state agencies, along with local school districts, serve as additional determiners of what is taught in your school. The influence of these groups is directly related to money. Both the federal and state governments can set aside monies for special incentives in curriculum development. One major historical event that saw millions of dollars poured into our public schools to improve mathematics and science education was the launch of *Sputnik* by the Soviet Union in 1957. Immediately, it was determined that schools needed to revamp and reconstruct their science and mathematics programs. Money was available through federal grants to rewrite the curriculum, retrain teachers, and implement the new curriculum in schools.

Currently, in some sections of our country, schools have access to large amounts of federal dollars for the training of teachers and the adoption of curriculum programs to ensure that students who do not speak English as their native language can get help in their schools. Special education is another area that has benefited from massive amounts of federal dollars infused into the public education system to meet the special needs of these children.

Some federal dollars are no longer directly distributed to individual schools or districts through grants but are sent to the states for distribution. In these cases, the states may have their own priorities for how they want those federal dollars distributed to meet the needs in their states. The states send out calls for proposals for the programs they deem necessary, and each school or each school district may apply for the funds if it meets the criteria for the available grant. Through such distribution of dollars, schools have had special reading programs, mathematics programs, character education programs, arts programs, physical education programs, and a host of other types of curricular opportunities. The major disadvantage of both the federal grants and those funneled through the state is that good programs often disappear once the federal or state subsidies are gone.

Under local control, schools frequently find themselves dealing with parent groups that are great lobbyists and demand that certain materials and programs be a part of the school curriculum or not a part of the curriculum. Frequently, a few very vocal parents are able to have books banned from the library or have sufficient influence to get programs placed at the school, such as safety programs or after-school programs. Anyone who has ever gone to or taught in a high school knows the power of the band association and the importance of the band to the curriculum of a high school. Band parents are a formidable force to contend with. Their hearts are often in the right place, but sometimes schools succumb to the demands of band parents over the curricular needs of other students within the school.

All of these agencies, groups, and persons influence what teachers have access to with respect to curricular choices. But even before anything can be implemented or placed in Saylor's curriculum plans reservoir, the programs and materials must meet constitutional and statutory law and especially Supreme Court decisions regarding what is appropriate to include in a school's curriculum. In 2004, we celebrated the 50th anniversary of the *Brown v. Board of Education of Topeka* court decision, which was designed to end segregated schooling in the United States. The court ruling, for some schools, dramatically changed the curriculum that students received. With the integration of the schools, students, both black and white, had access to the same materials and resources, which was not necessarily true under the dual school system. Although there is still controversy over whether our schools are still segregated, the 1954 ruling brought the inadequacies of the dual system of education to the foreground. It was also through court action and the eventual passage of law that exceptional education students were allowed to be mainstreamed into our public school classrooms. Through bilingual education rulings and consent decrees, students who do not speak English have more educational opportunities in our schools.

Once the curriculum options are filtered through state and federal screenings, teachers in the schools can plan their curriculum. Usually this is done in grade-level teams in elementary schools, interdisciplinary teams in middle schools, and departmental teams in high schools. After the various teams determine what will be taught at each grade level and subject—assuring that state and national standards are met and that all special needs requirements are accounted for—the individual classroom teacher can make his or her plans for what will be taught in the classroom and how it will be taught.

Although this seems like a complicated process and the teacher seems to have little choice, in reality, teachers have a great deal of options and control over what and how they teach. They can take the guidelines and massage them according to the needs and interests of their students. They are not limited by the methodologies they choose, nor are they confined to using only the textbook that has been adopted. Most schools have a multitude of resources from which a teacher may choose to enhance the curriculum in the classroom. But to do this, teachers need to do a great deal of planning.

The pre-active phase of teaching involves planning your lesson.

COMPLEXITY OF TEACHING

Teaching is a highly complex activity. It takes much planning, it requires teachers to think rapidly on their feet, and it requires teachers to be self-reflective to determine what is and is not working in the classroom. Teaching is not something you can do effectively without some training—specifically, how to work with the variety of students you will encounter in your classroom and how to make your subject matter interesting and engaging for those students. Too often, the critics of our schools assume that anyone can teach and that teaching is easy to do. Granted, for some teachers, it is easier than for others, but good teaching is both an art and a science. Well-trained teachers stay in classrooms longer than ill-prepared teachers and better meet the needs of their students. Let's look at the complexity of teaching as diagrammed in Figure 3.2, which is adapted from Kysilka and Davis (1988).

The first thing you should notice in this diagram is that there are three phases to teaching: the pre-active, interactive, and post-active phases. The pre-active phase is the of planning your lessons, both long term (some schools insist that teachers do yearly or semester-long plans) and

FIGURE 3.2   *Complexity of Teaching*

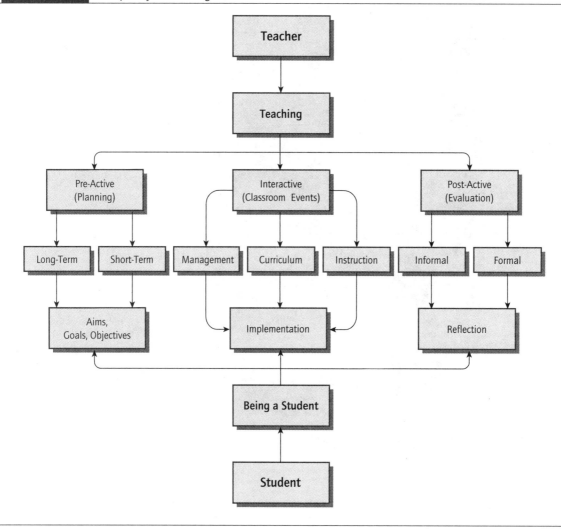

short term (units and daily lesson plans). The interactive phase is the activity that occurs within the classroom once the lessons have begun. This phase focuses on the strategies you choose to use to maximize the potential for learning of your students, as well as your classroom-management techniques and the content you are teaching. The post-active phase occurs once the teaching and learning have been completed—this is the assessment or evaluation phase.

Assessment has two parts to it: First, you need to determine how to assess the actual learning that has occurred for each of the students. The second part of assessment is your reflections on what worked and what did not work in the classroom. This is what happens as you drive home and evaluate what went well, which students failed to pay attention, which activity was a disaster, how you recouped, etc. At the end of each day, a good teacher will reflect on the day's activities and make a note of what needs to be done differently. We hope that students will also reflect on what happened during the school day.

Also important to the three phases of teaching are the backgrounds, abilities, and interests of the teacher and the students, that is the "baggage" each carries into the classroom. As a teacher, you will bring to the classroom your pedagogical knowledge as well as your personal knowledge. Pedagogical knowledge deals with content, learning theories, classroom-management strategies, teaching strategies, etc. Personal knowledge is your knowledge of how you learn best; your personal philosophy of what you expect your classroom to be like; your preferences for content, topics, and books; and your own needs and expectations.

Likewise, your students will enter the classroom with their identified goals and preferences. Some students will simply hope they can get through the class because they really hate English. Other students will be afraid that they cannot succeed because they have never been very good in science. Still other students will expect to rise to high levels of accomplishment. Some students will have so many personal problems that their likelihood of learning anything may be seriously jeopardized. How well your classroom functions depends a great deal on how your goals and objectives mesh with those of your students. The closer aligned they are, the more successful everyone will be. The further apart they are, the more challenging the classroom will become for you and your students.

SETTING YOUR GOALS AND OBJECTIVES

To set your goals and objectives for planning, you need to understand the difference between goals and objectives. *Goals* are defined as long-term desired outcomes. These are broad statements that may take a year or more to accomplish. Their purpose is to provide vision and direction for curriculum planning. The Goals 2000: Educate America Act (U.S. Department of Education, 1994) provided educators with expectations of what students should be able to accomplish by 2000. This document listed eight specific goals that schools were expected to meet by that year:

1. All children in America will start school ready to learn.

2. The high school graduation rate will increase to at least 90%.

3. All students will leave Grades 4, 8, and 12 having demonstrated competency over challenging subject matter, including English, mathematics, science, foreign languages, civics and government, economics, arts, history, and geography, and every school in America will ensure that all students learn to use their minds well, so they may be prepared for responsible citizenship, further learning, and productive employment in our nation's modern economy.

4. The nation's teaching force will have access to programs for the continued improvement of their professional skills and the opportunity to acquire the knowledge and skills needed to instruct and prepare all American students for the next century.

5. U.S. students will be first in the world in mathematics and science achievement.

6. Every adult American will be literate and will possess the knowledge and skills necessary to compete in a global economy and exercise the rights and responsibilities of citizenship.

7. Every school in the United States will be free of drugs, violence, and the unauthorized presence of firearms and alcohol and will offer a disciplined environment conducive to learning.

8. Every school will promote partnerships that will increase parental involvement and participation in promoting the social, emotional, and academic growth of children.

As you can see, these statements set long-term expectations for schools. But in order to meet these expectations, educators needed to turn these broad statements into measurable and achievable educational objectives and more specific instructional objectives. States and school systems across the country took the Goals 2000 objectives and rewrote them to provide guidance to their schools and teachers in the restructuring of the curriculum in the schools. Teachers were then presented with the state's or district's set of goals along with their educational objectives for implementation in the classroom.

According to Lorin Anderson and David Krathwohl (2001), educational objectives are those that can be accomplished in weeks or months and are used for unit planning. Instructional objectives are those that can be accomplished in days or hours and are used for daily lesson planning. To help teachers translate goals into educational and instructional objectives, we need to have a framework that provides organizational strategies for effective planning.

In 1956, Benjamin Bloom and his colleagues Engelhart, Furst, Hill, and Krathwohl published their *Taxonomy of Educational Objectives; Handbook I: Cognitive Domain,* which has served, for more than 40 years, as a set of guidelines for teachers to use in planning their classroom activities. Since its publication, the handbook has been translated into many languages and used as a basis for curriculum planning and test design all over the world (Anderson & Krathwohl, 2001). Over the years, surveys conducted to determine significant contributions to education have identified Bloom's work as among those writings that have had major impact on teaching and learning, not only in the United States, but worldwide (Shane, 1981; Kridel, 1999).

In his initial publication, which was designed to write educational objectives that could serve as a basis for proper assessment of learning, Bloom described three domains of learning: cognitive, affective, and psychomotor. The *cognitive domain*, which was thoroughly developed in the handbook, refers to the content or subject matter to be taught. The *affective domain*, which was further developed in 1964 by Krathwohl, Bloom, and Masia, refers to attitudes, emotions, and feelings—the aesthetic learning of students. The psychomotor domain, which specifically addresses the kinesthetic aspect of learning, was developed by both Simpson (1966) and Harrow (1972).

In this section, we are going to focus specifically on the cognitive domain, which is extremely important in helping you relate educational and instructional objectives to national and state curriculum standards, which are content or subject matter based. The other domains are worth exploring and would prove very helpful to you as a teacher; however, at this point in time, your primary responsibility as a teacher is to establish learning outcomes that reflect the national and state academic standards by which students' achievement is measured. The success of students in meeting these standards will determine how "effective" their education is as defined by the No Child Left Behind legislation.

BLOOM'S COGNITIVE DOMAIN

Anderson and Krathwohl (2001) updated and revised Bloom's *Taxonomy of Educational Objectives: Cognitive Domain* to better reflect what we now know about teaching, learning, and assessment. The revision, *A Taxonomy for Learning, Teaching, and Assessing,* is in keeping with Bloom's own belief that if the taxonomy is to be useful to educators, it must change according to the uses and needs of educators and the fields in which they worked (Bloom, Hastings, & Madaus, 1971).

For those of you who have worked with the original taxonomy, you will find some differences in the revised version. The major changes from the original are that the lowest level of the taxonomy, which was called *knowledge*, has been renamed *remember,* and the order of the two highest cognitive levels of the taxonomy have been reversed, from *synthesis* (Level 5) and *evaluation* (Level 6) to *evaluation* (Level 5) and *create* (synthesis, Level 6). Knowledge is now defined as that which is acted on and includes four major dimensions: factual knowledge, conceptual knowledge, procedural knowledge, and metacognitive knowledge. The first three dimensions of knowledge are from the original taxonomy; the fourth dimension was added, again, based on what researchers know is important with respect to learning (see Table 3.1).

TABLE 3.1   Knowledge Dimensions

Major Types	Examples
Factual knowledge	**Basic elements students need to know to understand a subject**
Terminology	Technical vocabulary; musical or mathematical symbols
Details and elements	Reliable sources of information; map legends; elements of the solar system; the five senses
Conceptual knowledge	**Interrelationships among basic elements within a larger structure that enable them to work together**
Classifications and categories	Periodical tables; classification of plants and animals; types of genres in literature
Principles and generalizations	Law of supply and demand; Rules of grammar; theorems in geometry
Theories, models, structures	Theory of evolution; gravitational theory; structure of U.S. government; sentence structure
Procedural knowledge	**How to do something; methods of inquiry and criteria for using skills, algorithms, techniques, and methods**
Subject specific skills and algorithms	Knowing the skills of using watercolors or acrylics; order of operations in mathematics; multiplication and division algorithms
Subject specific techniques and methods	Interviewing techniques; problem-solving techniques, scientific method
Criteria for determining when to use appropriate procedures	Knowing when to apply a procedure; applying criteria to judge the appropriateness of a specific method; using a specific procedure to determine profit margins
Metacognitive knowledge	**Knowledge of cognition, particularly one's own cognition**
Strategic	Outlining skills as a means of identifying main ideas; use of heuristics
Cognitive tasks; appropriate contextual and conditional knowledge	Knowing the types of tests teachers prefer to use; knowledge of the cognitive demands of particular tasks; knowing how to tackle different kinds of exams
Self-knowledge	**Recognizing mathematics is easier than English; knowing that writing essays is easier than poetry; awareness of one's own knowledge level**

Factual knowledge is defined as knowledge that is basic to understanding the discipline and to problem solving within the discipline, such as terminology and specific facts and details. *Conceptual knowledge* is defined as knowledge that explains the interrelationships among data within a discipline, such as classification schemas and categories, principles and generalizations, and theories, models, and structures of the discipline. *Procedural knowledge* is knowledge that explains how to do something within the discipline, such as subject-specific skills and algorithms, techniques and methods, and criteria for determining when to use them. *Metacognitive knowledge* is the knowledge of your own cognitive processes: how you organize information (strategic knowledge), what kinds of tests you prefer and why (cognitive task knowledge), your learning strengths and weaknesses, and how you "psych out" a teacher (self-knowledge).

Another major change in the revised taxonomy is its use. Bloom's original taxonomy was designed to aid educators in the construction of assessment instruments, but it found greater use among educators in planning for instruction and learning how to phrase questions in the classroom. The purpose of the revised taxonomy (Table 3.2) is its "emphasis on planning curriculum, instruction and assessment, and the alignment of these three" (Bloom et al., 1956, p. 263). With the change in focus, the revised taxonomy is much more useful to teachers and curriculum planners and requires less interpretation by the reader. It is written in user-friendly language that is the vernacular of the field, and it provides many examples of how to effectively use the taxonomy and its matrix for effective planning.

The revised taxonomy is still hierarchical. The levels, from lowest to highest, are as follows:

1. Remember: Retrieve relevant information from long-term memory; recognize and recall

2. Understand (formerly referred to as *comprehension*): Construct meaning from instructional messages; interpret, exemplify, classify, summarize, infer, compare, and explain

3. Apply: Use information; execute and implement

4. Analyze: Break material into parts and determine the relationships among the parts; differentiate, organize, and attribute

5. Evaluate: Make judgments based on internal and external criteria; check and critique

6. Create: Synthesize; put elements together to form new ideas, patterns, or structures; generate, plan, and produce

In Bloom's original taxonomy, it was assumed that you could not work at Level 4 unless you had worked through Levels 1, 2, and 3. Likewise, it was impossible for you to effectively create new ideas if you had not taken the time to analyze existing ideas. In the revised taxonomy, the hierarchical categories are based on the complexity of the skills in each category, not necessarily the relationship of one level to another. Knowing the levels of the taxonomy can help you to plan lessons that will require students to work at more complex levels of thinking. Research over the more than 50 years that Bloom's taxonomy has existed indicate that much of the instruction that goes on in classrooms is done at the lowest or least complex levels of learning, remembering and comprehending (now called *understanding*). Teachers at all grade levels are encouraged to plan their lessons so that students experience all levels of the taxonomy. Not only should students be expected to engage in activities that require more complex learning, but also they should be assessed at those higher levels of learning. Writing specific objectives focused on the complexity of learning tasks will help teachers to choose activities and assessments that are appropriate for the complexity of learning demanded by the objectives.

| TABLE 3.2 | Bloom's Revised Taxonomy |

Cognitive Level	Alternate Names	Examples
1. Remember		**Retrieve knowledge from long-term memory**
1.1 Recognize	Identify	Recognize dates and names from history and rules of operations
1.2 Recall	Retrieve	Recall names, dates, places, and arithmetic facts
2. Understand		**Construct and comprehend meaning**
2.1 Interpret	Clarify, represent, paraphrase, translate	Change from one form of representation to another e.g., symbols to words, verbal to numerical)
2.2 Exemplify	Illustrate	Find specific examples or illustrations
2.3 Classify	Categorize	Put information into groups, classes, or categories
2.4 Summarize	Abstract, generalize	Find a general theme, write a summary, or list major points from a communication
2.5 Infer	Conclude, extrapolate, interpolate, predict	Draw logical conclusions from presented information; approximate a number between two given points; determine what might be next given a specific sequence of events
2.6 Compare	Contrast, map, match	Detect relationships between ideas, objects; compare historical events to current events; find similarities between sets of words
3.0 Apply		**Carry out or use a procedure in a given situation**
3.1 Execute	Carry out	Apply a procedure to a familiar task (e.g., add two-digit numbers with no regrouping)
3.2 Implement	Use	Apply a procedure to a new task (e.g., use graphing skills learned in geometry to illustrate data from economics)
4.0 Analyze		**Break material into its constituent parts and explain how the parts relate to each other**
4.1 Differentiate	Discriminate, distinguish, focus, select	Determine relevant and irrelevant information; select only prime numbers out of a list of numbers; determine cause and effect
4.2 Organize	Integrate, outline, structure	Determine how ideas fit within a structure (e.g., complete an outline, create a timeline, find evidence for and against a particular issue)
4.3 Attribute	Deconstruct	Determine a point of view; identify bias or political correctness; explicate values from an essay or speech
5.0 Evaluate		**Make judgments based on criteria and standards**
5.1 Check	Coordinate, detect, monitor, test	Find inconsistencies or fallacies in a communication; determine the effectiveness of a process or procedure; determine the correctness of deductions from a given set of data

(Continued)

[handwritten margin note: Expansion ASL compare list or what it is not]

TABLE 3.2	(Continued)	
Cognitive Level	Alternate Names	Examples
5.2 Critique	Judge	Detect inconsistencies between a product and the external criteria for the development of the product; determine the appropriateness of a procedure for a given event; determine the best way to solve a problem
6.0 Create		**Put elements or information together to form a new idea, pattern, or structure**
6.1 Generate	Hypothesize	Come up with new ideas; create alternative hypotheses for an observed event
6.2 Plan	Design	Devise a plan to accomplish a task; plan and write a research paper; design a class presentation
6.3 Produce	Construct	Invent a product; build a model; paint a picture; create a collage

According to Anderson and Krathwohl (2001, pp. 34–36), writing objectives and categorizing them according to the framework provided by the revised taxonomy serves six purposes:

1. Categorization within the framework permits educators to examine objectives from the student's point of view.

2. Categorization within the framework helps educators to consider the panorama of possibilities in education, plan for higher-order thinking, and develop metacognitive knowledge.

3. Categorization within the framework helps educators to see the integral relationship between knowledge and cognitive processes inherent in objectives. For example, can students really apply knowledge without knowing procedural knowledge? Does analysis of factual knowledge lead to understanding of conceptual knowledge?

4. Categorization makes life easier; it helps educators to choose appropriate instructional and assessment strategies.

5. Categorization makes apparent the consistency among stated objectives of a lesson or unit plan, that is, the way it is taught and how student learning is assessed.

6. Categorization within the framework helps educators to understand the variety of language used in education to describe learning.

WRITING OBJECTIVES USING THE TAXONOMY

To write objectives using the revised taxonomy, you need to get acquainted with verbs that best describe the actions performed at each of the respective levels of the taxonomy. The list of verbs provided here is not inclusive, but it will provide you with sufficient knowledge by which to develop instructional objectives at various levels of the taxonomy.

Write explicit objectives that convey what should be accomplished by meeting that objective.

1. Remember: define, describe, find, identify, list, name, retrieve, recall, repeat, state, specify

2. Understand: arrange, interpret, clarify, paraphrase, translate, illustrate, exemplify, classify, categorize, summarize, abstract, infer, conclude, extrapolate, interpolate, predict, compare, contrast, map, match, explain, construct, sort

3. Apply: demonstrate, execute, carry out, illustrate, implement, sketch, solve, use

4. Analyze: appraise, differentiate, discriminate, focus, select, organize, integrate, outline, deconstruct, determine

5. Evaluate: assess, defend, detect, evaluate, monitor, predict, support, test, judge

6. Create: compose, generate, hypothesize, formulate, plan, design, produce, construct

When you start writing your instructional objectives for your unit or daily lesson plans, you will want to write them so that they are explicit and convey to you and your students exactly what you expect the students to do or accomplish by meeting the objective. The objective should be written so that you can choose appropriate strategies and learning activities for the students to engage in to meet the expectations you have set for the students. You also should be able to determine how best to assess your students by the way you have written your instructional objectives.

Suppose you want your students to use the law of supply and demand to analyze the current price structures of gasoline in the United States. This may seem like a very simple application objective, but let's examine it a little more carefully to determine exactly what you will need to do to ensure the students will be able to meet this objective. If students are going to use this law to analyze, they will first need to have knowledge of the principle (conceptual knowledge), and they will need to implement the principle (procedural knowledge) through the process of analysis (organizing information into a coherent communication). Thus, the students will be using a variety of skills to accomplish this one objective.

What will you need to plan in your lessons to ensure students' success? First, you need to know whether the students have preexisting knowledge of the law of supply and demand or whether you need to teach the law of supply and demand. If they have the knowledge, you may simply have to remind them of that fact and have them recall the information. If you need to teach the concept, then you need to determine how best to teach the concept: Do you tell the students what the principle is and give examples? Do you have the students examine a series of events in which the law is in effect and ask the students to find a pattern in the events to see whether they can "discover" the law? Do you have the students track the price of gasoline at the local pumps over a period of a month and then provide them with data on how much oil is imported, the cost per barrel, how much oil is produced in the United States, and its subsequent cost per barrel, and ask the students to draw conclusions?

Once the students understand the principle (i.e., they can state the law in their own words), how do you plan to have them apply the law? Will you have students work on projects? Will you have them go on the Internet to see what the economists are saying about the cost of gasoline and how that cost is determined? Will you ask them to interview members of their families and neighborhoods to see what the general public thinks about the cost of gasoline in local communities? Will you have the students examine what the media has to say about the cost of gasoline? These are the data-gathering techniques students will need to get information, which they can then organize and interpret to come up with a coherent communication about the effect of the law of supply and demand on gasoline prices.

Although you may have started out with a rather simple instructional objective, once you examine it carefully, you will realize that it is much more complex. What you actually want the students to do to demonstrate their understanding of the law of supply and demand and its implications for gasoline prices and what you know about their prior knowledge of the concept will determine what your lesson or lessons will look like. And how you construct your lessons will ultimately determine how you will assess your students. The key here is that the explicit statement of your instructional objective provides you with the necessary guidelines for developing your lesson plan. Thus, it is imperative that you think carefully about your instructional objectives and how you write them. You also need to realize that you do not need multiple instructional objectives for your lesson plans, particularly your daily plans. Focusing on fewer objectives during any given lesson is sometimes better than having many, which you might not be able to address. Also, you need to recognize how the lesson plans you write for each day relate to a unit plan and to the state standards that you are required to address in your planning.

UNIT AND DAILY LESSON PLANNING

There are several levels of lesson planning that you engage in as a teacher. Lesson plans need to be based on the state and national standards for each subject at each specific grade level, as well as any district or local standards advocated by your school. Depending on which state you live in, the extent of these standards is different. For example, Florida has extensive standards that must be met at each grade level in each subject. The standards not only indicate what the content should be but also include grade-level expectations for each of the standards. The state provides frameworks and suggested lesson plans for the standards. On the other hand, Montana has a very simple, straightforward set of standards for each subject at each grade level, and the specific objectives and grade-level expectations are left up to the individual teachers in each of the school districts within the state.

Your first step in planning for instruction is to acquaint yourself with the standards used in your state for the content and grade level you are going to be teaching. Read through your state documents and determine which standards are deemed essential and what the expectations are for student achievement of those standards. You also might want to determine whether there are special recommendations to teachers regarding the implementation of the standards for specific groups of students, such as special needs students or at-risk students. A thorough understanding of your state standards is the place to begin your planning. Most school districts have curriculum handbooks or websites that indicate the state standards and the district's interpretation of how they plan to have the teachers meet those standards.

Once you are acquainted with your state standards, the next thing you need to do is find out whether your district or school has a designated form for planning your lessons, both long term and short term. Some school districts require their teachers to follow a format that the district deems important and give a copy of their plan to the building administrator. Other districts do not provide any specific model for lesson planning. However, one thing is certain: Lesson plans include four major divisions regardless of how a district expects the plan to look. The four basic parts of a lesson plan are as follows:

1. Instructional objectives stated in measurable terms

2. Strategies or activities designed to meet the instructional objectives

3. Materials and resources needed to carry out the lessons

4. Assessment of the students' learning

Instructional objectives are derived from the goals and educational objectives determined by the state and district standards. Remember, goals are broad statements of what you want the students to be able to do at the end of a year or semester. Those broad goal statements are translated into specific educational objectives for unit planning and then converted into instructional objectives for daily planning purposes.

A unit plan requires a longer period of time to complete—for example, a week or a month. Unit plans are usually based on chapters in a book, broad concepts to be taught (e.g., genres in English), or interdisciplinary topics that several teachers focus on over a specified period of time. This last-named form of unit plan is popular in middle schools and in some elementary schools, where teams of teachers work together with a specified group of students. When you do unit planning, you are going to identify the goals you set and the specified educational objectives that relate to those goals. You will also determine the methods you will use to teach the objectives, the materials and resources you need to have for the unit, and the assessment plans for the unit. You will develop a timeline for completion of the unit.

Assessment plans are established for the completed unit, that is, what culminating activity do you want the students to engage in to prove to you that they accomplished the goals and objectives of the unit? For example, the culminating activity for the unit may be a group project that will be presented to the students in the class by each of the groups. These presentations will represent the assessment of the unit. Or you may decide that the best way to assess students' understanding is through a unit examination. In other words, the unit plan provides a schema from which you will organize your daily lesson plans. Unit planning provides four advantages over daily lesson planning:

1. Units provide a time frame for more integrated, holistic learning. Examining a topic for three to four weeks allows the students to engage in a variety of activities that can clarify and enhance their learning

2. Units provide flexibility in the use of time in the classroom. If an activity does not work well one day, the teacher has time to regroup and try something else the next day. Or, the teacher may discover that some of the students need more time to comprehend the ideas and others need less time. Again, such knowledge can help the teacher to readjust the lessons to benefit all students.

3. Units provide a context for interpreting daily activities. By acknowledging that daily objectives and activities are tied to broader ideas, both students and teachers can see the relevance to some of the activities they engage in on any given day.

4. Units provide sufficient time for more complex learning strategies such as analysis, evaluation, and creativity (Anderson & Krathwohl, 2001, p. 112).

Daily lesson plans are designed by breaking the unit plan into specific single lessons. Each lesson focuses on one or two very specific instructional objectives derived from the educational objectives of the unit. For example, if the educational objective for a unit on nutrition that is being taught to seventh graders is "Students will understand the importance of good nutrition to their cognitive and physical growth," several instructional objectives could be derived from this broader concept:

- Students will recognize the different foods in the food pyramid approved by the U.S. Department of Agriculture.

- Students will be able to explain which foods provide healthy choices for the development of strong bones and teeth, good eyesight, good thinking strategies, and sustained energy.

- Students will be able to construct a week's worth of menus that will ensure they are receiving proper nutrition for appropriate cognitive and physical growth.

Each of these instructional objectives is much more specific than the educational objective of the unit. Each of these objectives can drive a lesson for one to three days, depending on the time devoted to the objective each day and the previous knowledge of the students. But for our purposes, let's assume that Objective 1 can be introduced in one day, Objective 2 will take two days, and Objective 3 will take two days.

If students are going to be able to recognize the different foods that belong to each level of the food pyramid, what types of activities should they engage in? First, they need to be introduced to the pyramid, so you will need to have a classroom-size chart of the pyramid or individual charts to examine. Second, you will need to engage the students in a conversation about each level and the kinds of foods that fit into each level. Then, you might select one level—for example, fruits and vegetables—and ask students to identify foods that are classified as fruits and vegetables. You might have pictures of various fruits and vegetables to help the students identify the members of this food group. You will need to be prepared to help the students understand why some vegetables, such as potatoes, are classified as starches rather than vegetables in this pyramid.

As you work your way through the pyramid and you become reasonably sure that the students understand the pyramid, you will need to design some type of activity that will allow you to assess their knowledge of the pyramid and the placement of different foods into each of the categories of the pyramid. The assessment can take a variety of forms, such as a quiz, game, relay race, pair-share thinking groups, or a multitude of other activities. There is no need to continue on to Objective 2 unless you know that the students can perform the first objective accurately.

The second instructional objective you want to focus on is "Students will be able to explain which foods provide healthy choices for the development of strong bones and teeth, good eyesight, good thinking strategies, and sustained energy." To plan your lessons for this objective, you will need to think about the essential knowledge the students need to meet this objective. They will need to know something about the nutritional value of food groups and how that value relates to the development of strong teeth and bones, good eyesight, etc. So how will you plan your lesson to relate nutritional value to cognitive and physical growth? What are vitamins and minerals, and how do they relate to cognitive and physical growth? What are sources of calcium, and how is calcium related to physical growth? What is beta-carotene, and how does it relate to physical growth? What nutrients does the brain need to function? What does our body need to produce energy? How do you know which foods have certain vitamins and minerals? What can we learn about vitamins and minerals from reading food labels? There are many questions that need to be asked and answered. Each question you can think of provides you with some guidelines to structure your lessons around this objective.

Once you determine the activities that the students will engage in to accomplish this objective, you will also need to decide which assessment strategies you intend to use to ensure that your students can meet this objective. Again, the type of assessments you choose should reflect the knowledge and skills that are most important for the students to know when working on Objective 2. Knowledge learned in Objective 2 will make it much easier for your students to meet Objective 3, "Students will be able to construct a week's worth of menus that will ensure they are receiving proper nutrition for appropriate cognitive and physical growth."

The final objective asks the students to apply their knowledge of specific facts about nutrition to the creation of a week's menu that is designed to help them to nutritionally meet their cognitive and physical growth needs. In order for the students to plan the menu, you will need to think about the steps they need to follow to do this task. You will need to provide them with appropriate guidance to get the menus developed. Before you begin this phase of your unit, you might want to check with parents or guardians to ensure that the menus the students are planning are in accordance with any food preferences or requirements that parents or guardians deem essential because of religious beliefs or medical dietary limitations.

This lesson will require you to review the food classifications and the information related to which types of foods are essential and in what quantities to meet the nutritional needs for appropriate cognitive and physical growth. Once this is reviewed, then students can plan their menus. This can be done individually, in groups, or in pairs. You might have the class plan at least one day's menu based on some activity the class has or will be engaged in, such as a study of Mexico or France. The assessment strategy that is appropriate for this objective is the actual menus developed. A rubric (a scoring device that lists criteria you think must be evident in a menu) that you design and give to the students to help them plan the menus could also be used to evaluate their success at meeting the objective.

If you examine your plan for each of the objectives in this part of the unit on nutrition, you will determine that the objectives include several levels of the revised taxonomy. Students will be expected to recall information and use the knowledge (application) to create the menus. The students will be engaged with knowledge of facts and processes or procedures. They will also become aware, if you question the students as they engage in their activities, of metacognitive processes, recognizing how they think and which strategies they need to engage in to work effectively on the tasks they are expected to do. Consequently, as a teacher, you can assure yourself that you have asked the students to work in higher-order, complex thinking.

Before you complete your thinking about this unit and these lessons, reexamine the lessons and objectives and think about adjustments or alternatives you need to make to help students in your classroom who have learning or language difficulties. How can you help students in your room whose native language is not English? If their lack of language skills will interfere with their ability to achieve the objectives of your lesson, then you need to have options for them to engage in to demonstrate that they can learn the content of the lessons. Also, which activities could you include in your lessons to help students who have diagnosed learning problems? Many school districts will require you to put these adjustments in the lesson plan that you need to turn in to your building administrator. Again, you need to know what is required in your school and district related to alternative strategies and assessments for special needs students.

Some schools and school districts will require you to write very specific lesson plans that follow what is referred to as the "ABCD" form of objectives. This format was particularly popular when schools were working with competency-based curriculum materials and experimenting with computer-assisted instruction. Robert Mager (1962) introduced this concept of writing instructional objectives in his publication *Preparing Instructional Objectives*. Teachers were encouraged to write specific instructional objectives that addressed the audience (A), whom the objective was written for, that is, the students; the behavior (B), what specifically the students were expected to do; the condition (C), the circumstances under which the students were expected to perform; and the degree of expected accomplishment (D). An objective written using this pattern might be, "Given 10 two-digit by two-digit multiplication problems (C), students (A) will be able to complete the multiplication problems (B) with 85% accuracy (D)." Another example might be, "All seventh-grade students (A) will be able to write five structurally correct sentences (B) containing six or more words (C) with no errors (D)."

Whether you are expected to write your instructional objectives with this degree of specificity or whether you have the option of writing them in a less formal way, the important issue is that when you write your instructional objectives, the students should have no doubt as to what they are expected to do at the completion of the lesson. The more explicit you are, the better you will be at planning how you will organize your instruction to help the students accomplish the instructional objectives. Specificity will help you to properly assess your students' progress toward meeting the objectives. As you examine your instructional objectives, if they are written clearly and explicitly, you will be able to determine the cognitive levels at which your students are functioning.

By now, you may feel overwhelmed by what is required to plan your lessons for your students. The feeling is a natural one for novice teachers, but as you gain experience, as you get acquainted with the resources available to you as a teacher, and as you get to know your students and all of their idiosyncrasies, you will eventually find that the enormous amount of time and energy you spend in initial lesson planning will subside. You will learn how much detail you need and how to create shortcuts for yourself. However, as you start your career as a teacher,

EXHIBIT 3.1   Fourth-Grade Lesson Plan

COMPOUND WORDS

Expected duration: One or two lessons of 30–40 minutes

Instructional objectives: Students will be able to do the following:

- Define compound words
- Identify compound words in their reading
- Form compound words
- Explain the difference between "valid" compound words and "creative" compound words. (Valid compounds are found in the dictionary; creative compounds are formed by two words and cannot be found in the dictionary but may be funny, silly, or have unique meanings.)

Materials:

Compound worksheet

List of compound words

Individual words written on small pieces of paper to be drawn from a container to form compound words

Container to hold the words

Procedure:

1. Write a list of simple compound words on the chalkboard (e.g., airport, baseball, bedtime, catfish, cowboy, doormat, jigsaw, ladybug, oatmeal, runway, shortcake).

2. Ask students whether they see any pattern to these words (each word is made up of two other words).

3. Ask students to contribute more examples and write them on the board.

4. Look at all the words. Which compound words derive meaning from the two words used to form them? Which compound words have very different meanings from the words used to form them? Which compound words are formed by combining two nouns? Which compound words are formed by combining a noun with an adjective or adverb?

5. Have students give a definition of a compound word.

6. Have students complete the compound word worksheet.

7. Play "Making Compound Words."
   - Create a list of compound words and print them in large type on the computer.
   - Cut the compound words into their separate words.
   - Place all the separate words in a container.
   - Have each student draw two words from the container and form a compound word. Have the students determine whether the word is a "valid" or "creative" word and provide a definition of that word.

You could turn this activity into a team event by putting students into teams and having them form and define the words. Give points to students who form more valid words or more creative words, or give two points for a valid word and one point for a creative word.

Assessment:

- Formal assessment is the worksheet.
- Informal assessment is the "Making Compound Words" activity.

Suggested websites:

www.rickwalton.com/curricul/compound.htm
www.quia.com

EXHIBIT 3.2   Ninth-Grade Lesson Plan

HEALTH: THE SENSES

Expected duration: 2–3 class periods

Instructional objectives: Students will be able to do the following:

- List the five senses
- Describe how the senses work
- Explain the function of the sensory systems
- Teach others about one of the five senses

Materials:

Internet access

PowerPoint or some form of electronic presentation program

Display boards or overhead transparencies

Construction paper, pens, and markers

Procedure:

1. Ask students to identify the five senses (hearing, sight, smell, taste, and touch).

2. Ask students to describe how they use their senses.

3. Ask students to discuss how other mammals use their senses.

4. Break the class into teams of four or five students.

5. Have each student on each team select one of the five senses. (Some students may have to do two senses if the team has fewer than five students.)

6. Ask students to search the Internet for information on the selected senses. (One source is www.kidshealth.org/kid/body)

7. Have students take notes on how the sensory systems work and how they keep us safe and healthy.

8. Instruct students to work in their groups to create a presentation for the class (e.g., a bulletin board, presentation using the overhead projector, skit, or PowerPoint presentation). Each presentation must use words and pictures or diagrams.

9. Ask students to have their presentations done on the last day of the lesson.

Assessment:

- Formal assessment is the presentation, accuracy of information, quality of materials used in the presentation, and presentation skills. (You might want to construct a rubric to identify the specific things you will look for in the presentation and give that to the students before they begin planning the presentation.)
- Informal assessment is your observation of the students as they search the Internet and create their presentations.

Learning how to observe while the class is interacting is very important.

you will best serve yourself and your students if you spend a lot of time thinking about what you are going to teach, how you are going to teach it, and, most important, how you are going to assess it. You need to realize that you must use a variety of methods and materials with your students to ensure that all the students can learn the material. As you gain experience, you will also find that lesson planning and curriculum planning can be fun and that your classroom can be an exciting place for you and your students.

ASSESSMENT

Earlier in this chapter, we talked about the importance of assessment. We defined assessment as having two parts: assessment of what the students learned and your reflections on how your lessons and classroom activities worked. First, we are going to address the assessment of learning.

The assessment of learning is vital in any classroom. How you choose to do that assessment should be directly related to what you are trying to teach and how you taught it, that is, how did you plan to have the students engage in their learning? As previously indicated, the assessment and the objectives and methods of any lesson must be aligned. Too often, students are not assessed properly because the planned assessment strategy has little to do with what was designed to be learned. As a student, how many times did you end up leaving a classroom saying, "That test had nothing to do with what I studied" or "I had no idea that the teacher was going to grade the paper on how many different resources we used to write it. If I knew that's what she wanted, I would have done my paper differently." These typical comments occur when assessment is not aligned with the learning activity and with the instructional objective.

Sometimes, students are guilty of not paying attention or listening carefully to what the teacher said, but more often than not, teachers are guilty of not making their intentions clear to their students.

As you do your planning, you must give serious attention to your assessment strategies, whether they are formal or informal ones. Formal assessments imply planned assessment. You plan to give a quiz or a test. You will use a departmental examination, or you need to administer a standardized test of some sort. Tests are formal assessments. You may have students work on projects, book reports, or laboratory assignments. With these, you will also use formal assessments, but rather than use written tests, you might establish rubrics—formal, criteria-based checklists—that you will use as you read or listen to the presentations from your students. These rubrics allow you to apply the same criteria to the work of each student with a reasonable amount of consistency. The rubrics can also be used as guidelines for the students to follow in preparation for their presentations. You might choose to have students keep portfolios, usually thought of as a collection of students' work. Journaling is another assessment strategy you may want to use with your students. In journaling, students reflect on their learning: what was hard, what was easy, and what they perceived that they learned.

Informal assessments are generally done through observation. You notice which hands go up during class discussion. You note which students get immediately to the practice problems and which seem to hesitate. You see a pattern in homework completion. You recognize that some students are reluctant to go to the chalkboard or read aloud. You learn to read the blank faces on the students as you try to explain some concept or content. Through these observation techniques, you can determine who is having problems in your class, who is excelling, who is trying hard but does not seem to get it, and who does not seem to be trying at all. You will know when the class is lost and when you have to backtrack.

Learning how to observe while the class is interacting is very important. The faces and body language of students will convey more information to you about where they are with respect to your plans for their learning than anything else they may do. You certainly do not want to formally assess your students if they are not ready for the assessment. Often, the only way you will know how ready they are is to engage in informal assessment. The informal assessment may not identify specific problems, but it will tell you there are problems that you must deal with before you go any further with your plans.

Assessment is a huge part of teaching. In this time of accountability, assessment is what schools are all about. We may have different ideas about the kinds and importance of assessment in schools, but we would be terribly remiss if we did not try to help you understand that, at times, assessment may control your life in school. You need to learn how to adjust and accommodate to ensure that the instructional decisions you make are in the best interest of the students assigned to you.

As you progress through your education, you will learn and hear more about assessment, technology, standards, curriculum, No Child Left Behind, and other legislation that ultimately has an impact on what you are expected to do in your classroom. But if you keep in mind that the objectives you establish, the methods you choose to use, and the assessments you design must be aligned to maximize the potential for learning of your students, much of the frustration and aggravation that you confront related to assessment will be manageable.

Chapter 5 will provide you with guidelines for designing a variety of formal assessment strategies that you can use in your classroom.

TECHNOLOGY

Teachers of the 21st century have many more resources available to them than teachers at any other time in history. Many of the curriculum materials you have in your classroom may come with multimedia presentations, online materials, and CD-ROMs filled with extra activities that can be used for remedial work or for enrichment work. Many textbooks now come with test banks that make the construction of classroom tests, whether they are chapter tests, unit tests, or quizzes, easy to do. These materials are particularly useful when you have students who have missed school because of illness, when students have transferred to your classroom from another school and may be ahead of or behind your students in the curriculum, or when you simply want to do something different from what you have done in the past. School libraries have a great deal of materials useful to teachers. Supplemental materials in the form of books, magazines, films, CDs, and videos abound in many schools. Finding the time to preview and select them might be a problem for you, but the materials are there for your use.

The educational media specialist can be your best friend in the school. As you plan your units and daily lessons, you should work collaboratively with the educational media specialist, who can direct you to materials that are appropriate for you to use in your classroom. The worst thing you can do as a teacher is to use some form of media in your classroom without previewing it or knowing exactly what the content of the material is. Sometimes, you might not want to use the entire video or CD but might strategically use an excerpt from it. To do this, you need to know what is in the material and how it fits in with your plans. You need to prepare so that you do not fumble around during class to locate the exact information you want to share with the students.

The Internet is another valuable source of information for you to use as a teacher. Not only can you find interesting material on the Internet to help you plan lessons, but also there are excellent sources of information on the Internet that students will find engaging and motivating. If you are going to use this tool wisely, once again, you must plan how you intend to incorporate its use in your classroom. Just turning students loose on the Internet is not a wise idea. You need to focus their exploration and make sure that the time spent is directly related to the lessons and not an opportunity for them to entertain themselves with sites that have nothing to do with your lessons. Monitoring student Internet use can be a problem and will require your diligence. Most schools have built-in firewalls and blockers that prevent students from getting to sites that are not appropriate for school use. Sometimes, however, the control is so secure that students cannot always get to resources that are useful to them. Again, you need to find out how your students can access the Internet from school and the rules for use. Your best source of information is your educational media specialist, or some schools may have a technology specialist who can help you not only with finding appropriate materials to use but also with hardware and software problems.

Technology can be used in other ways in the classroom. First, you can use it as an instructional tool. Whether you choose to use an overhead projector to focus your students' attention on ideas you are trying to share with them or prefer to develop PowerPoint presentations, the use of technology can change the routine of a classroom and keep students focused on the lessons. But, like everything else, too much of the same thing can become boring and ineffective. If every class presentation you do is in the form of an electronic presentation, after a while, students will pay no more attention to that form of presentation than if you lectured all day or made them participate in group work all year long. Variety is the spice of life in your classroom.

Technology should be looked at as a wonderful tool to use in your classroom to enhance what you do as a teacher. Students should be taught how to use technology to help them both in their learning process and in their sharing process. Technology is here to stay and can make the classroom an exciting place to be. But sometimes, a good old-fashioned class discussion can be just as exciting, if not more so, than a multimedia presentation with all the bells and whistles available to you. As a teacher, learn how you like to use the technology available to you and then use it wisely and appropriately.

Summary

This chapter explored the numerous factors influencing what you teach in your highly complex classroom, specifically as it relates to national and state standards. In addition, you learned about the importance of varying the cognitive expectations of your students as you write your instructional objectives. Also addressed was the importance of adjusting your planning to meet the diverse needs of your students. Guidelines for unit and daily lesson plans were shared.

Thought to Action

1. Find an old course outline or syllabus from a previous class. Examine the objectives, the activities, and the assessment strategies. Can you determine whether they are aligned? If not, what would you do to align them? If so, what other activities or assessments could you include to provide for individual learning styles that may be evident among your classmates?

2. Examine a textbook that you might use in your K–12 classroom. Look at the objectives, then look at the quizzes or chapter reviews at the end of each chapter to see how closely they align with the objectives. If your textbook comes with a test bank, examine the questions and determine how closely it aligns with the objectives of the chapter.

3. Design a lesson to be taught to a grade level you plan to teach. Work from an educational goal to your instructional goals. Select one instructional goal and plan one lesson that focuses on that instructional goal. What methods do you plan to use with the students? What materials will you use? How will you assess the students, formally and informally?

4. Go online and search for unit and daily lesson plans that are appropriate for the content and level at which you plan to teach. Examine the lesson plans to see whether the developers have written instructional objectives that provide focus for strategies and assessment. How would you have to modify this lesson plan to accommodate a non-English-speaking student or a special needs student? Here are some suggestions for online lesson plans:

   www.lessonplanspages.com

   www.lessonplansearch.com

   www.lessonplanet.com

   www.edHelper.com

   www.kidzonline.org

   www.col-ed.org/cur

   www.teachnet.com/lesson

   www.LessonPlanz.com

5. Check your state's curriculum standards, then find those from another state. How do they compare? Look at the detail of the standards, the expectations for the students, the assessment requirements, etc. Does your state provide teachers with lesson plans, curriculum

frameworks, and other materials to help you incorporate the standards into your curriculum?

6. Pick a school district that you would like to work in. See whether you can find out what type of planning it expects its teachers to do. Will you have to do long-term planning that is turned in to the principal of the school? Will you be expected to turn in daily lesson plans? What will you need to put into your lesson plans to accommodate students with special needs? Does the district provide any help for the teachers in making these adjustments? Does your district require grade-level exams? How are they related to what is expected to be taught at each of the levels?

ON YOUR OWN

Log on to the web-based student study site at http://www.sagepub.com/holt for access to a Standards-Based Student Project that will help you connect what you have learned in this chapter to your state's standards; study aids, such as electronic flashcards; and research recommendations, including journal article links and other Web resources.

4

Classroom Organization and Management

THE CONTENT YOU TEACH DOES NOT MAKE YOU A GOOD MANAGER OF THE CLASSROOM. HAVING all the content knowledge in the world in an academic discipline does not guarantee that you will be able to manage the students. You were hired by the school to keep students interested in learning and to create a well-managed classroom. So what are the skills that you need to know to manage a classroom, to discipline the students, and to maintain a safe and orderly environment? We will address these questions and issues in this chapter.

According to Cangelosi (2004), to establish a positive classroom with a businesslike atmosphere, it is important to consider the following five steps:

1. Set the stage for cooperation in the classroom.

2. Model preparedness, organization, and "with-it" behavior.

3. Minimize transition time.

4. Use a communicative style that encourages a comfortable, nonthreatening environment that is free of the fear of embarrassment, harassment, or harm.

5. Clearly communicate the expectations for conduct.

Surveys given to college of education graduates following their first year of teaching ask, "What were you least prepared to do when entering the profession of teaching?" Year after year, the overwhelming response is classroom management. This may indicate that classroom management can only be learned on the job because it is often difficult to transfer into practice all the things about running an orderly classroom from a college course, a book, or a workshop. Classroom management is a hands-on activity and varies from teacher to teacher and classroom to classroom. Classroom management involves learning not only how to prevent

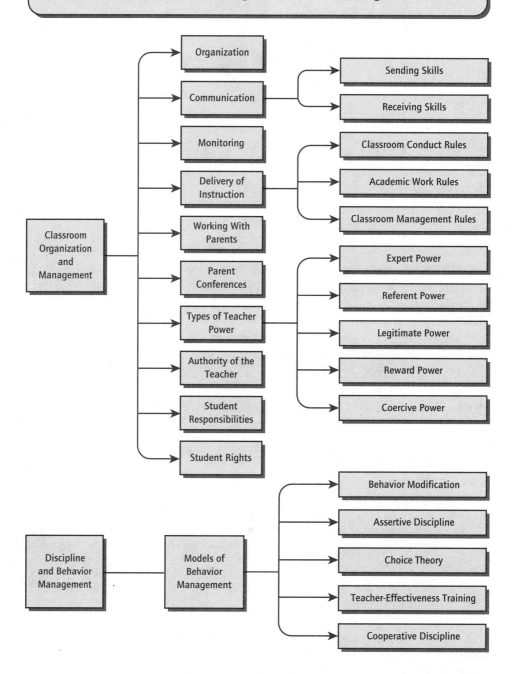

Chapter 4 Classroom Organization and Management

problems from occurring but also how to respond effectively when problems do occur. The most effective decisions in classroom management are based on a clear concept of the expectations you have for student behavior and how well you have communicated those expectations to your students. These outcomes can be organized into four headings: organization, communication, monitoring, and delivery of instruction.

Be sure that your students understand the consequences of breaking rules or ignoring procedures.

ORGANIZATION

Classroom routines should be established by the teacher on the first day of class. These routines should include general operating procedures in the classroom, such as how to enter the classroom, how to turn in papers, how to line up for lunch or recess, etc. These rules and procedures should be developed with your students to help meet their personal and academic needs and should be clearly communicated to them. It helps when the parents or guardians of your students are also informed of your classroom rules and procedures.

There are procedures you can establish that may prevent some behavior-management problems.

- Arrange seating in a U shape, in rows, or in a circle for easy access and eye contact with students.

- Post a daily schedule and discuss any changes each morning.

- Engage students until you have given clear instructions for the upcoming activity.

- Encourage students to take responsibility for their learning by determining not to do tasks that can be done by students.

- Establish routines for collecting homework, distributing papers, etc.

Other ideas that can help you to maintain an organized classroom are the following:

- Move around the room and attend to individual needs.

- Provide simple step-by-step directions for any new activity or assignment.

- Remind students of key procedures associated with the upcoming lesson.

- Use group competition to stimulate more orderly transitions.

- Develop transition activities.

Be sure that your students understand the consequences of breaking the rules or ignoring the procedures. Also, be certain that classroom rules are equitably applied to all students, regardless of whom they are. Often, teachers who lose control in the classroom do so because they play favorites and make it clear that some students do not have to follow the same rules as the rest of the students. Such inconsistent application of classroom rules and procedures establishes the seeds of discomfort in the classroom and makes it much harder to keep the classroom in control.

COMMUNICATION

The second consideration that is a foundation for effective classroom management is *communication*. Communication skills can be divided into two categories: sending and receiving.

Sending Skills (Skills Used When Speaking to Someone)

- Deal in the present. Information is more useful when it is shared at the earliest appropriate opportunity.

- Talk directly *to* students rather than *about* them. When teachers do this, students are shown respect and receive accurate information about adults' feelings.

- Speak courteously. This creates positive role models for students.

- Take responsibility for statements by using the personal pronoun "I." For example, you might say, "When I am interrupted, I get distracted and have difficulty helping other students."

- Make statements rather than ask questions. When dealing with student behavior, questions often create defensiveness. For example, say, "Tom, our classroom rules for participation are to raise your hand—I know you forgot because you were excited" rather than, "Tom what is our rule for participating in class discussion?"

Receiving Skills (Techniques for Becoming a More Effective Listener)

- Use empathic, nonevaluative listening. This makes students feel that they have been clearly heard and that the feelings expressed are acceptable.

- Use paraphrasing and active listening when responding to student contributions. Such a technique allows the students to become involved in the dialogue.

- Make eye contact and be aware of nonverbal messages.

- Suggest strong leadership by using body carriage, facial expressions, and gestures.

Sending and receiving skills are important for teachers and students. As a teacher, you can model appropriate speaking and listening skills for your students regardless of their age. For younger students, you might want to create posters that reflect appropriate speaking and listening behaviors and hang them in a permanent place in the classroom to help the students learn how to have effective conversations.

MONITORING

Often, misbehavior occurs because students find acting out more interesting than a boring lesson or more rewarding than another failure. Students may misbehave when they are not involved in the learning activity, do not understand the task, or cannot obtain assistance when it is needed. The following techniques are useful for responding to minor classroom disruptions:

- Scan the class frequently to notice and respond to potential problems.

- React calmly and quickly to a student's disruptive behavior to create a positive ripple effect.

- Make positive initial contact with students by praising the positive behavior that competes with the negative behavior.

- Remind students of the classroom rule or procedure that they are not demonstrating.

- Remind students of the rules and procedures and the consequences for violations.

- Give students clear cues indicating that the continuation of inappropriate behavior will result in the specified consequences.

- Employ consistent consequences for misbehavior.

- Inform students that they are choosing the consequence of their behavior.

- Use consequences that are educational in nature. For example, if students have not completed their work, then they must look up two Internet sites on a topic that is relevant to the subject they are working on and write a description of what they have learned. (Use this sparingly, especially if the student views computer time as fun.)

- When one or two students are being very disruptive, focus other students in the class on their task. Then find a time to talk quietly with the disruptive students.

Please see Table 4.1, Matrix of Infractions and Consequences for guidance on dealing with disruptive students.

DELIVERY OF INSTRUCTION

Leading educators over the past several years have emphasized that the quality of instruction is a key factor in influencing students' behavior and achievement. Your response to student misbehavior is most effective when it maintains or enhances your policy that the student is responsible for his or her own behavior.

TABLE 4.1   Matrix of Infractions and Consequences

Infractions	1	2	3	4	5	6	7	8	9	10	11	12	13	14	15	16	17
Aggression		O					O	O			O	O	O	O	O	O	O
Arson															M	M	M
Assault of staff member															M	M	M
Battery of staff member															M	M	M
Battery															M	M	M
Bomb threat															M	M	M
Breaking and entering/burglary															M	M	M
Bus rules/procedures violation	O						O	O	O	O	O	O	O	O	O	O	O
Cheating	O		O							O	O	O	O	O	O		
Computer/calculator misuse	O		O							O	O	O	O	O	O	O	O
Confrontation	O	O					O	O	O	O	O	O	O	O	O	O	O
Contraband			M				O	O	O	O	O	O	O	O	O	O	O
Disrespect	O	O					O	O		O	O	O	O	O	O		
Disrupting class or campus	O	O			O					O	O	O	O	O	O		
Dress code violation	O		O							O	O	O	O	O			
Drug/alcohol violation			M												M	M	M
Drug paraphernalia			M												M	M	M
Explosives			M												M	M	M
Extortion				M											M	O	M
Failure to report to detention/ Saturday school											O		O	O	O		
False accusation against staff														O	O	O	O
False alarm															M	M	M
Fighting													O	O	O	O	O
Firearms violation			M												M	M	M
Forgery			M				O	O		O	O		O	O	O	O	O
Gambling											O	O	O	O	O	O	O
Gang-related activity											O		O	O	O		M
Harassment							O	O	O	O	O	O	O	O	O	O	O
Horseplay	O	O					O	O	O	O	O	O	O	O	O	O	O
Hazing	O										O	O	O	O	O	O	O
Illegal organization violation											O		O	O	O		M
Inappropriate or obscene act	O	O	M				O	O	O	O	O	O	O	O	O	O	O
Inattentive behavior	O									O	O	O	O				
Insubordination		O					O	O	O	O	O	O	O	O	O		O
Lying/misrepresentation	O	O					O	O	O	O	O	O	O	O	O		
Medication policy violation	O		M							O	O	O	O	O	O		
Offensive touching of staff member							O	O	O	O	O	O	O	O	O	O	O
Off-campus felony															O	O	O
Open defiance							O	O				O		O	O	O	
Repeated misconduct							O	O	O	O	O	O	O	O	O		
Robbery			M	M											M	M	M
Sexual battery															M	M	M

TABLE 4.1

Infractions	1	2	3	4	5	6	7	8	9	10	11	12	13	14	15	16	17
Sexual misconduct												O			M	O	O
Skipping class										O	O	O	O	O			
Stalking															M	M	M
Substantial disruption of school															M	M	M
Tardiness										O	O	O	O	O			
Theft	O	M	M				O	O	O	O	O	O	O	O	O	O	O
Threat/intimidation		O				O	O	O	O	O	O	O	O	O	O	O	O
Tobacco products violation			M					O	O	O	O		O	O	O		
Trespassing													O	O	O	O	M
Unauthorized area	O	O								O	O	O	O	O	O	O	O
Unauthorized assembly										O	O		O	O	O	O	O
Unauthorized items	O	O	O				O	O	O	O	O		O	O			
Unauthorized publication			O							O	O	O	O	O	O	O	O
Unsafe act		O			O		O	O	O	O	O	O	O	O	O	O	O
Vandalism				O				O	O	O	O	O	O	O	O	O	O
Vehicle/parking violation	O				O	O				O	O		O	O	O		O
Weapons violation			M												M	O	M
Zero tolerance															M	M	M

Consequences

1. Verbal reprimand
2. Time out
3. Confiscation
4. Restitution
5. Revocation of parking decal
6. Towing of vehicle at owner's expense
7. Bus probation
8. Bus suspension
9. Bus expulsion
10. Work detail
11. Detention
12. School behavior contract
13. Saturday school
14. In-school suspension
15. Out-of-school suspension
16. Recommendation for expulsion
17. Referral to law enforcement

Directions

To identify appropriate sanctions, locate cells found at the intersection of the column numbers. The column numbers correspond with the consequences listed in the box to the right of the matrix.

Mandatory consequences are indicated by **M.**

Optional consequences are indicated by **O.**

When students are involved in evaluating their own work, ownership of the material to be learned can be enhanced.

- Involve students in evaluating their own work as well as your instruction.

- Hand out outlines, definitions, lecture notes, or study guides to focus students' attention on the task at hand and to organize their thoughts.

- Ask questions and give ample wait time before calling on a student. Wait time should be a minimum of three seconds after calling on a student and after a student has given his or her response.

- Vary the style as well as the content of instruction to address diverse student learning styles.

- Provide work of an appropriate difficulty to match varying ability levels.

- Relate materials to students' lives whenever possible.

- Be animated, create anticipation, and use activities to catch student interest or increase student motivation to participate.

- Engage student learning through cooperative group work, competitive teams, group discussions, debates, and role playing (Florida Department of Education, 2002).

Your students will arrive in your classroom with some perceived notions about what to expect and what is expected of them. Kindergarten students enter at their level knowing that teachers will correct antisocial behavior. Secondary-level students have learned from school experience that students who talk out of turn, yell, or scream, leave the classroom without permission, and those who are blatantly rude will be corrected and reprimanded by the teacher and school officials.

The better you know your students and their developmental, emotional, social, and physical level, the better chance you will have of succeeding with them. In 1970, Jacob Kounin established a term he called "withitness." Based on his observations of hundreds of teachers, Kounin concluded that successful teachers are the ones who are aware of what is going on in the classroom. Teachers who are aware are perceived by their students as "with-it" and can accurately detect classroom events. Students who perceive their teachers as with-it see the following characteristics:

- When discipline problems occur, the teacher consistently takes action to suppress misbehaviors of students who instigated the problem. This response displays that the teacher knows what is happening. If, on the other hand, the students expect the teacher to blame the wrong person, they will conclude that the teacher is not with-it.

- When two discipline problems arise concurrently, the teacher typically deals with the more serious one first.

- The teacher decisively handles instances of off-task behavior before the behavior gets out of hand or is copied by others. For example, if a third grader, Bernie, begins folding paper to make an airplane when he is supposed to be using the paper to validate answers to multiplication exercises, a with-it teacher will likely take action to get Bernie back on task before other students begin folding paper to build their airplanes (Cangelosi, 2004).

Being with-it is a perception that your students have of you. It is when they know that you know. It also means being able to handle classroom-management problems that may occur concurrently.

According to Wong and Wong, "classroom management refers to all the things that a teacher does to organize students, space, time, and materials so that instruction and student learning can take place" (1998, p. 84). Further characteristics of a well-managed classroom include the following:

- Students are deeply involved with their work, especially with academic, teacher-led instruction.

- Students know what is expected of them and are generally successful.

- There is relatively little wasted time, confusion, or disruption.

- The climate of the classroom is work oriented but relaxed and pleasant.

Teachers who create a learning environment that encourages positive social interaction, active engagement in learning, and self-motivation employ actions that describe effective classroom management (Burden & Byrd, 2003). A point of clarity is needed here: Classroom management and discipline are not the same. Discipline is not defined the same way as management. A discipline problem is behavior that (1) interferes with the teaching act, (2) interferes with the rights of others to learn, (3) is psychologically or physically unsafe, or (4) destroys property (Levin & Nolan, 2004). Management, on the other hand, describes how a classroom is organized and structured to prevent potential behavior problems. To prevent behavior problems, it is best to consider ways that you can organize the learning environment by thinking through classroom procedures and classroom organization. Classroom organization can be further divided into two categories: rules related to classroom conduct and rules related to academic work.

Classroom Conduct Rules

The following rules related to classroom conduct need to be communicated on the first day:

- What are the seating arrangements?
- How do we respond and speak during class?
- How much movement is allowed in the class?
- Are there rules for gum, drinks, and food?
- What are the procedures for using the washroom?
- What happens if I am tardy or absent?
- Am I allowed to come up to the desk?
- What do we do when a visitor comes to the door?
- How do we leave the classroom?
- What are the consequences of rule violation?

Academic Work Rules

Rules related to academic work include the following:

- What materials are required for class?
- How does the homework count, and what are the rules for completion?
- Am I allowed to make up work?
- Can I get partial credit for incomplete work?
- What happens if I miss a quiz or an examination?
- How are my grades determined?
- Will I be allowed to take notes?
- Will we work in cooperative learning groups and share with others?
- Are there separate rules for the learning center and reference material?
- How do we communicate during group work?
- Does neatness count?
- What are the lab safety rules?

Classroom Management Rules

Other rules about how to proceed and set up a classroom—specifically, how students respond and speak out—include the following:

- Will we raise hands?
- When are nonverbal signals to be used?

- What are the rules for students when speaking in the class?
- How will I know the appropriate loudness of my voice in the class?

Determining Grades

- What percentage will quizzes and tests contribute to my total grade?
- What percentage will class participation contribute?
- When will notification be given of failing performance?
- How much will homework count?

Violation of Rules

- What happens if I break the rules more than once?
- If I am absent, how will I know the due dates of my assignments?
- What happens if I am caught copying an assignment that is not my work?
- Can I make up work?

As you develop the organizational patterns and classroom routines, it is important to inform your students' parents of your plan of action. Keeping all players involved is important for your success. Consider these issues when communicating with parents.

WORKING WITH PARENTS

There are many ways to communicate with parents. Don't let your first communication with them be about a behavior problem. The means of communication may be affected by the purpose. Much communication with parents occurs at the start of the year in the form of an introductory letter, a back-to-school night, or a request for membership in a parent–teacher organization. At different times during the year, there may be other forms of communication with parents through the school office, such as open houses, newsletters, phone calls, special events, homework bulletins, and grade cards.

In the event that you must communicate with parents about an infraction that has occurred, there are several things that you should keep in mind. Visualizing the interaction with them in advance of the conference and knowing what to say and how to say it are important. Understand that without the support of the student's family or legal guardian, there is little chance that interventions at school will have a lasting effect in deterring the misbehavior. Parents have the ability to ask their son or daughter to be in at certain times, ground them from social activities, and perform extra chores around the house. The parents' ability to punish or reward their son or daughter will have more impact than any aversive measure that can be administered at the school. So as you think through the parent–teacher conference, it is vital to enlist the support of the parents or legal guardian of the student who has been disruptive in your classroom.

PARENT CONFERENCES

The notification that a conference is desired is usually your responsibility and should consist of a call or letter to the parent or guardian expressing the following:

- A statement of the purpose of the conference and the joint goal of supporting the student's success in school

- The role that the parent plays in the discipline-management process

- Possible dates, times, and locations for the conference

- A contact name and number in the event that the parent cannot reach you (Borich, 2004).

When conducting the conference, make sure that you use lay English and eliminate the education "alphabet soup" jargon. This is especially true when referring to acronyms such as IEP, TESOL, CRT, and LEP. In other words, make sure that you are clearly communicating with the parents at their level. Additionally, parents are not going to understand terms such as "norm-referenced tests," "higher-order thinking," and "brain-based learning." Using this sophisticated language will not enhance your credibility with your student's parent.

One of the most fundamental parts of the conference is your ability to listen. Parents need to express their hurt or anger, and you must listen and indicate that you are hearing them. This can be accomplished by eye contact, nods, and a lack of interruption. Remember, wait to add your comments when the parents have finished. Repeat what the parents have said: "Do I understand you correctly that . . . ," "So you feel that . . . ," or "I do understand . . . ." The use of "I" messages is characteristic of active listening and is important during parent conferences. When you feel upset about the actions of a parent's son or daughter in your classroom, it is important to express your feelings with "I" messages. For example, "When Fantasia blurts out or talks back to me, her behavior is disruptive to the class and that makes me angry. I have to take time away from what I am saying or from the other students to deal with her actions."

Following the parent conference, make sure you agree to an action plan to help with the situation at hand. There should be a list of actions that can be supported by the parent and a list of actions that you can implement to help resolve the discrepancy. Try out the plan and then check back with the parent or guardian. Checking back with them about the plan can be accomplished by a note, phone call, or home visit, if necessary.

Immediately following the parent conference, reflect on how well it went and take a moment to go through the interactions you had with the parent. This time of reflection will assist you with your parent-interaction skills.

We have addressed several classroom-management suggestions in this section, including the establishment of routines, organizational patterns, and communication with parents. Before we explain the different forms of behavior management, it is important to understand teacher power.

TYPES OF TEACHER POWER

In 1959, French and Raven, two social psychologists, theorized that all effective leaders must establish a sense of trust to gain the respect from students. They identified five types of social power a teacher can strive for: expert power, referent power, legitimate power, reward power, and coercive power (Levin & Nolan, 2004).

Expert Power

Individuals who are perceived as leaders are also perceived as experts. Teachers who are successful have expert power. This is power that you earn, not power that is bestowed on you because of your authority as a teacher. You have expert power when you are competent, have content knowledge, show enthusiasm for what you do, and are self-assured. Students will challenge you if you reveal a lack of self-confidence and appear to be unsure of yourself.

Referent Power

Referent power is power that is bestowed on you because students "refer" to you. In other words, you are liked because you are fair and trustworthy, and you care about your students—and they know that.

Legitimate Power

Your role, your influence, and your authority, by their very nature, carry legitimate power. Judges, police officers, and elected officials exert social power and leadership by their very titles. Influence in such cases may be conferred by the role itself rather than the nature of the person assuming the role. Students should respect you, give you their attention, and follow your requests because you are the teacher. Ideally, most families will talk to their children about listening to their teachers. When you begin your first day on the job, you begin exerting that legitimate power.

Because of your position, students may obey and accept your authority for the first few days of school. But after a few days, as they "psych" you out, they may challenge that legitimate power, and you will need to use your referent power and expert power to interact effectively with your students.

Reward Power

As a teacher, you can exercise your authority in the classroom by giving rewards to the students in the form of privileges, approval, or compensation (e.g., extra credit). However, many of the rewards that are available to teachers are often rejected by students who do not care about grades or teacher approval. Therefore, it is difficult to lead solely by exerting reward power.

Coercive Power

The term *in loco parentis* means that teachers are allowed to act in place of the parent, and this right is provided through the state and local governments. Consequently, within certain limits, schools can punish students who defy the authority of the teacher. Coercive power may stop misbehavior for a time, but the consequences of its use can result in disrespect or lack of trust, making it difficult to maximize students' potential for learning. Overdependence on coercive power may lead to antagonism and disengagement from the learning process.

AUTHORITY OF THE TEACHER

You may be wondering, what rights do I have as a classroom teacher? How do I know when to use my authority appropriately? After reading about the types of teacher power, you may be wondering, what other authority is granted to me? Authority granted to teachers is disseminated through the local school district according to the laws, rules, regulations, and policies of the state and the local school board. While students are on school property, attending school, or being transported to or from school or school-sponsored events, students are subject to the immediate control and direction of school employees, to whom such responsibility has been assigned by the principal or the principal's designee. State statutes grant teachers and other school staff the authority to control and discipline students who are assigned to them on campus or in other places where they may supervise students. Therefore, students are expected and required to follow the requests and directives of all teachers, school staff members, school volunteers, and chaperones when they are on school-owned property or other places where they are under the supervision of school personnel.

Teachers are expected to make every possible effort to control classroom disruptions. If the disturbance is severe, there are specific guidelines the teacher must follow that are established by the district according to other policies.

STUDENT RESPONSIBILITIES

Understanding the role that you play as a teacher means understanding the student's responsibility to you and to the learning process. When students are attending school, they have a responsibility to behave in a fashion that allows teaching and learning to take place.

Students have a responsibility to do the following:

- Attend school regularly

- Treat others with respect

- Treat school property and the property of others with respect

- Respect the privacy of others

- Have in their possession only those items allowed by law or by school board rules and policies—for example, in many schools, students are not allowed to carry DVD players, cell phones, or other electronic devices because of the disruptions they cause in the classroom

- Listen courteously to the opinions and points of view of others

- Come to class with all necessary materials and be prepared to learn

- Maximize their learning opportunities

- Report hazardous or dangerous situations to an adult in authority

- Report threats to do harm to an adult in authority

Although these may seem like reasonable responsibilities for students, many students do not take them seriously.

STUDENT RIGHTS

Understanding your students' rights will make clear the appropriate action to be taken by you, the teacher. By law, students have the right to a free and appropriate education, which includes the right to equal educational opportunities without regard to race, national origin, gender, disability, sexual orientation, or marital status. Other vested rights of each student include the right to be

- in a safe and orderly environment in which to learn
- treated with dignity and respect
- able to express opinions and personal points of view
- able to peaceably assemble
- secure in their personal privacy
- secure in the knowledge that there will be limited access to their personal records
- informed of the rules of conduct
- treated reasonably and fairly

The rights of students, like the authority granted to teachers, are a part of a local school district's policy and are maintained as law.

MODELS OF BEHAVIOR MANAGEMENT

Teachers need to consider the elements that affect classroom management before selecting or committing to a behavior-management strategy. Elements to consider are found in one of three categories: the student, the teacher, and the environment. One size does not fit all when considering an appropriate discipline or behavior-management model. The developmental level of the student is important, as is the kind of environment. We have discussed the school district's policy, the teacher's need for law and order, and the amount of freedom allowed for solving problems and making decisions. Additionally, the types of power used change as students mature and schools allow students greater freedom. Figure 4.1 illustrates behavior-management models in relation to the amount of freedom allowed and the developmental level of the student. Teacher power is denoted by the curved line that extends around and through each management model. Choices for appropriate management models depend on the developmental level of the students, the consideration for power, and the amount of freedom that is allowed in the environment (Sprinthall & Sprinthall, 1987).

Behavior Modification

Behavior modification is a type of behavior-management strategy that uses behavior analysis to appropriately discipline students. Behavior modification is based on B. F. Skinner's theory of *behaviorism* or *operant conditioning*. The techniques used in behavior modification derive from the theories of Mather and Goldstein (2001).

FIGURE 4.1 The Development–Freedom–Power Model

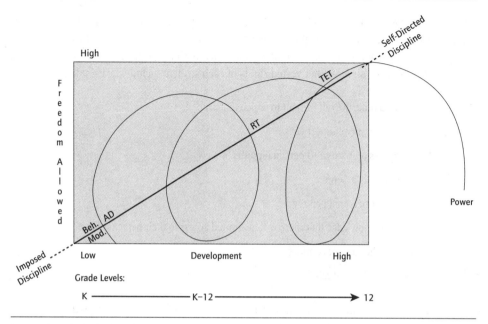

Source: Esler and Sciortino (1991).

Behavior modification assumes that observable and measurable behaviors are good targets for change. All behavior follows a set of consistent rules. Methods can be developed for defining, observing, and measuring behaviors, as well as designing effective interventions. According to theorists who espouse this theory, behavior modification rarely fails unless it is applied inefficiently or inconsistently. All behavior is maintained, changed, or shaped by the consequences of that behavior. *Reinforcers* are consequences that strengthen behavior. *Punishments* are consequences that weaken behavior. Student behavior is managed and changed by the consequences of classroom behavior. To manage behavior through consequences, use this multistep process:

1. The problem must be defined, usually by count or description.

2. Design a way to change the behavior.

3. Identify an effective reinforcer.

4. Apply the reinforcer consistently to shape or change behavior.

Each of the following techniques are parts of behavior modification and are related to teacher power.

- Positive reinforcement: When you, as a teacher, give rewards to your students, you are using reward power. A reward is given to a student if he or she complies with your wish. For example, you may grant students extra time on Friday if they line up quickly for lunch.

- Negative reinforcement: Negative reinforcement is related to coercive power. Negative reinforcement occurs when the frequency of a behavior is increased by ending or terminating something that is undesirable or uncomfortable. In a classroom environment, learners often want to avoid classroom experiences or things that are boring to them. So they disrupt the class in hopes of getting removed from the classroom by the teacher. Some psychologists believe that negative reinforcement is applied by teachers more often than positive because teachers react to the negative behavior in the hopes of stopping it but rarely react to positive behaviors in order to teach them.

- Punishment: Punishment is related to coercive power. An unpleasant consequence is applied by the teacher to the student in an effort to change his or her behavior.

- Contracts: In the negotiating stage with students, contracts can be used to improve behavior. A contract is an agreement among the student, teacher, and parents made in an effort to make specific expectations and rewards.

- Modeling: When students view teacher behavior that is consistent and fair to everyone in the classroom, they see referent power. Teachers create a positive model for their students to imitate.

- Token economy: Schools or individual classroom teachers that use behavior modification techniques may set up a token-economy system. This type of agreement allows students to earn prizes for positive behavior. Phony money may be exchanged for items desired by students in a store located in the school or classroom. A positive-reinforcement strategy that makes use of immediate rewards in the form of currency that can be redeemed for prizes is called a "token economy."

- Satiation: Satiation occurs when a teacher rewards an undesirable behavior to the extent that the student becomes bored with it. For example, if you have a student who repeatedly talks in class, you may ask the student to go to a time-out spot and talk, talk, and talk. The undesirable behavior grows tiresome to the student, and he or she does not talk inappropriately again.

- Extinction: At certain times during teaching, students may cause interruptions. At this moment, teachers need to decide whether to stop teaching or to stop the behavior. The term "extinction" is used when behavior is ignored. Behaviors that are ignored and not rewarded cease.

Behavior modification has the goal of changing a student's behavior. Management systems advocate ignoring negative behavior and rewarding positive behavior. It is believed that disruptive students have learned misguided ways of satisfying their need for recognition. These disruptive behaviors will become less frequent when the students learn that they will gain recognition and rewards (receive positive reinforcement) only when they behave. Another assumption of behavior modification is that students learn desired behavior most efficiently when adults immediately punish inappropriate behavior and immediately reward positive behavior.

The next model for classroom management was developed by Lee Canter during the 1970s but is still used widely in classrooms today. He calls it *assertive discipline*.

Assertive Discipline

Assertive discipline, developed by Lee and Marlene Canter (1976), is based on assertion training. This systematic approach is designed to help individuals learn to express their wants and needs more effectively while not abusing the rights of others. In assertion training, individuals

Lee Canter and Marlene Canter Assertive discipline is a structured, systematic approach that is designed to assist educators in running an organized, teacher-in-charge classroom environment. Lee Canter and Marlene Canter, when consulting for school systems, have found that many teachers are unable to control undesirable behavior that occurs in their classrooms. They attribute this, rightfully so, to a lack of training in the area of behavior management. Based on their research and the foundations of assertiveness training and applied behavior analysis, they developed a commonsense, easy-to-learn approach to help teachers become the captains of their classrooms and positively influence their students' behavior. Today, it is the most widely used packaged behavior-management program. Assertive discipline has evolved since the mid-1970s from an authoritarian approach to one that is more democratic and cooperative.

Source: "Assertive Discipline," retrieved June 29, 2004, from http://maxweber.hunter.cuny.edu/pub/eres/EDSPC715_MCINTYRE/AssertiveDiscipline.html.

have one of three general response styles. A *nonassertive response style* is one that is wishy-washy. It does not clearly communicate or express the wants or feelings of the individual, nor does it back up the individual's words with the necessary positive action. A *hostile response style* is one in which individuals express their personal wants and feelings in a way that puts others down or abuses their rights. By contrast, an *assertive-discipline response style* is one in which individuals express their wants and feelings and back them up with positive actions as necessary (Canter & Canter, 1976). Assertive discipline has a low level of freedom and can be used with lower and upper elementary-grade students.

Assertive discipline is about catching children when they are being good as much as when they are wrong. It involves an exchange of trust; like a bank account, deposits are made that praise and encourage.

To be assertive is to

- be calm

- be unemotional

- use a lot of eye contact

- give praise and do this methodically

Not to be assertive is to

- react

- beg

- plead
- show emotion
- show inconsistency

Assertive discipline needs a plan of action that is based on the *right to learn* and the *right to teach*. The following is taken from Lee Canter's book about the actions of teachers (Canter & Canter, 1976).

Assume an Assertive Attitude

To manage student behavior effectively, your words and actions must reflect an assertive attitude in the classroom: "I am the boss. I have a right to teach. You have a right to learn. You will not stop me from teaching or other students from learning."

Develop a Classroom Discipline Plan

To maintain and support your assertive attitude, you must preplan what you will do when students misbehave. This is accomplished by developing a *classroom discipline plan*. The plan consists of three elements: rules, disciplinary consequences, and positive reinforcement. Your classroom discipline plan should be communicated to the principal, the students, and the parents.

Teach the Classroom Discipline Plan

Before using the plan, teach it to your students. Carefully explain the rules, disciplinary consequences, and positive reinforcement so that students know what is expected of them and what the consequences of their behavior will be. To be sure they understand what you've explained, question students about the plan.

Implement the Classroom Discipline Plan

The implementation of your classroom discipline plan requires that you follow these steps:

- Clearly communicate general classroom rules.

In order for students to behave appropriately, they must know the rules of your classroom. At all times, you should clearly and firmly communicate to students exactly what you want them to do. For example, you might say, "I want you to stay in your seat unless you are given permission to get up." To be effective when communicating, remain calm and speak in a soft but determined voice.

- Provide disciplinary consequences.

Whenever students misbehave, you must provide disciplinary consequences in accordance with the discipline hierarchy that you have developed. It is important to be consistent and discipline students every time they are disruptive.

- Use positive reinforcement.

They key to changing student behavior is to provide positive reinforcement whenever students behave appropriately. You should balance your disciplinary actions with frequent praise and other forms of positive reinforcement (such as marbles, points, coupons, privileges, or prizes).

William Glasser's path has been a continuing progression in private practice, lecturing, and writing, culminating in the publication of more than 20 books. After writing the counseling book *Reality Therapy* in 1965, he wrote *Schools Without Failure* in 1969, greatly expanded the understanding of motivation and behavior with *Choice Theory* in 1998, and finally helped people improve their own mental health or happiness with *Warning: Psychiatry Can Be Hazardous to Your Mental Health* in 2003.

Source: "Who We Are," retrieved June 28, 2004, from www.wglasser.com/whoweare.htm.

A part of behavior modification and assertive discipline is the idea of praise. When praise is provided to the entire class, a token-economy system can be set up. With this in mind, an elaborate system of desired behaviors and comparable rewards is established using a type of phony currency. Students who demonstrate the desired behaviors are rewarded with play money. Class currency can be redeemed for items in a school store, such as pencils, erasers, paper tablets, etc. Other rewards may include free time, time in a learning center, or a weekend free of homework if the student is maintaining high achievement. This system works well with exceptional education students and with students at lower developmental stages.

Choice Theory (Control Theory)

Choice theory or control theory, described by William Glasser (1986), allows students a medium amount of freedom to make decisions and solve problems. Choice theory works best with upper-elementary, middle, or high school students. For this theory to work, students must be able to make decisions and solve interpersonal problems using inductive and deductive thought at a beginning level. Praise and success are important aspects of choice theory. As students begin to struggle with value questions such as fairness and loyalty, their cognitive and moral abilities are tempered by loyalties they have developed—to peers, adults, and their own developing conscience. Nevertheless, they have the ability to begin the struggle, the need to struggle, and the right to struggle. There should be no punishment by the teacher in choice theory.

According to Glasser (1986), people are driven by six basic needs. All of our choices and behaviors are based on the urgency of survival, power, love, belonging, freedom, and fun. Glasser asserts that 95% of all discipline problems are the misguided efforts of children trying to achieve power. By understanding the drives for survival, power, love, belonging, freedom, and fun in people, we can become more conscious of the need for our world to be a quality world of our choosing. The axioms of choice theory are as follows (William Glasser Institute, 2005):

- The only person whose behavior we can control is our own.

- All we can give another person is information.

- All long-lasting psychological problems are relationship problems.

As a last resort, teachers may refer students to the principal's office.

- The problem relationship is always part of our present life.
- What happened in the past has everything to do with who we are today; we can only satisfy our basic needs right now and plan to continue satisfying them in the future.
- We can only satisfy our needs by satisfying the pictures in our quality world.
- All we do is behave.
- All behaviors are "total behaviors" that are made up of four components: acting, thinking, feeling, and physiology. All total behaviors are chosen, but we only have direct control over the acting and thinking components.
- We can only control our feeling and physiology indirectly through how we choose to act and think.
- All total behavior is designated by verbs and named by the part that is the most recognizable.

When problems arise in the classroom, Glasser (1990) advocates saying something to the disruptive student such as the following:

> It looks like you have a problem. How could I help you solve it? If you'll just calm down, as soon as I have time, I'll talk it over with you and I think we can work something out. As long as you're doing what you're doing now, we can't work anything out. (p. 140)

If the student refuses to work it out, then Glasser recommends that you say,

> Well, I see that you are still angry and you will not calm down. I hope we can get together later and work this out, but if you are not willing to settle down, it's better that you leave now. (p. 142)

Saying something such as this leaves the door open, and there are no threats or hassles. The disruptive student is looking for someone to blame to justify keeping his or her grievance alive. But it's hard to stay angry at a teacher who is saying, "I want to work this out. I am not looking to punish you. I just want us to solve the problem." If the student calms down in class, then you need to find time to talk with the student. If the infraction is not severe, then you should be able to spare a few minutes between classes or after school to speak. If you need more than five minutes, you will have to arrange a special time. When you have the time, what you say should always be about the same. An example is provided here:

> What were you doing when the problem started? Was this against the rules? Can we work it out so that it doesn't happen again? If this situation comes up in the future, let's work out what you could do and what I could do so we don't have this problem again. (p. 143)

According to Glasser (1990), when students perceive that you are trying to make the classroom a better place to be, they will try to solve their own problems and go along with you to help each other. Glasser says that teachers should not try to be the boss in the classroom; instead, try to be a teacher who, with the students' help, can work through problems that may occur.

Another type of behavior-management model that supports working out problem situations with students is *teacher-effectiveness training*. The components of this model are explained in the next section.

Teacher-Effectiveness Training

Teacher-effectiveness training is a total classroom-management program designed to increase the amount and quality of teaching and learning time in the classroom (time on task). The program was developed by Thomas Gordon (1974). Central to Gordon's method is trust in the individual to exercise power to identify the problem, accept ownership of the problem, discover a solution to the problem, and carry out that solution. The teacher's role is to facilitate the student's behavior in a nondirective manner.

According to Gordon, there are three responses generally provided to students. The first is authoritarian; the teacher asserts his or her position of power over the student. The second is permissive; the student assumes power and the teacher is passive to the extent that students assert that they will get their way. This is indicated when a student nags at a teacher (or parent) to get his or her way. The no-win, no-lose method assumes a position that neither the student nor the teacher should have power; rather, they negotiate ownership of the problem and then expect the owner to find an appropriate solution. Related to this is an analysis of the problem of determining ownership: Is the problem the student's, the teacher's, or does a third party own the problem?

Gordon's method requires the use of well-developed communication skills. Users of this method must listen as well as hear the other's statement. Hearing is a physical act, whereas listening is an intellectual and emotional one. The message must first be filtered through the listener's emotional state and intellectual history. To communicate effectively, "I" messages rather than "you" messages should be used. For example, "I am angry" is an "I" message. "You are clumsy and stupid!" is a "you" message.

Thomas Gordon (1918–2002) was a leading clinical psychologist and founder of Gordon Training International who gained acclaim for his work in conflict resolution. Before serving in the U.S. Army and Air Force during World War II, he earned a bachelor's degree from DePauw University in 1939 and a master's degree from The Ohio State University in 1941. After leaving the military as a captain, he studied at the University of Chicago, where he graduated with a Ph.D. in 1949.

Gordon taught at the University of Chicago for five years before joining Edward Glaser & Associates in California as a consultant in 1954. It was there that he developed his theories about conflict resolution. Going into private practice as a psychologist in 1958, he began counseling others on conflict resolution, and in 1968, he founded the Solana Beach, California–based Effectiveness Training, Inc., which later became Gordon Training International. Gordon's ideas about conflict resolution are expressed in his best-selling book *Parent Effectiveness Training: The No-Lose Way to Raise Responsible Children* (1970). He later applied the same principles used in parent–child relationships to educators in *T.E.T.: Teacher Effectiveness Training* (1974); to businessmen in *Leader Effectiveness Training, L.E.T.: The No-Lose Way to Release the Productive Potential of People* (1983); to salesmen in *Sales Effectiveness Training: The Breakthrough Method to Become Partners with Your Customers* (1993, with Carl D. Zaiss); and to doctors in *Making the Patient Your Partner: Communication Skills for Doctors and Other Caregivers* (1995). For his groundbreaking work, Gordon was nominated in 1997, 1998, and 1999 for the Nobel Peace Prize, and he received lifetime achievement awards from the American Psychological Foundation and the California Psychological Association.

Source: Contemporary Authors Online; reproduced in the Biography Resource Center (Farmington Hills, MI: Thomson Gale, 2005).

A key element of this method is self-responsibility. Students are responsible for their problems. Teachers are responsible for theirs. The following five steps of Gordon's method form the core of a no-win, no-lose problem-solving method (see Table 4.2).

1. Identify and define the problem. Using active listening and "I" messages, the teacher facilitates the student's struggle to properly identify and state the problem by asking eliciting and probing questions. This step assumes that the student has accepted ownership of the problem. Using the infraction of smoking on school grounds, the following example shows how you might solve the problem using Gordon's method. To identify the problem, the student would state that he was smoking in the school building after skillful listening and perhaps some questioning by the teacher. The student may remark, "I am so mad at the principal for making dumb rules."

2. Help the student list possible solutions to the problem. For the problem of smoking in school, the student may generate the following solutions:
    Stop smoking.
    Smoke away from school
    Continue to smoke in the building but don't get caught.

TABLE 4.2   Teacher-Effectiveness Training

1. Identify and define the conflict. Whose problem is it?
2. Generate alternative solutions.
3. Evaluate each alternative solution.
4. Choose the best solution.
5. Create an action plan for the chosen solution.
6. Evaluate the solution that was carried out.

3. Help the student to evaluate alternative solutions. The outcome of the solution must be considered because the possible outcome of continuing to smoke in the school building may not be acceptable to the teacher because this may violate a fire code, the state school code, the school district's policy, or parental wishes expressed in a school policy handbook. You must express the inability to support the choice of that decision with an "I" message. The student should also use an "I" message in this conversation.

4. Choose the best alternative. This step involves both student and teacher in creating ways to make an action plan for the chosen solution.

5. In the last step, both teacher and student evaluate how the solution worked. They look at the results of the implemented solution and the timing of the implementation and, if necessary, recycle step two, generating alternative solutions, through the last step, evaluation.

Gordon's work became well-known in the nation when several training sessions were conducted by both teachers and parents. He explains that active listening techniques and "I" messages get results. He believes that when the guidelines are followed, less fighting, more mutual respect, and warm feelings are the outcomes of his techniques.

The last discipline model that we will explore is called *cooperative discipline*. Like the other models, it is dependent on the teacher understanding the degree of freedom and the developmental level of the students. The components of this model are explained in the next section.

Cooperative Discipline

According to Linda Albert (1990), cooperative discipline is a comprehensive, easy-to-implement discipline program that helps teachers achieve order and control in today's classroom in a manner that is consistent with optimum student growth—academic, social, and psychological. The program invites cooperation. It provides concrete strategies that encourage teachers, parents, administrators, and students to work as a team to help students choose appropriate behavior. Cooperative discipline challenges teachers to accept the enormous power that they have in influencing students' behavior and shows them how to channel this power into practical, effective skills that promote positive interactions with students.

This model advocates the development of a school plan. Implementing a plan that is consistently applied, no matter what the situation, is beneficial for students and school personnel.

Linda Albert was a teacher in the public schools in Ithaca, New York from 1968 to 1972; a teacher-specialist in the diagnosis and remediation of behavioral and learning problems from 1972 to 1981; director of the Family Education Center of Florida in Tampa from 1982 to the present; and adjunct professor at Elmira College from 1978 to 1986. She presents workshops, is a spokesperson for teacher and parent education and an educational consultant, has appeared on local and nationally syndicated television programs.

Her writings include *Coping With Kids* (1982), *Coping With Your Child's Education* (1984, with Elaine Shimberg), *Coping With Kids and Vacation* (1986), *Strengthening Stepfamilies* (1986), *Quality Parenting* (1987), *A Teacher's Guide to Cooperative Discipline: How to Manage Your Classroom and Promote Self-Esteem* (1989), *An Administrator's Guide to Cooperative Discipline: Strategies for Schoolwide Implementation* (1992), and *Cooperative Discipline* (in press).

Source: Contemporary Authors Online; reproduced in the Biography Resource Center (Farmington Hills, MI: Thomson Gale, 2005).

The school action plan is an important component of cooperative discipline, and no school is complete without one. The goals of cooperative discipline are achieved through a five-step diagnostic, corrective, and supportive system. Thoughtful responses and guidelines that are specific to an individual student's behavior are devised. Each step builds on the information gathered in the previous step; the completed plan is not only an individualized discipline plan but also a process for guiding teacher–student interactions and teacher–parent conferences.

It is recommended that the school action plan be communicated to the parents and become familiar to all students and teachers at the school.

The five steps of the school action plan are as follows:

1. Pinpoint and describe the student's behavior.

2. Identify the goal of the misbehavior.

3. Choose intervention techniques for the moment of misbehavior.

4. Select encouragement techniques to build self-esteem.

5. Involve parents as partners.

Cooperative discipline asks teachers to think about the rationale for the student's misbehavior. Is the student misbehaving because he or she seeks attention, power, revenge, or avoidance of failure? Table 4.3 describes the techniques teachers can use when students misbehave. A general strategy is suggested in the middle column, and appropriate techniques that match each behavior problem are listed in the third column.

TABLE 4.3	Cooperative Discipline Strategies	

Behavior	General Strategy	Techniques
Attention-seeking behavior	Minimize the attention	Ignore the behavior Give "the eye" Stand close by Mention the student's name while teaching Send a secret notice
	Legitimize the behavior	Make a lesson out of the behavior Extend the behavior to its most extreme form Have the whole group join in the behavior
	Do the unexpected	Turn out the lights Lower your voice Change your voice Talk to the wall Cease talking temporarily
	Distract the student	Ask a direct question Ask a favor Change the activity
	Notice appropriate behavior	Thank students Write well-behaved students' names on board
	Move the student	Change the student's seat Send student to time-out

Power and revenge behavior	Make a graceful exit	Acknowledge the student's power
		Remove the audience
		Table the matter
		Make a date
		Use a fogging technique:
		    Agreeing with the student
		    Changing the subject

	Use time-out	In classroom, another room, a special room, office
	Set the consequences	Loss or delay of activity Loss of objects or classroom materials Loss of access to classroom or special activities Required interactions with others
Avoidance of failure	Modify instructional methods	Use concrete learning materials Teach one step at a time Cooperative groups

TABLE 4.3

Behavior	General Strategy	Techniques
	Provide tutoring	Extra help from counselor
		Peer tutoring
	Teach positive self-talk	Post positive classroom signs
		Require two "put-ups" for every put-down
		Encourage positive self-talk before beginning tasks.
	Make mistakes okay	Talk about mistakes
		Equate mistakes with effort
		Minimize the effect of making mistakes
	Build confidence	Focus on improvement
		Notice contributions
		Build on strengths
		Show faith in students
		Acknowledge the difficulty of a task
		Set time limits on tasks
	Focus on past success	Analyze past success
		Repeat past success
	Recognize achievement	Applause
		Clapping and standing ovations
		Awards

Source: Albert (1990).

Teachers are faced with problems that occur on a daily basis. These problems may include simple infractions of school or classroom rules. When they involve more serious events, including disrespect, cheating, or obscene words and gestures or the open display of hostility, it becomes necessary to have a plan of action. We have presented a sample of five discipline models here. Table 4.1 depicted one central Florida school district's matrix of infractions and the recommended consequences. This matrix is a part of the district's code of conduct, which is given to each parent and signed and returned to the school. This process communicates the seriousness of appropriate behavior and emphasizes to everyone the actions to be taken by the parties involved.

Mr. Stennet is starting his first day with eighth-grade language arts students at Memorial Middle School. He is waiting at the door as each student files in. He greets each student with a smile and asks the students to sit down anyplace they like. He announces that later in the week, a seating chart will be set up and students will be assigned seats, but today, they may sit wherever they are comfortable as they enter the classroom for the first time. Once the students are seated, Mr. Stennet welcomes all the students to his class and provides background information to the students. Then, he proceeds genuinely by saying he would like to get to know all of them and quickly organizes a four-square (icebreaker) activity to find out his students' names, interests, and hobbies. Following this activity, Mr. Stennet clearly communicates the rules of his classroom: be prompt, be prepared, be polite, and be positive. He calls these rules the "four P" principles.

Principle rule number one is *be prompt*. When the bell rings, Mr. Stennet expects the students to be in their seats and to copy the agenda from the whiteboard for the day's class session. The agenda identifies the goals, the materials, and the order in which the activities will take place for the day. He explains that an agenda like the one on the board will become routine for their class. While the students record the agenda, Mr. Stennet will take roll. If any students are late, they must immediately sign a tardy roster by the classroom door and take their seats. The penalty for unexcused lateness is 30 minutes of detention after school. If students feel that they have a valid excuse for being late, then they should check the "please excuse" column on the tardy roster and place their excuse in the tray next to the roster.

Principle rule number two is *be prepared*. This requires the students to bring the necessary materials and completed homework assignments to class. Late work is not accepted, and only partial credit will be granted if work is not finished.

Principle rule number three is *be polite*. Mr. Stennet reviews what his definition of polite means. Because these are eighth-grade students who have been through at least seven years of schooling, he understands that the students will not need a list of classroom rules for every possible infraction because the code of conduct of his school district covers this quite well. His definition is that no student is allowed to be disrespectful to another student or to him.

The last rule is *be positive*. This is important because Mr. Stennet wants to boost his students' confidence in themselves. He understands that remaining positive will help the class get through all the trials and tribulations that may happen during the year. Mr. Stennet proceeds with an icebreaker activity to create a warm classroom environment and to begin to learn his students' names.

Summary

The relationships you establish with your students are among the most important in your teaching career. You enter into this relationship with them and learn the uniqueness of each student and his or her cultural background, socioeconomic background, and abilities. Students become your allies in the teaching and learning process and can be a valuable resource in the classroom. It is your students who will help you to establish the rules, procedures, and routines of the classroom.

Your success as a classroom teacher is dependent on your learning community. The people who make up your learning community all contribute and become resources as you develop the interactions of your daily life in the school. Remember, you are not in this alone. Members of your community include the administrative staff, peer teachers, specialists, service providers, students, and parents from the surrounding region of your school. You will want to establish cooperative, friendly, collaborative working relationships with everyone you work with in the learning community. Be a team player who is willing to seek help and give help to others.

Research suggests that teachers who follow the principles of democracy as part of their classroom routine and allow students options for rules, procedures, modifications to the curriculum, and activities have fewer discipline problems. If you engage students in choices about the learning environment, they will thrive in understanding and problem solving and will learn to manage freedom responsibly.

As we stated at the beginning of this chapter, you cannot learn all there is to know about classroom management and discipline by reading a book or taking a workshop. Interacting with the students and gaining experience from this interaction, along with the support of school personnel, will help you gain a repertoire of behaviors that can assist you when working with all students.

Thought to Action

1. What is your greatest classroom management fear? Why? Explain which approach you would select for your student population.

2. Using a search engine, find Internet sites that have information about classroom management. Find examples of how to work with culturally diverse learners.

3. If you were to meet with a student's parents about a discipline problem that occurred, how would you handle the parent conference?

4. Explain the importance of understanding the developmental, physical, social, and emotional needs of your student population in relation to classroom management.

5. Explain why you agree or disagree with the premise that management techniques should be used to allow students to develop their own sense of freedom and decision making.

ON YOUR OWN

Log on to the web-based student study site at http://www.sagepub.com/holt for access to a Standards-Based Student Project that will help you connect what you have learned in this chapter to your state's standards; study aids, such as electronic flashcards; and research recommendations, including journal article links and other Web resources.

Classroom Assessment and Accountability

IN TODAY'S ACCOUNTABILITY ENVIRONMENT, IT IS IMPERATIVE THAT YOU UNDERSTAND THE relationship between what you do in your classroom and what is expected with respect to content standards, high-stakes testing, and the ultimate grading of your school according to state and federal criteria, particularly the rules and regulations of the recent No Child Left Behind (NCLB) legislation. This legislation requires schools to measure student progress at regular intervals and to report the annual yearly progress (AYP) of the various subgroups of children who attend each school. School districts must report this data to the federal government to show overall and subgroup progress in the achievement of the students at each school. When a school does not meet the AYP indicators, the school is assigned a failing grade with respect to student achievement. If a school receives a failing grade for three consecutive years, the school is subject to a variety of measures, including the replacement of the principal and teachers, that are designed to improve the performance of the students at the schools.

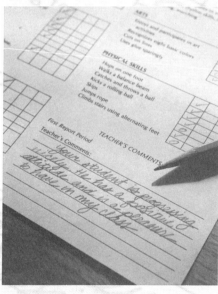

The NCLB legislation is quite extensive and needs to be reviewed by teachers so that they know what is expected of them and their students. Teachers who work with special needs students, diverse students, students whose primary language is not English, or students from inner cities face particularly difficult challenges to ensure that these students meet the requirements set forth in the NCLB legislation.

In some districts, schools have abandoned good learning strategies in favor of test-taking strategies. Teachers are required to review their students for the high-stakes tests frequently, provide tutoring opportunities for the students, institute remedial skill-building classes, and devote more time to reading, writing, and mathematics—at the expense of other areas of the curriculum—to ensure that the students perform well on the high-stakes tests. What is so unfortunate about this approach to solving the achievement problems of our students is that students may learn more about how to take tests and perform on specific tests, but they may not become good learners. One fourth-grade student shared her concern with one of the authors: "All we do is take

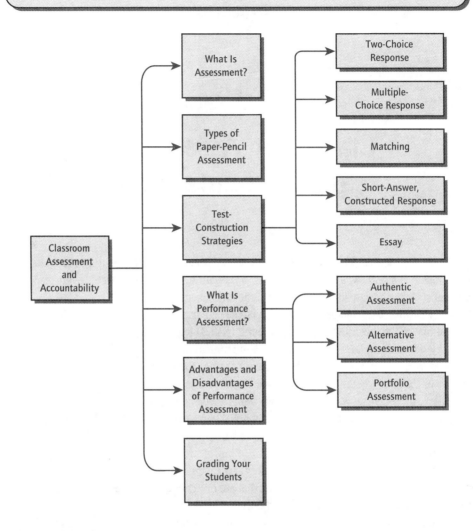

Chapter 5 Classroom Assessment and Accountability

- Classroom Assessment and Accountability
  - What Is Assessment?
  - Types of Paper-Pencil Assessment
  - Test-Construction Strategies
    - Two-Choice Response
    - Multiple-Choice Response
    - Matching
    - Short-Answer, Constructed Response
    - Essay
  - What Is Performance Assessment?
    - Authentic Assessment
    - Alternative Assessment
    - Portfolio Assessment
  - Advantages and Disadvantages of Performance Assessment
  - Grading Your Students

tests, we don't learn anything new." Another secondary student simply said, "School is no longer a fun place to be, it's all about the FCAT." (The FCAT is the Florida Comprehensive Achievement Test, which is administered at various grade levels in Florida. High school students must pass the mathematics, reading, and writing portions of the FCAT to graduate from high school).

Having criteria for students to meet in order to graduate from high school or progress from one grade level to the next is certainly not a bad idea. Having tests related to the curriculum standards for each subject area and grade level is also not a bad idea. But teaching to the tests instead of helping students learn how to learn and making the passing of the test the main objective of education is simply a bad idea. There needs to be a compromise—that compromise can be met by classroom teachers in the way they construct their lesson plans and assessment strategies. If the lessons are designed to meet the curriculum standards, as we indicated in Chapter 3, and student assessments are aligned with those objectives, then most students will not have trouble passing the high-stakes tests, provided that those tests are appropriately designed for the grade levels and the content standards required at those grade levels.

In this chapter, we will examine more closely the concept of assessment, types of assessments, ways to improve assessment, and the grading of students.

WHAT IS ASSESSMENT?

Before we engage in an in-depth discussion of assessment, it is imperative that we have common language to work from. At one time in education, when the word "assessment" was used, it was relegated to the work done by school psychologists and school counselors, who used various instruments to determine the emotional, personal, or academic problems that were preventing students from functioning normally in a given classroom or for the placement of students in gifted or learning-disabled classes. However, in recent years, the term "assessment" has become preferable to "testing" to describe what a teacher does in the classroom to determine the achievement of students.

Assessment is a formal procedure used to determine students' progress with respect to desirable learning outcomes or objectives. This broad definition encompasses the many activities that teachers engage in while working with their students. Students may be assessed using tests, performances, or demonstrations. They may have their participation in group activities and individual projects assessed. They may be assessed cognitively, affectively, or kinesthetically. Using the term "assessment" simply provides the teacher with more options for describing student progress toward desired learning outcomes.

Other terms that have been used to indicate student progress include "test," "measurement," and "evaluation." Let's examine these terms and see how they are related to assessment.

Tests imply some form of paper-pencil examination. Usually the test is designed to cover a specific amount of content, administered during a specific time period, and structured as either a forced-choice or free-response format. Tests designed by teachers may be short (referred to as quizzes) or fairly long (chapter, unit, semester, or end-of-year examinations). Standardized tests are professionally developed examinations that have been normed over a given population and are used to determine how a group of students performs in comparison to similar groups of students. Standardized tests are typically used to determine reading skills or readiness for different courses (such as algebra) or to qualify for entrance into universities (e.g., the SAT, ACT, GRE). They are used to determine intelligence and aptitude. Most of you took a variety of standardized tests during your careers as students. Sometimes you may have been pleased with your scores on these tests, other times you may have been disappointed. Most states' high-stakes tests are standardized tests.

"Measurement" is a term that implies the gathering of quantitative (numerical) data such as test scores, ratings, or rankings or physical attributes such as height, weight, blood pressure, and heart rate (Gallagher, 1998). When the data are gathered, evaluation occurs. Based on the data collected by your doctor, for example, you may get a clean bill of health, or you may be told that you have a physical condition that needs attention. Based on the test scores you receive in a college class, you may determine that you will get a B in the class. Based on your individual scores in your bowling league, you may be ranked in the top 10 in your league. Measurement is precise, numerically based analyses. It certainly has value, but is far too narrow a term to use in today's educational environment.

According to Bloom, Englehart, Furst, Hill, and Krathwohl (1956) and Anderson and Krathwohl (2001), evaluation is a judgment about the worth or value of something according to established criteria. The criteria may be internal—for example, following the rules of logical argument—or the criteria may be established externally—for example, the accreditation guidelines used by regional accreditation organizations or the teacher education standards used by the National Council for Accreditation of Teacher Education. Thus, evaluation is a form of assessment that judges the usefulness, value, appropriateness, or quality of products, procedures, policies, or programs based on established criteria. Schools typically evaluate the effectiveness of a reading program or mathematics program by the improvement in students' reading and computational skills. Teacher education institutions frequently evaluate aspects of their program, such as student internships, to determine how well they are preparing the students for the reality of the K–12 classroom.

As you can see, clarity of terminology is important when you are trying to provide information to parents and students about the achievement of the students. The term "assessment" is currently popular because it is more inclusive and allows for multiple means of testing, measuring, evaluating, and thus assessing student progress.

TYPES OF PAPER-PENCIL ASSESSMENT

In today's classrooms, there is a proliferation of assessment strategies in use. These strategies include the typical paper-pencil tests, as well as newer ideas such as performance assessments, observational schemas, and portfolios. However, the most commonly used strategies are still the paper-pencil tests or their computer equivalents. There are two basic formats for these paper-pencil tests: selected response and constructed or free response.

Selected-response forms, also referred to as forced-choice forms, are tests that require the student to select answers from a given set of choices. The most common forms are true-false or two-choice items, multiple-choice items, and matching items. Selected-response forms are excellent for assessing knowledge level and learning outcomes. They can be used to help students clarify terminology, apply the rules of grammar, or recall sets of historical facts or literary characters. Selected-response items rely heavily on students' ability to recognize the correct response. Selected-response items can also be used to assess students' comprehension of ideas and concepts or their ability to apply knowledge to other situations.

The higher you move on Bloom's taxonomy, the more difficult it is to structure effective selected-response items. Thus, teachers tend to use this format for lower level knowledge assessment. Constructed or free-response items include fill-in-the-blank items or short answers and essays. These items not only expect students to recall information but also require them to use principles, concepts, and strategies to formulate their responses. Thus, much more than recall is assessed in this form of response.

CONSTRUCTION STRATEGIES FOR SELECTED-RESPONSE ITEMS

Strategies for Designing Two-Choice Response Items

Although the most common two-choice item is the true-false test, you probably have taken tests that used other two-choice options, such as yes-no, supported–not supported, or cause-effect items. Regardless of the type of two-choice item, there are some fundamental guidelines for constructing these items. James Popham (1999, p. 116) has a succinct list of rules to follow for the design of appropriate two-choice items:

- Phrase items so that students who do not really understand the material will be guided to the wrong answer.

- Do not use negative statements or double negatives in your items.

- Include only one concept in each item.

- Divide items evenly between true and false statements.

- Write all items so that they are of similar length.

Gallagher (1998) adds two other suggestions: Make sure the items are entirely true or entirely false and avoid specific determiners (e.g., always, all, or never). Test-wise students know that such terms generally make a statement false, whereas other words, such as "generally," "usually," and "sometimes" will make a statement true. The purpose of these questions is to determine students' knowledge, not their test wisdom (p. 160).

If you think about these statements and previous tests that you have taken, you will begin to understand the importance of these simple statements. The purpose of assessment is to determine what the students know. Creating test items that are "tricky" because they break the fundamental rules of good test construction is simply not fair to your students and will not tell you what they know.

Strategies for Designing Multiple-Choice Items

Multiple-choice items are by far the most commonly used selected-response items in our country. By the time a student leaves elementary school, he or she is well versed in the use of multiple-choice items. Unfortunately, many students who immigrate to the United States are not as familiar with this form of assessment and may find the format confusing and difficult. Multiple-choice testing is more of an American phenomenon; thus, if you are working with diverse populations, be sure to spend some time helping students to understand how to take multiple-choice tests.

Multiple-choice items assess basic knowledge as well as higher-order thinking. These items force students to distinguish between the relative correctness of responses, thus assessing students' thinking strategies as well as knowledge level. A typical multiple-choice item presents a problem, statement, question, or task that is followed by a series of choices from which the student must choose. The first part of the item is called the *stem*; the choices are *alternatives* or *options,* and the wrong choices are called *distractors.* The following guidelines should help you to design multiple-choice items (Gallagher, 1998, pp. 167–175; Popham, 1999, p. 121):

- Write the stem of each question in clear, concise, and focused language; it should be long enough to provide the student with all he or she needs to know to make a good choice of response.

- State the stem as a question rather than an incomplete sentence.

- Avoid writing negatively stated stems.

William James Popham was a leading figure in the movement that promoted criterion-referenced measurements and was active and productive in the area of educational test development.

W. James Popham was born July 31, 1930, to William James and Anne I. Popham of Portland, Oregon. He grew up in Portland and attended the University of Portland, where he graduated cum laude with a bachelor's degree in philosophy in 1953 and received his master's degree in education a year later. After receiving his doctorate from Indiana University in 1958, Popham accepted an assistant professorship at Kansas State College in Pittsburg, Kansas. He stayed there for two years. He then accepted a position at San Francisco State College, where he taught for two years until he was appointed as an assistant professor in the Graduate School of Education at the University of California, at Los Angeles (UCLA).

A professor emeritus at the University of California, Los Angeles and a former test maker, Popham is a noted expert on educational testing. He has spent the bulk of his educational career as a teacher, first in a small, eastern Oregon high school, then in the UCLA Graduate School of Education and Information Studies. In his nearly 30 years at UCLA, Dr. Popham taught courses in instructional methods for prospective teachers and courses in evaluation and measurement for master's degree and doctoral candidates. He has won several distinguished teaching awards. In 1992, he took early retirement from UCLA (lured, he claims, by the promise of free parking for emeritus professors). In January 2000, he was recognized by *UCLA Today* as one of the university's top 20 professors of the 20th century. Dr. Popham has written 20 books, 180 journal articles, and 50 research reports and presented 150 papers before research societies. In 1978, he was elected to the presidency of the American Educational Research Association. He was also the founding editor of *Educational Evaluation and Policy*.

Source: Google Scholar, retrieved May 22, 2005.

- Keep the choices from which the students have to pick of equal length and complexity to prevent clues as to what the correct answer might be.

- Use logic in arranging options—for example, put names in alphabetical order or dates in chronological order.

- Randomly assign correct answers to different positions with the choices (i.e., correct answers are not always in the "a" position).

- Refrain from using choices such as "all of the above," or "a and b, but not c and d." "None of the above" can increase the item difficulty and can be used as a legitimate response, particularly as you try to measure the completeness of a student's knowledge; however, this rarely should be used. It is better to measure completeness of knowledge another way, such as asking more than one question.

- Use reasonable and plausible distractors.

The number of alternatives you choose to use in multiple-choice examinations is up to you. Four is a very common choice, but you can use three or five just as easily. What you must not do is alternate the number of choices on the same examination. The number of choices should be the same for each test item. If you cannot create viable choices in equal numbers for your test questions, you might want to rethink your questions.

Strategies for Designing Matching Items

Matching items are essentially multiple-choice items for which two things are true: There is a theme to the question (e.g., matching inventors with their inventions), and the answers serve as both appropriate responses and distractors. Matching items have two columns or sets of words or phrases from which students must find the given relationship. The students must match the entries in one list with those in the other list. Entries on the list for which a match is sought are called *premises* and the list from which selections are made are the *responses*. Matching items are best used when your intent is to measure knowledge acquisition. They are an efficient way to assess a lot of knowledge in a few questions.

To design good matching items, there must be a pool of premises and responses that make selections reasonable. Matching items are fairly easy to construct, assuming that there are sufficient premises and responses. Constructing a matching-item test is relatively easy, but often the tests do not work because the construction is confusing to the students. There are a few fundamental rules for constructing matching items (Gallagher, 1998, pp. 185–192; Popham, 1999, pp. 126–129):

- Write clear directions describing what the students are to do with List A and List B. For example, List A provides the names of Academy Award–winning films. From List B, select the name of the person who was the director of the film in List A and place the letter of that response in the blank provided. No director's name can be used more than once.

- Use brief, homogeneous lists of 5–10 items.

- Place the shorter words or responses (names, dates, places, etc.) on the right side and the premises on the left.

- Use more responses than premises so that students cannot get answers through the process of elimination.

- Place your responses logically (e.g., alphabetically or chronologically).

- Title each list according to the content of the premises and responses (e.g., names of Academy Award–winning films for premises and directors for responses.)

- Use longer phrases as premises and shorter ones as responses.

- Place all premises and responses on the same page.

When you look at the rules for matching items, you will begin to realize that a good matching test needs to be well constructed to provide a reasonable measure of student knowledge. Like other selected-response items, you need to spend time creating your questions, answers, and choices to ensure a fair and valid assessment of your students.

Strategies for Designing Constructed-Response Items

In constructed-response tests, students need to create the responses rather than simply recognize and choose an answer. Popham (1999) and Gallagher (1998) provide simple guidelines for constructed-response tests.

Short-Answer Items

Short-answer items require students to supply a word, phrase, or sentence to complete a question or statement. Much like the other tests, short-answer tests frequently focus on knowledge acquisition and recall; however, they can also be used to assess students' higher-order thinking. Many mathematical problems are short-answer questions that rely on students' ability to apply their knowledge. For example, a mathematical question such as, "How many square yards of carpeting will you need to replace the carpet in your bedroom?" is an example of an application short-answer question. The question requires students to recall the rules for calculating the square footage of a room and then apply that knowledge to the problem at hand. Many mathematical and science problems ask students to solve or complete: Deriving an algorithm, balancing a chemical equation, drawing a diagram, and using a formula are short-answer items requiring higher-order thinking skills rather than simple recall of information.

The following guidelines will help you to construct completion, fill-in-the-blank, and short-answer questions:

- Use direct questions whenever possible.

- Write the questions so that the responses are concise.

- Place the blanks for the responses to the questions in the margin.

- Place blanks for incomplete statements near the end of the statement; never use more than two blanks in any incomplete statement.

- Make the blanks for all the questions of equal length.

- Make the blanks long enough to accommodate handwritten responses.

- Understand what you want the students to know and create your own question or incomplete statement rather than taking a statement directly out of the textbook and removing a word or two to create the incomplete statement.

- State all items positively.

- Ensure there is only one possible brief answer for each item.

- Avoid language that gives clues to correct answers, (e.g., using "an" before a blank or gender-specific language that clues the students that the answer is a female or a male).

- Specify the degree of precision required in the answer (e.g., write your response to the nearest tenth, write the full names of the presidents, or make sure all responses are correctly spelled).

Short-answer items have several advantages. First, they avoid a common criticism of selected-response items: that they require students to produce answers rather than recognize information and avoid students guessing at answers. Short-answer questions are also easier to construct than multiple-choice items because you do not have to provide appropriate distractors. However, with these advantages come some disadvantages. Students can respond with a variety of words, phrases, or sentences, and often, very creative students present a response that is technically correct but not one you had thought of—thus, you need to be willing to accept correct but unpredicted responses. Student writing frequently calls for major deciphering on your part unless you make it very clear in your instructions that the legibility of responses is important. Because you have to do more interpretation of responses when you are grading short-answer items, grading time is longer than when you use selected-response items.

Essay Items

Essay items are very popular constructed-response tests. They are popular with teachers because they measure both the cognitive and affective dimensions of learning, as well as the higher-order thinking skills of students. Although we think of essay items as written questions requiring written responses, they are also used orally when teachers engage students in classroom discussions. For example, how often were you asked to clarify or elaborate on an answer you had given to an oral question? How often were you asked to iterate the characteristics of a particular person in the novel you were reading or explain the actions of the characters in that novel? How often were you asked to give your opinion of the actions taken by a world power in a conflict between that power and another nation? Were you ever asked to give your opinion about a controversial topic such as abortion, school vouchers, tax rebates, or censorship? In each of these cases, you were asked an open-ended question to which you had to construct a response and share that response orally with your classmates.

There are several advantages to using essay items in your classroom. First, they are a great tool for assessing higher-order thinking and affective dimensions of learning. Second, they force students to think, organize, and compose their thoughts into a coherent statement—an important set of communication skills for all students to learn. Third, they take less time to write than selected-choice items. But along with these advantages, there are several disadvantages. First, essay questions take much longer to answer, and thus fewer questions can be given to the students in the same amount of time. Second, because it takes more time to answer essay questions, less content may be assessed than when you use other forms of testing. Third, the scoring of essay tests is subjective and time-consuming. It is imperative, then, that you predesign a scoring rubric that you will apply to every examination you are reading. Fourth, because essay examinations require students to use a variety of skills and abilities, you may be unduly influenced by students' lack of attention to grammar, spelling, or neatness rather than their content knowledge and understanding.

The following set of guidelines will help you to design appropriate essay items to use in your classroom (Gallagher, 1998, p. 210; Popham, 1999, p. 141):

- Write your instructions so that the students know precisely what they are expected to do.

- Provide a time frame in which you expect your students to complete their task.

- Do not provide options for the students (e.g., "Answer three of the five questions."). When you do this, the choice you provide your students allows them to respond to different tests. Not all questions are created equal!

- Provide sufficient information so that the students recognize the quality of response you expect.

- Write an acceptable response to your question and then design a rubric that you will use to access your students' responses.

- Reserve essay items for higher-order learning outcomes that cannot easily be gauged by other forms of assessment.

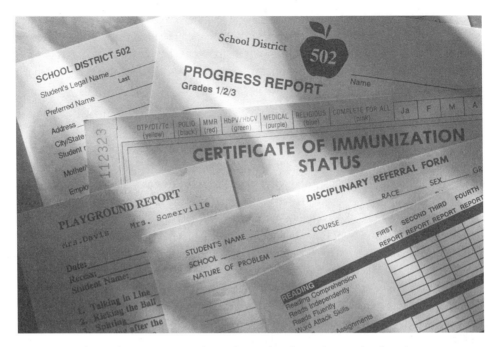

Using various forms of assessment strengthens what teachers know about student learning.

Reserve essay items for affective learning outcomes. Grading essays and essay items is very time-consuming. Having a preestablished rubric will help, but in no way will it cut down the actual time it will take you to read each student's paper. One of the reasons teachers avoid the essay format is the time required to grade the papers; however, in any subject area or any grade level, spending some time reading the free responses of your students will teach you a great deal about your students and their abilities. Thus, essay exercises are wonderful means to help you understand your students a lot better.

OTHER FORMS OF ASSESSMENT

Besides the typical classroom assessment instruments mentioned previously, newer ideas are permeating educational practice. The most common forms are performance assessment, observational assessment, and portfolio assessment. These strategies have become popular because of dissatisfaction with the typical testing done in our schools. Often, teachers and parents express their concern that students' performance on these teacher-made tests do not always reflect the students' skills and abilities. Also, newer information from the field of psychology has shed light on the way students learn and how they should be assessed with regard to that learning.

WHAT IS PERFORMANCE ASSESSMENT?

Performance assessment gained popularity during the 1990s as an alternative to traditional assessment techniques used in the classroom. Much of the interest in performance assessment is directly related to the concern with enhancing higher-order thinking skills and real-life applications of learning. This shift has increased educators' dissatisfaction with traditional multiple-choice and selected-response testing. If students are going to be engaged in activities such as problem solving, collaborative learning, cooperative learning, and other types of individual- and group-based learning, then assessment strategies are needed that better evaluate the process as well as the content.

Many terms are used in conjunction with the idea of performance assessment: *authentic assessment*, *alternative assessment,* and *portfolio assessment* are three of the most common terms used to describe assessment strategies that are different from the traditional ones used in classrooms. Performance-assessment strategies incorporate features that are unique to this form of assessment:

- Generally, the student's performance is judged by multiple criteria (e.g., a student's oral presentation might be judged on language skill, delivery techniques, media enhancement, and content).

- The evaluative criteria are known to the students prior to their performance.

- The feedback on the evaluation criteria are based on teacher and peer judgments.

- The evaluation is based on *observation* of students' actual performance or the final product of that performance.

Authentic Assessment

Authentic assessment suggests that the student's task should be a reflection of real-life situations and nonschool tasks. The word "authentic" refers to the context of the performance, suggesting that it is true to how students would be expected to perform in the real world—or at least in a highly simulated version of the real world. Many authentic tasks are designed to help students learn specific job skills, engage in service-learning projects, or engage in activities such as getting petitions signed to place a stop sign at a particularly bad intersection in the community, encouraging people to vote for the school referendum, or supporting the clean-up-the-environment campaign.

Alternative Assessment

Generally speaking, "alternative assessment" refers to assessment strategies that are different from or alternatives to the traditional assessments used in classrooms. The term is frequently used to include all options for traditional testing techniques used in classrooms, and thus it includes authentic assessment and portfolio assessment. As in other areas of education, we still struggle with language usage in assessment. According to Lyons, Kysilka, and Pawlas (1999, p. 148), effective alternative-assessment activities have the following qualities:

- Are open-ended
- Measure higher-order thinking skills and engage students in complex tasks
- Require extended time for completion, perhaps spanning several classes
- Are designed as group projects rather than individual projects
- Provide students with choices of how to demonstrate their learning

- Use judgmental scoring with predetermined guidelines given to students prior to the development of their projects

- Ask students to perform in accordance with real-life expectations

Alternative assessment relies more on students' personal experiences, their interactions with their peers, and their beliefs and advocacies than on their reading, writing, listening, and regurgitating skills.

Portfolio Assessment

Portfolio assessment is another way to assess student performance. Portfolios are systematic, organized collections of students' work. Although portfolios may be new to education, they are standard assessment strategies in areas such as art, architecture, journalism, modeling, and photography. The portfolio in education has become extremely popular with teachers who are trying to improve students' writing. Portfolios are also used by many teachers to help students track their progress in reading and mathematics skills. According to Lyons, McIntosh, and Kysilka (2003), there are three types of portfolios that can be used in a classroom: working, showcase, and assessment portfolios.

Working portfolios are designed to be ongoing exchanges between you and your students. These portfolios serve as collections of ongoing work. By examining the daily work of your students, you can diagnose their strengths and weaknesses and establish activities and remediation strategies to help them with their problems. The portfolios also help you to determine where you need to adjust your teaching. These portfolios work extremely well for long-term projects such as research reports or term papers. The main audience for the working portfolio, however, is the student. With regular feedback from you on his or her work, the student can develop reflective skills and learn self-evaluation strategies. He or she can correct errors more quickly and reinforce positive learning. This type of portfolio requires an iterative process between you and your students; thus, it is extremely time-consuming when done properly.

Showcase portfolios collect the best work of your students. Many of the projects that start in the working portfolio may be moved to the showcase portfolio once they are completed. The showcase portfolio can be an individual or a class activity. You might want to have each student develop a showcase portfolio for sharing during parent nights, or students could use it as a culminating activity for the year instead of having to complete a written comprehensive examination in the secondary schools. A class showcase portfolio could serve as a collection of the best work of each student, including both in-class and out-of-class activities, and it could be used to demonstrate to the principal and other faculty members what the class achieved during the year. Class showcase portfolios are very helpful to secondary schools when they undergo accreditation processes. The audience for showcase portfolios includes the students, faculty, administrators, parents, and potential employers. The main advantage of this portfolio is that students select their best work from a variety of experiences to demonstrate their learning.

The final portfolio is the *assessment portfolio*. The primary purpose of this portfolio is to document what students learned during the semester or year. The contents of an assessment portfolio should include assignments that demonstrate mastery of both content and specific skills. They should reflect the learning outcomes or objectives specified in the lesson plan for the class and the appropriate academic standards required by the district or state. The items must demonstrate that the students accomplished the intended outcomes. The contents of an assessment portfolio could include notes taken in class, homework assignments, book reports, lab reports, or any other pieces of work that document the students' learning of the given objectives. The audience for this portfolio is the teacher.

James Popham (1999) suggests that several steps are necessary for quality portfolio assessment:

- Understand that the material in the portfolios belongs to the students; it is their portfolio, not a collection of "stuff" you have graded.

- Help the students recognize which types of material go into the various portfolios and clarify the type you are using and why.

- Make sure students regularly collect and store their work samples in their portfolios.

- Select and share the criteria that you and your students will use to judge the quality of their work.

- Encourage students to continually evaluate and reflect on their work. One of the benefits of portfolio assessment is self-reflection.

- Schedule regular portfolio conferences with your students in which you provide feedback on products and students' self-assessments.

- Involve parents in the portfolio-assessment process. Make sure that the parents understand the portfolio-assessment process and ask for their perceptions as they view their students' work. When parents, students, and teachers work together on portfolios, the students understand the importance of this form of assessment.

ADVANTAGES AND DISADVANTAGES OF PERFORMANCE ASSESSMENT

As with other forms of assessment, there are advantages and disadvantages to performance-assessment strategies. The advantages include the fact that portfolios can be tailored to the individual learning needs, interests, and abilities of the students in your class. The portfolios provide a different perspective on student learning. They provide a sound documentation of the growth that is happening in your classroom in a way that teacher-made and standardized tests cannot. Portfolios can provide "authentic portraits" of student learning (Popham, 1999, p. 191). Portfolios and other forms of performance assessment encourage students to become self-evaluative and to take ownership of their learning.

The disadvantages relate mostly to the time-consuming nature of performance assessment. From the planning stage to the implementation stage to the evaluative stage, performance assessment takes up enormous amounts of your time. If you are going to use performance assessment, you not only have to determine what learning is best assessed through these strategies but also develop criteria for assessment prior to engaging students in this process. Developing the criteria and the corresponding rubrics can be very time-consuming. If you plan to use any of the forms of portfolio assessment, you will need to find the necessary time to engage with the students in individual, interactive exchanges to help them with their individual learning needs, as well as find time within the normal structure of your day to provide whole-class direction.

Technology has allowed us to make progress in assessment.

Performance-assessment strategies, even when accompanied by appropriate criteria and rubrics, may still create inconsistencies in judgment. The longer you review documents in the portfolios, the more stringent or lax you may become in applying the criteria. Because criteria become intense to follow, you and your students may tend to use broader, less precise criteria to assess the work because it seems easier to do. At the same time, such criteria can be interpreted very differently by different people, and thus the reliability of the assessment could be questioned.

IMPROVING ASSESSMENT—TECHNOLOGY CAN HELP

Classroom assessment can always be improved. In these days of increased accountability, you need to be very conscious of the assessment strategies in your classroom and how those strategies relate to the state and national standards that are in place in your school district. With the current emphasis on high-stakes tests, teachers are finding it more difficult to provide a variety of assessment strategies in their classrooms; however, it is essential that students have multiple opportunities to demonstrate their knowledge, skills, and learning strategies.

Our diverse classrooms encourage the use of more variety in assessment strategies because there are proven differences in the learning styles of different ethnic groups of children. You also will come into contact with many more students who have diagnosed learning disabilities, and you will be expected to accommodate those learning disabilities in your classroom. Sometimes, this will mean that written tests must be given in an isolated, quiet setting, require more time for the students, must be sent to the office to be enlarged if the student has a visual problem, or require an aide to read the test to the student. Some students may need to take the test orally. Students who have language problems or are enrolled in English for speakers of other languages (ESOL) or English as a second language (ESL) programs may require their tests to be translated into their native language, or may be expected to have access to a language dictionary, or may need more time to complete the examination. The more forms of assessment you use, the better you will be able to assess the different learning needs of your students. Some students may do better using portfolios, others may excel on essay tests, and others may prefer group projects or collaborative learning opportunities, and there will always be students who prefer traditional selected-response tests.

The key here is that whichever forms of assessment you choose to use, they must be directly related to the learning objectives or outcomes you established when you constructed your lesson plans, and those objectives or outcomes must be derived from the state or national curriculum standards expected of the content and grade level you are teaching. Once you have aligned the learning objectives and outcomes to the standards, then you can select class activities designed to meet those objectives or outcomes and create assessment strategies to match the activities, learning objectives, and outcomes. The important concept here is *alignment*. Standards, learning objectives, activities, and assessment must all be aligned.

Technology is a wonderful tool to help you do all this. First, most states have their curriculum frameworks on the state website. You can locate the standards for each grade level and content level on that site. In many states, there are links to suggested lesson plans and suggestions for how to adjust those plans to meet the diverse needs of your students. If your state does not have such extensive planning tools for you, there are other websites available that have preplanned lesson plans and assessment tools.

Do not overlook the resources that accompany the textbooks that you use in your classroom. In most cases, textbooks come complete with test banks, activities, and alternative assessment suggestions. Usually these are included on CDs that come with the teacher's edition of the textbook. Many secondary textbooks have CDs for the students as well, providing them with both remedial and advanced activities. A word of caution: If you plan to use the test bank that accompanies your textbook, make sure that you select items that measure what you taught. Often, teachers make up tests from the test bank questions without carefully ensuring that they effectively taught what the items assess.

Technology can certainly help you meet the requirements of your special needs students. With the current technology, many computers come equipped with voice-recognition software and speakers and can "speak" to the student. Most come equipped with earphones so that the noise from the computer will not disturb the rest of the class. Many computers can automatically increase the size of the print for students who have visual problems, or you can do that yourself. For students who need more reinforcement in their learning, you can design or install self-correcting exercises that provide immediate feedback to the students while they are trying to learn specific information. Some data banks will construct a number of practice exercises so that students can get as much repetition of concepts as they need to be successful.

It is important for you to know what the school has available for you to use with respect to technology. What software is available for your use? What are the capabilities of the hardware you have in your classroom? Does your school have a technology assistant or technology coordinator who can help you use technology effectively with your students? As frustrating as technology can be at times, it is a wonderful tool for assessment. Many teachers are now designing electronic portfolios for their classrooms. Students can keep their work in files on the computer, and the teacher can access them at his or her convenience and provide individual feedback to

Your grading schema is very much a reflection of your beliefs about your students and how they learn best.

the students without having to schedule specific classroom time to meet with the students. The editing tools of many word processing programs provide effective corrective feedback to students as they work on their writing skills.

GRADING YOUR STUDENTS

Once you have decided how you are going to assess your students, you then have to decide how you are going to grade your students. Grading your students means calculating a letter grade that will be reported on the report card that goes home with the student. Much of what you are allowed to do with respect to grading your students depends on what, if any, grading policies are in place in your school or district. Before you try to determine what your grading strategies are going to be, be sure you know what the school or district policies are.

Most schools or districts have a grading scale that determines the percentages that equate to an A, B, C, D, or F. In elementary schools, particularly primary grades, a school may use less ominous grades, such as excellent, above average, satisfactory, and needs improvement. Whatever the policies are, you must be aware of them before you establish how you are going to grade in your classroom. In some schools or districts, teachers are required to include attendance in their grading schemas. Some schools or districts have very specific statements related to tardiness, make-up work, and excused and unexcused absences. You need to know these rules before you determine how you intend to grade your students.

Your grading schema is very much a reflection of your beliefs. Operating within the guidelines of your school, you can devise your own personal marking practices that reflect your beliefs about assessing your students. A major factor in what and how you grade is the nature of your course and the level at which you teach. According to Wilen, Ishler, Hutchison, and Kindsvatter (2000), three general criteria apply to any system of evaluating your students: functionality, fairness, and clarity.

Functionality means that the system works effectively and efficiently for both you and your students. You want to be certain that you have a system that provides adequate feedback to your students but does not overburden you with excessive and complex paper grading. The system can comprise a variety of activities, some of which are simply recorded as completed, and others that require more extensive grading and analysis. You need to think about how you intend to weigh the various requirements in your course or program. For example, are you going to grade homework each night? If you grade homework, how much will the graded homework count toward the overall evaluation of your students—10%, 25%? Do you really want to "grade" homework? One of the authors was a secondary mathematics teacher. In her classes, homework was never graded because she believed that homework was a way to practice mathematical concepts and skills. However, she frequently collected homework to determine what kinds of mistakes students were making and used that information to inform her instruction. She also used the random collection to determine which students were and were not doing homework. She used unannounced and announced quizzes to determine students' knowledge and application skills. Quizzes constituted 25% of her grading.

She used practice tests before administering a chapter or unit examination. Thus, both the students and teacher knew whether the students were ready to take a major examination. She conducted review sessions prior to any major examination, focusing on the most difficult concepts for the students. She frequently included take-home tests and open-book tests to accommodate the learning needs of some of her students. Although her grading was typically based on quizzes and chapter and unit examinations, she provided multiple opportunities for students to assess themselves prior to taking tests that would count toward their grade for her class.

Another concern related to functionality is the number of points you assign to any particular activity or project. Basing everything on 100 makes a lot of sense to most teachers because grading schemas are traditionally based on percentages. But you might want to ask yourself some very basic questions. For example, if students are taking a spelling test consisting of 20 words, why is each correct spelling worth five points? Other than $5 \times 20 = 100$, there is no logic to making each word worth five points. Either a word is spelled correctly or not. There is no almost-correct spelling of a word. Thus, it would seem more logical to assign one point to each word, and the total number of points for the 20-word spelling examination would be 20. However, if you include spelling and usage in the test—that is, the students must not only spell the word correctly but also use it correctly in a sentence—then you might consider one point for spelling and one point for usage. What you really want to avoid is having to add up hundreds of points for each grading period. The more points you have to add, the more likely you will be to make a mistake. Keep your points simple. Know which activities are worth more and assign points accordingly.

Your grading schema needs to be *fair*. That means you have built into your assessment strategies various activities that meet the needs of your students. Remember, not all students learn the same way; some are verbal learners, others are visual, and others are kinesthetic, for example. Some students are extremely good at information recall, whereas others are better at the creative application of knowledge. Some students will excel in writing, others in performance. Students with special needs, whether they are learning disabilities or language limitations, need to have a variety of ways to demonstrate their knowledge and learning. You must keep this in mind as you structure your schema. You also need to have a clear policy on cheating and how cheating can affect a student's achievement.

Finally, your grading schema needs to be *clearly* communicated to your students and their parents. Students and parents need to know how the grading system works: the weighting of activities, the minimum expectations for achieving each grade, the makeup policies, etc. The more you share your schema with students and their parents, the easier it will be for you to explain grades if they are questioned by either the students or their parents.

The keys to successful grading of your students are as follows:

- Provide a variety of assessment strategies that match the variety of activities in your classroom and align with your objectives and standards.

- Establish a grading schema that is functional, fair, and clear.

- Base grades on student achievement only; do not let student behavior be reflected in the academic grade. If it is not against school policy, tardiness and absences should not affect the academic grade of a student. These issues ought to be dealt with in a different manner.

- Maintain a clear policy on cheating and keep cheating in check.

- Remain open and flexible with regard to your grading schema; if something does not work or appears to be unfair, change it.

Summary

This chapter included a large amount of information on assessment and grading; however, because of the limitations of this book, it was impossible to provide you with all the information you need to be successful in the area of assessment. Experience will teach you a great deal about which types of assessments work best for you and your students. But ideally, you will realize that there are many different ways to assess students; because of the diversity of students you will see in your classroom, you need to incorporate many different strategies in your classroom to meet the needs of all your students. You also want to ensure that your assessments are adequately aligned with the district and state standards and with the activities you have designed to meet those standards.

Assessment is a major part of teaching. You cannot ignore it or treat it lightly. Likewise, you need not be intimidated by the task. You have far more tools to use for assessment than ever before. Technology provides you with many opportunities to help you with the assessment process. And best of all, assessment serves multiple purposes: It provides you with knowledge that will help you adjust your teaching to better meet the needs of your students; it provides your students with tools for self-assessment; and it provides a way to communicate the achievements of your students to others.

Thought to Action

1. Think about the class you are currently teaching, one you hope to teach, or one in which you are enrolled. Is there any form of performance assessment being used? If so, how would you describe the effectiveness of that form of assessment? If not, how could a performance assessment be included as part of the assessment strategies in that class?

2. Think about a project or activity you want your students to participate in while enrolled in your class. Determine how you could structure a form of portfolio assessment for that project or activity. What kind of portfolio assessment would be most appropriate? What kind of guidelines will you provide for your students? How will this project affect the grading schema in your classroom?

3. Find out the grading policies of the school district you are working in, one you hope to work in, or the one you attended. (Note: most school districts have their policies listed on their websites.) Given those policies, how would you construct a grading schema for your classroom?

4. Look at an examination that was used in a classroom for K–12 students. What accommodations were made for students with disabilities or language problems? What options should a teacher offer to students with disabilities or language problems? How could this examination be adapted for students with disabilities or language problems?

5. Design an assessment activity that uses technology. How would this activity help you to properly assess your students' cognitive knowledge?

ON YOUR OWN

Log on to the web-based student study site at http://www.sagepub.com/holt for access to a Standards-Based Student Project that will help you connect what you have learned in this chapter to your state's standards; study aids, such as electronic flashcards; and research recommendations, including journal article links and other Web resources.

PART III

Teacher-Centered Patterns

Chapter 6:

Direct Instruction

Chapter 7:

Mastery Learning

T eacher-centered instruction occurs when instruction is focused on the actions of the teacher. Does the teacher begin the lesson on time? How many questions does the teacher ask? Does the teacher present the content knowledge? How does the teacher control the classroom? In this type of instruction, teachers have predetermined goals and objectives and plan their instruction in small increments or daily lesson plans that are parts of a larger unit. The actions of the teacher are paramount to the delivery of the lesson. The teacher should proceed in small steps, provide many examples, and provide for continued practice.

In this section, Chapter 6 covers direct instruction and Chapter 7 explores mastery learning. In each of these forms of instruction, the teacher is the purveyor of knowledge. The role of the student is more passive, and these forms of instruction assume that students are auditory learners. We will examine the research, theory, and instructional practices of each in Part III, "Teacher-Centered Patterns."

Direct Instruction

DIRECT INSTRUCTION (DI) IS USED MORE OFTEN THAN ANY OTHER INSTRUCTIONAL METHODOLOGY. It is not only the most used but quite possibly the oldest form of instruction. Ancient orators would pass knowledge from one generation to the next through a type of direct dialogue. Direct instruction is teacher-centered instruction. Whether it is used in training situations or in classrooms, the teacher is the purveyor of knowledge. In direct instruction, the teacher structures lessons in a straightforward, sequential manner. The teacher is clearly in control of the content and the skills to be learned. The teacher is in charge of the pace and the amount of interaction that occurs throughout the lesson. Sometimes, direct instruction involves highly rigorous, scripted lessons that are fast paced and provide constant interaction between students and the teacher. Direct instruction is often used when facts related to content need to be presented. The teacher begins with a statement that reflects the goals of the lesson: "Today, we are going to . . . " Many studies have found that students learn basic skills more rapidly when they receive a greater portion of their instruction directly from the teacher.

This form of teaching has also been described as *lecture format*, *didactic*, and *explicit teaching*. No matter what you call it, the method is characterized by teacher talk. The didactic teacher lectures, explains, gives directions, answers questions, drills students on facts, and generally uses direct teaching methods to transmit information. Direct or didactic teaching has generally been identified as an efficient method. A well-organized lecture delivered by a skilled teacher may cover a wide array of information and contain conceptual structure and applications from a number of subject areas. When learning objectives are narrowly defined as facts or skills, research indicates didactic (direct) instruction is especially efficient.

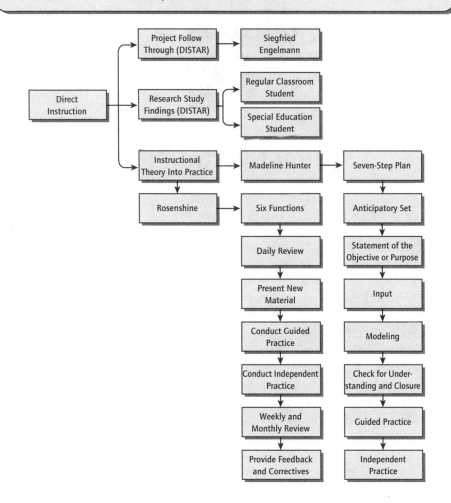

RESEARCH ANCHOR

Direct Instruction Research Projects

One of the most comprehensive direct instruction research projects to involve small-group, face-to-face instruction by teachers and aides using reading, arithmetic, and language was conducted by Siegfried Engelmann in 1975. This research, Project Follow Through, was published by Science Research Associates under the trade name DISTAR. This comparative study examined different instructional approaches to the teaching of economically disadvantaged children in the primary grades. The model was developed from Becker's work on the systematic use of reinforcement procedures in the classroom and from Engelmann's work in the Bereiter-Engelmann preschool program (Bereiter, 1967), a program that produced very dramatic results with disadvantaged children. Some of the children could read on third grade level and could perform on fourth grade arithmetic after two years of half-day preschool experience (Becker & Engelmann, 1978).

As a result of the success of this program, a variety of procedural manuals, observation tools, and child-assessment procedures were developed to ensure quality control during the 1970s. The final report of the national evaluation of Project Follow Through showed that direct instruction was largely successful in assisting disadvantaged children in catching up with their middle-class peers in academic skills.

Adams and Engelmann (1996) conducted a meta-analysis of research on direct instruction since the 1960s and analyzed a total of 173 comparison studies. They reported that 64% revealed a statistically significant difference favoring the direct instruction group. Out of the 173 comparisons, 35% showed no significant difference between the direct instruction groups, whereas 1% favored the non-DI groups (DI in this case is short for DISTAR).

CONTROVERSY REGARDING DIRECT INSTRUCTION

In some parts of the country, direct instruction is resurfacing. During the 1995 school year, Paul Vallas, chief executive officer of the Chicago Public Schools, talked of mandating direct instruction. This led to some disagreement among Chicago teachers, who stated, "It's rote, it's memorization, it's not good solid practice." Other comments included, "It's extremely authoritarian and can lead children to dependency on adults and resentment." Other states, such as California, excluded DISTAR from its list of approved reading programs in 1988 on the grounds that its stories in the early levels had no literary merit. More recently, the California board of education has called for more teaching of phonics but not necessarily DISTAR. Two of the reasons that direct instruction and phonics-based reading programs are resurfacing are the conservative times in which we are living and the rising popularity of highly controlled education systems. DI has a back-to-basics appeal. Principal Thaddeus Lott of Wesley Elementary in Houston, Texas, is running a nationally known DI school, and in his lectures to audiences, he states, "It's nothin' but old-time teachin' in a box" (Duffrin, 1996).

According to Duffrin, the controversy is more than a political battle between forward-thinking progressives and skill-and-drill conservatives. At the heart of the DI controversy is a far grayer matter—the human brain. In one camp, you have the cognitive psychologists, who believe that we approach learning from the inside out. They believe that learning takes place as the nerve cells of the brain process information. Because learning is not one size fits all, the challenge for teachers is to pick activities that best match the needs of individual students. In the other camp, you have the behaviorists, who believe that learning is a change in behavior. A person can be lead through a series of steps or through a set of activities. The proper activities can be identified by measuring the response of the learner at each step along the way and making appropriate adjustments (Duffrin, 1996).

In an elementary school in Milwaukee, Wisconsin, a principal named Sarah Martin-Elam was anxious to find a strategy that would help her kids learn. The faculty came together, explored direct instruction, and saw the potential for success. The number of fourth graders who scored proficient or better in reading on the state's standardized tests rose from 22% in 1997–98 to 57% in 1999–2000. In math, proficient or better scores rose from 11% to 48% over the same period. In social studies, scores increased from 13% to 61% (Lindsay, n.d.).

O'Conner, Jenkins, Cole, and Mills (1993) examined the effects of two phonetic reading programs, DISTAR Reading Mastery and the Superkids program, on reading achievement for one year. The findings did not reveal a significant difference between the two groups at the end of a one-year follow-up period. However, when the analysis focused on which group progressed further, the DI group showed the largest reading gains. Mosley's (1997) study showed a similar nonstatistical difference between the reading scores of students randomly assigned to DI and regular classroom groupings. The author concluded that DI must be taught for at least two years before a statistically significant difference can be realized.

The effects of DI on special education students have received attention in the literature, both through single studies and meta-analysis. Gersten (1985) reviewed six studies examining the effects of DI on handicapped students. The handicapping conditions identified among the six studies included the learning disabled, the moderately mentally challenged, high-risk students, students with low intelligence, and students with diagnosed minimal brain damage. The studies assessed language and reading programs based on DI. Gersten reported numerous methodological issues but concluded that the DI model tended to produce higher academic gains for handicapped students than traditional approaches to instruction.

A second researcher, White (1988), examined other outcomes of direct instruction with special needs children. His findings revealed that DI had an advantage of 0.84 standard deviation units over the comparison groups, with a total of 53% of the studies favoring DI. White noted that this figure significantly exceeded the 5% that would be expected by chance alone. In White's sample, only 14% of the comparisons indicated a negative effect for DI. None of the negative effects were statistically valid, so White concluded that DI appeared to be an effective method of instruction for both mildly and moderately to severely handicapped students. This appeared to hold true for all skill areas in which research was conducted.

Direct instruction is widely used by teachers from kindergarten through the adult years. It has proven to be an effective methodology for regular and special needs children. During the 1960s and 1970s, an educator named Madeline Hunter popularized the direct instruction method by marketing a lesson plan format along with staff development training for teachers. The training program, Instructional Theory Into Practice, is described here.

Instructional Theory into Practice (ITIP) was developed by Madeline Hunter (1984, 1994) and is perhaps best known for its eight elements of lesson design. As teachers plan a lesson, Hunter suggests considering three factors before instruction begins. First, teachers must decide what content to teach within the context of the grade level, student ability, and lesson rationale. Then, teachers must determine what students will do to learn and demonstrate that they have learned. In the final consideration, Hunter states that teachers must decide what research-based teaching behaviors will most effectively promote learning. The eight elements should be determined by the teacher as appropriate to the context for teaching. Each lesson does not need each element, nor should the steps necessarily be taken in sequence. When used as proposed by Hunter, ITIP is effective. Each of the steps has been supported by research, so it is no surprise that Hunter's work became popular with educators across the nation. Because her work has been widely adopted by many school districts, it sometimes has been implemented beyond the intended purpose. Some districts evaluated teachers according to whether all eight elements were present in their lesson plans. When used in this manner, ITIP became a teaching checklist and was no longer a tool for planning.

Another form of direct teaching reported in the research is *explicit teaching*. Explicit teaching has as its objective teaching students to master a body of knowledge. In the explicit teaching approach, the teacher must gain the students' attention, reinforce correct responses, provide feedback to students on their progress, and increase the amount of time that students spend

Madeline Hunter popularized the Instructional Theory Into Practice (ITIP) model for effective teaching, which was designed to "teach more faster" in all disciplines and all grade levels. Her training first as a practicing psychologist and later as a school psychologist served as the foundation for her ITIP model. This model translated her research in behavioral and social psychology into eight sequential steps for every teacher to follow in any given lesson. In 1985, Ron Brandt, executive director of the Association for Supervision and Curriculum Development, said that Madeline Hunter "has had more influence on U.S. teachers in the last ten years than any other person."

Source: "Madeline Hunter," *American Decades*; reproduced in the Biography Resource Center (Farmington Hills, MI: Thomson Gale, 2005).

actively engaged in learning course content. Rosenshine (1983) believes that this form of instruction is most beneficial for teaching mathematical computations, reading, decoding, the distinction of fact from opinion, science facts, foreign language vocabulary, and rules of grammar.

Ten general principles apply when developing an explicit teaching lesson (Rosenshine, 1987, p. 76):

1. Begin a lesson with a short statement of goals.

2. Begin a lesson with a short review of previous prerequisite learning.

3. Present new material in small steps with student practice after each step.

4. Give clear and detailed instructions and explanations.

5. Provide a high level of active practice for all students.

6. Ask many questions, check for student understanding, and obtain responses from all students.

7. Guide students during initial practice.

8. Provide systematic feedback and correction.

9. Provide explicit instruction and practice for seatwork exercises and, when necessary, monitor students during seatwork.

10. Continue practice until students are independent and confident (Burden & Byrd, 2003).

Within this framework, Rosenshine identifies six functions (introduced in Chapter 1). The framework presented from Rosenshine's work has been popularized as a summation of the process-product research of the 1970s and 1980s, and it is widely used today. Within an instructional cycle, the six teaching functions are as follows:

1. Providing daily review

2. Presenting new material

Planning prior to the lesson should ensure that objectives are selected at the correct level.

A. Consider the content (task analysis)
1. Identify the objective
2. Brainstorm
3. Weed out
4. Sequence
5. Form questions

B. Consider the learner
1. Administer survey
2. Interpret results
3. Form groups

C. Match the learner with the content

    I. Anticipatory set
        A. State the learning to be done.
        B. Relate the learning to past, present, or future experiences.
        C. Involve the learner.
        D. Establish a mental set and direction for the lesson.

    II. Statement of the objective or purpose
        A. Explain or show the *what* and *why* of the lesson.
        B. Define the lesson's outcome or what the learners will accomplish.

    III. Input
        A. Determine the techniques you will use to teach the lesson (demonstration, explanation, etc.)
        B. Tell the students how you plan to get the objectives across.
        C. Identify skills the students will need.
        D Use and incorporate into the explanation the principles of learning (motivation, reinforcement, retention, and transfer).
        E. Design the lesson in respect to Bloom's taxonomy.

    IV. Modeling
        A Demonstrate.
        B. Present examples (good and bad).
        C. Show a final product.
        D. Explain your expectations.
        E. Transfer the image in the teacher's head to the learner's head.
        F. Incorporate the principles of learning (motivation, reinforcement, retention, and transfer)

    V. Check for understanding and closure
        A. Ask students to explain the process to the teacher.
        B. Ask students to show you how to do it (check for covert behavior that is causing overt behavior).
        C. Ask students to tell again how they would proceed.
        D. Important: If the check for understanding reveals student weaknesses, reteach. We want to avoid students seeing the incorrect process or practicing the incorrect method. Say, "Let's go over this again. I must not have explained it well enough" (monitor and adjust).

TABLE 6.1

E. Respond in the language of the learner.

F. Summarize learning.

G. Involve the learners.

VI. *Guided practice*

A. Practice under the teacher's direct supervision.

B. Make sure students are practicing using the correct method or procedure.

C. At all costs, avoid students practicing an incorrect procedure or method. Be sure all students are doing the exercise correctly before moving to independent practice. Remember, it is just as easy to learn a wrong fact, concept, or habit as it is a correct one.

D. Students who do well on guided practice will be positively reinforced to do well on the next step, independent practice.

VII. *Independent practice*

A. Students practice individually in their seats.

B. Practice could be homework if the teacher is sure students know how to do it correctly.

C. Students could practice with another student without teacher supervision.

VIII. *Closure*

A. Summarize bridge to next lesson.

Source: Hunter (1994).

3. Conducting guided practice

4. Providing feedback and correction

5. Conducting independent practice

6. Providing weekly and monthly reviews

Providing Daily Review

An effective teacher will begin a new lesson with a review of what has been covered previously. The teacher who conducts the daily review can determine whether the students have obtained the necessary prerequisite knowledge or skills for the lesson. This practice informs the teacher about what the students remember and is an organizing device from which to spring forth the new content.

Presenting New Material

An effective teacher will begin a lesson by capturing the students' attention and explaining the goals of the lesson. In this way, the students are able to focus on the important parts of the lesson and can pay attention to the lesson purpose. After stating the goal of the lesson, a good teacher will present one point at a time within the lesson outline and incorporate concrete experiences or knowledge by which the students can understand the new material. Presentation clarity is important to avoid misunderstanding. While presenting new material, the teacher can ask questions and ask students to give a summary statement to ensure understanding. Rosenshine (1987) suggests following these steps when presenting new material:

- Organize material so that one point can be mastered before the next point needs to be introduced.

- State lesson goals.

The third step in explicit teaching is to present material in small steps and provide guided practice.

- Give step-by-step directions.
- Focus on one thought at a time, completing one point and checking for understanding before proceeding to the next.
- Model behaviors by going through the directions.

The step-by-step process of presenting material is recommended to teachers to prevent them from providing too much material at once. Additionally, it is recommended that teachers pause and assess student understanding.

Conducting Guided Practice

Guided practice is recommended following the presentation of new material to check students' understanding and to allow in-class practice with the content just learned. Reinforcement of the material is provided by the teacher during guided practice. Students often complete teacher-made worksheets or work on problems to demonstrate their skill level with the new content, and teachers monitor their in-class work during guided practice. Rosenshine (1987) reports that effective teachers have a 75% to 80% success rate during guided practice, suggesting that effective teachers combine success and challenge.

Provide Feedback and Correction

Clarifying students' work during guided practice is important to student success with the new material. Teachers can provide additional explanation of the material, summarize, or assess whether the student has correctly completed the assignment. It is recommended that as students seek additional explanation of the material through questions, teachers elaborate why something is correct or incorrect. Teachers may have to provide additional information in the form of hints or clues to aid with students' understanding.

Conducting Independent Practice

Independent practice follows guided practice and can be completed as homework. Its purpose is to reinforce the material learned with additional problems or study. For example, in a math class, the students would work the same kind of math problems that were completed in guided practice. However, this time, the teachers' cues are not present. If independent practice is completed in class, then the teacher should monitor the classroom environment by circulating the room.

Providing Weekly and Monthly Reviews

Reviewing can be completed in a variety of ways. However, structured reviews are important to remind students of the direction of the day's lesson and its relation to what has already been learned. Good and Grouws (1979) recommend that teachers review the week's work every Monday and the previous month's work every fourth Monday (Burden & Byrd, 2003).

Direct instruction assumes that students can learn information through auditory modalities; this may not work best for all students.

Scenario 1

Miss Hopkins is a first-grade teacher in a low-socioeconomic-status neighborhood in Detroit, Michigan. She is reviewing students' grammar by using SRA/DISTAR.

The lesson begins by using the teacher manual for DISTAR (Engelmann & Bruner, 1974). The students are seated on the floor in front of Miss Hopkins, and the book is open to Lesson 108. At the top of the page, in bold print, it says:

SOUNDS. Task 1: Teaching *p* as in *pat*.

a. Point to *p*. "Here's a new sound. It's a quick sound."
b. "My turn." [pause] Touch *p* for an instant, saying *p*. Do not say PUUH.
c. Again. Touch *p* and say *p*.
d. Point to p. "Your turn. When I touch it, you say it." [pause] "Get ready." Touch *p*. "*p*."
e. Again. Touch *p*. "p"
f. Repeat Step e until firm.

Miss Hopkins continues with Task 2, the individual test for each child in the group: pointing to the letter *p* and asking students to repeat the sound.

This scenario describes the scripted lesson used in the DISTAR material.

Scenario 2

Mr. Cullers's Stagecraft I class reached the end of a series of units related to theatrical lighting, and they were being asked to sign up for appointments to demonstrate their mastery of lighting design through a large and complex public demonstration. Mr. Cullers decided in advance the order, sequence, and prior knowledge of each student before he delivered his direct teaching lesson. While the students were busy negotiating time slots with each other, Mr. Cullers reflected on how far the students had come in just a short time.

For example, the students had already demonstrated mastery of the odd vocabulary associated with stage lighting equipment. Mastering this kind of jargon is difficult in most any area of specialized knowledge, but the field of stage lighting uses a number of very unusual terms from many languages, and there are a great many synonyms and near-synonyms for much of the equipment and techniques involved. Mastery of all this jargon was demonstrated through the combined use of free-response tests (in which students had to respond to questions such as "What type of instrument is most commonly used to illuminate scrims and drops, and why is this the preferred instrument?") and a practical demonstrations (in which students had to correctly identify and classify actual pieces of equipment). Mr. Cullers had thereby been able to confirm that each of these 21 high school students was fluent in the technical jargon necessary to communicate with their lighting project partners.

He also made sure that the students could demonstrate fluency in both the theoretical and practical application of the physics of electricity and optics. Through a similar test-and-practical-demonstration process, Mr. Cullers had worked the students through a variety of real-life problems, such as "How many 1000-watt ellipsoidal spotlights may be safely assigned to one 20-ampere dimmer?" and "What will be observed if a pale yellow set wall is illuminated at 80% current from 40 feet away with a 750-watt leko filtered with a dark blue gel?" The lesson leading up to this assessment included interdisciplinary direct lessons cotaught with art and physics teachers, which the students had found especially stimulating.

"I always figured physics was just for scientists," commented Kiva Wentworth, a sophomore with a decidedly artistic sensibility. "It never occurred to me that I might have to understand physics as an artist. It was great to have my art teacher and my physics teacher helping me with the same lesson." In fact, Kiva had been disruptive and resistant at the beginning of the course, but she became increasingly enthusiastic when she saw that Mr. Cullers was going to work with her directly until she mastered all the course content, no matter how long she needed to learn. She became even more enthusiastic about the course once she actually put mathematics and physics to use for something she cared about deeply. According to her physics teacher, her attendance and performance in her physics course had also improved somewhat.

All of this preparatory work was broken up into small, discrete units: One unit for subtractive color mixing, for example, was followed by a unit on additive color mixing. A part of the preparatory work included a unit on series circuit wiring. At one point, Mr. Cullers realized that several students lacked fluency with the mathematical concepts to convert formulas for ease of calculation (as in recognizing that amperes = volts/ohms can also be restated as volts = amperes x ohms). This discovery led Mr. Cullers to conduct a mini-unit on calculating and converting with formulas.

All of this preparatory work was intended to help students at this critical point in the stagecraft curriculum. From this point on, Mr. Cullers knew, the rate of learning would be swifter and the complexity of application would be greater than in the introductory stages of the course. He needed to be absolutely sure that all of his students had complete mastery of the basic skills necessary for independent learning in stage lighting design, and he took care to be sure that each student could respond correctly to any problem at any time.

Working through the curriculum framework for the course, and working from his own practical knowledge as a part-time stage lighting designer, Mr. Cullers had identified specific learning objectives for each of the preceding units. Mr. Cullers felt certain that each of his students had mastered the prior learning objectives. He was able to identify the intended outcome of the next lessons: The students will design, hang, gel, power, focus, and program a full-stage lighting setup according to a set of director's written parameters. This objective would involve a demonstration of the student's ability. To accomplish this objective, Mr. Cullers would need to focus on each prerequisite skill before the students could effectively complete the larger objective.

As a gateway unit into the more advanced portion of the course, this task involved separate skills: a sound working knowledge of electricity, a heightened awareness of safety issues, a firm grasp of color fundamentals, the ability to estimate and calculate, and an artistic sense of proportion and beauty. Each of these skills had been mastered by all of the students in separate lessons, but now students were going to have to apply all of this learning to an integrated public demonstration. To his surprise and satisfaction, Mr. Cullers noticed that the first student to sign up for the demonstration was Kiva.

ASSESSMENT

The assessment of academic content in the direct teaching model is systematic. Direct instruction requires mastery of every concept before instruction advances. Assessment is an ongoing and continuous process. The highly publicized kits of material that were used during the 1970s had the assessment component built in (DISTAR, SRA). Quite often, these kits would preassess the students' reading ability to determine the level at which to begin their instruction. When the unit is not a commercial product such as DISTAR, teachers generally design quizzes or test questions based on the concepts learned.

Direct instruction is largely structured around basic facts. So designing assessment to recall the basic facts through workbook pages, quizzes, or tests is routine. This assessment process prevents students from falling too far behind. The teacher must clearly define the specific objectives for each unit. The standard for this objective is that it be measurable in some observable and meaningful way and that the teacher be able to identify the manner and means in which student attainment will be measured. This form of assessment, which is conducted following information presented by the teacher, is called *formative assessment*. Other forms of formative assessment, in addition to workbook pages, quizzes, or tests, are teacher-made checklists. For each skill, the teacher checks or observes the process to see whether the student can successfully demonstrate the ability to complete each item on the checklist. *Summative assessment* monitors students' development over the course, and therefore it is to be administered at the end of the course. Summative assessment occurs just once and covers everything that has been presented and learned in one exam.

Assessments that determine the skill level of the students in order to properly align content with those skills can be conducted in the form of a pencil-paper test at the end of one unit or preceding the next unit. Demonstrations can also be used to assess student ability with concepts learned. What is important is that the teacher has accurate and reliable knowledge about the attainment level of each student. In Scenario 2 presented earlier, each student had to demonstrate fluency in electrical and optical concepts, expertise in color mixing, and other contributing skills. Class projects or group presentations should assess each member individually.

DISTAR includes charts in a kit of materials that assist teachers with the teaching of reading.

Group efforts such as theater should asses the ability of each individual student to determine whether that student is performing at the intended level. Various forms of assessment within direct teaching reveal which learners need remediation in the essential components of the lesson and which ones may engage in enrichment activities.

TECHNOLOGY

There are many forms of technology that can assist with the presentation of materials. Many classrooms are equipped with overhead projectors, whiteboards or blackboards, or even a presentation podium that is fully loaded with a computer, CD or DVD player, and VCR. Instructional materials such as posters, visual aides, pictures, or graphic organizers are all simple forms of technology that can boost interest in your lesson. Remember that visual aids, posters, pictures, graphic organizers are more easily encoded than text and teacher talk. Good lessons using the direct teaching pattern can be strengthened with the use of visual aids.

Learning Tenets
That Support Direct Instruction

The brain seeks to classify information and the things to be learned.

As teachers begin to present the concepts to be learned, students will listen to determine whether the material is familiar to them. This logical progression is the way the brain begins to classify the information to be learned. In the direct instruction model, the student is dependent on the teacher's ability to present the material in an organized manner. The lesson should begin with a statement of the objective. The lesson should have a hook or an anticipatory set used to connect the lesson with the learner.

This model assumes that students will attend to what is being said and will gain knowledge from your presentation. This means that your presentation skills are important. Your tone of voice is important, as well as your gestures. The amount of energy you put into the presentation is significant in the direct teaching presentation. Another important consideration is the pace of the lesson. Remember, you should only speak for a length of time that is equal to your students' age. Teachers who drone on and on will not be interesting to listen to, nor will they have the attention of their students. When delivering a lecture or a direct teaching lesson, consideration should be given to the order of what needs to be said. You should analyze the concepts to determine smooth transitions from one point to the next. Students will be able to gain an understanding of the relationship between ideas if the material is planned, articulated, and delivered free from distracting mannerisms.

The emotional system drives attention, and attention drives meaning and memory.

Connecting with the learner and making the day's objective relevant to them is vitally important to your success with this methodology. To enhance your direct teaching method, use music to establish the mood of the lesson. Music is emotional. It can be a powerful tool for enhancing your presentation techniques. If your lesson is about the War of Independence, disguise your voice and recite a relevant but famous passage, such as, "These are the times that try men's souls." Create excitement around the concepts that you are teaching by having students learn mnemonics from the direct lesson. When your students are engaged in a creative way in encoding direct skills and facts through the development of riddles, raps, or visual charts, emotional ties are developed that connect the student with the content through a creative process that peaks their interest. Setting the facts to be learned to music can assist students with recall.

Learning occurs in both conscious and unconscious states.

There will be students who cannot immediately indicate through their work or their expressions that they have learned. This type of learner may be a reflective thinker and may be processing and filtering the information presented without your knowledge. Do not assume that learning has not occurred despite the fact that some learners do not acknowledge with eye contact, verbal questioning, or nonverbal gestures that they are paying attention. At the end of the unit, you may discover that the students who did not show any sign of understanding during the lesson will score the highest on the test. It is possible that these students do not immediately and consciously process the content. This situation may be indicative of the student's learning style, but it also reminds us that learning is both conscious and unconscious. Learners are immersed in a vast sea of sensory possibilities. Although you may not get nonverbal cues from some students while teaching, that does not necessarily mean they are not learning.

The brain is designed for ups and downs, not constant attention.

Teachers who use the direct teaching phonetic approach illustrated in Scenario 1 are hoping for an instant response from the learners. We know that learning takes time. At times, students cannot keep up. If a teacher is on a roll with a scripted lesson, it is unlikely that every student will be able to keep up with the teacher's pace. There are occasions when brilliance occurs only after walking away from what we are concentrating on. When we walk away from puzzling situations, take a break, and then return, we have new insight into solving or understanding the task at hand. You may ask yourself, "Why didn't I get this before?" The same is true for your students. When you use fast-paced, scripted lessons that require an immediate response, students may become frustrated, disinterested, and unmotivated. Back away, change the instructional state, and start again. This short break will help to renew the students and help them adjust to the ups and downs of learning.

Learning occurs through processing and active engagement with visual, auditory, and kinesthetic modalities.

Following the rule about changing the instructional state in conjunction with your learner's age means adjusting your teacher talk. Think about ways to divide the instructional time so that you don't do all the talking. After pausing from direct teaching, use the following strategies to enhance your students' processing strategies, reflective thinking, and engaged time.

Turn to Your Neighbor: This takes only three to five minutes. Ask students to turn to a neighbor and ask something about the lesson; to explain in their own words a concept you have just taught; to summarize the three most important points of the direct teaching; or whatever fits the lesson.

Focus Trios: Before a film, lecture, or reading, ask students what they already know about the subject and questions they have about it. Afterward, the trios answer questions, discuss new information, and formulate new questions.

Book Report Pairs: Have students interview each other about a passage or what you have said. They read and then they report on their partner's understanding.

Elaborating Pairs: Ask students to elaborate on what they are reading and learning, relating it to what they already know about the subject. This can be done before and after a reading selection, listening to a lecture, or seeing a film.

Good teaching is about recognizing and selecting instructional patterns that match the context for learning and the students we are teaching.

Good teaching is about having a variety of instructional methodologies. Remember that even though direct instruction is the most frequently used mode of instruction, it should not be overused. Change the state as appropriate for the learner's age. Structure the direct teaching situations so that students are encouraged to learn from one another.

Summary

Direct instruction is the most popular pattern of instruction. It is teacher centered, and for that reason it is a part of this section of the book. The teacher is the purveyor of knowledge. We presented Madeline Hunter's research on lesson design and how to deliver effective lessons that match the content and the students. We support the idea that good lessons begin with a good opening (anticipatory set) and contain closure questions or summary statements. These two components are important because research says that your students will remember the first thing and the last thing you say. Remember to change the state of the lesson to match the age of the students. When you stop, select a processing strategy to ensure that the information shared will transfer to long-term memory. Use various forms of media to enhance the lesson delivery. The direct teaching pattern works best when the goal is for students to learn basic facts.

Direct instruction can be used with small children or with adults. It is not limited to any grade level or to any content or subject area. Therefore, it is widely used as a means to transmit knowledge. Remembering this will ensure learner success.

Thought to Action

1. Go to the curriculum materials center or to your university library and see whether any SRA kits are on the shelf. Examine the structure of the page for teaching reading. Do you think this form of direct instruction is still effective today? Why or why not?

2. Interview a high school teacher and ask for his or her opinion about direct instruction. Find out if the teacher divides the class period into time segments that are appropriate for the age of the students he or she is teaching.

3. Write three strategies that can be used to break up direct teaching. Label each strategy to identify whether the strategy is auditory, visual, or kinesthetic.

4. Find a teacher who works with exceptional education students and ask whether he or she uses direct instruction. Learn the routine of the class by making observations. What do you notice that is unique to this classroom?

ON YOUR OWN

Log on to the web-based student study site at http://www.sagepub.com/holt for access to a Standards-Based Student Project that will help you connect what you have learned in this chapter to your state's standards; study aids, such as electronic flashcards; and research recommendations, including journal article links and other Web resources.

7

Mastery Learning

MASTERY LEARNING IS A METHOD OF INSTRUCTION THAT SEPARATES CONTENT INTO UNITS, WITH an expected level of student performance for each unit. The unit contains goals with broad statements about what is to be accomplished and daily lesson plans with measurable objectives. The instruction is provided to students with the intent that they will master the content at a predetermined level of performance, usually 80% or above. On average, unit plans range between 5 and 10 days. Following the instruction of a unit plan, a criterion-referenced test is given to the students to determine their performance level or mastery of the content. Students who achieve 80% or above on the criterion-referenced test are allowed to proceed to the next unit. The students who do not achieve 80% are provided with corrective instruction.

Content areas that have used this approach the most are reading and mathematics, which are generally perceived as skills-based curricula. In these subjects, it is presumed that reading and mathematical skills are sequential and build on one another. You cannot read until you learn how to pronounce the words in a sentence, and you cannot solve a problem in division without knowing how to subtract. Therefore, if you plan to use mastery learning, content analysis must be done to determine which skills are prerequisite to more complicated skills. This practice has been given the name *chunking*. Content is chunked into isolated skills, and each skill builds on the last until all parts belonging to a unit are learned. Mastery learning is best used when specific skills need to be learned efficiently and thoroughly. Rules of grammar, spelling, basic operations in mathematics (addition, subtraction, multiplication, and division facts), state capitals, the periodic table in chemistry, and the bones of the body in biology or anatomy are all facts that can be taught using mastery learning. The focus is knowledge acquisition.

Providing instruction in this manner does not take into consideration the motivation of the learner. It is presumptuous on the part of the teacher to believe that every learner will be motivated to learn in this fashion. Often, teachers are so focused on the delineation of the skills

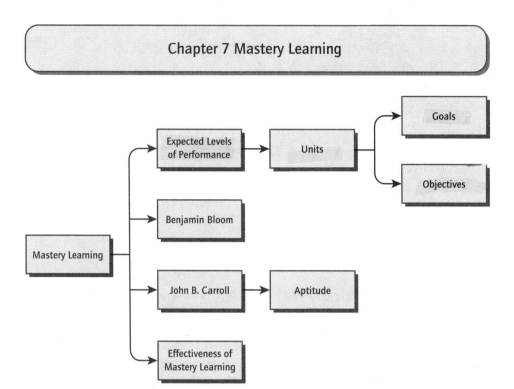

within a unit of study that little or no consideration is given to whether the learner cares about learning the skills. The teacher's goal is to determine whether the learner has accomplished mastery of the content. Beyond that, there may be little or no consideration of the learner's motivation and ownership of the content. Examining content with a skills-based approach to learning qualifies mastery learning as a teacher-centered approach.

Recently, neuroanatomists, cognitive psychologists, and medical technicians have combined forces to inform us about how the brain works. Technological advances that have occurred in the medical profession allow us to view the functions of the brain. Positron emission tomography (PET) and magnetic resonance imaging (MRI) are two brain-imaging methods that allow scientists to identify the anatomical areas that become active while a person performs various mental tasks. As we mentioned in Chapter 1, when we process or take in new information, the brain seeks an organizational placement of the new material. When we are seeing something for the first time, the brain begins to search existing schema and compares it to the new information to organize the new knowledge. Bits and pieces of isolated skills that are taught with the mastery learning approach may inhibit the brain's placement and organization of new knowledge. Failure to see the relationship between isolated skills and a larger goal or objective within a mastery learning unit may keep the learner from making the appropriate connections. "Why do we need to learn this stuff?" may be the learner's response to learning isolated skills within a unit of study. If the learner does not understand why isolated skills are important or how the skills are related to a larger goal, this teacher-centered skills approach to instruction may cause the learner to lose interest in the subject.

The mastery learning approach separates learners into two distinct groups: students who master learning and those who are "nonmasters." This separation creates a management

Mastery learning divides the content to be learned into simple and complex forms of knowledge.

problem for you. On one hand, you must provide new instruction for those who have mastered the content, and at the same time, you must provide corrective instruction to those who need the skills reinforced and retested. So the question becomes, how can you best practice the mastery learning approach given the fact that your learners will be divided by ability? The dilemma facing you is the amount of time it may take for corrective instruction versus continuing instruction for those who have mastered the content. One solution to this dilemma is the use of lists designed for mastery learning.

Several commercially made skills kits were produced during the 1960s, when the mastery learning approach was very popular. For example, SRA was a popular reading kit produced and marketed by reading associates (see www.sraonline.com). Each student was administered a pretest to determine his or her ability level. Once this was determined, students would be assigned to a colored skills box. Each of the stories within the box would be more complicated than the last story. Students were self-paced within their skills box. After reading a story, individual students could approach their teacher to ask for the criterion-reference test matched to the story. If the student scored 80% or better on the story, then the student could advance to the next story within the same box. When all stories were read in the box, the student would advance to a new color box within the skills set.

Although there may be some inherent problems in the use of mastery learning, it is probably one of the most frequently used forms of instruction and research and does indicate levels of success with certain types of learners. This is evident from the success of this approach with exceptional learners. Students with physical motor or mental deficiencies often benefit from this approach. The practice of breaking down steps to master rudimentary actions matches the lock-step objective approach and chunking used in individualized education plans for exceptional learners.

For students who are physically challenged, forms of mastery learning are used for rehabilitation.

RESEARCH ANCHOR

During World War II, the general feeling was that army recruits were not sufficiently prepared to handle the tasks required of them. This perception led to a multitude of studies involving intelligence testing and instructional approaches. What was learned through the military translated into more forces and later to more study in teaching and learning in public schools.

Tyler's *Basic Principles of Curriculum and Instruction* (1949) proved to be one of the landmark works of its day. The "Tyler rationale" outlined steps for the planning of curriculum and instruction. The first step in his plan was the creation of educational objectives. With the introduction of Tyler's book, the objectives movement was born. Objectives were then broken down into three major areas—the cognitive, affective, and psychomotor domains—in Bloom's 1956 book, *Taxonomy of Educational Objectives, Handbook I: Cognitive Domain.* This book classified levels of cognition and affectivity in a hierarchical fashion. Bloom posited that learners must proceed in an orderly progression through six levels: knowledge, comprehension, application, analysis, synthesis, and evaluation.

Bloom's second handbook systematically classified types of human reactions—feeling, attitudes, and emotions—and reduced them to behavioral equivalents of such feelings. This volume, *Handbook II: Affective Domain* (written in 1964 with David Krathwohl and Bertram Masia) suggested that the affective domain of student behaviors consisted of receiving, responding, valuing, and organizing those values into a system. Bloom suggested that students attain mastery learning when they reach the top of both the cognitive and affective domains.

Robert Gagné published *Military Training* and *Principles of Learning*. He demonstrated a concern for the different levels of learning. His differentiation of psychomotor skills, verbal information, intellectual skills, cognitive strategies, and attitudes provide a companion to Bloom's taxonomy. Later, he extended his thinking to include nine instructional events in *The Conditions of Learning and Theory of Instruction* (1965), which detailed the conditions necessary for learning to occur.

Source: Washburne (1922).

In 1965, Robert Gagné outlined the link between educational objectives and instruction in his book *Principles of Learning*. Adding to what had already been learned from Tyler's work on lesson design and Bloom's material on educational objectives, Gagné elaborated and linked educational objectives to the process of instruction.

Mastery Learning and Programmed Instruction

Mastery learning and programmed instruction were direct results of the objectives movement. Instruction in both settings occurs when a student is presented with a specific skill to master. B. F. Skinner worked with such instructional techniques during the latter part of the 1960s. At the time, behaviorists such as B. F. Skinner thought that programmed instruction would take over education. The objectives movement sought to create a "teacher-proof" curriculum. A teacher-proof curriculum is one that uses ironclad objectives and lock-step teaching strategies. The thought was that if teachers would only stick with the program as outlined by the curriculum experts, then all the ills of education would be fixed. Later, two forms of mastery learning materialized. One form, called *learning for mastery*, adapts well to various curricula. In this form, the teacher presents the units, and the students move through them at a uniform pace controlled by the teacher. The other form is called the *personalized system of instruction* or the Keller Plan. The units are self-instructional and students proceed at their own pace, moving to the next unit only when the previous unit has been passed using preset criteria (Lai & Biggs, 1994).

The Influence of Benjamin Bloom

In 1971, Bloom extended his influence in the field of education when he published his *Handbook on Formative and Summative Evaluation of Student Learning* (Bloom, Hastings, & Madaus, 1971), a monumental work that outlined precisely how educational objectives should be formulated and tested in every content area, from literature to industrial arts. The term "formative evaluation"

Benjamin S. Bloom published the *Taxonomy of Educational Objectives.* In *Handbook I: Cognitive Domain* (1956), Bloom dealt with knowledge and the development of intellectual skills. Bloom set forth a hierarchy of learning, beginning with factual knowledge and leading through comprehension, application, analysis, synthesis, and evaluation. Bloom posited that learners must proceed through each level in an orderly progression. *Handbook II: The Affective Domain,* written with David Krathwohl and Bertram Masia in 1964, systematically classified types of human reactions—feelings, attitudes, and emotions. The affective domain receives, responds, values, and organizes values in a system. Bloom contended that students reach mastery when they have reached the top of both the cognitive and affective domains.

Source: *University of Chicago Chronicle,* retrieved June 29, 2004, from chronicle.uchicago.edu/990923/bloom.shtml; "Bloom's Taxonomy," retrieved June 29, 2004, from www.nwlink.com/~donclark/hrd/bloom.html.

refers to Bloom's suggestion that student learning be monitored in the intermediate stages of mastering a topic rather than waiting for the summative evaluation that comes only at the end, when it is to late to modify instructional methods if the student has not learned appropriately. This approach was as back-to-basics as one could get. When steadily falling test scores became the hallmark of the 1970s, Bloom's orderly classification and objectives were seized on as a possible cure for an ailing system.

If you attended elementary school during the 1960s or 1970s and you happen to be a baby boomer or a Generation Xer, then you may recall certain mastery learning curricula. You may not have known it at the time, but you may have experienced mastery learning. Let's take a look into one such school setting from 1968 to see how the students would have experienced a mastery learning curriculum.

The Influence of John B. Carroll

Carroll recognized that an important component of instruction is time. In Carroll's theory, the difference in aptitude among students results form the amount of time spent learning the material. Traditionally, aptitude has been thought of as a characteristic that correlates with a student's achievement. The more aptitude one has, the more one is able to learn. Carroll, however, viewed aptitude as the amount of time it takes to learn the material rather than the student's capacity to learn. Therefore, students with low aptitude need more time to learn or master the content than students with high aptitude. Thus viewed, aptitude becomes the primary guide to how much time a learner needs and suggests how to instruct. For any given objective, the degree of learning achieved by any student is a function of the time allowed, the perseverance of the student, the quality of instruction, the student's ability to understand instruction, and the student's aptitude.

The eighth-grade students file into the reading classroom and take their seats while Mrs. Baron takes attendance. Mrs. Baron says after attendance, "Okay class, you will continue working independently in your respective reading books, advancing through each color in the index. As you know, you must take the pretest to determine whether you have to read the entire passage. Then, following the pretest, bring your questions to me for scoring. If you score 80% or better on this portion of the test, you can advance to the next story. If not, you must go back and reread the passages at the end of the story until you understand."

"Okay, everyone get quiet and begin."

This classroom scenario is an example of how self-paced mastery learning would be framed using the SRA material. This type of curriculum is an example of mastery learning, which assumes that when students are given enough time, they can master the skills associated with reading. This type of instruction is self-paced and would be considered a personalized system of instruction. The students operate independently working from one story to the next in color-coded boxes.

The steps in the program are designed to do the following:

- Allow each student to operate independently, giving them more than one chance to succeed with the material

- Develop demonstrable mastery in each student level

- Develop self-initiation and self-direction for learning

- Foster the development of problem solving through processes

- Encourage self-evaluation and motivation for learning

The core theoretical ideas in mastery learning are credited to Benjamin Bloom and John B. Carroll.

Mastery Learning Research

During the latter part of the 1980s, several debates about the effectiveness of mastery learning were reported in the literature. Robert Slavin (1987) was critical of the mastery learning approach and the studies that had reported its success. The criticisms that Slavin cited included the following:

- Unequal time: If one part of the class accomplishes mastery of the content, it creates a problem between the masters and nonmasters. The teacher must devote additional time to the students who need corrective instruction.

- Unequal objectives: Studies of mastery learning use experimenter-made summative achievement test as the criterion for learning effects, which by nature focuses teachers and students on a narrow and explicitly defined set of objectives.

- Unequal value: There is no evidence that mastery learning will be of value to those interested in achieving broader outcomes.

Several rebuttals to Slavin's criticism of the mastery learning approach subsequently appeared in the literature (Block, 1988; Guskey, 1988; Walberg, 1988).

John B. Carroll was influential in the use of factor analysis to study cognitive abilities. He conducted seminal work in applied linguistics and made significant contributions in the areas of linguistics and the teaching of foreign languages, educational psychology, and individual differences in cognitive abilities.

Source: Plucker (2002).

Although the concept of mastery learning has come under some criticism, its impact on learning is widespread. In numerous studies, researchers have demonstrated the effectiveness of the mastery learning method as measured by criterion-referenced and teacher-made tests (e.g., Block & Burns, 1976; Guskey & Pigott, 1988; Kulik, Kulik, & Bangert-Drowns, 1990). In a study equivalent to 18 years or 36 semesters, Whiting and Render (1987) provided information regarding the effectiveness of mastery learning in real-world classroom experience. The study investigated the cognitive and affective student learning outcomes in high school distributive education classes ($n = 7,719$ students). Student achievement in the cognitive area was represented by increasing grade point averages, and test scores were presented to show the consistently high level of academic achievement of students. Affective information (attitudes toward school and learning) was also elicited from the entire sample and presented to show positive changes.

A study in Yale, Michigan, examined a field experiment in implementing mastery learning (Anderson et al., 1992). The results indicated that mastery learning could have a significant positive impact on achievement, and as predicted, the students' perceptions of themselves improved as recorded by the Brookover self-concept scale.

More than 30 years have elapsed since Bloom's article on mastery learning appeared in the literature, and more than 2,000 citations now appear in the ERIC documents on this topic. Increasingly, there is evidence that mastery learning is being used in combination with other instructional models and educational approaches. Mastery learning has been compared with such methods as cooperative learning, constructivist teaching, and computer technology (Motamedi & Sumrall, 2000). Other studies reported by Hymel and Dyck (1993) examined the use of mastery learning in an international context. Mastery learning has been put forth as an instructional model that works well with low-achieving students (Kulik et al., 1990).

One of the criticisms of the mastery approach is that when objectives are preselected by the teacher, the quality of the learning is affected. In 1981, Satterly stated that mastery learning trivializes learning by reducing content to what is easily measured rather than what is most valuable. This brings to light the fact that the context for learning and the students' perception of learning can change. According to Tang (1991), students are adept at switching from high-level to low-level assessment depending on the expectations and strategies presented to them. Lai and Biggs (1994) further stated that there may be a difference in surface learning (predetermined teacher objectives) compared to deep learning (examining the process of learning). The perception of the learner and the educational context in which the learning occurs indicate whether a student will approach the task of learning in a surface or a deep way, adjusting their learning according to the task. Understanding this difference has implications for how teachers approach mastery learning. As we learn more about how the brain functions, we can begin to understand the utility of the mastery learning approach and its usefulness for the group of students we are to teach. The following scenario describes how two teachers working with the same group of students used the mastery approach to learning.

CLASSROOM SCENARIO

Ms. Holcomb and Ms. La Hart wanted to test the use of mastery learning in their fifth-grade math class. They first decided which objectives in the math book could reasonably be mastered by their students. Then, they researched and listed activities in these areas that could be used for reinforcement and enrichment. In addition to teaching the basic skills suggested by their adopted curriculum, they wanted to incorporate a variety of manipulative and learning styles to help master the concepts. After their objectives and methods for meeting the objectives were listed, they created two similar tests for fractions and geometry.

Ms. Holcomb gave the class the self-concept of ability scale. Then she began the mastery units. She began by immersing the class in several activities to develop the concept of fractions. (Most had not yet learned fractions in their elementary school careers.) The teachers then proceeded to teach the objectives they had decided on using the activities and materials they had chosen. When all activities and objectives were completed, Form A of the test was administered. Eight students did not score at 80%. However, of these eight, none scored below 65%. Then the teachers retaught the

objectives that were missed and gave the other students enrichment activities. Several students complained that the enrichment activities were hard, and they wished they had not done well on the test.

Ms. Holcomb and Ms. La Hart noticed that when they paired students who had mastered the concepts with those who were nonmasters, better results were achieved. Four days later, Form B was administered, and all but one achieved the 80% level. That one student received 78%, which both teachers agreed was pretty close and not so disappointing. The geometry unit was taught in the same manner, but the Form A test found all students scoring at 80% or above.

When all the tests and units were completed, the teachers readministered the self-concept scale. Both Ms. Holcomb and Ms. La Hart felt empowered using the mastery approach because it gave them permission to take the time to reteach the students who had missed out the first time around. They also believed that with some topics, students might have done better with mastery learning if they had prior knowledge of the concepts to be learned.

Drill and practice assessments should be part of a teacher's repertoire for mastery learning.

ASSESSMENT

Assessment in mastery learning is built into the system. The point of mastery learning is to acquire content at the lower levels of the cognitive domain, recall and understanding. Students practice until they reach the predetermined level of mastery.

The concern raised by many educators is that mastery learning and its built-in assessments limit the students' acquisition of information and do little to help them use or analyze the information. That criticism is valid, but we must respect the purpose of mastery learning—selecting a groundwork of knowledge on which other skills may be built.

In the tenets that we introduced in Chapter 1, we said that learners seek to organize information as they learn new concepts. As teachers use the mastery learning approach, which isolates skills into daily lock-step chunks to be mastered, keep in mind that students who cannot master the content may lose sight of the overall ideas associated with the purpose for learning. Learning must be relevant to the students, and teachers may need to help students understand how the concepts they teach are meaningful and relevant to their lives.

Overuse of mastery learning kits or drill-and-practice curricula can become drill and kill. As a teacher, you should combine mastery learning with other teaching strategies to avoid boredom on the part of the students and to enhance their repertoire of learning skills. In addition to varying the instructional format, you may seek ways to assess student knowledge above and beyond the prescribed multiple-choice, criterion-referenced tests that come with the mastery learning kit or curriculum. Assessment activities can be fun activities for the students. Because much of mastery learning is based on students' ability to recall (or regurgitate, as some educators claim) facts, names, places, dates, timetables, grammar rules, capitals of states, etc., the assessment activities can be quite creative. Crossword puzzles can be used to assess vocabulary. Using maps, students can place the names of capitals on the right states. A body diagram can be used on which students label the body parts. If you want to use less formal assessment, you can have math fact relays in which students are divided into teams, and teams get points when their runner provides the correct answer before any member of another team.

Assessment for mastery learning is not hard to do, but without some creative thinking on your part, assessment can be relegated to routine, which can lead to boredom. Adjusting the traditional testing format may be necessary for English as a second language students or exceptional education learners. These students can demonstrate their knowledge and their ways of knowing the material through alternative forms of assessment such as portfolios, visual diagrams, interviews, or rubrics. These variations will make learning more interesting for your students, and chances are, they will increase the students' success with the selected mastery learning curriculum.

TECHNOLOGY

Technology is a wonderful asset for mastery learning. Much of the drill and repetition needed for mastery can now be done with appropriately selected software programs. For students who have not mastered the facts, independent time with the computer to reinforce the skills can be arranged while the teacher progresses with students who have mastered the content. Additionally, software that is appropriately matched to the mastery curriculum can be used as enrichment for all students.

Learning Tenets
That Support Mastery Learning

The brain seeks to classify information and the things to be learned.

One of the benefits of mastery learning is the format of the material itself. The commercial products that were developed to enhance mastery learning provide a systematic way of introducing the content. The mastery learning kit breaks the skills into separate units of study, and within each unit, there are teacher guidelines for presenting lesson plans on various skills. Everything is self-contained as a guide for the teacher or designed to be used by students to independently track their progress. During the 1960s and 1970s, this material was used often because one of the goals of American education was to ensure that all students were minimally competent in basic skills. Mastery learning is an ideal way to build minimum competencies.

Even though the brain seeks to classify information and the things to be learned, some of the mastery learning organizational formats promote surface learning and not deep learning (Satterly, 1981). The outcome may trivialize learning by reducing content to what is easily measured rather than what is most valuable. The context for learning and the student's perception for learning are important. According to Tang (1991), students are adept at switching from high-level to low-level assessment depending on the expectations and strategies presented to them. Lai and Biggs (1994) further stated that there may be a difference between surface learning (predetermined teacher objectives) and deep learning (examining the process of learning).

**The emotional system drives attention,
and attention drives meaning and memory.**

One of the advantages of mastery learning is the option of self-paced material. If the material is not presented in a direct teaching format but rather as a self-paced process, the student's motivation for learning may be positively influenced. Achieving the learning outcomes independent of your guidance can boost your students' confidence in their abilities. When students feel affirmation for what has been accomplished, the emotional system is engaged—a positive outcome of mastery learning.

Learning occurs in both conscious and unconscious states.

Maybe your goal for a lesson was for students to learn that Columbus discovered America. However, instead of learning that goal, they learned how to spell Columbus. Sometimes, despite the fact that we may have defined our goals and objectives and we have presented in our mind the most brilliant lesson, there are other learning circumstances that may have occurred. As teachers, these outcomes are not the ones that we expect. Can we say that learning has occurred? Yes! However, the learning does not reflect what we had planned for the students to learn.

In this chapter on mastery learning, you read that according to John B. Carroll, students have different aptitudes for learning. This means that not all students learn the same thing at the same time or have the same capacity to learn. This is an important consideration when we consider this tenet regarding conscious and unconscious states. Unconscious learning may include the learning outcomes that are not reflected as a part of the learning goal. Conscious learning represents the concepts that are learned and reflected in the goal for learning. To assist learners with mastery of the content, we must be aware of these differences. More important, how we treat the student after we discover what was learned versus what we intended for them to learn is paramount. We should not look down on the incidental components that were learned by the students. We should continue to boost the students' confidence in their learning despite the fact they learned something that was incidental to what we had planned. At this point, with the mastery learning model, we refocus the student's attention and reteach the lesson. Own up to the fact that the approach you took with the students may not be the best one considering each learner's uniqueness. If reteaching is in order, redesign the approach of the lesson to meet the learners' needs.

The brain is designed for ups and downs, not constant attention.

You should be cautious about the pace of the mastery learning material you choose to use in your classroom. As we stated in the Research Anchor, aptitude plays an important role in your students' ability to master certain concepts. Therefore, your use of mastery learning must not engage in long, concentrated sessions that force the skills down the students' throats. That is not the intent of mastery learning. Following an assessment of what the students learned, you may find yourself in a bind—some students may not have achieved mastery whereas others have. Remember to concentrate on the positive outcomes your students have made and realize that, with time, those who have not mastered the material will catch up. Humans constantly do more then what we are consciously aware of. Even now, you are performing the very complex task of interpreting the marks on this page without consciously examining the shape of the letter or sounding out each syllable. If you were aware of the complexity of what you were doing, you would not be able to do it. In fact, in some instances, drawing conscious attention to some interactions can cause them to fall apart. Drill-and-kill techniques that focus attention on the same skills do not necessarily help students to progress through the curriculum at the same rate or at the same time.

Learning occurs through processing and active engagement with visual, auditory, and kinesthetic modalities.

When applying mastery learning curricula, it is important to consider instructional time. Within the unit, there are several lessons. Time measures for these lessons are important. How much time should you spend explaining the new material? Remember that the brain is better equipped to attend to information that is presented in time intervals that are equal to the learner's age. Following the explanation of the concepts, time should be allowed for processing. When students engage and interact with each other and the content, the chances of encoding the concepts are enhanced.

The following are suggestions for helping your students engage in processing content:

Turn to Your Neighbor: This takes only three to five minutes. Ask your students to turn to a neighbor and ask something about the lesson; to explain in their own words a concept you have just taught; or to summarize the three most important points of the discussion. You can structure this activity to fit the content of the lesson.

Focus Trios: Before a film, lecture, or reading, ask students what they already know about the subject and questions they have about it. Afterward, provide time for the trios to answer questions, discuss new information, and formulate new questions.

Fan 'n Pick: Prepare cards in advance that ask content questions related to the material being studied. Have your students work in groups of four. In each group, Student 1 fans, Student 2 picks, Student 3 answers, and Student 4 evaluates the answer. Students then rotate roles.

**Good teaching is about recognizing and
selecting instructional patterns that match
the context for learning and the students we are teaching.**

Mastery learning has had much success in many different settings. It has been combined with other instructional techniques, such as cooperative learning, to assess the performance level of students in various content areas. It has been documented in the research as being successful with exceptional education children and for teachers who use individual education plans that identify performance objectives. Mastery learning not only indicates the progress that is being made but also allows you to plan appropriate goals and objectives for your students.

Summary

Mastery learning is a systems approach to instruction. It is well positioned in Part III, "Teacher-Centered Patterns," because it is the teacher who guides the content expectation for the learners in this approach. During the 1960s, several systematic kits of curriculum materials in the areas of reading and mathematics were sold to school districts. Some of the kits required the students to take a pretest on a topic. If the student scored 80% or better, then the student could advance to the next set of skills within the kit. Mastery learning has been successful when used in this way for thousands of learners. It breaks down the content into parts to provide a process for obtaining skills. Mastery learning is useful for learners with special needs. Because mastery learning has proven to be successful, it will be around for many years to come.

Thought to Action

1. How might the mastery learning approach conflict with what we have learned about the way the brain works?
2. Find a school district that is using the mastery learning curriculum. Examine the school's content objectives and the state standards. Is there curriculum alignment?
3. Find a person who has experienced the SRA reading kit and interview him or her to get a reaction to this form of instruction.
4. Find a private school that is using the mastery learning or programmed instruction approach. Ask how the school tracks student progress using this curriculum.
5. Using the descriptor "chunking," search the Internet for additional information related to this approach. Analyze and synthesize the research found and explain what you think about it.
6. Identify some content within your field of expertise that would be appropriate for mastery learning. Create at least two assessment strategies that you think students would enjoy doing to illustrate their knowledge.

ON YOUR OWN

Log on to the web-based student study site at http://www.sagepub.com/holt for access to a Standards-Based Student Project that will help you connect what you have learned in this chapter to your state's standards; study aids, such as electronic flashcards; and research recommendations, including journal article links and other Web resources.

PART IV

Teacher–Student Interactive Patterns

Teacher–student interactive instruction occurs when the ownership of what is to be learned is shared by the teacher and the students. This form of instruction examines more than the behavior of the teacher; it also examines the process of learning. Which forms of interaction are needed to enhance the learner's understanding of the content? If the teacher provides a learning experience for the students, will the things learned be retained more easily? How can the teacher balance the ownership of what is to be learned? Which instructional practices will influence the students' feeling of ownership in relation to the content? The patterns of instruction that best represent the process of learning are included in this section of the book. Chapter 8 examines cooperative learning and Chapter 9 focuses on role play.

Ownership of the content is often shared in these forms of instruction, and these instructional types consider how students can work in groups. The focus is the process rather than a predetermined set of teacher objectives. In these patterns of instruction, student learning outcome objectives are often activities that permit the learner to examine the things to be learned with the teacher.

8

Cooperative Learning

COOPERATIVE LEARNING IS NOT A NEW IDEA. THROUGHOUT HISTORY, INDIVIDUALS WHO COULD organize and coordinate their efforts to achieve a common purpose have succeeded by using the ideas of cooperative learning. However, simply placing students in groups and telling them to work together does not guarantee the competence needed for cooperation. To begin to understand cooperative learning, it is important to distinguish between informal grouping arrangements and formal cooperative learning groups and to identify the major types of cooperative learning.

Cooperative learning can be employed at any grade level and in any content area. In fact, most formal cooperative learning structures can be used successfully with students age six through adult. Within a classroom, the teacher may use both informal and formal groups. A formal group is given an assignment to complete and stays together for specified period of time, usually dictated by the topic under investigation, such as a unit of study lasting one or more weeks. An informal group is given an assignment for a short discussion task and may stay together for only a few minutes or one class period. Another grouping structure is base groups, which are long-term groups whose purpose is primarily to provide peer support and accountability. Such groups stay together for at least one week.

Informal cooperative learning groups are temporary, ad hoc groups that stay together for a few minutes to one class period. The purposes of these groups are as follows:

- To focus the student attention on the material to be learned
- To set a mood that is conducive to learning
- To organize in advance the material to be covered during a class session
- To ensure that students cognitively process the material that is taught
- To provide closure to an instructional session

Informal cooperative learning groups are often organized so that students can engage in focused discussions before and after a lecture, film, or presentation. "Turn to your partner"

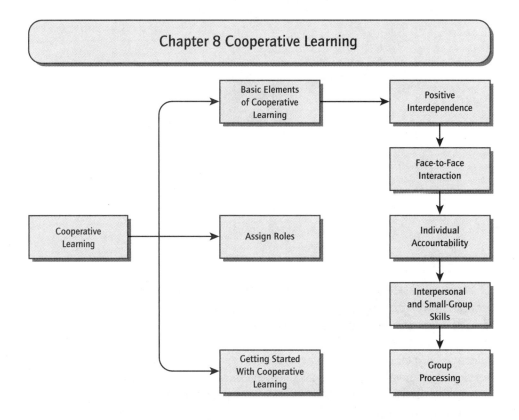

Chapter 8 Cooperative Learning

discussions can be interspersed throughout the presentation to help students retain what has been shared. The information presented by the teacher is then immediately discussed by the students, thus overcoming the problem of the traditional lecture.

Formal cooperative learning groups may say together for one class period to several weeks for the purpose of instruction that is focused on one specific task or assignment (i.e., solving a set of problems, completing a major unit, writing a report, conducting an investigation, or reading or comprehending a story). To form formal cooperative learning groups, the teacher must do the following:

- Decide on group size and how to assign students to groups

- Teach the academic concepts, principles, and strategies

- Assign a task to be completed cooperatively

- Monitor the functioning of the learning groups and intervene

- Teach collaborative skills

- Provide assistance when needed

Students are taught to look to their peers for assistance, feedback, reinforcement, and support. Students are expected to share materials, interact, and encourage each other's academic performance. Students may orally explain what was taught to them and elaborate on the strategies and concepts. In this way, students hold each other accountable for completing the assignment.

Base groups are long-term, heterogeneous cooperative learning groups with stable membership (e.g., one might consist of one high, one low, and two average academic level students). The purposes of the base group are as follows:

- To support, help, assist, and encourage members to make academic progress

- To develop students in cognitively and socially healthy ways

- To allow the group to stay together for much of the day and regularly work together to complete cooperative learning tasks

- To formally meet and discuss the academic progress of each member, provide help and assistance to each other, and verify that each member is completing the academic assignments

Base groups may also be given the task of letting absent group members know what went on in the class during their absence. The use of base groups tends to improve attendance, personalize both the required work and the school experience, and improve the quality and quantity of learning (Johnson & Johnson, 1991).

Cooperative learning tends to promote higher-level thinking and is most clearly seen in conceptual learning and problem-solving tasks. Cooperation, cognition, and metacognition are all intimately related. Cooperative learning provides the context within which cognition and metacognition take place. The oral and interpersonal exchanges among group members and the intellectual challenges that result from conflicting ideas and conclusions promote critical thinking, higher-level reasoning, and metacognitive thought. The divergent thinking and inspiration that spark creativity result from the oral explanations and elaboration required within cooperative learning groups. Explaining what one knows to one's groupmates facilitates the understanding of how to apply one's knowledge and skills to work and community settings (Johnson & Johnson, 1991).

Developing interpersonal skills within a cooperative learning group helps to ensure learning success.

RESEARCH ANCHOR

Cooperative learning is the instructional use of small groups so that students work together to maximize their own and each other's learning. In order for teachers to successfully use cooperative learning in their classrooms, teachers should observe the following five basic elements advanced by Johnson, Johnson, and Holubec (1988).

BASIC ELEMENTS OF COOPERATIVE LEARNING

The first element is *positive interdependence*. Students must perceive that they sink or swim together. This may be achieved by assigning mutual goals (goal interdependence); dividing labor (task interdependence); dividing materials, resources, or information among group members (resource interdependence); assigning students roles (role interdependence); and giving joint rewards (reward interdependence). For a learning situation to be cooperative, students must perceive that they are positively interdependent on the other members of their learning groups.

The second element is *face-to-face interaction*. No magic exists in positive interdependence in and of itself. Beneficial educational outcomes result from the interaction patterns and verbal exchanges that take place among students in carefully structured cooperative learning groups. Oral summarizing, giving and receiving explanations, and elaborating (relating what is being learned to previous learning) are important types of verbal exchanges.

The third element is *individual accountability*. Cooperative learning groups are not successful until every member has learned the material or has helped with and understood the assignment. Thus, it is important to stress and assess individual learning so that group members can appropriately support and help each other. Some ways of structuring individual accountability are to give each group member an individual exam or randomly select one member to give an answer for the entire group.

The fourth element is *interpersonal and small-group skills*. Rarely do students come to school with the social skills they need to collaborate effectively with others. So teachers need to teach the appropriate communication, leadership, trust, decision-making, and conflict-management skills to students and provide the motivation to use these skills in order for groups to function effectively.

The last basic element is *group processing*. Processing means giving students the time and procedures to analyze how well their groups are functioning and how well they are using the necessary social skills. This processing helps all group members to achieve while maintaining effective working relationships among members. Feedback from the teacher and student observers on how well the group worked together may help processing effectiveness.

As teachers, we are interested in having students acquire the ability to maximize their learning, develop a positive attitude toward school, and think critically. Although these are all important expectations of the students we teach, cooperation is as basic to human survival as the air we breathe. The ability to work collaboratively with others is the cornerstone of building and maintaining stable marriages, families, careers, friendships, and communities (Johnson et al., 1988). The skills of reading, speaking, listening, writing, computing, and problem solving are of little value if one cannot apply them in cooperative interaction with other people. People today—whether they are engineers, secretaries, accountants, teachers, mechanics, or medical professionals—are required to work cooperatively on the job as well as in their families and communities.

To ensure that students are appropriately using the basic elements of individual account-ability in cooperative learning environments, roles must be assigned. The roles assigned within the group may be stated as the need arises. As students begin working in groups, members learn how the roles assigned complement and interconnect with the task at hand. Usually, the roles are rotated daily so that each student obtains considerable experience in each role. Roles are assigned to create positive interdependence and to teach students new skills. Roles assigned may be working or social-skill roles depending on the needs of the group. Students will learn new roles if those roles are carefully defined, watched for, and rewarded.

Role assignment may vary according to the classroom environment, age, ability, and social skills present in your student population. Decide for yourself which roles are most appropriate for your class and spend some time explaining the rationale and definition of the roles with your students. The following list defines several possible roles for students (Johnson et al., 1988):

- Reader: This student reads the group's material out loud to the group, carefully and with expression, so that group members can understand and remember it.

- Writer/recorder: This student carefully records the group's best answers on the worksheet or paper, edits what the group has written, gets the group members to check and sign the paper, and then turns it in to the teacher.

- Materials handler: This student gets any materials or equipment needed by the group, keeps track of them, and puts them carefully away.

- Encourager: This student watches and makes certain that everyone is participating and invites reluctant or silent members to contribute. Sample statements include,
  "Jane, what do you think?"
  "Robert, do you have anything to add?"
  "Pedro, help us out."
  "Leroy, what are your ideas on this?"

- Checker: This student checks the comprehension or learning of group members by asking them to explain or summarize the material learned or discussed. Sample statements include,
  "Terry, why did we decide on this answer for number two?"
  "James, explain how we got this answer."
  "Anne, summarize for us what we've decided here."

- Praiser: This student helps members feel good about their contributions to the group by telling them how helpful they are. This is a good role to assign to help combat put downs. Sample statements include,
  "That's a good idea, Al."
  "Sharon, you're very helpful."
  "Karen, I like the way you've helped us."
  "Good job, John."

- Prober: This student keeps the group from answering questions superficially by not allowing the members to agree too quickly. The prober agrees when he or she is satisfied that the group has explored all the possibilities. Sample statements include,
  "What other possibilities are there for this problem or question?"
  "What else could we put here?"
  "Let's double check that answer."

- Relater/elaboration seeker: This student relates the new information presented in the lesson with what was previously presented. Sample statements include,
  "How does this compare with what we already know?"
  "What is the purpose behind what we have just learned?"
  "How does this relate?"

There are other ways that roles can be assigned depending on the needs of the group. Additionally, nonworking roles may be assigned to increase the social-skill awareness among group members. Some social-skill roles might include the noise monitor, who uses nonverbal signals to quiet the group down; the energizer, who energizes the group when it starts to lag; the observer, who keeps track of how well the team members are collaborating; and the asker for help, timekeeper, question asker, or paraphraser. Come up with roles that fit the task and your students.

During the past 90 years, more than 600 studies have been conducted to compare the effectiveness of cooperative, competitive, and individualistic efforts to learn. These studies come from a variety of researchers, examine participants of varying ages, and focus on different subject areas. More is known about cooperative learning than about lecturing, departmentalization, instructional technology, or almost any other aspect of education (Johnson & Johnson, 1989). The results of this research indicate that cooperative learning increases student achievement, creates positive relationships among students, and promotes students' healthy psychological adjustment to school (Johnson & Johnson, 1989).

David Johnson, a social psychologist, and his brother Roger, a science educator, developed several methods of cooperative learning. Learning together and structured controversy are two methods that focus on the practice of collaborative skills. These researchers recommend that every cooperative learning lesson include a collaborative skill and an academic task. Collaborative skills are stressed because students do not magically work well together. Johnson and Johnson strongly believe that students need to be taught the collaborative skills needed for group work.

Robert Slavin of Johns Hopkins University has developed several group learning methods (Slavin, 1990; Slavin, Karweit, & Wasik, 1994). Two of these methods are Jigsaw II and Student Teams Achievement Division. Both methods are tutorial frameworks. Jigsaw II, which is based on a method first introduced by Aronson, Blaney, Stephan, Sikes, and Snapp (1978), is a tutorial structure in which students learn material individually and then combine their knowledge with others, as if the separate information were pieces of a jigsaw puzzle (see Figure 8.1). Jigsaw II has been found to be an effective cooperative learning structure for improving students' comprehension and retention of written material (Nesbit & Rogers, 1997). According to Yager, Johnson, and Johnson (1985), if written information is restated and summarized by students, there is a greater achievement and longer retention of this information. Klatzky (1975) has noted that rehearsal of information, which is an integral part of any tutorial method, is needed for information to be stored in long-term memory. Additionally, Scott and Heller (1991) have advocated using this method when students are given difficult material to read.

Spencer Kagan (1989/90) of the University of California at Riverside has developed several dozen cooperative learning structures that are informal and adaptable. Each can be introduced easily into any subject area or grade level at various points during a lesson. These structures include *think-pair-share*, the *three-step interview*, and the *roundtable*. Students' language and listening skills are developed in all three models. In think-pair-share, students work

FIGURE 8.1   Jigsaw Strategy

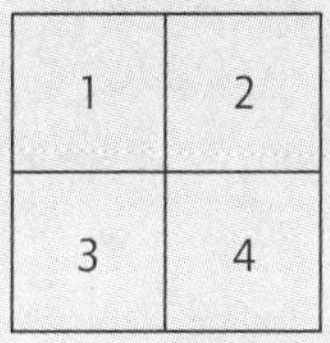

Step 1: Home Group

1	2
3	4

Arrange students in equal groups at a table or ask them to put desks close together. Ask group members to number off.

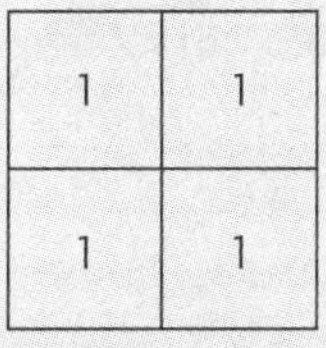

Step 2: Expert Group

1	1
1	1

Assign a section of the text or a summary of a principle or concept to be learned. Group members with like numbers meet together and record their summary.

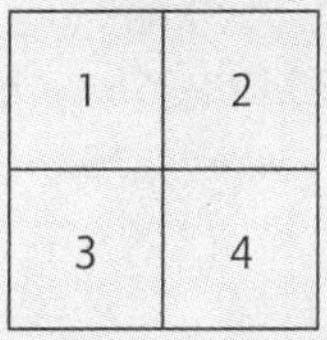

Step 3: Home Group

1	2
3	4

Members return to their home groups and teach the other members the section they were responsible for learning.

in pairs to solve a problem, analyze a paragraph, or debate a point and then share their findings with the larger group. In the three-step interview, students form groups of four. Teachers then assign the interview questions. In Step 1, students conduct one-way interviews in pairs. In Step 2, students reverse roles in each pair. In Step 3, the two pairs report to the group what their partners shared during the interview. There is a guarantee that all students participate equally because all students must listen, write what they hear, and talk with one another. Kagan (1989/90) has stated that this method is very effective at encouraging divergent thinking.

Because cooperative learning promotes higher-order thinking and problem solving, it is imperative that students become aware of their cognitive abilities and understand how they think. Cooperative learning provides the context within which cognition and metacognition can take place. The oral and interpersonal exchanges among group members and the intellectual challenges that result from the exchange of ideas and conclusions promote critical thinking, higher-level reasoning, and metacognitive thought. The divergent thinking and inspiration that spark creativity result from the oral explanations and elaboration required within cooperative learning groups. Explaining what one knows to fellow group members facilitates the understanding of how to apply one's knowledge and skills (Johnson & Johnson, 1991).

GETTING STARTED WITH COOPERATIVE LEARNING

The importance placed on social skills in today's work world is growing. Employers value interpersonal skills, verbal communication, decision making, and initiative as desirable

David W. Johnson is Professor of Educational Psychology at the University of Minnesota, where he holds the Emma M. Birkmaier Professorship in Educational Leadership. He is codirector of the Cooperative Learning Center. He received a master's and doctoral degree from Columbia University. He is a past editor of the *American Educational Research Journal.* He has published more than 350 research articles and book chapters.

Johnson is the author of more than 40 books, most coauthored with R. Johnson. His works include *The Social Psychology of Education, Social Psychology: Issues and Insights, Reaching Out: Interpersonal Effectiveness and Self-Actualization, Joining Together: Group Theory and Group Skills, Learning Together and Alone: Cooperative, Competitive, Individualistic Learning, Productive Conflict Management: Perspectives for Organizations, Circles of Learning: Cooperation in the Classroom, Teaching Students to Be Peacemakers, Creative Controversy: Intellectual Challenge in the Classroom, Cooperation and Competition: Theory and Research, Active Learning: Cooperative Learning in the College Classroom, Meaning and Manageable Assessment Through Cooperative Learning,* and *Learning to Lead Teams: Developing Leadership Skills.*

Source: University of Minnesota, Cooperative Learning Center, retrieved June 29, 2004, from www.co-operation.org/pages/dwj.html.

Roger T. Johnson is Professor in the Department of Curriculum and Instruction, with an emphasis in science education, at the University of Minnesota. He holds a master's degree from Ball State University and a doctorate in education from the University of California, Berkeley. His public school experience includes teaching in kindergarten through eighth grade in self-contained classrooms, open schools, nongraded situations, cottage schools, and departmentalized (science) schools.

He is the author of numerous articles and book chapters and coauthor (with David Johnson) of *Circles of Learning* (1984), *Cooperation and Competition: Theory and Research* (1989), *Active Learning: Cooperation in the College Classroom* (1991), and *Learning Together and Alone* (4th ed., 1994).

Source: University of Minnesota, Cooperative Learning Center, retrieved June 29, 2004, from www.co-operation.org/pages/rj.html.

Robert Slavin has been the director of the elementary program at the Center for Research on Effective Schooling for Disadvantaged Students, Johns Hopkins University, since 1975.

His writings include *Using Student Team Learning* (1978, 1986), *Teams-Games-Tournament: The Team Learning Approach* (1980, with D. L. DeVries, G. M. Fennessey, and others), *Cooperative Learning in Student Teams: What Research Says to the Teacher* (1982, 1987), *Student Team Learning: An Overview and Practical Guide* (1983, 1988), *Cooperative Learning* (1983), *Research Methods in Education: A Practical Guide* (1984, 1992), *Learning to Cooperate, Cooperating to Learn* (1985, edited with S. Sharan, S. Kagan, C. Webb, and others), *Team-Accelerated Instruction: Mathematics* (1986, with N. A. Madden and M. B. Leavey), *Educational Psychology: Theory into Practice* (1986, 1994), *School and Classroom Organization* (1989), *Effective Programs for Students at Risk* (1989, edited with N. L. Karweit and N. A. Madden), *Cooperative Learning: Theory, Research, and Practice* (1990), *Success for All: A Relentless Approach to Prevention and Early Intervention in Elementary Schools* (1992, with N. A. Madden, N. L. Karweit, and others), *Preventing Early School Failure: Research, Policy, and Practice* (1994, edited with N. L. Karweit and B. A. Wasik), *Education for All* (1996), *Every Child, Every School: Success for All* (1996), *Show Me the Evidence! Proven and Promising Programs for America's Schools* (1998, with O. S. Fashola), *One Million Children: Success for All* (2000, edited with N. A. Madden), *Success for All: Research and Reform in Elementary Education* (2000, edited with N. A. Madden), *Effective Programs for Latino Students* (2001, with M. Calderon), and *Title I: Compensatory Education at the Crossroads* (2001).

Source: Contemporary Authors Online; reproduced in the Biography Resource Center (Farmington Hills, MI: Thomson Gale, 2005).

qualities of employees. A question that is on the minds of employers when they are seeking new applicants for a position is, can this person get along with other people? Technical competence is not enough to ensure a successful career. Cooperative learning can assist students with the social skills that they will need in today's work world. Students learn the importance of communicating, building and maintaining trust, leading others, and managing conflicts. One of the greatest advantages of cooperative learning is that important life-survival skills are required and can be mastered within a task-structured classroom environment. Social-skill development should be a prerequisite to academic skills because achievement will improve as students become more effective at learning from each other.

There are four assumptions underlying the teaching of cooperative skills. The first is that prior to teaching cooperative skills, a cooperative classroom environment must be established. An effective teacher will make students aware of the need for specific skills for working in cooperative situations. It is important to establish a feeling tone within the group that students are dependent on one another and must be involved in maximizing their own learning, as well as their groupmates' learning.

Second, cooperative skills have to be taught. Children are not born instinctively knowing how to cooperate with others. Teachers who fail at cooperative learning are those

Students have an uncanny ability to learn from each other; cooperative learning supports this type of learning.

who try to structure cooperative lessons without attention to the feeling tone of the classroom and the teaching of collaborative skills. Learning how to interact with each other is no different from learning basic skills associated with mathematics, science, social studies, or language arts.

Third, although it is the teacher who structures cooperation within the classroom and initially defines the skills required to collaborate, it is the group members who largely determine whether the skills will be learned and internalized. Peer support and feedback and the processing of group work are the responsibility of the group. Students who learn to monitor and reflect on their ability to work in groups will develop effective social skills.

The fourth assumption is that the earlier students are taught cooperative skills, the better. Students who begin to learn cooperative skills in the elementary grades will have competencies in collaborative working relationships. These skills can be enhanced in the middle grades if these competencies are reinforced as the maturation process unfolds. Adults who are engineers, supervisors, secretaries, or medical professionals frequently are the most difficult to work with, particularly if their work experience has not been dependent on collaboration. According to Johnson et al., "There is a direct relation between schools demanding that students work alone without interaction with each other and the number of adults in our society who lack the competencies required to work effectively with others in career, family, and leisure settings" (1988, pp. 7–8).

How do you decide which cooperative skills to teach? Which skills are learned formally and informally? The answers to these questions depend on the cooperative skill level of the classroom. Students with prior experience in cooperative learning will have fewer needs than those who are just starting, regardless of age.

Some of the cooperative and collaborative skills associated with positive group relationships include the following:

Encouraging each other

Praising each other

Describing feelings

Paraphrasing or summarizing

Expressing support

Giving direction to the group

Listening to each other

Being positive

Sharing materials

Teaching social skills to students is as important as teaching basic concepts in mathematics, science, social studies, or language arts. Students are not magically going to work together in the classroom without attention to cooperative and collaborative skills.

The kind of learning required for successful group work is called *procedural learning*. It is no different from playing golf or tennis, learning how to work on a car, or learning how to ride a bicycle. The difference between factual learning and procedural learning is the degree of feedback given to the learner. The process is not automatic but gradual. Trial, error, and sometimes failure are all a part of the learning process. Success is guaranteed with practice. Once the process is learned, your students will perform without having to think about it.

Learning cooperative skills results from the following process:

1. Engaging in the skill

2. Obtaining feedback

3. Reflecting on the feedback

4. Modifying one's enactment and engaging in the skill again

5. Repeating steps 2, 3, and 4 again and again until the skill is appropriately used in a more automated fashion

The performance of the learners is based on their willingness to trust each other and to talk frankly about each other's performance. Expertise cannot be obtained unless students are willing to recognize each other's lack of expertise. The teacher must monitor the performance of the group and identify students who are having difficulty. Students not only obtain a valuable set of skills for life but also have an excellent chance of raising their achievement.

Students who work well in cooperative learning share materials.

Now that the basic elements of cooperative learning have been explained, let's take a peek inside a classroom to see how Mr. Watson applied his knowledge of cooperative learning in his classroom.

According to research (Treicher, 1967; Lyons, Kysilka, & Pawlas, 1999), we learn

10% of what we read

20% of what we hear

30% of what we see

50% of what we see and hear

70% of what we discuss with others

80% of what we personally experience

90% of what we teach to someone else

The scenario that follows outlines a powerful tool for assisting the learning process. Think back to a time when you had to teach something to someone else. As you began to plan, you realized that you were responsible for getting all the facts straight—that you really had to know the ins and outs of what you were to explain to someone else. After rehearsing your explanation to yourself, you realized that, with practice, you knew the material inside out and upside down. This experience is realized only when you are responsible for teaching the material to someone else. We learn when we teach. Mr. Watson knew there was no point in talking

Mr. Watson had assigned his seventh-grade students to read Chapter 4 in the social studies text. He explained that he would be discussing the chapter with them in today's lesson. Now, the students are slowly walking to their seats, which are arranged in groups of four. Some focus questions are written on the blackboard to guide today's discussion. Mr. Watson begins, "Good morning class. Today I want to discuss Chapter 4 on landforms from our text. Who can tell me, What is a landform?"

Mr. Watson is getting no response from the students. He rephrases the question: How many students have seen a butte? In what state are you likely to find a butte? Still there is no response from his students. Mr. Watson begins to notice that his students are ignoring him. Students are placing their heads down on their books to avoid eye contact with him. Others are looking away from the front of the room and are trying not to be noticed. Finally, Mr. Watson says, "Okay, class, I get the message. It is obvious to me that you are not ready to discuss this chapter on landforms because you have not read it. Is this right? Well then, we will have to try another strategy for learning this material."

"At your tables, please number yourselves from one to four." Students begin to talk and complete the numbering. "Now, I would like for everyone to take out a piece of paper and your book, opened to Chapter 4. All those with the number one will examine the first five pages of Chapter 4, pages 46–51. Your task is to meet and write a summary of this material. You will have 20 minutes to complete your work. Those with the number two will summarize pages 52–56. Number threes will take the next five pages, pages 57–61, and finally, the number fours will summarize pages 62–66. Everyone should take a piece of paper and your book. You will first survey, read, and then summarize the most important parts of the section you have been assigned. Remember to highlight and write the definitions for any boldfaced vocabulary words in your section. Each group will be given 20 minutes to complete its task. You may now move to meet with your group."

During the time that Mr. Watson's class is meeting in groups to review the various sections of the chapter, he monitors the work of the groups and listens as students first read and then discuss each section. After approximately 15 minutes, Mr. Watson asks the groups to write a summary statement of their section of the chapter and record the vocabulary words. Following the 20-minute time block, students are asked to return to their original tables. Each team member is now responsible for teaching his or her section summary to the other members of the group. Five minutes of time is allowed for each person to teach his or her section to the others seated at the table. Students can record notes as the information is presented from their team members. Mr. Watson then discusses with the entire class the sections of the chapter he would like the students to remember, and he clarifies any questions or concerns from the students. Mr. Watson has learned that a discussion of the chapter without students' knowledge of the material is not a good use of class time. However, allowing members to work together to learn the material benefits all students involved.

to himself because the students had not read the chapter. He switched his plan to focus on student learning, and what better way to get the students to learn than to ask them to teach the material to one another? Remember that we learn 90% of what we teach to someone else. This cooperative grouping arrangement is a powerful learning tool.

ASSESSMENT

One of the problems that teachers raise when engaging students in cooperative learning strategies is assessment. There is a myth that students are granted a group grade whenever cooperative learning is used. However, most teachers who regularly employ cooperative learning use a combination of group and individual assessment. You may apportion 20% of each individual's overall grade to their ability to function cooperatively, but a group grade should not be a part of the individual's overall assessment. How do you determine the individual learning, as well as the success of the group activity? Depending on the purpose of the cooperative learning activity and the age level and experience of the learners, you can construct a multiple-assessment strategy:

- Each individual could be responsible for summarizing his or her contribution to the group.

- The group project could be assessed as a whole, addressing the equal contributions of members.

- Individual's self-assessment and assessments of each other are other ways of determining who did what in the project.

- A typical quiz or test can be used to evaluate the content learned by each individual.

The important consideration here is making sure that each individual had the opportunity to learn the content you desired. Thus, assessment should focus on the student's ability to recall the content or apply the content to another activity, project, or topic. Remember, when you are using cooperative learning, you want to capitalize on students' learning from one another. Your task is to monitor that learning and ensure that what the students are learning academically is correct and matches your goals and objectives for the students.

At the beginning of the book, we outlined several tenets that are important for learning to occur. In the cooperative learning model, the most important tenet to consider is that the emotional system drives attention, and attention drives meaning and memory. If you are able to successfully establish a positive learning environment in which students respect each other, then asking students to work together can be a powerful learning tool. They will appreciate the opportunity to learn from one another. They will learn mutual trust. They will learn to share materials. They will become considerate of team members and develop empathy, respect, and admiration for each other and for the tasks to be learned. Emotions are remembered best, and students will never forget the feelings they had in your classroom as they learned. These emotional responses to their learning are likely to stay with them for life.

TECHNOLOGY

We would be remiss if we did not address how technology can be used effectively in the classroom. How you incorporate technology into your classes will depend on your skill with technology. Recognizing that technology is just another tool available to you and your students will help you to focus on how this tool can aid instruction.

In the cooperative learning environment, technology—specifically, the computer—can be used as a research and presentation tool. As a research tool, groups can access the Internet to get the content they need to complete their projects. They can learn effective and efficient research skills by using the search options available to them on the Internet. They can find original documents, video clips, pictures, essays, and research reports that will help them develop the content of their projects.

Depending on their skills, students can use the software available to them to develop the presentation. Whether the result is a written report highlighted with pictures and diagrams or a PowerPoint presentation is irrelevant as long as the content is correct. As a teacher, you need to be sure that you are not influenced by the presentation mode but by the quality of the content presented as you assess your students. Too often, as a teacher, you can be impressed by the technology skills of your students and overlook the academic quality of the project. Establishing a grading rubric prior to the final presentation of the projects will not only help your students to understand what is expected of them but also keep you on track while you are grading each student's work.

Learning Tenets
That Support Cooperative Learning

The brain seeks to classify information and the things to be learned.

Sometimes, content information cannot be understood when it is stated by the teacher. The reason this happens may not be clear, but it is true. Reflecting on my experience, I can remember stating what I thought were explicit directions to my middle school students. No sooner had I finished providing them with directions when two or three students were at my desk asking, "What I am supposed to do?" As the teacher, I would stare at them in disbelief, thinking to myself, "What planet were you on when I gave the directions?" The students would giggle. After more classroom experience, I discovered the phenomenon of cooperative learning. If you structure the academic task around cooperative learning groups and provide each group with a verbal or written summary of what is to be done, the teacher does not have to repeat the directions. Giving directions, stating learner expectations, and following procedures is much easier and can be better understood when students tell each other. Somehow, information coming from the teacher is not always heard or understood.

As we learn new things, we classify the new information with what is already stored. We use patterns in our spoken and written language. Information communicated from student to student is recognized, processed, and perhaps encoded more easily than if it is communicated from teacher to student. Communication between students is a pattern that can be more easily categorized and classified by students. Students approaching adolescence often create their own nonverbal signals or unique verbal language that is all their own. By using cooperative learning, communication between students becomes more efficient and possibly better understood.

The emotional system drives attention, and attention drives meaning and memory.

Cooperative learning and the emotional system go hand in hand in many ways. Cooperative learning affirms for students the importance of friends, mutual trust, and positive interdependence. When we work with others, we enjoy learning. The grouping arrangements supported by cooperative learning engage students' emotions and help them to attend to the learning task. However, if the learning arrangements are not positive, then the stress of learning in groups can impair students' potential. Therefore, it is important for the teacher to model appropriate positive emotions. Additionally, it is appropriate to model the social skills that support group work. Praise, encouragement, and sharing of materials are all affective qualities that are influenced by our emotions and necessary for successful cooperative groups.

Learning occurs in both conscious and unconscious states.

A good cooperative learning group is like a well-oiled machine. When it is working, the operation is automatic and sometimes unconscious. Students emote to one another. They have mutual trust, and they share materials. They enjoy the interaction with one another. When students are working well together, they are focused on the task at hand. Patterns of interaction are recorded in the brain as episodes. This episodic memory is cued by students' interactions with one another and the experience of working together. These patterns may or may not be conscious, but once they are cued, the conscious learning experience can be successfully recalled.

The brain is designed for ups and downs, not constant attention.

Teachers using cooperative learning begin with an overview of what the students will do and the specific behaviors that indicate success. In the overview, the new skills are explained and followed by guided practice. This routine divides the class time devoted to the specific content and allows for transitions to occur. Adding this dimension to the instructional routine is beneficial to students and to teachers planning instructional routines matched to the learners' ages. Remember, brief transitions between explanations of new skills followed by guided practice in cooperative learning support the learning and should not be a constant drill. Learning is best remembered when teachers consciously take a break from long explanations and change the state to support the downtime needed by the brain.

Learning occurs through processing and active engagement with visual, auditory, and kinesthetic modalities.

One of the advantages of using cooperative learning is that processing is built in as a basic tenet. According to Johnson and Johnson, students should process how well they are working together to monitor their progress while working in groups. Processing is one of the basic elements of successful cooperative group arrangements. Students working together must have ways to monitor their own progress as a group.

Processing is aimed at providing accurate, nonthreatening feedback on the procedures that the group is using to achieve its outcome goals. The feedback gives group members information that helps them to improve performance. Group processing depends on the following:

- Student-to-student interaction

- Observations to provide feedback to group members as individuals and to the group as a whole

- Reflection on feedback to identify problems the members are having in functioning effectively

- Plan for how to be more effective next time the group works together

Every learning experience is a lesson in collaboration when the group members process how well their group is functioning. Although a great deal of time and attention has been paid to structuring team materials and organizing instruction, little attention has been focused on training students to promote group processing to achieve collaborative efforts. Teachers must discuss which collaborative skills are and are not being used in the group and plan how they will improve their students' performance. Cognitive skills are matched with collaborative skills as group members learn group dynamics and interact with each other. Sometimes, processing will be quite brief. At other times, processing will be thorough and take more time. Whether the processing is thorough or brief, an integral part of group work is having groups reflect on their effectiveness.

Some of the most important reasons for having groups process include the following (Johnson et al., 1988):

- If students are to learn from their experience working in groups, they must reflect on that experience. Unexamined experience rarely benefits anyone.

- Problems in collaborating effectively may be prevented by group processing.

- Systematic processing of group functioning promotes the development and use of cooperative learning.

- When groups first begin to work together, they tend to be very task oriented. Processing gives the group the time it needs to maintain effective working relationships.

There are two basic options for providing members time to process how well they are collaborating. The first is to provide a few minutes at the end of each working session for immediate feedback. The second is to take a longer period of time and invite observers to watch the interaction of the group during a work session. When groups are being formed at the beginning of the year, it is best to allow the group to examine itself and reflect on its ability to work together. This emphasizes the self-examination and reflection that are necessary for the groups to be effective. It also provides an opportunity to discuss the group process while it is fresh in the group's memory.

Informal processing can be completed within the group in the following way. A prepared checklist or questionnaire could be used to record group members' impressions of how well they or the group functioned. The focus of the questions could be what the group member did (I, me), what other members did (you, they), or what all members did (we). After the group has completed the checklist following a planning session together, the group summarizes its perceptions.

A sample checklist or "stem" statement can be used. At the end of each work session, ask the group members to share their impressions verbally within the group. One of the following stems can be selected for each work session:

I observed . . .

I liked the way . . .

I saw . . .

I heard . . .

I noticed . . .

Ask each group member to complete one of the following . . .

I appreciated it when you (we) . . .

I liked it when you (we) . . .

I admired the way we . . .

I enjoy it when you (we) . . .

You really helped out the group when you . . .

Group members need to reflect on and analyze the group session they just completed to discover what helped and what hindered them in completing the day's work and whether specific behaviors had a positive or negative effect. Such reflection and analysis is generally structured by the group member assigned the role of checker or encourager.

If formal observation of the group's working relationships is desired by a visitor or observer, you must decide which skills and behaviors you are will emphasize and observe. Appoint observers and prepare an observation form for each one. The group that is being observed should be informed of the collaborative expectations that are to be demonstrated. The observer then reports to the group the information gathered, and group members report their impressions of how they behaved. Group members reflect on and analyze the effectiveness of their behavior by comparing their observed behavior with their own impressions and expectations for their performance. Group members publicly set goals for performing collaborative skills in the next group session.

Remember, group processing, group dynamics, and social-skill development are processes. Students need instruction in procedural learning to work successfully in groups, and time must be allowed for reflection so that group interactions can be enhanced.

Good teaching is about recognizing and selecting instructional patterns that match the context for learning and the students we are teaching.

Cooperative learning can be used effectively with second graders to adult learner and higher education classrooms. However, the context for learning and the students you are teaching make a difference and should be taken into consideration. Children with exceptionalities who are mentally or physically impaired cannot always work in groups or communicate with one another using class grouping arrangements. Obviously, adjustments for special needs populations must be made. However, some of the social skills associated with cooperative learning are universal to every classroom. The identification of these norms must be the job of the classroom teacher and must be implemented appropriately given the skills and abilities of each classroom.

Teachers will not become proficient in using cooperative learning by reading this book or taking a workshop. Teachers become proficient by doing. Developing expertise in cooperative learning procedures requires conscious planning, thought, and practice. One of the most important contributions that you can make to your school is to encourage cooperation among teachers and the use of cooperative learning in the classroom. Cooperation in your own classroom is easier to accomplish if there is a sense of cooperation in your school.

Summary

Cooperative learning is an interactive pattern of instruction that allows students and teachers to share the responsibility for learning. For this reason, it is best situated in Part IV of this book, "Teacher–Student Interactive Patterns." Roger and David Johnson emphasized the importance of social skills to learning outcomes. Robert Slavin stressed the mechanics of cooperative learning and developed several classroom structures. Five elements of cooperative learning are important to the success of this technique: positive interdependence, face-to-face interaction, individual accountability, interpersonal and small-group skills, and group processing.

If you choose this organizational pattern for your classroom, you will benefit from reading the section "Getting Started With Cooperative Learning" provided in this chapter.

Thought to Action

1. Select a chapter of material and plan a jigsaw strategy: Divide the content and assign students to become experts by teaching the sections to one another.

2. Identify the social skills that your class needs and create a lesson plan that supports how you will teach those social skills to your students.

3. Write letters to teachers in your area and interview them about their success with cooperative learning.

4. Examine several different models of cooperative learning and decide which would best suit your skills and content area.

5. Analyze your content area and identify at least three topics that could be taught using cooperative learning strategies.

ON YOUR OWN

Log on to the web-based student study site at http://www.sagepub.com/holt for access to a Standards-Based Student Project that will help you connect what you have learned in this chapter to your state's standards; study aids, such as electronic flashcards; and research recommendations, including journal article links and other Web resources.

9

Role Play

ROLE PLAY IS ONE OF THE MOST CREATIVE WAYS TO ENGAGE STUDENTS IN THEIR LEARNING. ROLE PLAY in its simplest form means asking the students to imagine that they are either themselves or another person in a particular situation. The role players are asked to behave exactly as they feel the other person would behave. As a result of engaging in this activity, the player, the class, or both will be in a better position to empathize with, understand the reactions of, and clarify the feelings, values, and attitudes of the person or the situation.

Role play is defined as the spontaneous practice of various roles that exist in society. Role play provides an opportunity to study social behavior and values in a safe environment. It is a way for students to discover and learn about human relation problems. When students engage in human interaction by acting out problem situations, they perceive other people's points of view and often see themselves and their behavior in a new light. Role play is referred to as "reality practice." Having students identify with others and recognize how their behavior affects others through role play is a major focus of the activity.

When you use role play, you will change the environment of your classroom. One of the basic assumptions about the use of role play is the belief that students have the ability to cope with their life situations and grow in their capacity to deal with problems intellectually in a safe, open environment. Role play demands that teachers patiently guide the activities and discussions so that students make their own discoveries and gradually move to higher levels of personal decision making. Important to the success of the role-play situation is that the enactment is neither good nor bad; rather, it is the best idea that is available to the students at the time.

The technique of role play can be used with a variety of ages. As you may know, children around age five use it naturally as part of their games when playing. However, using role play with young children in a classroom environment may have some drawbacks. Young children not only lack enough life experience to provide options and choices to situations, but also they have little knowledge of how to predict outcomes or draw conclusions about the consequences of their behavior. If you choose to use role play, you will need to (1) design the enactment, making

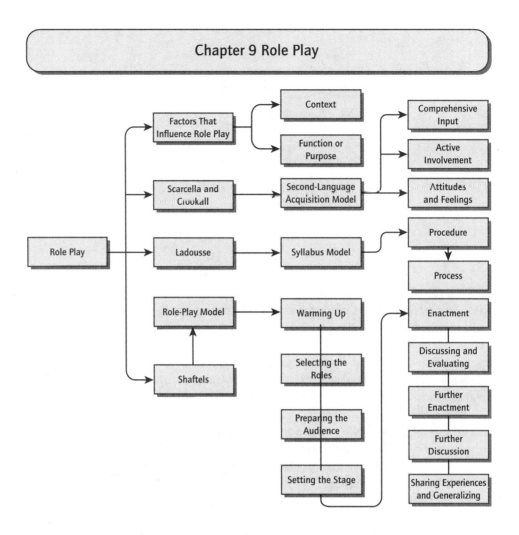

Chapter 9 Role Play

sure it is appropriate to the age and developmental level of your students; (2) describe when the enactment needs to stop; and (3) conduct a debriefing that will help the students to understand what happened during the enactment and what they learned. The debriefing and evaluation of each role play session are the most important steps in the role play. In fact, the ability to discuss the actions of the players within the roles is as important as the enactment itself.

As the teacher, you are responsible for guiding the enactment and creating a climate in which it is safe for pupils to explore behavior. You must help the group to respect the ideas and feelings of all members. Role play can engage an entire class, it can be fun, and it may lead to better learning. At the same time, role play is time-consuming and, if not planned appropriately, can be viewed as frivolous and may feel threatening to you and your students.

RESEARCH ANCHOR

The word "role" derives from the word used to describe the roll of parchment on which an actor's part was written. Therefore, role play descends from theatrical use, meaning an actor's part in a

This teacher is conducting a class meeting with the students to inform them of how they will use role play to resolve a classroom conflict.

drama. The extension of this concept of role to the way people behave in everyday life comes from a need in real life to summarize or condense what may be the complex perceptions of the constituent details of another person's appearance or behavior (Van Ments, 1983). Even though the word "role" is descendent from an actor's part in a drama, role play should not be confused with acting. Acting is the bringing to life of a dramatist's idea (or one's own idea) to influence and entertain an audience. Role play, on the other hand, is the experience of a problem situation under an unfamiliar set of constraints so that one's ideas may emerge and one's understanding may increase.

ROLE PLAY AND PERCEPTIONS

When your brain codes and groups information so that you can make comparisons and decisions, you are forming *perceptions*. As you examine the way different people behave in different situations, you form a perception of the role those persons play in those situations. Roles, then, act as a shorthand way of identifying and labeling a set of appearances and behaviors, with the assumption that these appearances or behaviors are characteristic of a particular person and predictable within a given situation. Roles may be ascribed to people in a variety of ways. In everyday life, for example, roles may be allocated by social position, such as teacher, wife, clerk, auto mechanic, priest, infant, or juvenile delinquent. In this way, roles may have reciprocal relationships: husband and wife, mother and child, doctor and patient, delinquent and parole officer. A role, then, is a way of expressing group norms and social pressures acting on an individual or a group. It characterizes a person's social behavior (Van Ments, 1983).

Factors That Influence Role Play

Context, or the surroundings in which you find yourself, can influence your role behavior. When you see yourself or other role players as members of a congregation, an audience, or participants in a parade, then the way you behave—your role—changes in accordance with your surroundings. Your behavior in church, for example, would be much more formal and serious than your behavior at a parade. Your behavior at a rock concert would certainly be different from your behavior at a symphony.

Roles can also be influenced by a person's *function* or *purpose.* People who are found in a hospital may be carrying out the tasks of a doctor, administrator, patient, visitor, or chaplain. People who are found in a school may be carrying out the tasks of a teacher, counselor, cafeteria worker, administrator, bus driver, student, or volunteer. Because roles are dependent on context, function, and purpose, when you plan to use role play in your classroom, you need to carefully think though the enactment, the roles, how you plan to have the students engage in the enactment, how you will assign roles, how long you will allow students to engage in the enactment, and how you plan to debrief once the enactment ends.

There are several interchangeable terms associated with this instructional pattern, and there is literature that compares and contrasts role play with other types of instruction. Interchangeable terms include "simulation," "game," "role play," "simulation game," and "role-play game." There does not seem to be agreement in the research on which term is preferred. However, Ladousse (1987) views simulation as complex, lengthy, and relatively inflexible. Role play, on the other hand, is simple, brief, and flexible. Simulations recreate real-life situations, whereas during role play, the participant represents and experiences some character type known in everyday life (Scarcella & Oxford, 1992). However, within a good simulation, there are

This group of students is brainstorming how they will perform during a role play.

elements of role play. Differences and similarities become evident when these two instructional patterns are compared.

Role play and simulations clearly promote effective interpersonal relations and social transactions among participants. For a simulation to occur, the players must accept the responsibilities of their roles and functions and do the best they can in the situation in which they find themselves (Jones, 1982). To fulfill their the responsibilities of their roles, the players must focus on utilizing effective social skills.

ROLE PLAY RESEARCH AND APPROACHES

Over the years, role play has been used to teach language content according to two different approaches. Research by Scarcella and Crookall (1990) shows how comprehensive input, active involvement, and attitudes and feelings are all components that facilitate second-language acquisition. The dialogue within the role play used to teach language can be specified (convergent) or unspecified (divergent). Patterns are specified within the convergent exchange and left unspecified in the divergent exchange. The difference is explained in Table 9.1.

The approach and outcomes involved in role-play situations can take various forms depending on the goals or objectives for the lesson. Considering the goal or objective is the first important step in planning the role play. For example, if the objective is to demonstrate proper etiquette while dining at a formal restaurant, the outcomes will benefit from genuine communication, active involvement, and positive attitudes. The simulated real-life problems help students to develop their critical-thinking and problem-solving skills. When considering this approach, as the classroom teacher, you must focus on the specific outcome or objective that you hope to accomplish with the role play.

Another approach, which uses a combination of procedure and process, is called the *syllabus model* (Ladousse, 1987). In this approach, explained by Skehan (1998), learner activities are included, but the activities are chosen by the teacher. For example, if the teacher selects an icebreaker activity called Famous People, described in Ladousse (1987), the students learn by guessing as one student adopts the role of a famous person. The other students ask questions of the volunteer to guess his or her identity. This game is more procedural in its design, but it is helpful for introducing students to role play and may ease their tension about role-play situations.

TABLE 9.1	Convergent and Divergent Patterns in Role Play
Convergent Model	*Divergent Model*
This is the problem, how shall we solve it?	This is the situation, what will we do?
The action has a "past."	The action takes place "on stage."
Roles are given in detail.	Roles have no constraints.
The organizer processes the action.	There are no formal steps or sequences.
The focus is what will happen.	The focus is what the players do.

Source: Christopher and Smith (1990).

The opposite of the procedural role play is the process role play, which may take place over several class periods. In the process model, the students are allowed to control the nature of the interactions that take place (Skehan, 1998). An example may be a singing competition. In this simulation, students might create a competition similar to the *American Idol* television show and designate a panel of judges and singers who will audition. When the roles and activities are defined by the teacher, the procedural syllabus is used. When the goals and activities are student driven, the process syllabus is used.

Learner roles have to be specifically defined, either through verbal directions or by role cards. Researchers such as Kaplan (1997) argue against role play that focuses solely on scripted theses because there is a loss of spontaneous flow and interaction.

The teacher generally defines the structure of the role play but does not actively participate once the structure is set. The topic of the role play should be relevant to the students to keep their interest and to stimulate their motivation. Jones (1982) describes the teacher as a traffic controller, helping to avoid bottlenecks but not telling students which way to go. Again, you do not want a teacher-centered classroom using this model. The teacher keeps a relatively low profile, and students are free to interact with each other spontaneously. This reduces anxiety and facilitates learning.

Other related research to role play is appearing in the literature. For example, role play has similar learner outcomes to storytelling. Both patterns of instruction have emotional elements that support meaning and attention. Bruner's research (1986) identified three components of good storytelling: *characters* taking actions with *goals* in settings using *means*. Characters who take on personality attributes and then take action toward an intended outcome or goal follow the steps in role play. The *means* refers to the tools used to accomplish the goals. The setting is also important to the role play, especially in the case of simulations of historical events. Storytelling is an engaging method of communicating and remembering information that dates back to the beginning of most civilizations. If the storyteller assumes the role of the person in the story, it brings the events in the story to life. Thus, the storyteller plays the role of a person or situation that is different from the current one to convey information to an audience.

The context of the classroom environment is a consideration for the type of effect or outcome of the role play or storytelling event. Considerations must be made given the ability and developmental level of the learners, the environment, and the skill of the teacher who is facilitating and processing each role-play enactment.

When the emotional system is exposed to role play and matched with appropriate learning outcomes, then the potential for attending to learning and meaning is accomplished.

Fannie and George Shaftel conducted research on the use of role play and authored the book *Role-Playing for Social Values: Decision-Making in the Social Studies* (1967). Their rationale for the use of role play is that it enables groups to relive critical incidents, explore what happened in them, and consider what might have happened if different choices had been made in the effort to resolve problems. They believed that young people need to learn from their mistakes under conditions that protect them from any actual penalty and have the advantage of group members who can help to explore the consequences of various choices of behavior. They proposed the following steps for the role-play enactment:

1. Warming up the group (problem confrontation)

2. Selecting the participants (role players)

Fannie Raskin Shaftel (1908–1999), professor emerita of education at Stanford University, died on March 21, 1999, at age 90. She had been an active member of the Stanford faculty for 27 years until her retirement in 1974. She specialized in social studies in elementary and secondary curricula. Her dissertation on the use of role playing in the teaching of American ideals provided a basis for her work at Stanford. Her particular interest was guiding youngsters to grasp the different viewpoints of other people and even to sympathize with those views.

In their classic book *Role-Playing for Social Values*, published in 1967, Fannie and George Shaftel offered curricular materials that simulated typical real-life situations of children and early adolescents. These ended with dilemmas to be solved by the children. When these stories are explored through role playing, the child makes a trial decision, confronts the consequences of that decision for oneself and others, and analyzes the values underlying the behavior. For example, in one situation, the child must choose between loyalty to the group and honesty. Through practice and analysis of their own decisions, children are educated in ethical behavior, integrity, and citizenship.

Source: *The Stanford Report*, Memorial Resolution: Fannie Raskin Shaftel, retrieved June 29, 2004, from http://news-service.stanford.edu/news/1999/december8/memshaftel-128.html.

3. Preparing the audience to participate as observers

4. Setting the stage

5. Role playing (enactment)

6. Discussing and evaluating

7. Further enactment (replaying, revising roles, playing suggested next steps, or exploring alternative possibilities)

8. Further discussion

9. Sharing experiences and generalizing

An elaboration of each step will help you to understand how important it is to follow such procedures when you plan to use role play as a learning strategy in your classroom.

The *warming-up stage* is used to develop an awareness of the students, to get the students emotionally familiar with the problem situation, and to help them identify with the individuals involved in the situation and the complexity of human relations that may arise while trying to find a solution to the problem. You should talk with the students about human characteristics such as embarrassment and dishonesty, and you should describe occasions when these characteristics might come into play.

The problem under discussion must be important to your students and one they can identify with immediately. The details of the specific problem should be presented to the students to get them emotionally involved in the enactment. You may allow the students to draw on situations they have experienced or use an actual incident they are familiar with. You may use a scene from a film, a television show, or a selection of literature. An effective way to introduce

The second step in the role play is selecting the participants.

the role play is to read the problem story to your class and stop at the dilemma. The problem story should be believable and interesting, and the basic situation should be real for the group. When you stop at the dilemma, a brief discussion should be held to lead the class into the role play. You can clarify any facts concerning the players before the role play begins.

Selecting the participants is done by you, the teacher. You know your students and can predict which students will be effective role players. You are aware of your students' personalities and can select the students who will do the best job. Avoid having classmates choose players for the roles because their motivations may not always be understood by themselves or by you. You are the only person who should assign roles. If you have adequately discussed the situation with the students, you may select students who identify with the characters or have asked questions about the players.

Setting the stage means that the students briefly plan what they will do. They do not plan the specific dialogue that will be said, but they plan, in a general way, a course of action. You may need to clarify for your students the physical props on the imaginary stage or remind the players of the roles they are to take. You must help the players get inside the situation as best they can to follow the line of action decided on.

Preparing the audience to be participant observers is important to the success of the role-play enactment. The audience must be trained listeners. Understanding another's point of view means taking a position regardless of whether you support or oppose the player's position. Taking a position is one of the best benefits of using role play; you hope that students will see things from a different perspective. Students need to listen to others' feelings and ideas in order to learn from another person's stance. Ideally, the students will go beyond listening and will be able to explore alternative positions in solving the problem under discussion in the enactment. To help students understand the necessity of good listening, you may assign specific observers' tasks to different students. If you are working with a beginning group, you may want the observers to focus on specific questions: How realistic was the enactment? Could this really happen? Do you think that the actors were behaving in a way that matched their assigned role?

During the *role playing* (enactment), the players will try to live the enactment. They will respond to one another's ideas and actions as they feel the people in those roles would behave. There is no set plot, only a moment in time, and players are thinking on their feet, spontaneously reacting to the developing action. No player is expected to present his or her role flawlessly. Slips or awkward moments are taken for granted. When real feelings are being portrayed, language can become vernacular. You should ensure that you do not judge the student who becomes an actor in a situation. No player is evaluated for his or her acting. Make sure your students know they will not be chastised for their interpretation of a role as they see fit. Remember, enactments are representations of real-life situations that are being explored, not performances that are being judged. You and your students should be concerned with whether the portrayal was true to life.

One of the most vital phases of role play is the *discussion and evaluation* that follow the enactment. During the discussion, the give-and-take of the problem-solving procedures are refined and learned. If the students have an emotional tie-in with the situation, they will usually be excited about sharing their opinions and reactions. You may want to consider some open-ended questions—What is happening? How does John feel?—to elicit responses from your students. The questions and discussion should guide your students toward consequential thinking, that is, looking ahead to the consequences of their behavior. If the discussion leads students to make statements such as, "I don't think I would have responded that way" or "People don't behave that way," then you need to guide the group's thinking by asking other questions: What would you have done? How do you think the people would have acted? If no alternatives are offered by the group, then you might ask, "Are there other ways of dealing with this situation?" This will lead to the next step of the process.

The advantage of role play over real life is that it provides multiple chances to solve a dilemma in a safe and positive environment. Facing problems on a practice level develops broader understanding. Different students may assume the roles so that other interpretations and solutions can be explored. Moving from the enactment to the discussion to the *reenactment* may be the most effective learning sequence for the students. A player who thinks that he or she has a rational way of solving a problem may find in an actual role play that his or her feelings get in the way of rationality. Eventually, students seek a balance between their feelings and their rational behaviors and are able to analyze their impulsive responses.

Once the same role-play situation has been reenacted with new players, *further discussion* can be held. A comparison of the first and second enactments can be made and more questions can be asked. Depending on the age group of your students, the same role-play situation can be reenacted as many as five times during one hour. The length of the discussions cannot always be predicted, so you should use good judgment in allowing multiple reenactments and follow-up discussions. When you believe that further discussion will not reveal any new ideas or points of view, you should stop.

The purpose of the final stage in the process, *sharing experiences and generalizing*, is to determine the relevancy of the enactment to the students' lives. You may start by asking, "Has anything like this happened to you or to someone you know?" By engaging your students in discussions that are more personal, you can help your students to see that they are not alone in their lives, that other people may share the same experiences and problems. Role play can also help your students to understand that classroom experiences and out-of-school experiences can be dealt with in a manner that brings these two separate parts of their lives together. Ideally, the discussion will lead students to conclude that general principles of conduct do exist regardless of where you are or what you are doing. Students may discover that getting away with some things that are deemed inappropriate in the adult world does not make them feel good once they really think about it. This may lead them to conclude that opportunistic solutions are not worth the loss of self-respect.

As the teacher, you must be aware that not all enactments will lead to these types of generalizations. Some enactments may only delineate the full detail of the nature of the problem. Even if no further generalizations can be drawn, addressing the social problems and conflicts that students may encounter during their lives will provide students with opportunities to learn about and better prepare for them. Maybe they will see a different way of looking at their world. Maybe, with further role play, a group will develop insights into problems that lead to generalizations. According to Shaftel and Shaftel,

> It is the opportunity to explore, through spontaneous (that is, unrehearsed) improvisational and carefully guided discussion, typical group problem situations in which individuals are helped to become sensitive to the feelings of the people involved, where the consequences of choices made are delineated by the group and where members are helped to explore the kinds of behavior that society will sanction. In this process, young people are guided to become sensitive to feelings, to the personal consequences of the choices they make, and to the consequences of those choices for other people. The group members practice many roles, or different approaches to roles, and gradually they develop skills for solving problems of social conduct and interpersonal relations. (1967, p. 84)

CLASSROOM SCENARIO

We are in a fifth-grade classroom in Northern Indiana. The students have just returned from lunch and are excitedly talking about what has just occurred in the lunchroom. Their teacher, Ms. Ralston, asks the students to settle down and take their seats. Ms. Ralston says, "Students, one at a time. Please raise your hand if you want to speak."

Apparently, two students from the class got into a squabble on the way to lunch. There was a race to see who could line up first to be served. Then, there was an argument about where the students should sit once they got their trays. This included an argument about whether girls should be allowed at certain tables. Once lunch began, there was an argument about trading slices of pizza. After listening to all the students who wanted to complain, Ms. Ralston displays her disappointment with her class. She is not only angry over the incidents that had occurred, but also she is disappointed that these kinds of incidents happen over and over again.

Finally, Ms. Ralston says, "We really have to face these problems. I'm sure many of you are growing tired of these same events occurring each day. So, we are going to discuss a technique that can help resolve our problems. We need to learn to operate successfully in our school so that we can resolve these issues and talk about them. We are going to divide up into groups of five, and each group is to write down the types of problems we've been having."

The students begin with the issue of how to line up for lunch and the race to be served. Then each group outlines other problems that have occurred. One person from each group reports the issues that his or her group came up with to the larger class. Some of the problems that the groups identified have consistently bothered the entire class. After examining the list of problems identified by class, the students are asked to group the problems by type. One issue has to do with the struggle for power. Another type has to do with being courteous. Another problem has to do with being fair to all people. Another problem is not having rules to deal with these problems.

Ms. Ralston assigns one problem to each group and asks the students to come up with situations in which these problems occur. After examining all of the situations in which these problems might occur, the students vote on one issue they want to talk about. The first issue they select is being fair to all students. Together, the class talks about how the problem develops. It begins when one group is left out. One group believes that it doesn't need to include the other group. The class explores some questions related to this problem. Together, the class answers some of the questions posed by Ms. Ralston, and then the students are asked to act out an incident using role play.

Several students are selected to enact the situation. Others are asked to be observers. The observers are asked to recall what was said during the enactment and how the development of each point occurred. After a short period of time, when the students are shouting in the middle of the room to each other, Ms. Ralston calls time. Then the students are asked to explain what occurred and what was going on. At this point, everyone is eager to talk. Many students point out that the attitude of the role-play participants was not fair and that unfair judgments were being made. No one was listening to the other person's point of view. No one had a real solution to the problem or could say how to resolve these disputes.

Ms. Ralston begins to explore questions with the group. She asks for ways that people might behave in this kind of conflict. Finally, an important question is raised by the group: Can we develop a policy about being fair to each other? The class decides to reenact the scenario, allowing one group to rule the other. The enactment takes place. This time, the players attempt to follow the policy that one group should have power over the other. Once again, the enactment results in a shouting

match. This time, the observers point out that the role players acted as if there were no solution to the problem and that power can be a problem when one group forces power on another.

Ms. Ralston poses more questions, and the students are asked to explore their feelings. Each side explores what it is like to have power and not to have power. Students recognize their behavior is much like what happens to people in real life. Students then decide if they are to be fair to each other, then attitudes and behaviors must change. They decide to try a third enactment, this time with new role players. After the third enactment, the students point out that within their classroom, a system to ensure order must be in place and that their attitudes must change. This means resolving conflicts systematically and establishing a set of guidelines for behaving and treating each other fairly.

The discussion continues as Ms. Ralston opens up another set of issues for the students to explore. The exploration of other areas of dispute continues until students realize that a basic set of values governing individual behavior must be in place as an operating principle for their classroom. Pretty soon, the students begin to see the problems of communal living, and they begin to develop policies for governing their own behavior, as individuals and as a group. Students begin to negotiate. They decide there should be a judge and a jury within their class so that problems can be aired. The judge and jury will be allowed to decide the punishment for students who do not behave according to Ms. Ralston's rules and the school's student code of conduct.

After the class establishes this policy for monitoring student behavior, only two incidents of bad behavior occur. The students who had been previously locked in conflict gradually learn that if they behave and change their attitude, others may also modify their behavior, and problems will become easier to solve.

ASSESSMENT

If you review the steps of the role play proposed by George and Fannie Shaftel, you will note that the assessment is built into the role of the observers. In most classroom environments, observers are asked to watch for certain details of the enactment as a means of assessing the process. The teacher can pose some guiding questions for each observer as the enactment takes place. These questions allow for good discussion as the group processes what has occurred. These outcomes are a part of the process for learning, but an additional outcome of role play may be students' ability to see things from another point of view. The kinds of outcomes that students benefit from learning include objectives in the affective domain such as empathy, self-concept, and what makes people angry, sad, or disappointed. Having students identify with others and recognize how their behavior affects others through role play is a major focus of the activity. When you use role play, you will change the environment of your classroom. One of the basic assumptions about the use of role play is the belief that students have the ability to cope with their life situations and grow in their capacity to deal with problems intellectually in a safe, open environment. The following is a sample assessment technique called "PMI":

- The observers in the class sit in groups of three or four with a large sheet of chart paper.
- Ask the students to divide the chart paper into three columns: P, M, and I.

   P stands for the pluses.

   M stands for the minuses.

   I represents the things that were the most interesting.

This provides an excellent way for the students to process and discuss their reactions to the role-play enactment.

TECHNOLOGY

Many advances have occurred in technology that have influenced the use of role play and role-play environments. One such environment, *massively multiplayer online role-playing games* (MMORPGs), creates virtual worlds that have the capability of holding thousands of players at once. The online environments *Everquest* and *The Realm* are both popular MMORPGs. These online games have become so popular because of their role-playing aspects. Players enter virtual three-dimensional worlds in which they can become warriors, magicians, or heroes. Players keep coming back because the enactments occur at different skill levels, and players cannot complete tasks until they master certain skills. People in MMORPGs complete goals in a scenario set out by the game designers by role playing characters and using their means. Players learn to solve problems in environments set by the game designers. As players become involved in MMORPGs, they search the World Wide Web for clues to solve the problems posed by the game. The online collaboration of these games increases their lifespan. Manufacturers continue to add new content to extend the player's duration of engagement. One drawback of MMORPGs is that they do not allow players to author new content.

Other types of environments are called *multi-user domains* (MUDs). These MUDs include Sony's *Virtual Fighter,* Capcom's *Street Fighter II,* and Midway's *Mortal Kombat.* Often, MUDs are spaces provided on the Internet that are used for social interaction (Geier, 1998). When playing, a user assumes the role of a fighter and possesses the ability to win tournaments or defend himself or herself. The outcome goal is the same for each of these games, which is a limitation for the user. The idea is to win or to reach the goal within the design of the game. Unlike a role-play enactment, in a classroom environment, the outcome is always the same; therefore, these games may cause boredom on the part of the user.

Other software products that support the use of role play are Tom Synder's *Decisions, Decisions 5.0.* In this program, students learn history by assuming the role of a mayor, president, or a noble during a time of war. The software is designed with scaffolds for decision making and critical thinking about topics from various eras. The purpose of this software is to assist the learner with decisions and to relate these decisions to everyday life.

In the *goal-based scenarios* developed by Schank, Fano, Bell, and Jona (1994), students role play an important figure in a situation in order to learn skills related to certain occupations. For example, learners role play news anchors to develop a news broadcast; this exercise is designed to motivate them and provide a context for learning about current events.

Aside from software and online Internet uses, several examples of role play can be found in the entertainment Industry. Reality shows that depict individuals in various real-life situations have become increasingly popular. *Big Brother* and *Survivor* are two television programs in which viewers tune in each week to watch as players depict roles in a house or particular outdoor setting, all vying for money. Immersive environments for entertainment capture the attention of the audience better than passive environments. The Court TV network has become popular, as have talk shows that feature people trying to resolve their personal or legal problems on air.

Television has had quite an influence on students. Though not related to role play in a classroom environment, students often view television and witness through the entertainment world examples of role play. Role playing from the entertainment world may include television dramas, movies, or comedy acts. Television has become a standard for storytelling in modern culture. The viewing audience watches television programs that involve stories and role plays. Dramas, both fictional and nonfictional, portray moral dilemmas in 30-minute segments. Movies are extended forms of dramas that also convey messages through many scenarios, sometimes happening all at once within the same story. Comedians who role play politicians are entertaining viewers but at the same time portraying the many nuances and personality traits of the political figurehead. The American public is probably persuaded and informed through television more than print forms of media such as newspapers. Therefore, the entertainment world, through the use of television and movies, is having a profound effect on the culture of our society.

Learning Tenets
That Support Role Play

The brain seeks to classify information and the things to be learned.

Humans learn to classify information from the experiences we have had and from our ability to see interactions with one another. Learning depends on prior conceptions that the learner brings to the experience. As teachers allow students to explore structured role-playing activities, the learner is provided with a means to construct new knowledge and meaning based on the observation of role-play enactments or participation in them. Another advantage of role play is that learning is dependent on the shared understandings of what learners negotiate with each other.

Teachers can use role-play strategies to facilitate conceptual change depending on the congruence of the concepts with student understanding and conceptualization. One of the key elements of role play is that conceptual change can be used as a teaching method, resulting in a unique classification of information.

The emotional system drives attention, and attention drives meaning and memory.

Role play evokes our emotions from the beginning to the end. Whether students are engaged in the enactment or serve as focused observers, the emotional benefits of the experience are likely to be remembered. When students' emotions become overstressed, you need to intervene to maintain a comfort level that is appropriate for all. Role play should be seen as a practical way to explore ideas, learn from them, and incorporate that learning into one's repertoire of skills for active living.

Learning occurs in both conscious and unconscious states.

Human understanding and one's level of acceptance of others are often determined during the first five years of life. A student's belief system is shaped by his or her cultural and family background, and this, in turn, influences his or her interactions with others. When it comes to discriminatory practices and judgments, students may not be conscious of their prejudices. Role play can help students to develop other points of view by putting themselves in another person's shoes, in turn influencing their conscious and unconscious views. Increasing the sensitivity to others is an important goal for all learners, and one way to do this is through the role-play pattern of instruction.

Learning occurs through processing and active engagement with visual, auditory, and kinesthetic modalities.

Processing of the enactment is built into the steps of the role-play model. The sixth stage is about discussing and evaluating. Providing the observers with some leading questions before the enactment begins focuses the role players so that the situation can be discussed. Leading questions might include the following:

What did you notice?

What kind of emotion was expressed?

If this situation were real, how might you feel?

A technique that can be used to assess the enactment is called "PMI." This technique allows students to provide feedback in a nonjudgmental format using the highest level of thinking evaluation. Students can work in groups or as individuals. If you have students work in a group, assign a recorder, a summarizer, and two encouragers for groups of four. If you have five-member groups, also assign the role of checker. Students divide a piece of paper (chart paper works best for groups) into three distinct columns: P, M, and I. Following the role-play enactment, the students record the positive outcomes in the P column, negative outcomes in the M column, and the most interesting things in the I column. This allows students to evaluate the role-play enactment.

Good teaching is about recognizing and selecting instructional patterns that match the context for learning and the students we are teaching.

Knowing your students and understanding whether they can handle the role-play technique is important. There are many other ways that you can address important values and questions of behavior and citizenship without using the role-play model. Not all students can deal with this type of format. In the end, it is your classroom, and you must make the decisions about what is best and whether this strategy will work with the class of students you have. Knowing what works with them is truly a characteristic of an effective teacher.

Summary

Role play is best suited to Part IV of this book, "Teacher–Student Interactive Patterns," because learning outcomes are shared between the teacher and the student in this interactive pattern. Effectively administering role-play sessions in the classroom requires many skills on the part of the teacher. You must know your students well enough to understand the appropriateness of role play as an instructional pattern. When used appropriately, role play can have a powerful influence on students and can assist them with problem situations.

Thought to Action

1. Select the student code of conduct from a local school or school district. Partner with a friend from class and write a role play about how a teacher might handle the following conflicts. Use the school's code of conduct to facilitate the appropriate action. In your description, provide the demographics of your classroom, the role players, and the enactment.
   - Negotiating differences of opinion with your students
   - Designing contracts for improving student behavior
   - Explaining the discipline infraction of a child in your classroom to his or her irate parent.

2. Select an academic standard from the state and design a role-play lesson to meet that standard. Identify the subject and grade level and write the enactment.

3. Psychology tells us that people do not behave the same way with different groups of people. Students may behave one way in the classroom and a different way at home or with friends. Explore why people may not behave the same way in every situation. For example, you would not behave the same way in front of your parents as you would in front of your friends. Why?

4. Role play can be used to explore conflicts between groups of people. Imagine that a student has used inappropriate language in your class. Role play this incident as if you were the teacher. Explain how you would communicate this incident to the student's parent or guardian. Explain how you would tell your school administrator what occurred. Put yourself in the place of the student and explore this incident from his or her point of view. Examine the similarities and differences between the approaches and how the enactment differed depending on the individuals involved.

ON YOUR OWN

PART V

Student-Centered Patterns

Chapter 10:
Nondirective Learning

Chapter 11:
Self-Taught Instruction

S tudent-centered instruction occurs when the learner comes first. The approach is based on psychology as a human science rather than a natural science. Chapter 10 explores nondirective learning and Chapter 11 looks at self-taught instruction. These chapters reflect a pattern of learning that is focused on helping each student "actualize" and become an emotionally healthy person. The rationale is that learners seek knowledge as they need it and make wise personal decisions independently throughout their lifetimes when presented with these patterns of instruction. Teachers are facilitators who may provide a rich array of materials, give emotional support, and clarify dialogue but do not instruct the learner or present a predesigned curriculum. The learners guide their own progress in self-taught instruction.

Nondirective instruction, a model advocated by Carl Rogers, is considered student centered. When learners depend on their own motivation for the completion of an instructional task, then this type of learning is regarded as student centered. Motivation and task independence may exist within other instructional patterns, but when the learner is the primary focus, these instructional patterns are considered student centered.

10

Nondirective Learning

NONDIRECTIVE LEARNING IS A STUDENT-CENTERED MODEL OF INSTRUCTION. PETERS (1994) PLACES it at the crossroads of the personal and emotional learning paths because the model incorporates personal insight and learning preferences with emotional involvement. Nondirective learning is considered democratic in that it focuses on the unique feelings and experiences of each person involved, and no one can prohibit feelings (Coulson, 1989). It also emphasizes responsibility and intention in human behavior (Clark, 2000), encouraging learners to move toward valuing themselves and expressing feelings honestly (Daniels, 2002). Major personal learning decisions are made by the student; the teacher functions as a facilitator, providing resources, emotional support, and feedback. There is challenge as well as freedom in the approach because learners are expected to rise to their highest possible potential with the support of facilitating professionals (Warmoth, 2002).

Although nondirective learning has roots in several educational and counseling traditions and has been incorporated into the work of numerous contemporary educational theorists, it is indelibly identified with therapist and university professor Carl Rogers. Rogers is also credited with creating the modern concept of counseling psychology, establishing the study of humanistic psychology with Abraham Maslow (Kirschenbaum, 1979), and developing the encounter group. However, his main contribution to both counseling and education was that he "turned the social system upside down" (Gendlin, 1988, p. 127) with his revolutionary method of letting the client (or learner) take charge and work out his or her problems without direct intervention or instruction from the therapist (or teacher).

RESEARCH ANCHOR

Rogers built his own clinical theory around "actualization," the idea that all creatures naturally strive to make the very best of their existence and themselves. Mental illness, criminality, and

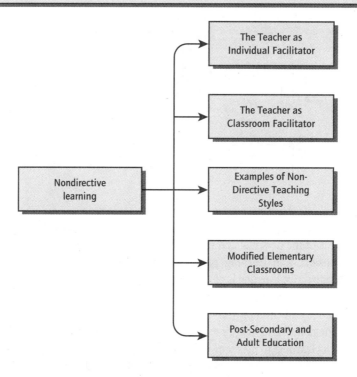

Chapter 10 Nondirective Learning

The Teacher as Individual Facilitator

The Teacher as Classroom Facilitator

Examples of Non-Directive Teaching Styles

Modified Elementary Classrooms

Post-Secondary and Adult Education

Nondirective learning

lack of motivation, Rogers believed, are all distortions of this natural tendency and can be overcome through therapy of the correct variety (Boeree, 1998). A person is effective in achieving self-enhancement to the same degree that he or she is open to experiencing what is truly happening within (Rogers, Stevens, Gendlin, Shlien, & Van Dusen, 1967). People who accept and incorporate new experiences and listen to themselves will become increasingly complex and survive better because they are more tolerant and flexible; those who shut out change instead became rigid (Boeree, 1998).

Many people live conflicted lives because they internalize the judgments made by others, which makes them avoid new experiences and ideas that do not fit their imagined or "ideal" selves. Resisting change and experience—and therefore, actualization—clients never reach their mythical ideal, and so condemn themselves to constant failure and frustration (Vavrus, 1999). Although culture is an important part of the individual—and Rogers made a point of accepting minority, gay, and female clients without any judgment or conventional advice—he acknowledged that culture can take on a life of its own and interfere with actualization, making worth, regard from others, and self-regard conditional on conforming to norms (Boeree, 1998).

The most radical part of Rogers's theory, however, was his conviction that the client usually knows how to proceed better than the therapist. As described by Gendlin (1988), in the nondirective counseling theory, every person makes internal sense, even if he or she appears severely psychotic to others, and that sense evolves and becomes healthier as the person's self-actualization develops. If the therapist has genuine honesty (congruence), the ability to see life from the client's view (empathy), and acceptance of whatever feelings emerge as well as respect for the other as a person (unconditional positive regard or prizing), then the client will improve (Boeree, 1998). Rogers (1969) further explained that when a person finds someone who listens acceptingly to the feelings he or she is expressing, that person starts to listen to himself or herself as well. Anger or fear can be recognized and accepted. Allowing the client to control the process permits deeper steps, circumvents defenses, and actually permits the therapist maximum closeness without imposing on the client.

Rogers discovered through his own experience that his clients progressed faster if he avoided dealing with what the patient had said, pushing the person in some way, or agreeing and disagreeing with certain statements. Instead, he simply listened and checked his comprehension immediately and out loud, attempting to grasp exactly what the client intended to convey (Gendlin, 1988). Rogers called this *reflection*: mirroring the immediate statement concisely, no matter how violent or outrageous, to inform the client what he or she appeared to be communicating (Boeree, 1988). The client would correct Rogers, refine the statement (calmly or not), then think silently and eventually produce a deeper insight without prompting or hints (Gendlin, 1988).

Rogers (1961) came to believe that the important question is not, "How can I cure or treat this person?" but, "How can I provide a relationship which this person may use for his personal growth?" (p. 32). He realized that an authoritarian approach might work well at first, but would leave the client dependent. A better idea would be to let the client develop insights and try them in real life beyond the therapist's office (Boeree, 1998). This technique would require great restraint from the therapist, but the client would benefit most from expressing attitudes and feelings until insightful understanding spontaneously appeared (Coulson, 1997).

Rogers envisioned clients moving away from facades, "oughts," and pleasing others as goals (Rogers et al., 1967, p. 25) and eventually becoming "fully functioning"—being open to experience without being defensive, being creative, living in the present, trusting the inner self, and taking responsibility for all decisions. The client could then comfortably choose to conform to or live outside conventional boundaries while accepting personal responsibility for the choice. As one client stated, "I don't know what I'm gonna do, but I'm gonna do it!" (Rogers et al., 1967, p. 144). Rogers first called his theory "nondirective," but later he changed it to "client-centered" (because he realized that clients read direction into his remarks even when he was not directing them) and finally to "person-centered" to avoid the connotation of illness and the all-knowing doctor (Boeree, 1998).

Accepting a full professorship at The Ohio State University in 1940, Rogers began to look for broader application for his theories. He felt that his model had the most impact in education and nursing, both fields that he believed were lacking in compassion, relevance, and practical experience (Gendlin, 1988). Education and medicine, Rogers felt, were stifled by excess dependence on tradition, reputation, and dogma. As he later told Robert Evans, "[C]onventional education from primary school to graduate school is probably the most outdated, incompetent, and bureaucratic institution in our culture. It's also pretty much irrelevant to the interests of the students" (Rogers, 1975, p. 37).

Typically, Rogers started his education research with his own teaching—his personal experience. He had already begun recording individual therapy sessions during the 1930s (much to the dismay of his professional colleagues), both to be able to review exactly how and to what a client had reacted and to share experience with his interns. He brought in both models and failures and invited group analysis so that the young therapists were not afraid to admit their own

Carl Ransom Rogers (1902–1987) was the most influential psychotherapist in American history. He pioneered a major new approach to psychotherapy, known successively as the "nondirective," "client-centered," and "person-centered" approach. He was the first person in history to record and publish complete cases of psychotherapy. He carried out and encouraged more scientific research on counseling and psychotherapy than had ever been undertaken anywhere. More than any individual, he was responsible for the spread of professional counseling and psychotherapy beyond psychiatry and psychoanalysis to all the helping professions—psychology, social work, education, ministry, lay therapy, and others.

Rogers was a leader in the development and dissemination of the intensive therapeutic group experience, sometimes called the "encounter group." He was a leader in the humanistic psychology movement during the 1960s through the 1980s, an idea that continues to exert a profound influence on society and the professions. He was a pioneer in applying the principles of effective interpersonal communications to resolving intergroup and international conflict.

Rogers was one of the helping professions' most prolific writers, authoring 16 books and more than 200 professional articles and research studies. Millions of copies of his books have been printed, including more than 60 foreign-language editions of his works.

Source: "About Carl R. Rogers," retrieved July 1, 2004, from http://www.saybrook.edu/crr/papers/valhow.html; "Personality Theories," retrieved July 1, 2004, from http://www.ship.edu/~cgboeree/rogers.html.

confusion or mistakes. Rogers found preworded diagnoses to be "inadequate, prejudicial, and often misused" (Gendlin, 1988, p. 128), so he simply eliminated them from his records and vocabulary, preferring to picture each client as a unique experience, and he taught his trainees to do the same. He applied his nondirective therapeutic model of honesty, empathy, and acceptance to his classes. When he met with his graduate students, he handed out lists of available resources, asked for suggestions as to the direction of the syllabus, and pursued the logic of each student's proposal. He discovered that without specific assignments, the students actually worked harder and read more than conventional peers (Gendlin, 1988).

Moving to the University of Chicago, Rogers put his theories to work in the university's laboratory school, with mixed political and clear academic results. In 1951, when a committee from the University Council evaluated the school, its report was critical of Rogers's educational philosophy and demanded concrete demonstrations of growth in knowledge and "not such concern for happiness, socialization, and democratic principles" (Kirschenbaum, 1979, p. 183). However, the members did admit that lab school students were about three years ahead of their peers in basic intellectual skills.

Rogers quietly continued to refine his research and his student-centered teaching model, including it in his book *Client-Centered Therapy* in 1951 and finally presenting his classic model

Carl Rogers believed that developing a relationship with a person was an important step in growth.

in *Freedom to Learn: A View of What Education Might Become* (1969). Rogers's theory was hailed as the beginning of inclusion and diversity in educational philosophy because his emphasis on unconditional positive regard "at least implies tolerance, and ideally acceptance" (Warmoth, 2002, p. 1). Informal and special educators were among the first groups to be attracted to Rogers's educational work because his counseling-based model and emphasis on the person instead of the subject matter seemed more relevant to their work and their struggling students (Smith, 2002). A wave of international interest followed. Rogers became a featured speaker at national conferences of the Association for Supervision and Curriculum Development, and he was invited to contribute articles to such prestigious publications as the *Harvard Education Review, Educational Leadership,* and *The National Education Association Journal* (Kirschenbaum, 1979).

Like most ideas, Rogers's nondirective learning was met with controversy. Rogers was both a gifted teacher and a committed practitioner who looked to his own experience, so he was difficult to dismiss as a mere theoretical academic (Clark, 2000). However, controversy swirled. Journal articles suggested that Rogerian nondirective learning would only work for students who were already independent learners, just as Rogerian therapy would only work if the client "desires change and is willing to do the work" (Rowan, 2002). Critics insisted that Rogers's view was naive and simplistic, especially after a large-scale experiment with an entire Catholic school district in California yielded some emotional benefits but also caused hostility and disintegration that required large-scale conflict-resolution and staff counseling from a third party (Kirschenbaum, 1979). A former associate accused Rogers of substituting feelings for reason and teaching students to replace moral absolutes with "running the risks of personal growth" (Coulson, 1989, p. 18), making them susceptible to fringe ideologies and risk taking. Others pointed out that Rogers was denying or ignoring his own considerable teaching ability and stature when he claimed that the students directed his classes (Smith, 2002) and that practitioners who were less skilled and trained often turned individual or group sessions into pointless parroting that frustrated and insulted students (Coulson, 1989; Gendlin, 1988).

The model's lack of specific teaching techniques or academic training methods caused concern; inexperienced and insecure devotees of Rogers were accused of using coercion to make students follow the principles of congruence, empathy, and unconditional regard, a gross violation of those very principles (Zimring, 1994). Some educators worried about selfish "person-centeredness" in students (Smith, 2002), about the frustration of young students forced to make their own undirected choices among multiple and usually conflicting consequences (Evans, 1975), and about the length of time that might be needed to develop open emotions and then learn to control and shift away from those feelings "when further rumination is counterproductive" (Lopes & Salovey, 2001, p. 13). School districts' nervousness and parents' demands caused a schizophrenic reaction in teachers: "Schools may recognize the need to bolster socioemotional development, but educators are less likely to promote it unless they can see clear correlations to achievement" (Zins, Weissburg, Wang, & Walburg, 2001, p. 2). Throughout the running battles, Rogers did not argue with critics but simply listened carefully and with interest, stated his position politely and clearly, and followed through on his own actualization until his death following hip surgery in 1987 (Gendlin, 1988).

Rogerian concepts have been mirrored or incorporated by other prominent modern theorists, including Malcolm Knowles, D. A. Kolb, Thomas Gordon, Maxine Greene, and Paulo Freire. Kolb wrote an entire book on experiential learning, stating, "Learning is the process by which knowledge is created through the transformation of experience" (Pontius, Dilts, & Bartlett, 2000). Gordon, a student of Rogers, developed "parent-effectiveness training" and "teacher-effectiveness training," both based on the nondirective model of individual therapy (Coulson, 1997).

Knowles, a Depression-era Harvard graduate who parlayed a desperate first job running work-study and YMCA adult programs into a fortune, used observation and borrowed ideas, including those of Rogers, to design what he later called *andragogy*, or adult pedagogy (Carlson, 1989). The theory of andragogy states that adults have a psychological need to be self-directing. In pedagogy, the learner is dependent, and the teacher applies sufficient pressure and determines what, when, how, and whether learning takes place. Adults, however, learn only when they want to do so, and a teacher of adults must discover what they want to know (Pontius et al., 2000). Adults need to learn experientially, need to know why, and learn best if the information has immediate value for real-life tasks (Kearsley, 1999).

Knowles's interest began after a YMCA class with a noted professor dwindled to nothing. Another class with an amateur astronomer who asked what students wanted to learn and set up treks to the roof on clear nights was standing-room only. Knowles, intrigued, wrote an article called "The Day I Changed From Teacher to Facilitator of Learning" (Carlson, 1989, p. 3).

Knowles earned a doctorate, borrowed the term "andragogy" from visiting Yugoslav scholar Dusan Savisevic, and went on the road as a writer and lecturer. He held a prestigious adult education directorship at Boston University until concern over the free-form degrees that Knowles had approved forced him to North Carolina State in 1974. He continued to push his theory on the lecture circuit until his long absences and obvious commercialism finally culminated in his forced retirement in 1979. Andragogy faded in academia, but not in popular and informal educational circles (Carlson, 1989).

Noted philosopher Maxine Greene frequently incorporates the vision of the learner who is open to a personal world and experiential learning into her writing. Although Greene advocates a curriculum based on the humanities instead of nondirective choice, she is a fervent proponent of discovery as the basis of growth. In "Curriculum and Consciousness," she commented that literature is an author's effort to understand his or her own experience, and being a learner means "remaining in contact with one's own perceptions, one's own experiences, and striving to constitute their meaning" (Greene, 1978). Greene (1978) described prepared conclusions and explanations as weighting down learners and making them passive. Again advocating personal exploration and individual discovery in her 1995 book *Releasing the Imagination,* she commented, " [I]t is perhaps the refusal to control what is discovered as meaningful that strikes traditional educators as at odds with their conception of norms or their notions of appropriate cultural literacy" (p. 125). Greene viewed education as helping students realize the deep connection and responsibility they have to their own individual experience and to other human beings.

Other than Carl Rogers, the educational expert most closely aligned with nondirective learning is Brazilian theorist Paulo Freire. Freire, who called his book and the strategy outlined in it *The Pedagogy of the Oppressed* (1970), began his work in the slums of São Paulo, finding groups of displaced rural workers and providing them an "education of liberation" using materials of their choosing, with the goal of gaining political power (Facundo, 1984). In the 40 years since, projects from food-growing training, clowning, childbirth preparation, and massage to graduate degrees based on the literature of a cohort's ethnic group have been facilitated globally by Freire and his disciples, each project designed by the students and run according to their needs (Smith, 2001). Nondirective learning is alive and well around the world.

Carl Rogers based his educational model on the premise that the purpose of education is to produce emotionally healthy, actualized persons who learn by experience, make intelligent choices for their own situations, take responsibility for themselves, and are open to learning and change throughout their lives (Warmoth, 2002). The qualities that define true education are personal involvement (feeling as well as thinking), self-initiation (discovery), pervasiveness (a change in behavior or attitude), and self-evaluating acceptance (self-recognition that the knowledge is meeting the learner's needs) (Kirschenbaum, 1979, p. 375). In nondirective learning, students guide their own education (as clients guide therapy) according to their needs and interests, with teachers as facilitators who participate as equals and provide support and materials as needed. Rogers's model is "an explicit philosophy of learner-centered education, and an implicit philosophy of democratic power structure" (Warmoth, 2002).

Rogers described the process of learning as stating uncertainties, trying to clarify puzzles, and getting closer to the meaning of one's own experience (1961, p. 277). According to Rogers, there are two types of learning: meaningless (cognitive) and significant (experiential). Meaningless learning is rote memorization, such as multiplication tables and lists. Significant learning takes place when the knowledge addresses the needs or wants of the individual (Dover, 1999), when the content matters to the learner (Kirschenbaum, 1979), or when the subject is relevant to the personal interests of the student (Kearsley, 1998). It strengthens the student psychologically, enables him or her to deal with life and solve problems, and facilitates the setting and achievement of goals (Kirschenbaum, 1979, p. 374). Significant learning is self-directed and experiential, and it uses both intellectual and intuitive processes (Daniels, 2002).

Carl Rogers commented, "To know who won the battle of Poltava or when the umpteenth opus of Mozart was first performed may win $64,000" (1961, p. 281), but such knowledge is not learning. Significant learning must make a difference in the attitude of the person, pervading his or her behavior and actions.

TABLE 10.1	Carl Rogers's Basic Therapy Model: Definitions
Congruence	*Real, genuine openness and honesty*
Defenses	Denials and perceptual distortions used by persons to make a situation appear less threatening
Ideal self	Mental creation based on being forced to live without regard; unattainable myth
Incongruity	Gap between one's real self and ideal self; cause of mental suffering (neurosis)
Organismic valuing	Each person knowing best what is good for himself or herself
Positive regard (unconditional)	Emotional support and nonpossessive affection without conditions or terms
Positive self-regard	Sense of self-worth (esteem) created by the regard of others
Real self (fully functioning)	What a person can become with positive support

Personal experience is the only true means of education. Presenting secondhand conclusions is like retelling a personal adventure to a friend. The story is almost never as real to someone who was not there—it is just a listening exercise (Levine, 2002). One person's truth may not serve another person's best interests or even make sense based on another's life experiences. "Benefits from solutions just do not trickle down" (Sapp, 2000, p. 12). Eeva Reeder (2002) concurred: "No one can become a world-class chef simply by attending lectures . . . This isn't news, really. Back in 270 BC, Sophocles said, 'We learn by doing.'"

THE TEACHER AS INDIVIDUAL FACILITATOR

Your role as a nondirective educator is to engage in positive interaction with a single student. Your job is to act as a facilitator, following the student's thoughts rather than directing questions for the purpose of eliciting information and always focusing on the student's feelings, relationships, insights, and experiences (Joyce, Weil, & Calhoun, 2000). One-on-one teaching is not a simple process. Teachers must study both the student and the situation. Student needs cannot be determined ahead of time, and the teacher-facilitator must listen to the student's feelings and be ready with resources for what the student may need or become in the future (Thompson, 1998).

In a person-to-person situation, the nondirective teacher-facilitator exhibits the characteristics of congruence, defined as honesty; empathy, a sensitivity to how the educational and learning process seems to the student; and prizing, an unconditionally positive regard no matter what the student's feelings or perceptions may be (Rogers, 1961). The empathy must be accurate, reflecting the student's perceptions, and straightforward enough that the student realizes that you truly understand his or her feelings. The student must know that you have a genuine personal interest. An atmosphere of nonpossessive warmth—that is, one that is not threatening to the student and fosters trust—is also imperative (Rowan, 2002).

The role of a nondirective teacher is to engage in positive interaction with a single student.

Once an interaction has been planned, you may provide definition, explaining the initial problem perceived (such as concern about falling grades or a dispute with a classmate), the procedure (you will not make the student answer questions or accept advice), and permissions (the student may say whatever he or she pleases but may not control you or resort to physical violence, for example) (Joyce et al., 2000, p. 292). The student is then free to express his or her feelings about the situation. Even if the problem does not seem to be an emotional one, the non-directive model states that feelings must be released before an intellectual or behavior change can effectively be made (Joyce et al., 2000, p. 289).

You are to focus on three main areas: the student's present feelings, any distorted percep-tions, and alternatives that the student may not have explored because of an aversion or some other emotional block. With the teacher-facilitator reflecting statements to sharpen perception, the student can begin to explore and develop insight into the problem. This insight sometimes triggers more emotional statements, which may be followed by further insights. Eventually, the student may be able to understand and accept his or her feelings and reactions more openly, make decisions or plans, and clarify or establish new behaviors as time goes on (Joyce et al., 2000, p. 292).

The process is not always immediate or smooth, and it can be frustrating if you are ill prepared or time runs short. Rogers's former associate, William Coulson (1997), claimed that Rogers intended the individual approach only for the clinic, not for the classroom, because a teacher would not have the time to develop a deep connection. Speeding up the process when possible remains a priority in the crowded school day. Carl Rogers often gave some short, provoca-tive input to get a dialogue started or to startle a response in therapy (Smith, 2002), and you may give similar "lead-taking" responses to direct or maintain a faltering conversation. Actual inter-pretation may be used sparingly if the student seems at a loss to explain or articulate, but it is imperative that such statements promote and not hinder the dialogue (Joyce et al., 2000). You must, in short, "be selfless but active. You are not to provide invisible assistance, but to help students see their situation and what might be done to change it" (Thompson, 1998, p. 5).

It is important for you to keep the roles of educator and counselor separate; empathy does not mean getting deeply involved in every student's personal problems (Kahn, 2002). In this intense relationship, however, your personality may be the most potent factor of all. Smith (2002) has argued that the facilitator's ability to foster trust, exploration, and self-encounter is more important to the student's long-term actualization than memorizing an exact method or routine. "To some extent," Boeree added, "Rogerian [facilitators] are 'born,' not 'made'" (1998, p. 7).

THE TEACHER AS CLASSROOM FACILITATOR

The most widespread nonclinical application of nondirective learning theory has been the facilitation of actual classroom activities. Rogers provided educators with "fascinating and important questions on the way of being participants" (Clark, 2000) in learning and the processes to be used. Although the student is to initiate and pursue learning, Rogers is very specific about the requirements needed to be a teacher-facilitator, personally and professionally. His preconditions are first to understand and accept oneself and to have a clear understanding of the goals to be sought (Rogers, 1980, p. 49). The facilitator must be sufficiently secure to trust students to think for themselves—not be wounded or give in to the temptation to direct or judge (Warmoth, 1999)—and must recognize and accept his or her own limitations (Pontius et al., 2000).

You have several specific roles in Rogers's expanded theory: to set a positive climate in the room, to clarify the purposes of the learner through reflection, to organize and make available learning resources, to help the student balance the intellectual and emotional components of living, and to share feelings and thoughts with the learners but not dominate or override them (Dover, 1999, p. 1). The sequence of learning is similarly well-defined: You share information with others (students and perhaps parents and the community), provide resources (from within himself or herself or within books, materials, or community contacts), guide and reflect as the student develops a personal program, and maintain a positive and supportive climate that encourages further exploration (Warmoth, 1999, p. 2). You may serve as a support, a stimulus, and even an immovable object, but not an authoritarian influence (Thompson, 1998, p. 4). Rogers added that the teacher-facilitator may help put students in contact with meaningful resources but does not assign tasks (Rogers et al., 1967).

The classroom teacher-facilitator's personal conduct should follow the same three attributes: congruence, empathy, and prizing. Students need to see you as a real (congruent) person with dislikes and enthusiasms. It is acceptable for you to show boredom with topics or to be angry, as long as you accept the feelings as personal and do not impose them or blame the students. (For example, it is fine to say, "I am frustrated," but not, "You make me so angry! Put that down and be quiet!") The teacher is not a "sterile pipe passing knowledge" (Rogers, 1980, p. 287). If you do not feel empathetic or do not like or accept someone or something at the moment, then realness is most important. Students need to accept your feelings, too, and it is appropriate to indicate a limit when needed (Kirschenbaum, 1979, p. 376). It is also important for you to determine your personal congruence in tolerating extremes of behavior such as chaotic activity, fighting, or messes and to present those concerns (as personal statements) to the class for remediation. Student extremes need not violate your or other students' sense of well-being (Kirschenbaum, 1979, p. 375).

You should respect students, just as mutual respect is expected in the dyadic relationship. You are to speak from a single perspective and leave room for the views of others, to be welcoming and invite others to express opinions, and to acknowledge and attempt to understand what others are saying before disagreeing with them (Zimmer & Alexander, 2000, p. 42). Your thoughts do not demand or impose; rather, they are a personal sharing that the students may take or leave (Pontius et al., 2000).

Indiscriminate enthusiasm, though, is not the intent of prizing in nondirective learning theory. Having unconditional positive regard does not mean praise for nothing (Daniels, 2002) or automatic reassurance of success (Rogers et al., 1967) but acceptance of students as separate people with equal rights to their own feelings, experiences, and meanings (Rogers, 1980, p. 283). Neither unconditional positive regard nor empathy implies tolerance of abusive or coercive language or behavior. You should be able to tell a student that his or her behavior is unacceptable if the student wishes to remain with the group, although the hope is that a sense of safety in the classroom will reduce unacceptable actions to almost nothing (Zimmer & Alexander, 2000).

A distinction also needs to be drawn between empathy and permissiveness. You may understand why a student is behaving or responding in a certain way. In spite of this empathy, helping students to become fully functioning means making sure they meet their responsibilities, including their social responsibilities to the group. Flexibility will probably depend on prior experience with each student. A student in crisis may have much more latitude on a given day than one who habitually sees the classroom as a chance to ogle, harass, insult, or otherwise show a lack of respect to others (Kahn, 2002).

The issues you will struggle with most, however, are the precise aspects of how to be a professional in the classroom while applying nondirective theory. Daniels (2002) argued that letting the students learn—trusting them to take care of their own agendas and progress—is most difficult. Zimmer and Alexander (2000) identified the greatest conflict in learning as letting go of control given our competitive modern culture and the dogmatic nature of most teacher–student relationships. Teachers' reactions to the lack of student motivation most concerns Vavrus (1999), and he warned that student initiative is at the center of the theory. If a student takes no initiative, then you must respect that and not do something merely to fill time. Carl Rogers himself also viewed working with a person who has no desire to change as the greatest challenge. A teacher can only extend acceptance and wait, for there can be no learning without response and change (Rogers et al., 1967).

The two examples that follow illustrate the application of the nondirective teaching style to education settings.

A. S. Neill and the Summerhill School

A. S. Neill's book *Summerhill* (1960) describes the Summerhill School, founded in 1921 in the village of Leiston in Suffolk, England. The children who reside in the school are divided into three groups: The youngest range in age from 5 to 7, the intermediates from 8 to 10, and the oldest from 11 to 15. The principles underlying the school's practice are based on Neill's system of child rearing:

- Neill maintains a firm faith "in the goodness of the child." He believes that the average child is not born a cripple, a coward, or a soulless automaton but has full potential to love life and to be interested in life.

- The aim of education—in fact, the aim of life—is to work joyfully and to find happiness. Happiness, according to Neill, means being interested in life or responding to life not just with one's brain but with one's whole personality.

- In education, intellectual development is not enough. Education must be both intellectual *and* emotional. In modern society, we find an increasing separation between intellect and feeling. The experiences of man today are mainly the experiences of thought rather than an immediate grasp of what the heart feels, what the eyes see, and what the ears hear. In fact, this separation of intellect and feeling has led modern man to a near-schizoid state of mind in which he is almost incapable of experiencing anything except in thought.

- Education must be geared to the psychic needs and capacities of the child. The child is not an altruist. He does not yet love in the sense of mature adult love. It is wrong to expect something from a child that he or she can show in only a hypocritical way. Altruism develops after childhood.

- Discipline, dogmatically imposed, and punishment create fear, and fear creates hostility. This hostility may not be conscious and overt, but it nevertheless paralyzes endeavor and authenticity of feeling. The extensive disciplining of children is harmful and thwarts sound psychic development.

- *Freedom does not mean license.* This very important principle, emphasized by Neill, is that respect for the individual must be mutual. A teacher does not use force against a child, nor does a child have the right to use force against a teacher. A child may not intrude on an adult just because he or she is a child, nor may a child use pressure in the many ways a child can.

- Closely related to this principle is the need for true sincerity on the part of the teacher. Neill claimed that never in the 40 years of his work at Summerhill has he lied to a child. Anyone who reads this book will be convinced that this statement, which may sound like boasting, is the simple truth.

- Healthy human development makes it necessary for children to cut the primary ties that connect them with their father and mother (or with later substitutes in society) and become truly independent. They must learn to face the world as individuals. They must learn to find security not in any symbiotic attachment, but in their capacity to grasp the world intellectually, emotionally, artistically. They must use all these powers to find union with the world rather than security through submission or domination.

- Guilt feelings have the primary function of binding the child to authority. Guilt feelings are an impediment to independence; they start a cycle that oscillates constantly between rebellion, repentance, submission, and new rebellion. Guilt, as it is felt by most people in our society, is not a reaction to the voice of conscience but an awareness of disobedience against authority and fear of reprisal. It does not matter whether such punishment is physical or a withdrawal of love or whether one simply is made to feel like an outsider. All such guilt feelings create fear, and fear breeds hostility and hypocrisy.

Summerhill School does not offer religious education. This, however, does not mean that Summerhill is not concerned with what might be loosely called the basic humanistic values. Neill put it succinctly, "The battle is not between believers in theology and nonbelievers in theology; it is between believers in human freedom and believers in the suppression of human freedom." The author continues, "Some day a new generation will not accept the obsolete religion and myths of today. When the new religion comes, it will refute the idea of man's being born in sin. A new religion will praise God by making men happy" (Neill, 1960, p. xii).

The aim of education according to A. S. Neill is to work joyfully and to find happiness.

Neill emphasized that the kind of person we develop in present-day society is a "mass man." Neill does not try to educate children to fit well into the existing order but endeavors to rear children who will become happy human beings, men and women whose values are not to have much, not to use much, but to be much. "Neill is a realist; he can see that even though the children he educates will not necessarily be extremely successful in the worldly sense, they will have acquired a sense of genuineness which will effectually prevent their becoming misfits or starving beggars" (p. xiv).

Neill's philosophy—demonstrating courage to believe in what one sees and combining realism with an unshakable faith in reason and love—is rare today. Neill respects life and has respect for each individual. He mixes education with therapy. However, he does not view therapy as a condition to solve problems; rather, he views the process as demonstrating to the child that life is there to be grasped, not to run away from.

The New College of Florida

A second example of student-centered learning can be found in the goal or mission statements of education institutions. A liberal arts college in Sarasota, Florida, for example, has as its goal honoring the importance of the student's role in his or her own education. New College of Florida has the following goals and principles:

- To provide a quality education to students of high ability who, because of their ability, deserve a program of study that is both demanding and stimulating

- To engage in undergraduate educational reform by combining educational innovation with educational excellence

- To provide programs of study that allow students to design their educational experience as much as possible in accordance with their individual interests, values, and abilities

- To challenge undergraduates not only to master existing bodies of knowledge but also to extend the frontiers of knowledge through original research

New College pursues these goals through highly selective admissions, an individualized and intensive "academic contract" curriculum, frequent use of individual and small-group instruction, an emphasis on student–faculty collaboration, a required senior thesis, and innovative approaches to the modes of teaching and learning.

In particular, since its inception, the college has subscribed to and attempted to foster the following principles:

- Each student is responsible in the last analysis for his or her education.

- The best education demands a joint search for learning by exciting instructors and able students.

- Students' progress should be based on demonstrated competence and real mastery rather than the accumulation of credits and grades.

- From the outset, students should have opportunities to explore areas of interest to them in depth.

The mission and goals of New College evolved out of intensive dialogue about higher education at the time of the college's inception involving administration, trustees, and the charter faculty. Subsequently, the faculty developed a unique curriculum that would enable them to realize the four principles just described and to sustain the college's broad commitment to individualism, pluralism, flexibility, freedom, and excellence.

Modified Elementary Classrooms

Teachers or districts that are not prepared to support a totally nondirective learning environment can still incorporate many varied nondirective activities into traditional classrooms. The "experience" reading method found in South Africa uses student-dictated stories as initial reading materials and student-selected literature once reading competence has been established (Mafune, 2002). Allowing ample time for student-led discussion and sharing is a nondirective tool that shows respect for the contributions and opinions of the learners (Kahn, 2002). Even highly structured materials can be used in a nondirective way; Carl Rogers actually suggested using programmed instruction when this would help a student learn more efficiently—*if* the student chose that method (Kirschenbaum, 1979, p. 377).

Problem solving with multiple approaches and solutions is an excellent exercise in experiential learning at any level (Rogers, 1969). The problem solving may actually be a necessary prelude to any traditional academic learning if the students are surrounded by hostile forces in life, and the teacher will need to help construct knowledge incorporating the students' experience and unique perceptions (Thompson, 1998).

Sensitivity is called for in allowing students to choose alternative reading material: Keywords that are common in children's literature, such as "home" or "family," may trigger emotional pain in children in crisis. The teacher may need to directly help the children address problems and differentiate between the conditions at school and outside of school (Elias, 2001, p. 16). Summarizing the general attributes of a blended classroom, McCombs (2001) recommended practices that nurture empathy and self-discipline and attention to the role of students' perceptions. She emphasized that caring does not replace high expectations and standards for learning, but incorporating nondirective learning techniques will help to offset alienation, low self-worth, poor attendance, irresponsibility, and depression (2001, p. 9). For adult learners, there are other contexts that have been tried using the nondirective learning model. We will explore these contexts in the next section.

Postsecondary and Adult Education

Many levels and types of nondirective learning have been developed for adults, most focusing on eliciting response and choice. Teacher-facilitators are urged to seek discovery learning rather than specific results, provide resources and simulations to gain vicarious experience, use contracts, and permit self-evaluation (Kirschenbaum, 1979, p. 377). Rogers urged discussion, provided that the teacher is prepared to accept student conclusions or low opinions of the learning material (1969, p. 311). He also stated that expressing a highly controversial personal opinion and then endeavoring to understand and accept the divergent opinions offered in return can result in a very meaningful class (p. 173). Hesitant learners can be invited in with phrases such as, "I'd be interested in any insights you might have" (Zimmer & Alexander, 2000, p. 45).

If the students request a lecture, it is perfectly acceptable to give one, but the teacher-facilitator must be acutely aware of boredom or lack of relevance and prepared to cut off or modify the presentation. Expounding is not a high priority (Rogers, 1969, p. 290). Even in a highly traditional classroom, the professor can let students know that their contributions are valued by maintaining firm eye contact, paraphrasing and reflecting comments, writing down relevant information immediately, and allowing a short silence after a comment in case the students have anything to add (Sapp, 2000, p. 11).

When using handouts, rather than stating firm conclusions, professors can give handouts with a relevant teacher opinion and invite responses. Instead of a question-and-answer session after a lecture, a professor can ask for questions first and tailor the lecture, as the students may already know core information or may provide new insights or approaches (Kahn, 2002, p. 5). Dialogue rather than a direct person-centered approach may be better for some adults because both parties can look at the material and work toward mutual understanding instead of one person looking at the other (Smith, 2002, p. 3).

Scenario 1:
Individual Facilitation

Megan Carson, a sixth-grade English teacher, is concerned about her first-period student, Jake. She knows that Jake and his mother have periodically been homeless, but Jake's elementary school file describes him as bright, enthusiastic, and curious. Now, Jake is dozing through Ms. Carson's class. His grades have plummeted, and he rarely turns in work. Ms. Carson asks Jake to talk to her after school. She tells him that she is concerned about his current well-being and would like to help him sort out whatever is making his life difficult, but she will not push him to answer questions, and he is free to leave whenever he wishes.

Ms. Carson:	"Jake, when you sleep, I wonder if I'm not giving you interesting things to study."
Jake:	"Oh, no! It's not that. I just can't stay awake. That's really stupid, but I can't help it."
Ms. Carson:	"It's frustrating to fall asleep without meaning to at odd hours."
Jake:	"Well, kinda. It's more like I can't go to sleep at night."
Ms. Carson:	"Going to sleep at night is hard for you."
Jake:	[Pause] "Um, it's not that exactly. I'm at Diamond Lil's Café until midnight every night. I'm sorry about sleeping in class, Ms. Carson, but I got a job at Lil's, so . . . " [Shrugs.]
Ms. Carson:	"You'd like to be alert in the mornings, but it's more important to be at Diamond Lil's."
Jake:	[Loudly] "It's NOT that important to me, but I don't get a vote! It's just important to *them*!" [Long pause while Jake scrapes his shoe on the floor.]
Ms. Carson:	[Gently] "Someone wanted you to get the job at Lil's. Could you say more about that?"
Jake:	"It's not a real job. I just say that 'cause it sounds cooler. Lil lets me stack trays and carry nachos, and she gives me the extra chicken or a sandwich, and sometimes I get tips, too. She's real nice to me. I wish Lil was my mother—No, I don't! I don't!"
Ms. Carson:	"You like the way Lil treats you."
Jake:	[Silent]
Ms. Carson:	"You feel good about your work at the café."
Jake:	"Yeah, it's OK. It's a lot better than sitting in the bus station or something. I even get to watch the big screen. That always makes me laugh."
Ms. Carson:	"Watching TV is a lot of fun."
Jake:	"Nah, it's 'cause Mr. Slick Michael just has a little one. He tells me to get lost and I end up with the best view. Too bad I can't tell him that."
Ms. Carson:	"You're happy that you have a better television to watch than Michael does."
Jake:	"Damn straight. I wish I could get a real job and my mom and me a TV and a house and tell 'Michael dear' to get lost. No, I don't . . . Um, it's nice of him to take us in."
Ms. Carson:	"You aren't sure if you're happy about Michael."
Jake:	[Pause] "I dunno. He's my mom's boyfriend. It's his apartment, his TV, his life, his couch, his everything. That's why I can't sleep at night."
Ms. Carson:	"It's difficult having someone new in your life. When my sister married, I was angry with her new husband, even though I was in high school and he was a nice guy."

Jake: "I wish Michael was a 'nice guy.' He won't even get his fat butt off the couch all night!"

Ms. Carson: "The couch is important."

Jake: "Well, yeah, it's my bed. I guess that's important—to me, at least."

Ms. Carson: "You sleep on the couch at Michael's, then. It's hard not to have your own place."

Jake: [Jumps up and paces around.] "It's the pits, Ms. Carson. I don't mind not having a room, but wouldn't you think my mom would make sure I got a bed? Even at the shelters, I had a bed. I could do my homework, too. But no, we can't disturb Michael and his TV before midnight. He might throw us out! Big wow. I'd rather live on the street, or at Lil's. Maybe I should just burn the place down. I hate them both!"

Ms. Carson: [Quietly] "It really hurt when my sister got married. She had moved back home after college and we were close, and then all of a sudden, all she thought about was him."

Jake: [Pause] "I guess I don't really hate my mom, but I wish she'd spend time with me in the evenings and make Michael move his butt so I could go to bed. Lil's is fun, but I wish it was my mom there instead. I can't read there or nothing, either . . . I hate having people feel sorry for me. Lil thinks I'm brave, but I'm not. I should just push fat Michael off his couch and go to sleep when I want to."

Ms. Carson: "Being pitied is embarrassing, but it's not always easy to change the situation, either. That's a terrific insight, Jake. Could you follow that thought some more?"

Jake: "Guess so. I can't make Michael move, and there's just one bedroom. Do you think my mom would make Fatty go to bed earlier if I yelled at her?"

Ms. Carson: "Having a place to sleep when you want is seriously important to you."

Jake: "Duh. You think I *like* falling asleep in class? Too bad I can't just carry a bed around with me. [Pause] Hey, maybe I can. I could get blankets, or a sleeping bag. I could camp. Wow! The Sallies always have cheap stuff. Awright! Thanks, Ms. Carson. You have the best ideas! See you tomorrow . . . Oh, is it OK if I go? You said I could."

Ms. Carson: "Sure, Jake. You're an A+ problem solver. I'll see you tomorrow, and sleep well."

In follow-up conversations, Ms. Carson learned that Jake's mother had helped him buy a sleeping bag, and he staked out the dinette floor as his "room." Jake's grades improved some, and he usually stayed awake. Jake visited Lil's for big games and on weekends, earning spending money and adopting Lil as an unofficial grandmother. Jake and Michael never did get along.

Scenario 2: Classroom Facilitation

Brian Benz is introducing nondirective discovery learning in his fourth-grade science class. The state curriculum lists levers, reciprocal motion, gravity, and other physics concepts as topics. Mr. Benz is determined to let the students learn as they choose, so he has brought in a wide assortment of tools, machines, and materials, hoping to spark interest. A group gathers around an old-fashioned wood-and-metal metronome, obviously curious.

Rafael: "Hey, Mr. Benz, what's this thing for?"

Mr. Benz: "You're curious about it."

Rafael: "Yeah, that's why I asked. What's this bar thing on the box for?"

Mr. Benz: "Sounds like you would like to check it out."

Rafael: "Geez, is it a secret or something? My teacher last year told us everything we were supposed to know. Aren't you a real teacher?"

Mr. Benz: "It's a little scary to have to investigate for yourself when you aren't used to it."

Kristen: "Well, I think it's fun! Give me that, Rafael. I want to see what it does. Hey, look! It has a big key like a wind-up toy. Does it dance or something?"

Lin: "Try it and see, Kristen. Wind it and put it on the table here. Wow, the metal thing is swinging! That's what moves—the bar thing, not the box. Weird; it just goes back and forth and ticks. There's no clock, though, is there?"

Kristen: "Don't see one. You're right though, it ticks unless I grab it."

Rafael: "You're dumb. Clocks don't go that way. It's upside down."

Mr. Benz: "I get irritated when I hear people insulting each other."

Lin: "Me, too. I think we should all promise not to make fun of each other."

Rafael: "Very sweet. It's still upside down. No regular numbers or hands, either. All it's got are numbers going down the edge, and they're too big to be a clock. It's kinda cool, though. Why does it bounce back instead of just falling over? And see how it goes slower and doesn't swing as far when it's running down? What makes it do that? Crank it up again and watch."

Brett: "Maybe it's like when we do the Tarzan rope, Rafael. You know, the first swing is big, and then you swing back, but you end up just hanging if you don't jump right away."

Rafael: "Yeah, but this goes a lot of times before it runs down. And where does it get the start? Is there a little person inside? Eek! It's Martians!"

Mr. Benz: "You like to use your imagination. What do you think could make it go?"

Lin: "I still think it looks like a clock. My aunt has a big one in her hallway, and it has all kinds of little wheels with teeth that click around when the bottom swings."

Rafael: "He was asking *me*. You're right, though. I've seen those big clocks, too. The bottom is a pen, pen something."

Kristen: "Mr. Benz, have we got a chart or something with the pen thing on it?"

Lin: "Yes, would that tell us how it works?"

Mr. Benz: "Sounds like you want to look the word up."

Kristen: "That encyclopedia is huge! It would take a year when I don't know the whole word."

Brett: "Wait! Use the dictionary. We could just read the 'pen' words until one sounds right or the meaning has 'clock' in it."

Lin: "OK, got one." [Pause]

Rafael: "There it is—pendulum. I knew it was pen! OK. It says it makes the gear things move by 'reciprocal motion.' What's that?"

Lin: "You've got the dictionary, bright boy. Look it up!"

Mr. Benz: "I get irritated when I hear people insulting each other."

Lin: "Sorry. Couldn't resist. I guess we can both stop now—We're even."

Rafael: "The 'reciprocal' definition just says it responds or takes turns. That's no help."

Kristen: "Maybe we need the whole thing—'reciprocal motion.' Bet that's in the encyclopedia, not the dictionary. Try the R one, Rafael."

Rafael: "Here it is. There's diagrams and stuff. Help, I'm drowning! OK, I think it says that when an object is hung from one end and gets swung to the side, then it swings back the same the other way, until it runs down and stops. Look, there's the clock. Hey, there's the box thing, too. It's called a 'metronome.' It says it helps keep music going at the same speed."

Lin: "I *told* you it was like a clock. Clocks go at the same speed, too."

Brett: "Look what I found! I was looking at the CDs 'cause you had the books, and I found a song called *The Syncopated Clock*. Do you suppose it sounds like ticking?"

Kristen: "Nobody'd make a CD of ticking. What does clock music sound like, though? Can we play it to find out, Mr. Benz?"

Mr. Benz: "You sound really interested. I'm sure there is a CD player around. I would enjoy listening to the music, too. We've found out a lot of information, though. I didn't remember the precise definition of reciprocal motion. I'm going to write that down before I listen to the song, so I won't forget."

Rafael: "Good idea, Mr. Benz. Maybe we could make a sheet with all the stuff we looked up and put it on the wall. What about that rope thing Brett was talking about? Is that reciprocal motion, too? And what makes the metronome slow down?"

[And so on, and so on…]

ASSESSMENT

Because nondirective learning is so intensely personal, traditional assessment of an entire class through standardized exams and letter grades is highly impractical. In fact, one of Carl Rogers's basic tenets is that the only legitimate evaluation of self-directed learning must be self-evaluation. Only the learner knows whether the new knowledge was valuable, whether he or she pursued it thoroughly, and whether it made a pervasive difference in his or her behavior or attitude.

Rogers felt that testing to meet a teacher's criteria is contrary to significant learning (1961, p. 290) and that students who demand testing need to reassure themselves that they learned what they should, which shows a lack of self-trust on several levels (1961, p. 307). He described evaluation as "a ticket of entrance, not a club over the recalcitrant" (1961, p. 291). A person cannot develop film without knowing about the chemicals and cannot readily succeed in an honors English class without essay skills. However, students should be free to decide whether they want to earn the right to join any group or activity, and they should accept the consequences as a personal choice (Rogers, 1980).

Seymour Papert urged administrators that if they must evaluate students, they should do so by measuring the diversity of knowledge gained and what the learners can do with the knowledge, not how many answers they can give (2002, p. 2). Portfolio-based assessment is even more authentic, but it is limited unless the portfolio follows what the grading is based on (2002, p. 3).

In modified classroom programs such as Fairfield University's first-year English classes, planned negotiation is common. Students may choose some of the texts and the type of tests and vote on penalties and consequences; grades are often earned by contract between professor and student. In another university's undergraduate psychology class, in which structure and grading were required by the administration, the professor based the assessment on each student's choice of a mix of reading, writing a psychological autobiography, working with the elderly or homeless, taking psychological tests, receiving counseling, doing case studies, or creating independent projects (Kirschenbaum, 1979). When teachers are required to give letter grades in a nondirective setting, Zimring (1994) advises providing very clear criteria to the students before each assignment, commenting on drafts of papers, allowing the students to rewrite them before grading, and using peer evaluation as well as the teacher's evaluation if the age group warrants this.

In the pure nondirective model, though, no external evaluation is truly valid. Who can accurately measure the depth and value of learning for another person?

TECHNOLOGY

Carl Rogers used technology during the 1930s to record his client sessions, much to the dismay of his colleagues. Rogers was interested in reviewing his therapy sessions to examine how his clients behaved and how they reacted to interns. In his classes, he played the tapes and examined negative and positive examples of the sessions.

Today, sophisticated videotaping equipment has replaced the audiotapes, and client sessions can be viewed and reviewed to improve interactions.

Learning Tenets
That Support Nondirective Learning

The brain seeks to classify information and the things to be learned.

Rogers (1945) first sought to bring the cognitive and experiential hemisphere of the brain into a single, integrated relationship. Rogers insisted that only when the teacher is able to empathize (put oneself in place of another) with the student is significant learning likely to take place. The student must become the center of the process: Students, first and foremost, are being taught, and the subject matter (math and science) plays a more subordinate role. In the person-centered approach, three conditions must be present.

The first element has to do with genuineness, realness, or congruence. Whether we are speaking of the therapist–client, teacher–student, or any other relationship, there must be a close matching or congruence between what is experienced at the gut level, what is present in awareness, and what is expressed to the client or student.

The second element of creating a climate for change is acceptance, caring, or prizing—an unconditional positive regard. It is a nonpossessive caring in which the teacher prizes the student in a total rather than a conditional way.

The third facilitative aspect of the relationship is an empathic understanding. As the students are accepted and prized, they tend to develop a more caring attitude toward themselves and greater freedom to be the whole person that they are inwardly.

The classification of information in the brain is based on a climate of acceptance and a sense of empathy, caring, and positive regard.

**The emotional system drives attention,
and attention drives meaning and memory.**

Carl Rogers insisted that knowledge without feelings is not knowledge and only leads to public irresponsibility. Therefore, feelings are paramount to the success of the teacher in the nondirective model. For years, I have asked my students to write down the characteristics of their favorite teachers. After collecting their responses and recording them on a whiteboard at the front of the classroom, I ask questions about the list formulated by the group. What comes up more often than not are the affective components about the teachers that students remember the most. "The teacher was nice," "The teacher was funny . . . The teacher had a way of making everyone valued in the room." The things most remembered about our former teachers are their qualities as a person. The qualities defining true education are personal involvement (feelings as well as thinking), self-initiation (discovery), pervasiveness (a change in subsequent behavior or attitude), and self-evaluating acceptance (self-recognition that the knowledge is meeting the learner's needs). These are the qualities that were most important to Carl Rogers.

Learning occurs in both conscious and unconscious states.

We do not always know what our students are thinking. They may share views and perceptions that are different from ours. They may or may not be conscious of their feelings and how these shape their learning. As teachers, we need to be consistent, reliable adults. We must respect all individuals, and we must model appropriate behavior for our students. As students develop a view of their world and what is happening to them, they may look to us to know how to respond to a dilemma that is facing them. If we can model behavior for our students, this may help them to cope with difficult situations. So if we model appropriate responses to others in our own lives, we hope that students will learn how to make good, conscious choices from our example.

The brain is designed for ups and downs, not constant attention.

The interaction of therapist and patient or teacher and student does not force constant attention on either party involved with the interaction. In a person-to-person situation, the nondirective teacher-facilitator must exhibit the same characteristics as his or her therapeutic counterpart. This characteristic of congruence is reflected in open honesty, empathy, and a sensitive awareness of how the educational and learning process seems to the student. This process requires the therapist to listen. In the case of the teacher, it is best to approach the student after class or call him or her to the hallway to discuss an issue than to address the problem in front of the class. The idea, however, is to give the student your undivided attention.

Learning occurs through processing and active engagement with visual, auditory, and kinesthetic modalities.

Because each encounter is unique and fluid, the best way to internalize the nondirective model is to work with individuals or classes in real-life situations until the approach is ingrained and sensitivity is highly developed. By role playing, a teacher can become familiar with the emotions engendered on both sides of a dialogue, learn from personal successes and failures, and receive the feedback from a cohort (much as Rogers shared tapes with his clinical interns) under fairly Rogerian conditions—that is, reduced external threat to provide easier assimilation and pervasive behavioral change. Zins et al. (2001) highly recommend additional training in psychology and field experience in counseling to help beginning teachers learn to become skilled socioemotional facilitators.

Handouts may not be vital, although lists of strategic phrases for different situations might provide the same assistance as scripted opening chess gambits. Writing reflections for a sheet of feelings statements might allow mental practice in mirroring.

Modeling using peers, professors, actors, or simulations can provide a type of observational practice. Videotapes of exemplary classroom practices allow observation when real-time interaction is not feasible, although vicarious experience is never preferred. Readings from theorists and practitioners can stimulate ideas but cannot replace personal involvement. Good teaching is about recognizing and selecting instructional patterns that match the context for learning and the students we are teaching.

The context for teaching the nondirective model can be organized in many forms. One of those contexts is the open-school concept. Open classrooms are normally found at the elementary level, and they are partially based on the thinking of psychologist Jean Piaget. The American version is derived from the British open primary school; both provide a rich array of materials that the students can explore on their own and staff who help students set goals and carry on activities (Kirschenbaum, 1979).

Seymour Papert (2002), a leading open-school proponent, urged free-form groups incorporating learners of various ages but common interests bonded by powerful ideas. Papert claimed that age segregation is just as evil as any other type of segregation. He instructed would-be open classroom teachers to give up the idea of curriculum. He advocated disposing of a system in which certain things must be learned on given days and replacing it with a system in which learners learn what they need.

Joyce et al. (2000) define group work focused on creativity and self-knowledge as the norm of open classrooms (p. 295). Rogers acknowledged that students may at first be frustrated and angry over having to develop their own learning content after a teacher's "abdication" (1969, p. 304), but Levine (2002) assured that the teacher's time is better invested in helping learners identify the types of experiences they would like to explore and helping them get involved. Other applications and recommendations for teacher-facilitators in open elementary classrooms include responding to student feelings, using student ideas for ongoing projects, considering alternatives to discussion, praising frequently, using congruent conversation rather than clichéd teacher phrases, tailoring explanations carefully to the students' frame of mind and immediate need, and smiling often to communicate relaxation and positive regard (Huitt, 2001).

Summary

McCombs (2001) defined nondirective learning as valuing and supporting individual learners, as well as learning outcomes, based on the knowledge that education goes beyond academic competence. Rogers remembered his own teaching experience as hours of engrossed discussions, mellowed personalities, and a strong sense of community that outlived the length of the class (1961, p. 308). The most creative definition, though, may be that of Tom Peters. He pictures nondirective learning as "thinking outside the box, coloring outside the lines, and digging, digging, digging, in the sandbox of life!" (2002, p 1). The nondirective learning pattern is best suited for Part V of this book, "Student-Centered Patterns," because it represents a student-centered approach.

Thought to Action

1. Interview a professor of psychology to ask his or her opinion about Carl Rogers's work.

2. Discuss with school personnel whether they use or apply any nondirective techniques. If so, under what circumstances are nondirective strategies used, and with which students?

3. Explain how you will connect with the students you teach. Name three to five belief statements that you hold about students and your relationship with them. Would your belief statements be congruent with Carl Rogers's theory?

4. How has your personal family experience shaped your ability to empathize with others? Do you believe that you can put yourself in another person's shoes?

ON YOUR OWN

Log on to the web-based student study site at http://www.sagepub.com/holt for access to a Standards-Based Student Project that will help you connect what you have learned in this chapter to your state's standards; study aids, such as electronic flashcards; and research recommendations, including journal article links and other Web resources.

Self-Taught Instruction

THE SCHOOL REFORM MOVEMENT OF THE 1980S FOCUSED ON THE IDENTIFICATION OF FAILING schools and the characteristics they possess. Although the effort concentrated on why students fail, the often-overlooked question was, why do some students succeed? Enhanced and more efficient teaching efforts failed to bring about substantive changes, and researchers began to realize that to improve schools, studies were needed on success and learning (Marzano, 2003). Inevitably, the nature of success has become an integral part of many research projects and education reforms since the 1990s.

Motivational studies since 2000 have revealed that success is a result of a complex set of dynamics that interact to enable students to be highly motivated or extremely resistant (Marzano, 2003). Further, research on emotional intelligence, resiliency, and social relatedness has established the need for a healthy self-concept as a basis for personal growth. This instructional pattern, self-taught instruction, is a student-centered approach that examines psychology as a human science rather than a natural science. The student-centered pattern is intended to have the students develop richer states of growth and focuses on helping each student "actualize" and become an emotionally healthy person.

Alfie Kohn (2003) stated that classrooms should provide a rich environment, full of positive, engaging experiences at which students achieve a recognized level of success. Unfortunately, this has not always been the case. Many classrooms begin with the positive climate that Kohn described but erode to lesser forms of reality because of traditional assumptions and resource stresses. Kohn lists six errors that commonly occur that limit personal growth and self-esteem:

- Blaming the students
- Keeping control of the classroom
- Missing the systemic factors
- Ignoring problems with the curriculum

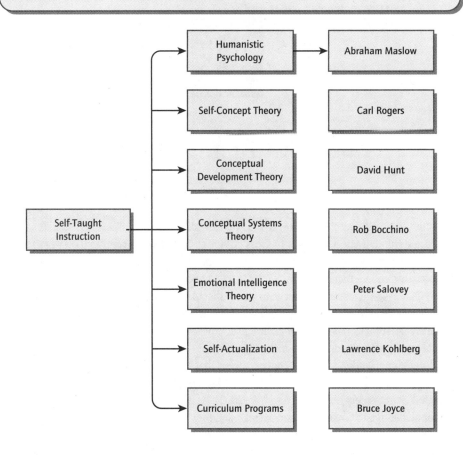

- Settling for self-discipline
- Manipulating with positive reinforcement

You should be aware of these errors and learn to ask the right questions, such as, "What do these kids need—and how can we meet those needs?" (Kohn, 2003, p. 27).

In an interview with *Curriculum Review*, Brenda Townsend, a professor of education at the University of South Florida who had recently published her work on techniques for teaching African American students the "reality classroom" concept, stated, "I firmly believe that, through a challenging, interactive curriculum, you can do both. You can affirm children's self-esteem as well as teach them effectively" (2003, p. 15).

RESEARCH ANCHOR

Humanistic psychologists such as Abraham Maslow, Carl Rogers, and David Hunt, as well as scholars Rob Bocchino, Peter Salovey, Lawrence Kohlberg, and Bruce Joyce, agree that the ability to

Humanistic psychologists believe that the ability to succeed depends greatly on an individual's self-concept.

succeed depends greatly on an individual's self-concept. Developmental, hierarchical models have frequently been used to describe personal states of growth from physiological to self-actualized. These developmental states of growth are related to states of learning that range from resistant to optimum.

Abraham Maslow focused on the concept of self. He felt that one's competence to relate to others and to our environment is dependent on the feelings we have toward ourselves. Many research studies have demonstrated the need for improved teaching on concepts of self. A motivational study on adolescent adjustment among seventh and ninth graders found that a student's low self-worth resulting from numerous discipline referrals, negative expectations, and doubts about the economic value of education was a high predictor of failure in high school (Murdock, Anderman, & Hodge, 2000). On the other hand, students who had high self-worth were predicted to succeed in high school.

Research on youth who have succeeded against all odds also demonstrates the need for program and curriculum development on self-concept and resiliency factors (Rink & Tricker, 2003). Why is it, for example, that two students with the same background, intelligence, and ability can be given the same set of circumstances, and one turns out to be a huge success, whereas the other is an absolute failure? The underlying factors have a lot to do with self-awareness and self-concept.

Programs designed to develop self-awareness, emotionality, sociability, morality, and character all share similar basic qualities. The goal of such programs is to instill in all students a high desire for a fulfilled life. Character education and service learning are two such programs that have been designed to develop personal states of growth and improved self-concept.

Character education programs have recently seen a rise in popularity based on disturbing statistics released by a number of research organizations across America (Gilbert, 2003). Program studies by Dr. John M. Doris at the University of California, Santa Cruz, and by Dr. Jerome Kagan at Harvard University show that moral development programs such as character education and service learning aid in the moral growth of young people. According to Kagan, neurons begin to connect the brain's hemispheres around age two, and emotionality becomes linked with judgment. It has been determined that this is the age at which individuals become aware of right and wrong and can link behavior with emotions.

Researchers have also noted attributes of success in the workplace. David Thornburg (2002) wrote about employment of the future, which he dubbed the "Telematic Age." According to Thornburg, the following are the most desirable workforce characteristics .

- Visual and information literacy

- Cultural literacy and global awareness

- Adaptability and the ability to manage complexity

- Curiosity, creativity, and risk taking

- Higher-order thinking and sound reasoning

- Teaming, collaboration, and interpersonal skills

- Personal and social responsibility

- Interactive communication skills

- Ability to prioritize, plan, and manage results

- Effective use of real-world tools

- Ability to create relevant, high-quality products

In addition, Thornburg stated that workers of the future should be prepared for short-term employment and comfortable with ambiguity, and they should be lifelong learners, highly mobile, highly entrepreneurial, and creative. There is not one mention of the knowledge base, achievement level, or intelligence quotient desired from workers of the future. These 11 workforce characteristics might all be classified in the affective domain, which is related to self-concept and social awareness.

Daniel Goleman, author of *Emotional Intelligence* (1995) boldly stated that 80% of success in the workplace can be attributed to emotional intelligence factors (EQ) and only 20% to intellectual ability (IQ). He added that indicators of emotional intelligence, such as the ability to cope with frustration and stress, delay gratification, and work cooperatively, were more powerful predictors of success in life than IQ.

In 1990, Salovey and Mayer defined emotional intelligence as the "abilities to perceive, appraise, and express emotion; to assess and/or generate feelings when they facilitate thought; to understand emotion and emotional knowledge; and to regulate emotions to promote emotional and intellectual growth" (Caruso, Mayer, & Salovey, 2002, p. 306). Further, they felt that emotionally intelligent people have the ability to discriminate among personal and social affective areas and can use this information to guide their own thinking and actions. According to the authors, there are three mental processes related to emotion that are involved in this thought process: (1) appraising and expressing feelings, (2) self-regulation of emotions, and (3) the ability to adapt to various situations.

Rob Bocchino, in his book *Emotional Literacy* (1999), discussed the differences between emotional intelligence and emotional literacy. He described emotional intelligence as a subset of factors that make up an EQ score, which is very different from IQ but is similarly based on a scale measuring potential from low to high. Like IQ, a normal emotional quotient would be 100. Emotional literacy is defined as the ability to functionally operate at high levels of social and emotional achievement. Emotional literacy is described as the richest state of growth on the emotional intelligence scale.

Other researchers have suggested different terms for a concept like emotional literacy. Skaalvik and Skaalvik (2002) used the term "academic self-concept" to refer to the frame of reference that individuals use to self-judge their academic ability. Academic self-concept comes from a student's self-perception of being capable, competent, and successful. Educational scholars David Johnson and Roger Johnson (1994) reported that three types of learning outcomes—namely, cooperative, competitive, and individualistic—have a wide range of effects on academic self-esteem. The most positive effect on self-esteem comes from cooperative learning environments. Johnson and Johnson attributed higher self-esteem to students who were able to formulate a positive self-concept and build processes through which they came up with positive conclusions about their self-worth. Self-esteem was determined to be composed of two parts: (1) one's initial level of self-worth level and (2) the processes through which individuals derive conclusions about their self-worth (Johnson & Johnson, 1994). They continued by describing five processes for deriving self-esteem:

- Basic self-acceptance: Intrinsic perception of oneself

- Conditional self-acceptance: Perceived acceptance based on competition

- Comparative self-acceptance: Compared level of attributes with peers

- Reflected self-acceptance: Opinion of self against the judgment of others

- Real–ideal self-esteem: Self-perception related to a desired state

Listed here in a somewhat developmental sequence, these processes illustrate the situational nature of self-concept. Self-concept must be described as being dependent on environmental and social conditions and affected across the time continuum (Johnson & Johnson, 1994). Major improvements in self-esteem have been identified as benefits of cooperative learning activities in research studies on special education and remedial students, who are usually considered to have low self-esteem (Jenkins, Antil, Wayne, & Vadasy, 2003).

In a meta-analysis of self-concept in students with learning disabilities, George Bear, Kathleen Minke, and Maureen Manning (2002) stated that self-concept is not affected as a function of the special education setting. However, academic self-concept reflected by the special education group is lower, based on reasonably accurate perceptions of their academic abilities when compared to regular education students. In contrast to a previous meta-analysis by researchers in the 1980s the results of this study indicated no differences in overall self-concept as a function of the special education setting (Bear et al., 2002). The implications of

Abraham H. Maslow (1908–1970) was the founder of humanistic psychology. His article "Dominance-Feeling, Personality, and Social Behavior in Women" (1939) applied his interest in primate dominance to humans. He concluded that highly dominant women, regardless of their sex drives, are more likely to be sexually active and to experiment sexually than less dominant women. In 1941, with Bela Mittelman, he published the textbook *Principles of Abnormal Psychology,* wherein he stated that his final shift to the humanistic view had occurred as he cried while watching a parade soon after Pearl Harbor: "Since that moment in 1941 I've devoted myself to developing a theory of human nature that could be tested by experiment and research."

In his most important work, *Motivation and Personality* (1954), Maslow did not repudiate classical psychology; rather, he attempted to enlarge its conception of personality by stressing man's higher nature. In contrast to "the analytic-dissecting-atomistic-Newtonian approach" of behaviorism and Freudian psychoanalysis, it emphasized the holistic character of human nature. It defined and explained "the need hierarchy," "self-actualization," and "peak experiences," phrases that have become part of the vocabulary of psychologists.

Source: Contemporary Authors Online; reproduced in the Biography Resource Center (Farmington Hills, MI: Thomson Gale, 2005).

this study confirmed teachers' rationale for providing engaging educational activities and evaluating academic achievement at a recognized level of success.

In his study of the discomfort of learning about the unknown, Bruce Joyce discussed how to help students become active seekers for new states of personal growth: "Self-actualization allows the individual the ability to maintain learning focus through the discomfort of the unknown" (1984, p. 27). In other words, when new learning takes place, students venture outside the realm of their comfort zone. This discomfort must be calmed with a level of high academic self-concept in order for the focus to be maintained.

SELF-CONCEPT THEORY

Abraham Maslow (1962) developed a *self-concept theory* based on a hierarchy of needs that included five sets of goals: physiological needs, safety, love, esteem, and self-actualization. In addition, he postulated that we are motivated by the desire to achieve or maintain the conditions on which these basic satisfactions rest and by more intellectual desires. The highest level is self-actualization, defined as the desire to be fully enriched in all of life's activities. These needs are based on prepotency, that is, the most potent goal will monopolize consciousness directing both thought and action.

FIGURE 11.1   Maslow's Hierarchy of Needs

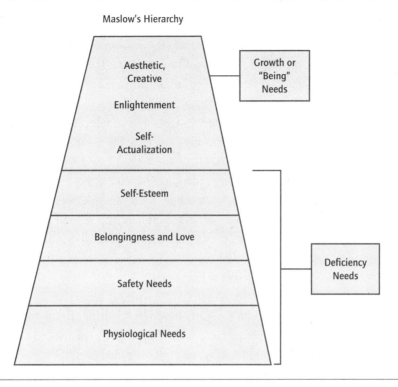

Maslow's Hierarchy

Source: Reilly and Lewis (1983).

According to Maslow, self-actualized individuals exhibit the following characteristics:

More efficient perception of reality and more comfortable relations with reality: Individuals have an exceptional ability to judge people, ideas, and information correctly and efficiently. Thus, people who are neurotic cannot be considered self-actualized because they lack judgment in the realm of reality.

Acceptance of self, others and nature: Individuals do not have extreme forms of guilt, shame, or anxiety; they accept all levels of love, safety, belonging, honor, and self-respect for themselves, for others, and for the environment.

Ability to act spontaneously: The behavior of the self-actualized is outwardly simple and natural. Their inner lives are more spontaneous than their outward lives.

Problem centered: Self-actualized individuals focus on problems outside themselves; they are problem-centered rather than ego-centered. This is based on their need to fulfill personal obligations, duties, or responsibilities.

Quality of detachment and need for privacy: Individuals may be considered solitary, but it is without harm to themselves or discomfort to others. They are not seen

(Continued)

(Continued)

as introverted but as more detached to attain the thought processing necessary for their problem-centered personality.

Autonomy and independence of culture and environment: These individuals are not easily influenced by external factors. They are considered very stable in the face of hard knocks, blows, deprivations, frustrations, and the like.

Continued freshness of appreciation: Self-actualized people retain a naive, childish appreciation for the little things in life even after the same stimuli may have become stale for the ordinary person.

Mystic experiences or oceanic feeling: Individuals have the ability to lose themselves or the transcendence of self through intense sensuous, self-sacrificing, musical, or artistic experiences. This feeling was described initially by William James.

Gemeinschaftsgefühl: This term, used by Alfred Adler, describes a deep feeling of identification, sympathy, and affection for others in spite of occasional anger or impatience; it is a genuine desire to help the human race.

Interpersonal relations: These people have deep and profound interpersonal relationships, a sort of unconditional love. However, this is not to say that hostile reactions do not exist in self-actualized people; their negative reactions to others are described as well deserved and for the good of the intended person.

Democratic character structure: Individuals are friendly with anyone of suitable character regardless of class, education, political belief, race, or color. Respect is given to any human being just because he or she is a human individual.

Means and ends: Individuals are strongly ethical with definite moral standards. They do right and do not do wrong, even if it can be legitimized.

Philosophical, unhostile sense of humor: Self-actualized individuals use witty remarks, puns, and thoughtful and philosophical humor that elicits a smile rather than a laugh.

Creativeness: This is a universal characteristic of self-actualized people; they are considered original and inventive.

Source: Adapted from Lowry (1973).

It is important to remember that some negative traits are associated with self-actualized people. They have been described as occasionally and unexpectedly ruthless because of their strong personalities and highly autonomous spirit. Another negative trait of self-actualized people is being "stuffy." Conventional people have often been insulted by the behavior of self-actualized people because social politeness becomes secondary to intense problem solving and creativity. Finally, self-actualized people are not free of guilt, anxiety, sadness, internal strife, and conflict. They experience these states like other individuals, but because of their self-actualized state, they are able to separate their negative feelings from conscious thought and action (Lowry, 1973).

David Hunt outlines four types of learners in his levels of student awareness theory.

CONCEPTUAL DEVELOPMENT THEORY

Conceptual development theory has been used to describe ways that people use information to structure and conceptualize the information they perceive from the environment. The conceptual development theory coordinates Piagetian levels with types of learners (Joyce, Weil, & Calhoun, 2000). Learners are described as gourmet omnivores, passive consumers, or reticent consumers. This theory not only explains that all students can learn but also that learning stages contribute to the need for reciprocal transactions. In other words, to optimize learning conditions, teachers must take into account the learning stages of their students.

LEVELS OF STUDENT AWARENESS THEORY

David Hunt outlined four types of learners in his *levels of student awareness theory*: (1) stereotype learners, (2) opinionate learners, (3) existential learners, and (4) creative learners (Armstrong, 1998). Hunt postulated that learners pass through several different levels of awareness during their years in school and beyond. Teachers are also considered to have levels of awareness that relate to these four levels. For example, problems may arise when a teacher who is an opinionate learner has a student who is an existential learner. In this case, the mismatch may lead to tension between teacher and student with regard to each other's role expectations.

Stereotype Learner

The first type of student, the stereotype learner, places the teacher in a quasi-parental role, with the expectation that he or she will be directed and may choose to reject those directions, with negative consequences. The teacher's role with this type of learner is to guide students and provide structure.

Opinionate Learner

The second type of student, the opinionate learner, composes approximately half of the K–12 population (Armstrong, 1998). This type of learner places the teacher in the role of lecturer, discussion leader, and assignment creator. This student's emphasis is the collection of content knowledge, but he or she does not choose to analyze, synthesize, or evaluate information.

Existential Learner

The third type of student, the existential learner, is concerned with present situations, the here and now. These students see the classroom as a place to debate issues not related to historical or futuristic terms merely for the quality of argument. Teachers can address the needs of the existential learner by allowing debate but then delineating the argument by providing choices and employing decision-making processes.

Creative Learner

Students at the fourth level of learning take charge of their learning experiences and view the teacher as facilitator. In Maslow's hierarchical model, creative learners would be considered to be self-actualized. In this case, you might allow your students to be self-directed, and you may use inductive models.

CONCEPTUAL SYSTEMS THEORY

Conceptual systems theory originated in 1961 with the publication of the book *Conceptual Systems and Personality Organization*. In that work, O. J. Harvey, David Hunt and Harry Schroeder described the relationship that individuals have with concepts, information, organization, and their world (Joyce et al., 2000). With regard to education and learning, the conceptual systems theory is similar to Hunt's levels of student awareness theory. It requires teachers and students to recognize and understand the states of growth achieved by others in their environment. To achieve higher levels of conceptual development, students and teachers must be able to analyze people and events from multiple points of view and make the appropriate accommodations.

EMOTIONAL INTELLIGENCE THEORY

The term "emotional intelligence" first appeared in Peter Salovey and John D. Mayer's 1990 treatise on the subject (Caruso, Mayer, & Salovey, 2002). Daniel Goleman (1995) popularized and

O. J. Harvey is Professor of Psychology at the University of Colorado. His writings (with David E. Hunt and Harold M. Schroder) include *Conceptual Systems and Personality Organization* (1961), *Motivation and Social Interaction* (editor, 1963), and *Experience, Structure and Adaptability* (editor, 1966). He contributed more than 50 articles to psychology journals.

Source: Contemporary Authors Online; reproduced in the Biography Resource Center (Farmington Hills, MI: Thomson Gale, 2005).

extended the application of the concept from psychology to other fields, such as business and marketing. Goleman postulated that 80% of one's success is based on factors other than IQ. These factors, such as social perception, patience, and persistence, make up the attributes of emotional intelligence. Mayer and Salovey detailed four levels of emotional states: (1) identification, perception, and expression in communication; (2) emotional facilitation of thought; (3) emotional understanding; and (d) emotional management.

UPDATE ON SELF-ACTUALIZATION

Recent educational theorists have argued that Maslow's self-actualizing theory does not go far enough to describe healthy social relationships (Hanley & Abell, 2002). Feminist psychologists and non-Western scholars believe that the problem with Maslow's theory is that it does not allow for different sets of values. The Western male bias toward self-actualization and the ability to detach from one's environment does not emphasize societal, value-driven interpersonal relationships, in which highly actualized behavior includes such things as "creative fidelity," a concept that is attained when an individual redefines himself or herself based on the life of another, as in parenting or marriage (Hanley & Abell, 2002). "Maslow never really represented his theory with a triangle and that the triangle may suggest an unnecessary endpoint to human growth and development" (Hanley & Abell, 2002, p. 43). Therefore, a new model is suggested that reflects three domains:

- Priority to family life and parenting as central opportunities for personal growth

- Neighborhood, community, and global issues as integral parts of the new self-actualized individual

- Spiritual component that defines a relationship of the person with a conceptualization of god or other supernatural power

These three things are paramount for the new model. In addition, the new model shows that a powerful interrelationship exists between belongingness, love needs and self-actualizing needs, which are connected through the creative fidelity. Finally, Hanley and Abell believe that achievements must come from symbiotic partnerships with others and cannot be attributed to one person alone.

Peter Salovey is the author of *Peer Counseling* (1983), *The Remembered Self* (1993), and *Psychology* (1993) and editor of *Judgment and Inference in Clinical Psychology* (1988), *The Psychology of Jealousy and Envy* (1991), *Emotional Development and Emotional Intelligence* (1997), *At Play in the Fields of Consciousness* (1999), and *The Wisdom in Feeling: Psychological Processes in Emotional Intelligence* (2002). He has served as of editor of the *Review of General Psychology* (1996–2002), associate editor of the *Psychological Bulletin* (1991–96), and *Emotion* (2000–02) and has contributed many articles to professional journals.

Source: University of Central Florida, Biography Resource Center, retrieved June 29, 2004.

STATES OF GROWTH

Bruce Joyce described states of growth in terms of professional staff development and adult learning models. He found that adult learners in professional development situations vary greatly along a continuum from low to high activity and from high-maintenance to self-driven, interactive individuals (Joyce et al., 2000). He listed three types: (1) gourmet omnivores, (2) passive consumers, and (3) reticent consumers. Approximately 10% of the adult professional development community can be described as gourmet omnivores (Joyce et al., 2000). These individuals want to learn everything possible and pass their knowledge along to others in a helpful way by bringing the ideas they learn back to their workplace. In contrast, the reticent consumer rejects opportunities for growth. They are reluctant to learn and practice new ideas that come from their professional development opportunities.

These theories relate to learners in several ways. First, learning states are developmental in nature. From simple to complex, from little interest to high interest, and from resistance to motivation, learners come to the table with a wide range of abilities to maintain an academic focus. These states of growth need to be identified by educators to optimize learning. Second, states of learning are directly associated with an individual's concept of self. Whether one uses the term "self-concept," "self-awareness," or "emotional intelligence," the way an individual views his or her self-worth is directly related to the ability to succeed. Self-actualization, self-esteem, academic self-esteem, and emotional literacy all describe individuals who feel good enough about themselves to perform at high levels of confidence and relatedness.

Bruce Joyce summarized the concepts of the self model by saying "the important message is that students can learn, not only academic content and social skills, but how to become integrated selves that reach out into the world and reciprocally contribute to and profit from their transactions with it" (Joyce et al., 2000, p. 301). In addition, educators model their own self-concepts in their daily transactions with students. This influence encourages many students to develop their own higher states of growth.

FIGURE 11.2   Interpersonal Model of Self-Actualization

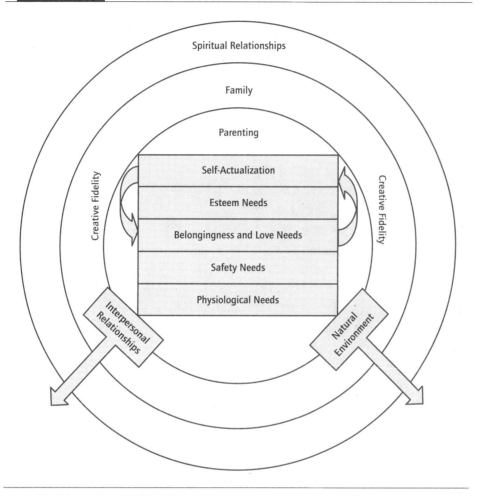

Source: Adapted from Hanley and Abell (2002).

MODELING SELF-ACTUALIZATION

Bruce Joyce stated, "If we model passivity, we encourage it. If we model activity and reaching out toward the world, we encourage active states" (Joyce et al., 2000, p. 324). Observational learning of self-actualized people develops a higher state of learning in the observer. A rich and active social climate that is full of positive substance and organization creates changes in learning states toward more outreach and production (Joyce et al., 2000). The tools for developing self-actualized students are climate, positivism, depth, and organization through interactive modeling with self-actualized teachers.

In his article "Moral Teachers, Moral Students," Rick Weissbourd (2003) reported that the moral development of students does not depend solely on creative teaching strategies or well-planned curricular programs, but on the moral development level of the adults who are

Bruce R. Joyce taught at Wayne State University, the University of Delaware, University of Chicago, and Columbia University and was the director of Booksend Laboratories in Pauma Valley, California.

His writings include *Strategies for Elementary Social Science Education* (1965), *Social Studies Extension Service: Grades K–12* (eight volumes, 1966–67), *The Structure of Teaching* (with Berj Harootunian, 1967), *Alternative Models of Elementary Education* (1969), *New Strategies for Social Education* (1972), *Perspectives for Reform in Teacher Education* (edited with Marsha Weil, 1972), *Models of Teaching* (with Marsha Weil, 1972; 6th edition with Marsha Weil and Emily Calhoun, 2000), *Performance-Based Teacher Education Design Alternatives: The Concept of Unity* (with Marsha Weil and Jonas F. Soltis, 1974), *Creating the School: An Introduction to Education* (with Greta G. Morine-Dershimer, 1976), *Selecting Learning Experiences: Linking Theory and Practice* (1978), *Information Processing Models of Teaching: Expanding Your Teaching Repertoire* (with Marsha Weil, 1978), *Personal Models of Teaching* (with Marsha Weil and Bridget Kluwin, 1978), *Social Models of Teaching: Expanding Your Teaching Repertoire* (with Marsha Weil, 1978), *Flexibility in Teaching: An Excursion Into the Nature of Teaching and Training* (edited with Clark C. Brown and Lucy Peck, 1981), *The Structure of School Improvement* (with Richard H. Hersh and Michael McKibbin, 1983), *Improving America's Schools* (1986), *Student Achievement Through Staff Development* (with Beverly Showers, 1988; 2nd edition, 1995), *The Self-Renewing School* (with Emily Calhoun and James Wolf, 1993), *Learning Experiences in School Renewal: An Exploration of Five Successful Programs* (edited with Emily Calhoun, 1996), *Creating Learning Experiences: The Role of Instructional Theory and Research* (with Emily Calhoun, 1996), *Models of Learning: Tools for Teaching* (with Emily Calhoun and David Hopkins, 1997), *Learning to Teach Inductively* (with Emily Calhoun, 1998), and *The New Structure of School Improvement: Inquiring Schools and Achieving Students* (with Emily Calhoun and David Hopkins, 1999).

Source: "Peter Salovey," Marquis Who's Who; reproduced in the Biography Resource Center (Farmington Hills, MI: Thomson Gale, 2005).

influential in their young lives. Research was presented showing that even when schools undergo massive restructuring efforts and curriculum changes, students remain oblivious to those changes. When asked about their school's reform or change, students often responded according to the strengths and weaknesses of their own teachers instead of the success or failure of the schoolwide change. Weissbourd suggested that schools and districts prioritize the mental health of their teachers by identifying not only the seriously depressed but also teachers who have mild forms of depression or disillusionment because of the nature of their jobs over time. Mentor teachers can help with disillusioned ones, and for severe cases, mental health counseling should be arranged. By developing richer states of growth in teachers, students will observe, interact with, and aspire to imitate adults who are self-actualized.

CURRICULUM PROGRAMS

There are many programs aimed at building self-esteem, emotional literacy, and richer states of growth in our students. Character education, peace education, conflict resolution,

Lawrence Kohlberg is the author of *The Philosophy of Moral Development* (1981). He also contributed articles to professional journals and texts, such as "The Just Community School: The Theory and the Cambridge Cluster School Experiment," with E. Wasserman and N. Richardson (1975), for the Harvard University Center for Moral Education.

Kohlberg's theory of moral development never gained wide acceptance in the field of psychology; like Kohlberg himself, many of his students were to teach in schools of education. Nonetheless, Kohlberg's approach has served as a foil for socialization theorists, who deny that individuals develop according to the same set of stages regardless of their social surroundings, as well as for behaviorists, who deny that what people say about moral dilemmas has a bearing on how they behave. Feminists have criticized Kohlberg's conception of moral development because it initially drew on an all-male sample and because it ranks moral judgments based on universal human rights rather than care for those one is closest to. Although it has been the subject of many disagreements, Kohlberg's theory of moral development is recognized as a distinctive psychological and educational philosophy.

According to friends, Kohlberg was physically unwell at the time of his death and slipping into another major depression. In January 1987, he attempted to take his life and was hospitalized. On January 17, 1987, he obtained a day pass from Mount Auburn Hospital in Cambridge and disappeared. His body was found on April 6, 1987, in Boston Harbor, near Logan Airport, an apparent suicide. He was cremated, and his ashes were scattered off the coast of Cape Cod, Massachusetts.

Source: "Lawrence Kohlberg," *Scribner Encyclopedia of American Lives, Volume 2: 1986–1990.*

antibullying, violence prevention, emotional literacy, social skills, personal skills, and at-risk curriculum programs are available, to name a few. Generally, these programs are aimed at students who find themselves on the lower portion of Maslow's hierarchy (Weissburg, Resnik, Payton, & O'Brien, 2003). Through social and emotional learning programs, students can develop skills in maintaining healthy, caring, ethical, and active lives.

Knowing and understanding the theories associated with self-concept and self-awareness, you now have the ability to use sound practices to develop healthier self-concepts with your students. However, Ross, Powell, and Elias (2002) have pointed out that there is a gap between theory and practice related to addressing social and emotional learning in schools. Although the importance of social and emotional learning has become increasingly well established and accepted, no discipline has stepped up to lead the process. The result has been a patchwork approach to moral development in the structure of schools, especially middle schools (Ames & Miller, 2001).

Ross et al. (2002) listed the following suggestions for improving school-level social and emotional learning:

- Professional development for teachers and administrators should address methods for social and emotional development.

- Collaborative efforts among education professionals should increase.

- School psychology should move into the field of practice (i.e., community and mental health psychology) rather than evaluation.

Not only can you affect the self-esteem and emotional health of your students, but also school psychologists, counselors, and other mental health professionals have created programs to develop better self-concepts in students. The increasing recognition of the need to incorporate social and emotional learning and emotional intelligence into the regular instructional program provides an exciting opportunity for school psychologists to redefine their roles. The program, as described by Ross et al. (2002), is aimed at the prevention of high-risk behaviors, violence, and other disruptive behaviors. Another successful program is a product of the U.S. Office of Special Education Programs called "Positive Behavioral Support." This program uses data to drive collaborative behavioral planning and aids professionals in making proactive decisions for students with behavioral disorders. Through this paradigm, students are involved in personal and social-skill building that empowers students with emotional disabilities to achieve success among their regular education peers, thereby improving their self-concept.

Class meetings are sometimes necessary to address social issues or conflicts in the classroom.

Dubbed a "movement" rather than a plan, the Philadelphia schools are working to increase the academic self-esteem of their students through more challenging academic courses and guidance services aimed at peer counseling programs and improved decision making in their students (Snyder, 2003).

Schoolwide projects to build self-esteem can be found in the 47 Nativity Schools, which are designed to close the achievement gap between needy minority students and their white middle-class peers. In these schools, inner-city youth are chosen to attend based on their motivation and emotional intelligence potential. These schools are parochial, operated by a branch of the Jesuit Catholic community, and most schools include religious teaching. The schools cap enrollment at 70 and limit class sizes to 15. Students chosen to participate in this program lag a minimum of one or more years in academic achievement. They are considered more for their motivation and emotional competence than their intelligence. Although most do not tout their successes, most of the Nativity Schools succeed in closing their students' achievement gaps within three years.

Probably the most interesting schoolwide system for developing self-actualized learners can be found at Memorial Junior High School in Valley Stream, New York (Melchior, 1994). The conceptual systems theory was adapted to teach students critical-thinking skills that could be attributed to creative learners and the higher-conceptual-level learner. The model encourages learners to resist their natural tendency to desire certainty, passivity, and impulsivity. The counterpoint thinking model encourages learners to tolerate ambiguity, interdependence, and the search for multiple answers. The program has been successful in developing self-awareness, responsibility, and a love of lifelong learning.

CLASSROOM SCENARIO

On a Thursday afternoon during the fourth week of the new school year, Mr. Snyder, a fifth-grade teacher, receives a notice in his mailbox that informs him he will be getting a new student in his class beginning on Monday. With this student comes a list of personal infractions that have been documented by the school psychologists. As he reads this news, Mr. Snyder thinks to himself, "Oh no, a new student—just what I need. I just established a routine with my students in the room, and things are up and running smoothly in my class. My students know our routine. Now I have to initiate a new student to the room and our daily procedures."

As he glances at the school psychologist's report, he is amazed reading about Eric's previous offenses. Mr. Snyder reads, "Eric Bracken has been expelled from Our Lady of Lourdes Catholic School due to his inappropriate behavior." "It is reported that Eric set the school on fire. Eric does not work well with other children. He lives with a foster family and he has had three different foster homes since his birth." "Eric has self-concept and self-esteem issues."

Learning this news during his lunch break, Mr. Snyder begins to reflect on what this may mean for the mix of current students in his class. How well will Eric fit in? If Eric is a bully, as the school psychologist's report reads, who in the class will challenge his authority? Mr. Snyder thinks about the other boys in the class who would not stand for Eric's bullying and would likely fight back. Mr. Snyder makes it through the afternoon and the rest of his day. But as he is driving home that night, knowing that Eric will begin class on Monday, he decides that he should hold a class meeting with his students on Friday afternoon.

It is now Friday afternoon, and the students are filing into the room after their lunch. Mr. Snyder begins, "I hope you enjoyed your lunch and your recess. Instead of our usual science class this afternoon, I am going to propose that we have a class meeting." Various whoops and hollers rise up from the back of the room. "Well," begins Mr. Snyder, "We have never had a class meeting. Here is what I propose that we do. When everyone is listening, we will begin." Students find their seats and quiet down.

"Let's begin with a question. I want you to think of the people whom you know in your life. How are they the same and how are they different?"

Vita speaks up: Well, some people I know are my relatives, and some are not my relatives."

Mr. Snyder replies, "So, if I understand you correctly, you mean that the people like you are your relatives?"

Vita says, "Yah."

Mr. Snyder says, "Can you have relatives who are not the same as you? In other words, are all of your relatives the same?"

Vita says, "Uh, some are and some ain't."

Mr. Snyder says, "Can we have relatives who are different from us?"

"Okay," says Mr. Snyder. "How else can be people be the same?"

Marietta says, "They can have the same color hair."

Mr. Snyder says, "Okay, how can people be different?"

After listing several personal attributes about people, including their similarities and differences, Mr. Snyder directs the discussion to a different line of questioning.

He asks, "Do all people have the same opportunities in life?"

Leticia says, "No."

Mr. Snyder says, "Can you explain your response?"

Leticia says, "Some people are lucky and some are not."

"Okay," Mr. Snyder says, "What makes you feel lucky, Leticia?"

"I feel lucky because I have a sister and a mom who love me," says Leticia

Mr. Snyder continues, "Okay, would others in here agree? We can be considered lucky if we have people who love us. So, people who are unlucky might be different from us because they may not have had the same opportunities. Would everyone agree?"

Several students nod their heads.

"So, you are saying that people are not always treated the same way?" Mr. Snyder probes.

Michael says, "Well, yes, that is right. Sometimes my little brother gets things that I don't."

"And why is that?" says Mr. Snyder.

"Well, he is smaller," says Michael.

Mr. Snyder continues, "So, he gets things that are unique to him because he is younger. You probably wouldn't want the same things he gets, right, because you are bigger and older. Right?"

Mr. Snyder states, "So, we are not in control of things that may happen to us. Is that correct?"

Everyone agrees and nods their heads. "Yes!"

"Well, on Monday, we are going to have a new student in our class, and he has not had the same opportunities that we have had," continued Mr. Snyder. "So, what could we do to help him get started in our room?"

"Oh, I can show him our routine, Mr. Snyder," said Jesus.

"Okay, that would be great, Jesus," replied Mr. Snyder. "Now, if everyone agrees that not all people are treated the same way, what could we say about how that would make us feel?"

Susan says, "Well, I would not feel good if someone got something that I did not."

"Okay, Susan, thanks for being honest," says Mr. Snyder.

"So, with our new student, if he were to be angry because of things that have happened to him in the past, how should we treat him? What could we do with someone who might be angry and wants to get our attention?" asked Mr. Snyder.

Jesus says, "We could ignore it."

"What do the rest of you think?" Mr. Snyder continues.

"I think we could ignore him if he gets angry with us," agreed the other boys in the class.

"Okay, everyone, let's remember that when our new student arrives, we are going to help him adjust as best we can. If he tries to be mad with us, let's ignore him and go on with our work. Thanks for the meeting," said Mr. Snyder. "Now, with the rest of time we have today, let's play some kickball outside."

"Alright!" said everyone as they lined up at the door.

Mr. Snyder did not know if having a class meeting would be the best way to handle this particular situation. He did not want to purposefully bring attention to Eric as a new student. But the more Mr. Snyder thought about Eric's background, the more he knew Eric would challenge the other students in the class and act out to get their attention. Having the group decide not to react during this time did help Eric to adjust to the class. Eric's self-confidence and self-esteem changed that year as he was given a second chance to be in a different school with a group of students who accepted him. Eric's motivation for learning improved as he and Mr. Snyder worked through the anger and resentment he felt inside.

ASSESSMENT

Dr. William Damon, director of the Center on Adolescence at Stanford University, reported that one way to know whether students are on the right moral and emotional track is for parents to look for a strong, passionate interest (Gilbert, 2003). Sometimes those interests are not exactly what parents' desire for their children, but as long as it supports positive behavior, he encourages it. The other indicator of healthy self-concept is having a mentor, or someone who inspires them. If these two things—interest and inspiration—are not in place by mid-adolescence, Dr. Damon recommended getting some help for the child (Gilbert, 2003).

Another way to assess the processing of self-esteem and emotional literacy curriculum is to ask the right questions. According to Kohn (2003), what matters most are the questions that educators ask in regard to fundamental learning. Past practice has often produced the wrong questions, such as "How can we get these kids to obey?" or "What practical techniques can you offer that will make students show up, sit down, and do what they're told?" (Kohn, 2003, p. 27).

Other researchers have stated that the assessment process can be determined if educators ask questions related to "getting it" (Eaker, DuFour, & Burnette, 2002). Educational outcomes in the social domain are not difficult to assess if data are measured by school discipline, suspensions, and guidance visits, for example. In addition, personal issues and self-concept could be measured by school climate and school safety surveys.

TECHNOLOGY

This instructional pattern, which includes the self-concept and self-esteem of the individual learner, has few technological applications. If you want to conduct an Internet search using the terms "self-concept," "learning style," or "self-help programs," you might be able to find an online learning style inventory. Using the computer in this manner is the only technological support that could assist students with discovering more information about who they are. A list of websites related to this area can be found in the text supplement.

Learning Tenets
That Support Self-Taught Instruction

The brain seeks to classify information and the things to be learned.

The brain operates on many levels simultaneously. As we take in information from our world, we process color, movement, emotion, shape, intensity, sound, taste, and weight. From this information, our brain assembles patterns, composes meaning, and sorts daily life experiences based on a number of cues. When we consider these factors and the motivation for learning, we realize that potential differences may exist in each one of us. Each individual is unique in the manner in which we process, perceive, and learn. If we could figure out the right combination for these variables, we could increase understanding of why some learners are self-starters, self-motivators, and prefer to be self-taught learners.

The emotional system drives attention, and attention drives meaning and memory.

School is not just about the things to be learned. School is a miniculture that is constantly being massaged by the students, school personnel, and parents in the community. The feeling tone of your classroom is controlled by you, the teacher. Many affective issues are dealt with on a daily basis in the school. In the Thought to Action section of this chapter, you will find some strategies that could be used in the classroom to assist students with their emotions. Emotionally literate people can employ strategies that make good use of these emotions through voice volume, tone, and rate of speech, for example. Vary your academic environment to maintain a happy, secure place for your students.

Remember, what students remember most about their school experience is often related to how they were treated by their teachers and other school personnel. Students will remember the "affect" of their school experience—their emotions and how they felt about school. Rarely do students remember their school experience because the teacher had good content knowledge. This does not mean that we think content knowledge is unimportant. It just means that in the lives of your students, getting along and having a positive emotional response toward school is vitally important.

The brain is designed for ups and downs, not constant attention.

When we think about individuals who are self-taught learners, we realize that many factors influence the ability to attend to information. Some of these differences are diet, emotions, and biological chemistry. Any one of these factors may cause fluctuations in attention. Each person has a natural learning pattern or pulse. Depending on the activity and the self-taught learner's characteristics, ups and downs may occur in the ability to attend. These rhythms and cycles may vary from one individual to the next.

Learning occurs through processing and active engagement with visual, auditory, and kinesthetic modalities.

Self-taught learners are very skilled in understanding how they learn. They are keen on knowing what it takes for them to recall material, and they practice the skills unique to them. They know, for example, that for learning to occur, they must read the material, then develop an outline, then write it, and finally reread it. This pattern for understanding material may vary from one self-taught learner to the next. However, skilled self-taught learners understand their own learning style and seek to rehearse and process what they must learn. Knowing your preferred learning style and understanding which modality is used to ensure learning is a skill of the self-taught learner.

Good teaching is about recognizing and selecting instructional patterns that match the context for learning and the students we are teaching.

Self-taught learners understand the amount of light, sound, and level of comfort they need to concentrate. When they need to learn, they will seek an environment or context that matches the manner in which they can learn best. Understanding oneself in relation to this process can benefit one's learning potential.

Summary

Self-taught instruction is best suited to Part V, "Student-Centered Patterns," because developing richer states of personal growth among all students is the goal. This goal is ambitious for schools, colleges, universities, and communities. Knowledge, high levels of cognition, and personal satisfaction are indeed worthy efforts for educators, but the application of effort should be more widespread than just those who have the ability to achieve higher states. The efforts of educators should focus on students at all levels of the continuum. In addition, whole systems should be designed to ensure that those with influential positions in the lives of the socially needy are at higher states of growth so that they can act as positive role models.

Thought to Action

1. For students who need to have their emotional reactions to school interactions recorded, try the traditional diary-style journal: Have students record daily events in a diary.

2. A format that is different from the traditional diary-style journal is the split-entry journal: Each page is divided in half by a vertical line. In the left column, students record their feelings, which correlate to their work in the right column.

3. Have students brainstorm or free write a list of single words or short phrases related to a series of directed topics. After 60 seconds, direct students to list words that describe the physical sensations that go along with their feelings.

4. For students who are visual learners, have them use the "Charting the Day" bar graph. Students create a graph of their emotions during a specific period of time or activity. (It looks like a multicolored bar graph.)

5. In "Speak and Feel Exchange" (SAFE), students verbalize their emotions and the physical sensations that accompany them. However, students must be able to identify and articulate how and what they are feeling in real time. This activity is not recommended for students at the lowest levels of self-awareness.

ON YOUR OWN

Log on to the web-based student study site at http://www.sagepub.com/holt for access to a Standards-Based Student Project that will help you connect what you have learned in this chapter to your state's standards; study aids, such as electronic flashcards; and research recommendations, including journal article links and other Web resources.

PART VI

Thinking and Organizing the Content

Examining the content and choosing the best way to approach the organization of the material is the focus of this final type of instruction. How can I best organize the concepts that belong to a subject to enhance the learning process? What do I need to know about the content in relation to the students' perceptions of the things to be learned? This section represents more than just the teacher's knowledge of content; it is the concepts within the content that determine learning outcomes. What patterns exist between and among the concepts that can be organized to enhance student learning?

In Part VI, Chapter 12 examines thinking patterns, Chapter 13 explores memorization, Chapter 14 looks at attaining concepts, and Chapter 15 investigates inquiry.

12

Thinking Patterns

AMERICAN SCHOOLS HAVE ALWAYS BEEN CONCERNED WITH PROVIDING THEIR STUDENTS APPROPRIATE education so that they can become productive citizens within our society. However, the way we define "productive citizens" has changed as American society has changed. As our public schools have accepted the responsibility of educating all children regardless of race, ethnicity, gender, or special needs and as laws and court decisions have struck down discriminatory practices in the hiring of personnel in our businesses and industries, schools have had to adjust and adapt their curricula to meet the learning potential of all of these students. Thus, the knowledge and skills that are necessary for equal access to employment have become a priority of public education. As schools strive to meet the demands of employers, the curriculum fluctuates according to the postsecondary needs of students, whether that means immediate employment or further education.

If you were to examine school curricula over the past 50 years, you would see an emphasis on basic skills, inclusion of vocational education and career exploration, attention to values clarification and character education, a push for the development of higher-order thinking skills, attention to (or sometimes a lack thereof) the fine arts, introduction of physical fitness into physical education programs, introduction of social justice and civil rights education, a huge push for more mathematics and science (particularly following the *Sputnik* launch), and all kinds of special needs programs. Currently, we find a rigid back-to-basics approach and high-stakes testing curriculum with few provisions for the variety of needs of today's students.

Many of the attempts to change the school curriculum were not necessarily good choices because there was little research that could tell educators what really works and what does not work. Many students were tracked into programs and deprived of educational opportunities because of decisions made about their academic potential. Some students, because of parental concern, were placed in programs that were not appropriate for their academic potential. Needless to say, all of our attempts to design curricula that meet the needs of all students have not always been successful and could be subjected to lots of criticism, some of which is justified.

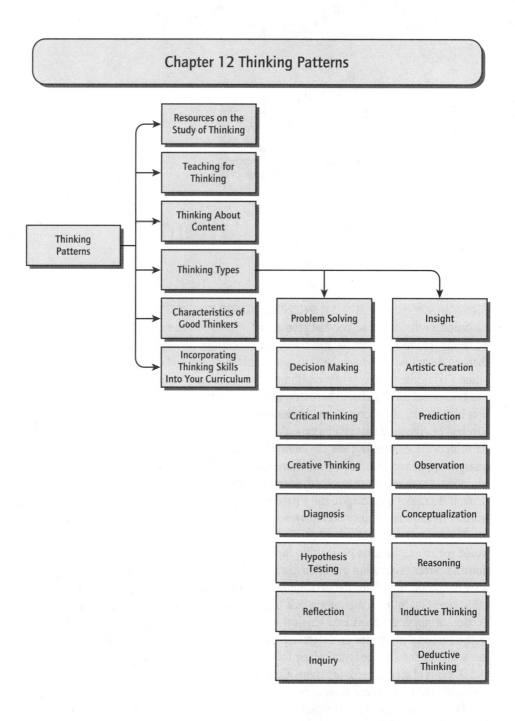

Chapter 12 Thinking Patterns

Thinking Patterns

- Resources on the Study of Thinking
- Teaching for Thinking
- Thinking About Content
- Thinking Types
- Characteristics of Good Thinkers
- Incorporating Thinking Skills Into Your Curriculum

Thinking Types:

- Problem Solving
- Decision Making
- Critical Thinking
- Creative Thinking
- Diagnosis
- Hypothesis Testing
- Reflection
- Inquiry

- Insight
- Artistic Creation
- Prediction
- Observation
- Conceptualization
- Reasoning
- Inductive Thinking
- Deductive Thinking

However, in all of these attempts to best meet the needs of the changing population of American schools and changing society, one fact is certain. Students cannot be successful in postsecondary environments unless they leave the K–12 system with strong reading, writing, arithmetic, and thinking skills. Much attention, particularly now, has been focused on the development and improvement of reading, writing, and arithmetic skills, whereas little attention has been devoted to the development and improvement of thinking skills. Too often, it is assumed that by having students work through English, science, social studies, and mathematics classes, they will develop appropriate thinking skills. The reality is that most students do not develop these skills without some instructional help from their teachers.

Students rarely see the transferability of thinking skills that are taught in one subject area—for example, problem solving in science—to other content areas, such as mathematics or social studies (Adams, 1991). Also missing from educators' understanding is the realization that thinking skills are not necessarily subject specific. Creative thinking should not be relegated to the domain of the English teachers and fine arts teachers. If scientists were not capable of thinking creatively and "outside the box," humans would never have walked on the moon; we would never have been able to view the exploration of Mars by rovers launched into space or see the rings of Saturn with such clarity and awe. We would not have the technology we now take for granted, nor would we have medicines to prevent the diseases that killed our ancestors. If our musicians and artists were incapable of solving problems or using critical-thinking skills, we would not have the variety of music we listen to, the fantastic films we watch, the computer-based graphics we have come to rely on, or the virtual tours of museums we can now enjoy.

This chapter will examine the types and ways of thinking that should be included in every curriculum and thinking-skills strategies that can be incorporated into different models of teaching. Because the organization of content and the thinking skills needed to use that content are inextricably connected, it is imperative that you understand the relationship between content and thinking skills. Different thinking-skills programs will be explored to inform you of the options if you are working with students who need a different approach to learning how to think. In addition, the concept of metacognition and its importance to your understanding of thinking skills will be addressed.

RESEARCH ANCHOR

Probably one of the best resources devoted to the study of thinking skills is a publication of the Association for Supervision and Curriculum Development titled *Developing Minds,* edited by Art Costa (1991). This two-volume publication sorts through the research on thinking skills, methods of teaching thinking skills, and programs for teaching thinking skills. In the introductory chapters, a case is made for teaching thinking skills in the curriculum based on statistics gathered from various sources: National Assessment of Educational Progress (NAEP) reports; the Education Commission of the States (1982); the Institute for the Study of Human Knowledge (Ornstein, 1980); the NAEP's *Mathematics Report Card—Are We Measuring Up?* (Dossey, Mullis, Lingquist, & Chambers, 1988), *Science Report Card—Elements of Risk and Recovery* (Mullis & Jenkins, 1988), and *Writing Report Card, 1984–1988* (Applebee, Langer, Mullis, & Jenkins, 1990); as well as books and reports such as *A Place Called School* (Goodlad, 1984) and *A Nation at Risk* (National Commission on Excellence in Education, 1983).

In addition, the annual Gallup Poll of Teachers' Attitudes Toward the Public Schools, published yearly by Phi Delta Kappa, consistently shows that teachers are very concerned about the need to teach thinking skills to students. The data gathered in these reports can be summarized as follows:

- Although students' performance in reading, writing, mathematics, and science proficiency is improving, that improvement is still relegated to the lower levels of Bloom's taxonomy. Students are not demonstrating sufficient skills at the higher levels of thinking (see the National Center for Education Statistics's Condition of Education indicators, available at http://nces.ed.gov/programs/coe/).

- With increasing societal pressures, such as energy production, population growth, environmental concerns, employment and health issues, and economic and social problems, students need to develop quality thinking skills to be efficient and effective problem solvers and decision makers in the future (Ornstein, 1980).

- Mathematics skills are improving, but for students ages 9, 13, and 17, most of the progress has been made at the lower levels; students need to develop higher-order thinking skills in mathematics (Dossey et al., 1988, p. 12).

- Recent improvements in science have occurred at the lower levels of thinking and basic knowledge acquisition. Few students demonstrate higher-level skills (Mullis & Jenkins, 1988, pp. 19–20).

- Although students ages 9, 13, and 17 can perform minimal responses, few students demonstrate reasoning skills and the use of higher-order thinking strategies (Applebee et al., 1990, p. 40).

- According to Goodlad's (1984) study of 1,000 classrooms in communities across the country, 75% of class time was spent on instruction. Seventy percent of that time was teacher controlled, and of that share, teachers only engaged students in higher-order thinking 1% of the time.

As you read through current literature on thinking skills, the concerns remain much the same. Teachers are working hard in the classroom to ensure that students can perform adequately on the high-stakes tests that are being used to evaluate our schools, but much of that testing is still focused on knowledge acquisition rather than the higher-order levels of thinking that are needed in today's complex society. The need for higher-order thinking is greater now than ever before in our history; it is imperative that you understand what the thinking skills are and how you can incorporate them into your teaching.

WHAT ARE THINKING SKILLS?

Children learn to think long before they ever come to school. In previous chapters, we explored how the brain functions and how we learn and develop knowledge. Young children, before they develop language facility of their own, learn by observation, sorting the input they receive, categorizing, and relating the information to previous observations, and they begin to build a knowledge base from which they can continue to learn. Language is learned through repetition and making relationships between sounds and objects. Young children do a great deal of experimentation and learn through trial and error as they grow up. For example, have you ever watched the "tasting habits" of young children? Mothers get upset as children keep placing objects in their mouths, but children instinctively do that and eventually, with some guidance from adults, discriminate edible objects from inedible ones. Through repetition, they learn the names of the objects they can eat. Children initially might call all four-legged animals dogs or cats (whichever is first known to them), but eventually they will distinguish dogs from cats, horses, cows, pigs, and other four-legged animals.

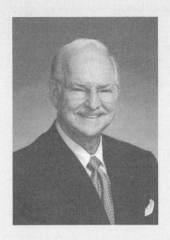

Arthur L. Costa is an emeritus professor of education at California State University, Sacramento, and cofounder of the Institute for Intelligent Behavior in El Dorado Hills, California. He has served as a classroom teacher, curriculum consultant, assistant superintendent for instruction, and director of educational programs for the National Aeronautics and Space Administration. He has made presentations and conducted workshops in all 50 states as well as Mexico, Central and South America, Canada, Australia, New Zealand, Africa, Europe, Asia, and the Islands of the South Pacific.

Dr. Costa has devoted his career to improving education through more thoughtful instruction and assessment. He edited the book *Developing Minds: A Resource Book for Teaching Thinking* and is the author of *The Enabling Behaviors* and *The School as a Home for the Mind*. He is the coauthor of *Techniques for Teaching Thinking* (with Larry Lowery) and *Cognitive Coaching: A Foundation for Renaissance Schools* (with Bob Garmston), and the coeditor of *Assessment in the Learning Organization*, *Assessment Strategies for Self-Directed Learning*, the *Habits of Mind* series (with Bena Kallick), and the trilogy *Process as Content* (with Rosemarie Liebmann). His works have been translated into Dutch, Chinese, Spanish, Hebrew, and Arabic.

Active in many professional organizations, Dr. Costa served as president of the California Association for Supervision and Curriculum Development and was the national president of that organization from 1988 to 1989.

Part of this ability to distinguish is the child's ability to examine characteristics and to place that information with the language heard from adults. All of this listening, trying, sorting, and naming are manifestations of various forms of thinking skills. Unless we are born with some physiological defect, most of our initial learning is created by the experiences we have in our environment and our ability to think about those experiences and put names on the various aspects of those experiences.

According to Howard Gardner (1982), much of our exploratory efforts to learn as young children are identical to the practicing that scientists and artists engage in when they create new knowledge and images. Unfortunately, however, this self-induced exploration ceases once we enter formal education. Current authors who support brain-based learning (Given, 2002; Jensen, 1998; Jones, 2003; Sprenger, 1999) all imply that what is wrong with what we do in school is that schools are "brain incompatible" (a term coined by Hart in 1975). To improve our students' learning and develop their thinking skills, you, as the teacher, need to create classroom conditions and activities that are conducive to student thinking. But what does this mean?

According to Costa (1991), teachers must teach for, of, and about thinking in their classrooms. Teaching for thinking means developing a classroom climate that engages students in their learning:

- You pose problems, raise questions, or create dilemmas and invite students to engage in problem solving.

- You positively respond to students' ideas, listen carefully to their thoughts, and help them to clarify and understand their thinking. You remain nonjudgmental as students explore ideas, and you encourage experimentation and risk taking.

- You model good thinking strategies in your teaching and interaction with students, colleagues, and parents.

By doing the above-mentioned activities, you establish a classroom climate that is conducive to teaching for thinking.

The teaching of thinking means direct instruction of specific thinking strategies. Some authors have indicated that separate courses specifically devoted to teaching of thinking ought to be included in the curriculum (e.g., de Bono, 1985; Feuerstein, 1980; Lipman, 1991), whereas others believe that the direct teaching of thinking skills can be incorporated into the existing curriculum (e.g., Beyer, 1987; Ennis, 1991; Marzano, 2003; Parnes, 1992; Pogrow, 1988; Presseisen, 1991). Regardless of whether a separate curriculum for the teaching of thinking skills is feasible, you need to be cognizant of your obligation to teach students how to engage in various forms of thinking while they are in your classroom. There are specific steps to follow to be a good problem solver, and students need to learn them and practice them. For your students to engage in creative thinking, they need to learn how to brainstorm and evaluate ideas. For students to be critical thinkers, they need to know the strategies of analysis, logical argument, and organization. These are all teachable skills that can be woven into your lessons and are not tied to specific content areas.

The third category of Costa's thinking is teaching about thinking. This is the *metacognitive* dimension of thinking. We have discussed metacognition in previous chapters, but as a reminder, metacognition is thinking about how we think. It is the self-awareness of how we process information and make sense out of what we are doing. Too often, teachers do not take the time to get their students thinking about what they have just done. Without this reflection, students often do not understand why they solved problems correctly or why their ideas about how to do something did not work.

Fundamental to metacognition is learning how to learn and helping students to understand which learning strategies work best for them. Are they auditory, visual, or kinesthetic learners? Are they good at problem solving but not creative thinking? Do they know how to ask questions to help them get on the right track before tackling an activity or assignment? Knowing about how they learn will help students make adjustments when they are confronted with tasks that ask them to work in areas that are not their strengths. Rather than getting frustrated and quitting, students can rearrange the tasks and clarify the expectations so that they can apply the skills that work best for them.

Two other areas that should be explored in teaching about thinking are knowing how our brain functions (this is particularly valuable as different learning strategies are introduced to students) and the study of how knowledge is produced (epistemic cognition). The latter knowledge was the basis for many of the curriculum reforms of the 1950s and 1960s in the areas of mathematics and science. The purpose of many of these programs—designed immediately after we were embarrassed by the Soviet Union's successful launch of *Sputnik*—was to help students think like scientists and mathematicians. The failure of these programs had much to do with the inability of teachers to teach science and mathematics from the perspective of the scientist or the mathematician. After all, they had not been taught that way, and most of them were not scientists or mathematicians. Although they were very knowledgeable about the subjects they were teaching, they did not work in the field or use science and mathematics to solve problems or create new ideas. Without a thorough understanding of how content is used in the real world, it is difficult to teach it through the eyes of the artist, musician, scientist, geographer, mathematician, writer, or composer.

In today's environment, however, through the use of technology, there is far more information available to you that will help your students understand how knowledge is used and created in various fields. By studying the lives of philosophers, scientists, artists, and composers, students can begin to make comparisons about the kinds of thinking used by various individuals. Epistemological questions can be related to these comparisons. Students can use the Internet to contact novelists and ask them about their strategies for writing, how they get their ideas, how they structure their time, and how they overcome writer's block. Students can examine why certain forms of inquiry, such as problem solving, might not work as well for solving social problems as they do for solving scientific puzzles. They can watch some of the programs presented on cable channels such as Discovery, Animal Planet, the History Channel, and Lifetime, which focus many of their programs on how we gather information, process it, and learn from it. Paul and Elder (2003) suggest that each subject have its own systematic way of thinking about the content within that subject, and these ways can be found by examining the following elements:

- The purposes of the content

- The questions and issues generally attributed to that content

- The information within the content and how it is used

- The ideas and theories appropriate to interpret data from that content

- The concepts, theories, definitions, laws, principles, models, and axioms of the content

- The assumptions about the content

- The implications and consequences generated by the content

- The perspectives or points of view attributed to that content

Although Paul and Elder identify these eight elements of thinking about content, they do not indicate that systematic ways of thinking about different content areas cannot overlap. Some of the same skills of thinking apply to a variety of content areas; however, it is imperative that students and teachers recognize that content is structured differently, and for us to be good thinkers about the content we are trying to learn, we must be cognizant of that structure. Knowing how content is structured, what kinds of questions need to be asked about that content, and what kind of thinking one needs to engage in to learn that content is also part of the metacognitive process—it is thinking about thinking.

Besides Costa's notion that we need to teach for, of, and about thinking, it is also important that we have a solid knowledge about the types of thinking that humans do. Various authors have chosen to define these types of thinking differently; the list that follows details the most common types of thinking that we do:

- Problem solving: resolving a known difficulty (Presseisen, 1991)

- Decision making: choosing a best alternative (Presseisen, 1991)

Metacognition is thinking about how we think.

- Critical thinking: understanding particular meanings, relationships, theories, and proofs (Presseisen, 1991)

- Creative thinking: developing new ideas or products (Presseisen, 1991)

- Diagnosis: troubleshooting (Glatthorn & Baron, 1991)

- Hypothesis testing: forming and testing hypotheses (Glatthorn & Baron, 1991)

- Reflection: searching for general principles or rules based on previously gathered evidence (Glatthorn & Baron, 1991)

- Insight: experiencing the "eureka phenomenon" or, as others have defined it, the light bulb going on; solutions come suddenly and with certainty (Glatthorn & Baron, 1991)

- Artistic creation: forming a synthesis, a deliberate search for goals that can be reproduced in a painting, poem, or musical composition (Glatthorn & Baron, 1991)

- Prediction: analyzing current evidence, placing it into the context of previous knowledge, and generating a position (Glatthorn & Baron, 1991)

- Observation: watching, listening, sorting, mimicking (Glatthorn & Baron, 1991)

- Conceptualizing: generalizing from specifics or inventing concepts or models (Beyer, 1987)

- Reasoning: inferring information systematically according to the rules of logic (Beyer, 1987)

- Inductive thinking: examining specific information to form a generalization according to the rules of logic (Beyer, 1987)

- Deductive thinking: reasoning from a known principle to an unknown or from the general to the specific according to the rules of logic (Beyer, 1987)

- Inquiry: having an awareness of problem-solving and critical-thinking skills and the ability to apply them to a given situation (Costa, 1991)

In addition to these types of thinking, you need only return to Bloom's taxonomy to see additional ideas about the types of thinking we do at the various levels of the taxonomy or revised taxonomy. The type of thinking that we do at the recall level, for example, is far different from the thinking we do at the application, analysis, evaluation, or synthesis levels. You need only look at the verbs that are used to form your learning objectives to realize there are different expectations for thinking at each level of the taxonomy.

As you examine the 16 different definitions of thinking listed here, you may begin to realize that they are not necessarily distinct—that is, in critical thinking, you would be expected to use reasoning skills, observation, and inductive and deductive strategies. In creative thinking, you would use skills of observation, prediction, artistic creation, and reflection. Likewise, problem solving and decision making incorporate some of the other identified thinking skills, such as inquiry, critical thinking, diagnosis, and conceptualizing, to name a few. Regardless of how we define thinking skills, the important thing to remember is that you need to help students develop their thinking skills across the curriculum areas. There are instructional strategies that are specifically designed to develop some of these thinking skills, whereas others are best developed by incorporating them into instructional strategies such as cooperative learning, direct instruction, and self-taught instruction.

In-service and staff development workshops facilitate ways that teaching can be taught.

CHARACTERISTICS OF GOOD THINKERS

If one of your goals is for your students to enhance their thinking skills, then you need to know the characteristics of good thinkers. Glatthorn and Baron (1991) developed the following list of characteristics of a good thinker:

- Welcomes problematic situations

- Tolerates ambiguity

- Is sufficiently self-critical

- Looks for alternative possibilities and goals

- Seeks evidence on both sides of an issue

- Is reflective and deliberative

- Searches extensively when appropriate

- Believes in the value of rationality

- Believes thinking can be effective

- Is deliberative in defining goals

- Revises goals when necessary

- Is open to multiple possibilities

A good thinker is someone who likes to engage in the thinking process and finds the process fun and exciting. A person may be a good thinker in one subject area but not necessarily in another, so you should not be quick to judge a student's ability to think. For example, it is not unusual to find a student who is an excellent thinker in mathematics but cannot analyze a story, find errors in grammar, or interpret a poem or sonnet. On the other hand, a student might be an extremely creative writer and storyteller but cannot make sense of chemical bond theory. It is possible that our inability to think effectively in some subject areas may have to do with Paul and Elder's (2003) notion that different subjects have different ways of thinking that are directly related to the structure of that subject; if we do not understand the structure of the subject, we may not be able to think effectively about the content. Much of how we think is influenced by what we are asked to think about. Subject matter has a powerful effect on one's thinking-skills development. That is why some researchers, such as Feuerstein (Link, 1991), have developed programs such as Instrumental Enrichment, which try to teach a variety of thinking skills in a "content-free" environment.

As you contemplate how you will infuse thinking-skills development into your curriculum, you need to set goals for your students. You need to assess where they are with respect to how they think in the content area you will be teaching. As you think about all of this, you can, as you write your lesson plans, determine where you might need to teach a certain type of thinking skill directly. You may need to think about alternatives if you assume that students have a thinking skill and come to discover in the course of your instructional strategy that they do not have the skill or cannot use the skill effectively. In planning your lesson, if you follow the guidelines suggested by Bloom's revised taxonomy, you will be able to determine where the teaching of thinking skills belongs in your program. As you write objectives at higher levels, you will be automatically involved in thinking-skills development.

There are many resources available to you for teaching thinking skills in the classroom. You need only go on the Internet and type in "thinking skills lessons," and you will be bombarded with ideas and suggestions for the integration of thinking skills into your curriculum. You also need to examine the materials provided to you by the curriculum coordinator or resource person at your school; many of these materials have provisions for the teaching of thinking skills. Look closely at the teacher's guide to your textbooks and any supplemental materials that come with the textbook. Usually, these materials will have suggestions for the teaching of thinking skills specific to the content you are teaching.

If all else fails, remember a few basic things: The questions you ask your students should fall into the *why* and *how* categories rather than the *where*, *what,* and *when* categories. Insisting that students explain a phenomenon or a procedure helps them much more than simply identifying it or describing when it might be used. For example, it is far more important for students to be able to explain the decisions made by a character in a novel than to identify all the characters in the novel or attribute lines of text to an individual character. How many times were you asked to memorize phrases from poetry or plays and recite them on demand in class? How many of these passages do you remember now? Of what value was the activity of memorizing and reciting those passages? What do you remember about the rest of the poem, play, or story? Why do you think you were expected to read the poem, play, or story in the first place?

The same could be said for the study of history. How many dates and events and people do you remember from your world history classes? Can you explain the causes of World War I or World War II and the dilemmas faced by the Allied forces and the enemies during those wars? Can you explain why enemies are now friends and allies are now enemies? How could this knowledge help you to explain to your students the current engagements in which we find ourselves in the Middle East? Are there any similarities? Do you think you could have been taught differently, so that what you learned in high school might now be of value to you as a teacher?

INCORPORATING THINKING SKILLS INTO YOUR CURRICULUM

To provide you with some easily adaptable techniques for incorporating thinking skills into the subject matter that you are teaching, we will focus on the four major categories of thinking: problem solving, decision making, critical thinking, and creative thinking.

Problem Solving

There are many different interpretations of problem solving, and part of the difference is directly related to how we use language in our subject fields. For example, in mathematics, we typically find the phrase, "solve the following problems," when what we really intend is for students to find the answers to these problems by applying the rules they just learned. Most of what is called "problem solving" in mathematics is not problem solving in the true sense of the term but the application of rules to find correct answers. Problem solving does occur in mathematics: for example, when we are working with word problems, or in higher mathematics, when we are attempting to prove theorems and ideas.

Too often, problem solving is thought of as a skill that is used specifically in the sciences and is directly related to the scientific method. The scientific method does, in fact, identify a procedure that is applicable in the laboratory and is taught to all science students:

1. Identify the problem.

2. Formulate hypotheses.

3. Test the hypotheses.

4. Analyze the data.

5. Draw conclusions.

Depending on whose version of the scientific method you use, you may include more or fewer steps. However, the purpose is to provide a systematic means of working through a problem or dilemma. However, teachers and students often erroneously assume that the scientific method cannot be used in subjects other than the sciences. Because terms such as "hypotheses" and "data analysis" are used, it is assumed that the procedure is only useful in experimental studies. Therefore, you might be more inclined to think of problem solving as it is described by George Polya in his seminal work *How to Solve It* (1957). Though Polya was a mathematician, in his book he described a four-stage method for general problem solving that is adaptable to any subject, from academics to life skills. His stages are as follows:

1. Understand the problem.

2. Devise a plan.

3. Carry out the plan.

4. Look back.

If the problem you are attempting to solve is a science problem, you can see how this general plan for solving a problem could easily be converted to the scientific method. If, on the other hand, you are trying to solve a word problem in mathematics, this plan works very nicely, as it does if you are examining a social problem, a literary dilemma, an architectural challenge, an engineering concern, or the production of an artistic piece.

There are many ways students can engage in understanding the problem—the key to solving the problem. They can draw diagrams, they can restate the problem in their own words and ask their teacher or peers if their translation is correct, or they can discuss the problem with their peers in pairs or groups. How students understand the problem is directly related to the complexity of the problem and the context in which it is presented. Research has shown that if the problem is not meaningful to the students, then they are less likely to be successful at finding a solution (Arnand & Ross, 1987; Ross, 1983; Wright & Wright, 1985).

Students need to be taught how to strategically design plans to solve problems. Again, what is taught in these strategic plans is usually directly related to the context of the problem. Different content areas may use different strategies to design a plan. Problems in the sciences are usually solved in a lab, where strict procedures are followed. In mathematics, different schema for

George Polya (1887–1985) was a mathematics educator at Stanford University from 1940 until 1953. Polya wrote *How to Solve It,* one of the most widely distributed mathematics books in history. The popular book has sold more than one million copies and has been translated into 15 languages. Polya made notable discoveries in probability, problem solving, geometry, numbers theory, and other fields, and his name is associated with several mathematical concepts. His 1925 book *Problems and Theories in Analysis,* which he wrote with Gabor Szego, is considered by many to be his most important work. It was written when Polya was working at the Swiss Federal Institute of Technology, where he taught for 26 years. Polya received the Mathematical Association of America's distinguished service award in 1963, for his constructive influence on mathematical education in the widest sense. His other writings include *Mathematics and Plausible Reasoning, Mathematical Discovery,* and *Mathematical Methods in Science.*

Source: Biography Resource Center, University of Central Florida, retrieved July 27, 2004.

translating language into mathematical symbols and establishing equations are used. When examining social problems, the procedures might involve collecting data in the form of written materials, newspaper reports, television documentaries, and personal interviews. Literary dilemmas might require a systematic analysis of the meaning of words and phrases used in the literary selection, particularly in a genre such as poetry. Because devising a plan is directly related to the subject matter at hand, it is imperative that you, the teacher, help your students to develop the necessary skills to do this effectively. According to Wood, Woloshyn, and Willoughby (1995), this takes direct instruction and time.

Once the plan is designed, students must carry it out and reexamine what they have done. In the reexamination stage, they need to think about the effectiveness and efficiency of their plan. If they were going to solve a similar problem in the future, what would they do differently and why? This last stage is very important in helping students to build their skills and confidence in problem solving. They also need to learn that finding a solution that *does not work* is just as important to their learning as finding one that does work. Much of our progress in science has been based on learning about what did not work.

Decision Making

Our lives are filled with decisions: what to eat for breakfast, what to wear on any given day, what books to read or television programs to watch, what movie to see, what classes to take, what car to buy, what college to go to, what job to accept, what insurance to buy, what house to buy, where to live, and so on. Some of the decisions we make almost automatically—for example, what to eat for breakfast. Rarely do we debate the alternatives and decide which is the healthiest or most economical. We eat either what we always eat for breakfast, what we can grab on the run, or all

TABLE 12.1	Decision-Making Model

Define the decision-making context:

- Identify the goal or purpose to achieve
- Identify values
- Understand uncertainty
- Identify alternatives
- Analyze alternatives
- Rank alternatives
- Evaluate alternatives
- Choose the best alternative

too often, nothing at all. This type of decision making is more of a habit than a thoughtful, deliberative process of sensible, objective, and rational examination of viable alternatives. What we are going to examine here is the latter form of decision making: having to choose among alternatives when we are faced with decisions that may have more complex outcomes.

There are a variety of models of decision making; the one presented in Table 12.1 combines the decision making models of Barry Beyer (1987) and Robin Gregory and Robert Clemen (2004).

In defining the context for decision making, it is imperative that you learn when to use a systematic process for decision making. That is, does the goal or purpose to be achieved warrant the time spent on following a systematic decision-making process? Not every decision you make requires this process. For example, there is no need to use this process to decide what you are going to wear or what you are going to have for dinner, but the process may be very important when you are buying a car, deciding which college to attend, or weighing job opportunities. Being able to clearly delineate the goal or purpose to be achieved is important because the desired goal or purpose becomes a criterion for judging the available alternatives. By defining your goal or purpose, you will examine the gap between your goal and your current situation and attempt to identify causes for that gap and means of closing the gap (Kysilka & Biraimah, 1992).

Decisions are not made in a vacuum; they are highly affected by the values that you hold, whether those values are societal or personal. When making decisions, the alternatives you think about lead to different consequences, some of which may be more satisfying to you than others, depending on the values that you hold. Thus, understanding your values is an important but often neglected part of learning how to make good decisions. When making decisions within a group setting, individual values and beliefs may be part of the reason that some groups have difficulty making decisions—their values may be in conflict. Knowing and understanding your values requires you to be introspective, to think carefully about what is really important to you and what pleases you the most. When you understand your values, you become more conscious of the values of others and begin to appreciate the different opinions that exist in a group. Understanding your values also empowers you to make better decisions (Gregory & Clemen, 2004).

Our lives are filled with uncertainty. Whether that uncertainty relates to the price of gasoline from week to week, whether your lost luggage from your recent holiday trip will ever be found and returned to you, or what the weather will be tomorrow, it can influence the decisions we make. Suppose, for example, that you are planning a road trip to North Carolina. Based on the number of days and the distance you have to cover, you estimate the cost of gasoline as part of your decision to make the trip. However, two days into your trip, the cost of gasoline escalates from $2.25 per gallon to $2.37 per gallon, and then, before your trip ends, to $2.86 per gallon. Was your decision to take the trip flawed? Not really—you had no way of knowing that the cost of gasoline would skyrocket during your trip. It was simply an uncertainty that you had little control over. The key to dealing with uncertainties is to identify them, get as much information about them as possible if you think they will have a negative impact on your decisions, then proceed with your decision-making process.

Identifying feasible alternatives to achieve your goal or purpose is a very important step in the decision-making process. Ways to determine alternatives include brainstorming, the use of analogous or similar case options, or the elaboration of possible alternatives.

Once you have a set of alternatives, you need to analyze them. The analysis should be based on relevant criteria. Those criteria are directly related to the goal or purpose you are examining, but most often include long-term and short-term consequences such as the costs (financial or opportunity) and resources needed for each of the alternatives (Kysilka & Biraimah, 1992).

The sixth step in this process is ranking the alternatives. Because the alternatives have been analyzed according to criteria, the ranking will be determined by how well they meet the criteria.

The next step is the evaluation of alternatives, which requires you to think about trade-offs (Gregory & Clemen, 2004). Dealing with trade-offs is a very difficult task: It means examining values in light of consequences and weighing equally viable alternatives with different consequences—maybe positive immediate results but not-so-positive long-term results. You need to ask yourself, what is most important as you attempt to rank your alternatives: knowing that you may be giving up immediate wants for long-term gains or vice versa.

The final step in this process is choosing the best alternative. Your final selection will be based on your best efforts to analyze, rank, and evaluate your alternatives. Once you have selected the alternative and put it into operation, you will experience the consequences of your decision making. Afterward, you may want to reflect on your decision to assure yourself that you made a good decision or reexamine what you did and what you might want to do differently if the consequences were not what you expected.

Obviously, decision making is not an easy task, but because you engage in so many decision-making activities in the course of a day, most of which require no in-depth thinking, you may not consider this an important skill to teach to your students. However, when teachers are asked about the thinking skills that students need, decision making is among the first that they mention, mainly because poor decision-making skills can affect students in all walks of life (Beyer, 1987).

Critical Thinking

Critical thinking can be defined as "reasonable and reflective thinking which uses a variety of skills to reach logical, unbiased and informed reasons or conclusions" (Kysilka & Biraimah, 1992, p. 119). This definition attempts to encompass the important aspects of critical thinking as defined by writers in the field of thinking skills. The skills required for critical thinking are reactive; that is, they are used to judge the acceptability of the opinions, conclusions, or responses you might have to a given situation. Critical thinking, then evaluates your own or another person's perceptions of reality. Like other thinking skills, critical thinking may manifest itself differently in different contexts and subject areas: In mathematics, deductive reasoning is very acceptable, whereas science generally prefers inductive strategies. Social studies uses cause and effect and informal reasoning to determine truth and falsities, and language arts may use language or character analysis to determine meaning in a piece of literature.

According to Robert Ennis (1991, 2000a), critical thinking involves both dispositions and abilities. He defines dispositions as characteristics of the thinker, such as the following:

- Caring about the truth and being willing to justify one's decisions
- Being well informed
- Considering other points of view
- Remaining open minded
- Maintaining a focus on the question
- Seeking and offering reasons
- Taking into account the total situation
- Caring about the dignity and worth of every person
- Avoiding intimidating and confusing others
- Being concerned about others' welfare

Ennis defines abilities as skills of thinking, such as the following:

- Identifying and formulating questions
- Formulating criteria for judging answers
- Identifying stated and unstated reasons
- Seeing similarities and differences
- Summarizing
- Asking and answering questions of clarification—why, what, how?
- Judging the credibility of a source
- Drawing inferences—deducing and judging deductions and inducing and judging inductions
- Explaining conclusions
- Making and judging value judgments
- Defining terms, judging definitions, identifying and handling equivocation (the context in which the language is used)
- Identifying assumptions

Ennis believes that a good critical thinker is disposed to get it right and to "present a position honestly and clearly, and to care about the worth and dignity of every person; furthermore the ideal critical thinker has the ability to clarify, to seek and judge well the basis for a view, to infer wisely from the basis, to imaginatively suppose and integrate, and to do these things with dispatch, sensitivity, and rhetorical skill" (2000a, p. 7).

Robert Ennis was a high school teacher in Fithian, Illinois, from 1951–54. Later, he was an instructor in the philosophy of education at Cornell University and a professor of philosophy at the University of Illinois–Champaign. His books include *Language and Concepts in Education* (1961), *Critical Thinking Readiness in Grades 1–12 (Phase I: Deductive Reasoning in Adolescence, Logic in Teaching,* 1969), *Ordinary Logic* (1969), and *Critical Thinking* (1996).

Source: Biography Resource Center, University of Central Florida, retrieved July 27, 2004.

As you examine Ennis's abilities, you will recognize the relationship of these statements to Bloom's revised taxonomy; both ask students to function at the higher cognitive levels of the taxonomy—application, analysis, evaluation, and synthesis.

Richard Paul and Linda Elder (2004) of the Foundation for Critical Thinking have indicated that students must master two elements of critical thinking: the identification of the "parts" of their thinking and the assessment of their use of these parts. The parts of thinking are as follows:

- All reasoning has a purpose.

- All reasoning attempts to figure something out.

- All reasoning is based on assumptions.

- All reasoning is based on information.

- All reasoning is dependent on concepts and ideas.

- All reasoning involves inferences used to draw conclusions.

- All reasoning leads somewhere and contains implications and consequences.

The assessment of these parts might depend on the context in which the thinking occurs, but generally it can be evaluated through assessment standards of clarity, precision, accuracy, relevance, depth, breadth, and logic. The quality of students' critical thinking is dependent on how they apply the standards of assessment to their elements of thinking.

As you can see, critical thinking is a complex activity, and no one teaching strategy can possibly help students to learn all the aspects of critical thinking. Thus, it is imperative that as a classroom teacher, you recognize when, where, and how you can include critical thinking in your teaching strategies. Because critical thinking functions differently according to context, you need to be aware of how a specific content area or topic addresses critical-thinking skills. Ennis (2000b) has provided some suggestions for the teaching of critical thinking skills:

- Always encourage your students to think about alternatives (hypotheses, conclusions, points of view, plans, and explanations).

- Emphasize the use of evidence and searching for reasons—why is an important question.

- Emphasize the importance of keeping an open mind.

- Engage students in asking questions and discussion—use controversial situations to encourage participation.

- Provide students with time to think.

- Encourage students to verify each other's answers and positions.

- Have students read each other's ideas and suggestions.

- Provide criteria for judging written position papers or have students develop the criteria that you will use.

An important concept to remember is that, although you interact with students, you should model critical-thinking skills. Modeling is a strong strategy to encourage students to participate in critical-thinking activities. If they see you thinking critically, they will be more likely to engage in critical thinking. At least they will know that the environment is safe for them to try.

Creative Thinking

What is creativity? This is a very complex question. There are numerous definitions of creativity, and they change constantly as we learn more about how the brain functions. There seems to be agreement that creativity is a combination of three factors: ability, attitude, and processing skills. We also know that creativity is something that can be measured on a continuum: There are degrees of creativity, and some people may be more creative at times than others depending on the context in which they are using their creative skills. Some students can be highly creative in the language arts but not in mathematics or history. Some students demonstrate

The information-processing skills of creative students are different from those of other students.

outstanding creative skills in art but not in science. Some students excel in creative thinking in science but not in music. We also know that some individuals have something that we might define as "general creativity"—that is, they seem to function creatively in a variety of contexts. If we look at the abilities of creative individuals, we might describe them as

- intrinsically motivated
- able to easily synthesize ideas
- able to exhibit original thought
- unorthodox in their thinking
- able to go beyond the obvious
- very imaginative
- able to see multiple perspectives easily
- flexible with ideas
- nonjudgmental
- inventive
- elaborative

These abilities (Kysilka & Biraimah, 1992) indicate characteristics that often get students into trouble in some classrooms but allow them to excel in others. For instance, some teachers might find unorthodox thinking problematic in their classrooms, particularly if the class is mathematics or maybe history; however, the ability to synthesize information and see multiple perspectives may prove to be a positive characteristic in the language arts, and having flexible ideas and nonjudgmental skills may prove to be positive traits in a science classroom. Just knowing about the abilities of students is not enough. How these abilities interact with student attitudes has much to do with the way these students are perceived by their teachers. Creative individuals often

- take risks
- are not inhibited by convention, tradition, or reality
- like to toy with ideas
- break rules
- challenge authority
- push boundaries
- break boundaries
- prefer to work alone

As you look at these attitudes, you can imagine the challenges these students create for some teachers. Students who challenge authority or push boundaries may frustrate many teachers, particularly less experienced teachers. Students who break rules and care little about convention or tradition often create havoc in a classroom. A risk taker with strong unorthodox thinking who is working alone on a project may create a project that is highly questionable as to its appropriateness for the classroom. Thus, when working with these students, you may find that you need to monitor them a little more closely than you had anticipated.

The information-processing skills of creative students are often quite different from the processing skills of other students (Kysilka & Biraimah, 1992). Creative students think

- divergently

- metaphorically

- analogically

- cyclically, reexamining ideas again and again

- analytically, examining experiences to satisfy their need to learn from them

- objectively and subjectively

- aesthetically, seeking to order, categorize, or rearrange ideas until they are aesthetically satisfying

These students frequently work at the edge of their competence, tolerate confusion and uncertainty, and are willing to accept a higher risk of failure than many other students (Perkins, 1991). Schools and the way classes are structured often work against creative thinking. This is particularly true in the current environment of high-stakes testing. Because teachers are expected to ensure that students excel on the high-stakes tests, they find little time to explore the aesthetic nature of their subject—for example, few teachers help students to see the beauty of the structure of mathematics because they are too busy getting students to compute. Little time is spent understanding the nature of history as a synthesis of hundreds of pieces of data; students are too busy memorizing the data. Even in science classes, time spent in the laboratory discovering scientific concepts is often replaced by students being told the concepts. And because of heavy teaching loads, many language arts teachers forgo writing-process philosophy for less labor-intensive grading activities.

Forty years ago, E. Paul Torrance (1966) described four aspects of creative thinking that can be incorporated into your teaching with relatively little effort and can enhance and encourage the creative thinking of your students:

- *Flexibility* refers to establishing points of view or developing multiple perspectives to a problem. Students can learn to be more flexible if you use strategies that encourage this—for example, asking students to redefine a problem, paraphrase an idea, or engage in forced associations. When you use forced associations, you give students two very different objects, such as a brick and a car, and ask them to determine how they are alike. By having to look beyond the objects and think about how they are used, students may come up with similarities they would never have thought about before. Once they get used to this type of "stretching the mind," they can use what they have learned as they approach other problems. How many times have you, when building a puzzle, walked around the puzzle or turned the puzzle to see how a piece might fit? How many times have you looked at a diagram and found yourself moving the paper around to get a different image? These are tactics for developing different perspectives or points of view—tactics that indicate your flexibility of thought.

- *Fluency* is defined as the ability to supply a variety of responses. You can encourage your students by directly asking them, how many different ways can we solve this problem? Or you might ask, how many invertebrates can you name? Or, how many different words can you think of that describe the color blue? Students need to be encouraged to offer multiple answers, not just one. Brainstorming techniques can help students to become more fluent. Fluency can be learned. Fluent thinkers are better at drawing conclusions and making generalizations than those who are less fluent.

- *Elaboration* is defined as the ability to embellish ideas and add detail. As we have indicated, elaboration is a characteristic of creative thinkers and can be taught. Again, you need to help students to develop this ability. In the primary grades, you can help students to develop their elaboration skills by giving them a picture that they are asked to enhance. The directions you may give them can be as simple as, "Take this picture of a house and make it look different. You can add objects to the picture, such as people or animals, change colors, or put in details that aren't there, such as putting lines on the roof to indicate shingles. Make this picture uniquely yours." Or as the children are reading, you might ask them to draw pictures about what they are reading. In secondary classrooms, you can ask students to elaborate on each other's ideas. For example, Bob made a statement in an economics class that the cost of gasoline has gone up because of the war in Iraq. You might then ask Tenitia, "Tenitia, can you explain Bob's idea about how the war in Iraq has caused our gasoline prices to go up?" Tenitia replies. "That's good Tenitia. Rae, can you add anything to Tenetia's explanation?" If you are teaching language arts and are engaged in writing activities, you might encourage students to add adjectives or adverbs to their sentences to enhance their message. Helping students to improve their elaboration skills is not hard to do.

- *Originality* is the ability to create unique ideas. You really cannot teach originality, but you can foster the original thinking that your students already have. Too often, students do not recognize that they have any original thought. You need to let them explore their originality. One activity that has always worked with students, regardless of age, is to give the students a paper plate, a glob of clay, and some toothpicks and ask them to make a sculpture. You will be amazed, as will they, by the different pieces of sculpture they create. There is no right or wrong to their creations. Another activity that can help students to recognize their original thinking is to give them a picture book and then ask them to write a story. What you want to do is convince your students that everyone has original thought; some may have more or more complex thoughts, but everyone is capable of creating ideas. They simply need the opportunities to do so.

As you can see, creative thinking is multidimensional and rather complex. It is both aesthetic and practical; it involves skills found in problem solving, decision making, and critical thinking; it requires students to work "outside the box"; it can be fun for some students and highly threatening for others; and it can be enhanced by helping students to understand some of the basic aspects of thinking creatively. As a teacher, you may find that the most challenging students you will ever work with are the highly creative ones; they are more likely to rebel against traditional teaching strategies than other students. Creative thinkers are explorers and questioners, and they want opportunities to do these kinds of activities in school. When such opportunities are not available, they become very frustrated and either disrupt classes or simply shut down. Some have learned how to tolerate school, but they do not necessarily live up to their

TABLE 12.2	Differences in Critical and Creative Thinking

Critical Thinking	Creative Thinking
Analytic	Generative
Convergent	Divergent
Vertical	Horizontal (lateral)
Probability	Possibility
Judgmental	Non-judgmental
Focused	Diffused
Objective	Objective and subjective
Left-brained	Right-brained
Verbal	Verbal and visual
Linear	Associative and circular
Reasoned	Novel

potential. You have an obligation to help these students get the most out of their time in school and maximize their potential for learning.

Robert Harris (1998) has provided a comparison of critical and creative thinking and indicated how both types of thinking are important to problem-solving and decision-making skills. The table is presented here with some slight modifications by the authors (see Table 12.2).

Edward de Bono developed a system of "six thinking hats," which is a quick, simple technique to help you improve and organize your thinking. His system identifies six "hats" that require you to consider the kind of thinking you are engaged in at any given time. As you are working on a problem, you "place" one of the hats on your head to determine what kind of thinking you are using or need to use. The six hats are as follows:

- The *white hat* calls for information known or needed. This involves data gathering and objective thinking.

- The *red hat* signifies feelings, hunches, emotions, and intuition. The red hat allows the thinker to use feelings and intuition without having to justify his or her thoughts.

- The *black hat* is used for judgment and caution. It is a very valuable hat. The purpose of black-hat thinking is to point out why suggestions might not be appropriate for the situation. This is the logic hat.

- The *yellow hat* symbolizes brightness and optimism. It is positive, logical thinking. This hat allows you to determine what will work and why it will offer benefits.

- The *green hat* focuses on creativity.

- The *blue hat* is used to manage the thinking processes. This is the metacognitive hat.

Using the six hats thinking process can help you to manage the types of thinking you need to engage in. It is an effective tool to help your students begin to recognize the kinds of thinking they are engaged in or need to solve a particular problem or situation.

The teachers at Seneca High School have just returned from a districtwide meeting at which the superintendent of schools indicated to them that, although he was pleased with their progress in improving students' scores on the exit exams required by the district at each academic level (elementary, middle school, and high school), he was very concerned that the National Assessment for Educational Progress reports revealed that the higher-order thinking skills of the students at each of these levels have not improved. The district has decided, therefore, to include higher-order thinking skills questions on future exit exams and expects teachers to do a better job of teaching these skills in their classrooms. The teachers are all abuzz about having to do more in their already packed curricula and indicate that they think the superintendent is asking them to do too much—there is no time to add thinking-skills instruction to their curricula.

Mrs. Pack, the principal, Mr. Jelicek, the assistant principal of instruction, and Miss Hernandez, the curriculum coordinator, decided that teachers needed time to talk about these new challenges and to decide how they will meet the expectations of the district. They organized a two-day retreat to tackle the problem. The retreat was held at a nearby state park that had lodging facilities, recreational activities, and great food service. Teachers were encouraged to bring families along to enjoy the park's facilities while the teachers engaged in academic conversations. Over 80% of the teachers came to the retreat. The principal used staff development monies to pay for the retreat and only asked the teachers to pay extra for their spouses, significant others, and children.

At the retreat, teachers initially grouped themselves into subject areas and identified the higher-order thinking strategies they were already teaching. They used Bloom's revised taxonomy to help them classify the thinking strategies. What they discovered was that, within their subject areas, they were already teaching most of the skills that would be included on the new tests. They also determined that they needed to help the students recognize that they were using these skills by placing more emphasis on metacognitive strategies—making the students aware of their thinking. Even though this was a great discovery for the teachers, they were still concerned that knowing this and emphasizing the skills within their content areas might not be enough to see improvement in thinking skills on a test.

Consequently, on the second day of the retreat, the teachers broke into different teams—this time, they were interdisciplinary. They wanted to know whether the thinking skills they were using in their subject areas were similar to or different from those used in other content areas. It did not take the teachers long to determine that the skills overlapped. The problem then became how to capitalize on the fact that the skills were overlapping between content areas.

The teachers began to look at which skills were present in the curriculum. They found that mathematics and science used problem-solving and decision-making skills in all of the various subjects in these fields. They also realized that critical-thinking skills were part of the process of problem solving and decision making. The mathematics and science teachers started to plan how they could emphasize the interrelationship of these skills in their subject areas. The language arts and social studies teachers said that these skills were also used in their subject areas, although they tended to focus more on inquiry, critical thinking, and creative thinking. The art, music, and drama teachers thought they could help in the areas of critical and creative thinking. The industrial arts teachers thought that decision-making and problem-solving skills were used extensively in their curriculum. The physical education teachers said that decision making and creative thinking were also part of their curriculum.

(Continued)

As the discussions extended into the afternoon, the teachers decided that, collectively, they were teaching a variety of thinking skills, but the impact was lost on the students because there was no coordination within the curriculum to help students realize that thinking skills span the curriculum and that what they learn in one setting could be applied to another. Too much time was wasted teaching and reteaching skills that students technically already new.

The teachers decided they needed to get a curriculum planning task force together that could examine all the suggestions from the teachers and design a plan for the incorporation and emphasis of higher-order thinking skills across the curriculum. They determined that through multiple subject areas and multiple perspectives, students would realize that thinking skills are used everywhere, all the time, and that these are essential survival skills. They also did not want one group of teachers to be held responsible for teaching these skills when it was evident that they were used in every subject area. They charged the task force with the following responsibilities:

- Synthesize the data on higher-order thinking skills and how they are taught in the various subject areas.

- Find areas within the curriculum that use similar skills at the same grade level—for example, problem solving in ninth-grade general mathematics, ninth-grade environmental science, ninth-grade social studies, and ninth-grade English.

- Where similar skills are used at the same grade level, have team members from these subject areas get together to determine how they can collaborate to ensure that students understand the thinking skills and see how they are used in the various subject areas.

- Determine whether any thinking skills that are deemed essential are not being taught in the curriculum or are relegated to a single subject area. If this is the case, provide suggestions on how these skills can be incorporated into the curriculum.

- Develop a set of generic guidelines that will help existing and new teachers to see where in their content areas different thinking skills are taught, how to coordinate teachers' efforts in teaching the skills among the different content areas, and how to emphasize the skills while students are using them.

- Create a series of activities that teachers can use to help students understand their metacognitive strategies.

- Complete the report and have it ready for teachers to read and revise by the next schoolwide retreat in four months.

The concern of the faculty was that the problem could not be resolved by the large group, but by putting together a task force, they were more likely to begin to make progress in planning for the teaching of thinking skills. What the teachers understood throughout the retreat was that they were already using higher-order thinking in their classrooms, but there was no specific emphasis on the skills or any attempt to coordinate their work with each other. They also realized that they did not have time to include a special course in thinking skills, so integrating them into the existing curriculum, where they are used anyway, was the most appropriate strategy.

The teachers recognized that they were teaching at the higher cognitive levels, but their efforts were frequently lost on the students, who knew that what counted was getting the correct answers on the multiple-choice exit exams, which required little higher-order thinking. And, students being the astute people that they are, they preferred to spend their time memorizing information they knew they would be tested on rather than thinking about that information and how it might be useful to them in the future. The teachers were determined to change the students' perspectives about what learning was all about, and they believed their plan was the beginning of restructuring their curriculum so that the students would learn how to learn and, in the process, improve both their lower- and higher-order thinking skills.

The teachers were excited about the prospect of getting help from each other on accomplishing a task they thought was important and would help them to do a better job of teaching for learning in their classrooms. All the teachers were willing to help members of the task force and were enthusiastic about having another retreat.

ASSESSMENT

Inherent in the use of higher-order thinking is assessment. As you engage students in higher-order thinking skills, you will be able to easily assess their use of these skills in the activities you plan. For example, if you are doing problem solving and students cannot find a suitable solution to the problem, you can use selective questioning to find out where their thinking went astray. More often than not, when viable solutions do not materialize, it is because the students did not have a clear definition of the problem.

If you ask the students to do a critical analysis of a piece of literature, you can determine from their responses whether they were able to do so successfully. But you might not want to wait until the students have engaged in a complex thinking process before you know whether their thinking is on track. To help the students, particularly as they are just beginning the process of systematic thinking, you might want to create a story guide that they can follow to keep them on track. This guide does not have to be dictatorial, but a means of helping them to focus on the processes they should be using to complete the task. For example, you might want the students to pay specific attention to the following ideas:

- Plot: What is the definition of a plot? How is it developed? Who are the most important people to think about in the development of the plot?

- Characters: Who are the characters? How are they related to each other? Which characters are most important to the story? Which characters provide an interesting diversion in the story? Are there any characters whose presence is not essential to the story?

- Story line: How is the plot established at the beginning of the story? What pieces of information are most important to remember as you progress through the story? As you became involved in the story, did you see the plot changing? If so, how? How did the characters' roles change as the story progressed? Was the ending of the story what you had expected? How did you think the story would end? Why do you believe the author chose to end the story the way he or she did? Do you think the ending was plausible?

- Evaluation: Based on your analysis, how would you rate this story? Do you think it had a message for the reader? If so, what was it? Was the story for pure entertainment, not focused on providing a specific message? Does all literature have to have a message? Would you recommend this story to one of your parents, a sibling, or a best friend? Why or why not?

If the students know ahead of time what they are expected to do in an analysis of a piece of literature, they will pay more attention to what they are reading and will not have to retrace their steps to answer questions. Remember, part of your responsibility in getting students to think at higher levels of cognition is to guide them to those levels. They will not automatically think at those levels; rather, they must be taught to do so through systematic processes.

You can also assess students' higher-order thinking skills through the tests that you administer to them. Unfortunately, most tests, whether they are standardized or teacher constructed, focus on lower rather than higher levels of thinking. It is much easier to construct factual, knowledge-based questions than thoughtful, higher-order questions. Lower-level questions are by far easier to grade—they are right or wrong, no in between. Higher-order questions that are not of the multiple-choice variety (yes, it is possible to construct multiple-choice items that measure higher-order thinking) are open to much more subjective analysis, particularly if the questions are not well phrased and do not clearly delineate what is expected. Subjective responses are open to many interpretations, and often students' intents and teachers' understandings are not the same.

Although testing for higher-order thinking is not easy, you should begin to think about incorporating higher-order thinking questions into your examinations. You might want to read up on how to become not only an effective test constructor but also a good assessor of learning by reading James Popham's (1999) book *Classroom Assessment: What Teachers Need to Know.*

TECHNOLOGY

No discussion of thinking skills can occur without thinking about how those skills can be enhanced through the use of technology. Typically, in most schools today, technology in many classrooms is relegated to review processes, remediation, or maybe curriculum enhancement. Even in the last-named use, however, students are frequently on their own to surf the Web to find the information teachers want they to use to provide depth to their understanding of a concept. Thus, students search, read, and respond. Although this is not a bad use of technology, it certainly does not use technology efficiently to help students develop higher-order thinking skills.

Much of the rhetoric in curriculum areas refers to authentic learning and authentic assessment. In this context, writers indicate how the use of the World Wide Web can provide the students with tools for authentic learning—real artifacts, access to expert knowledge, and interactive engagement with information. What does this mean? If you are teaching an art class, you can have students take a virtual tour of a number of major art museums around the world. In these virtual tours, students can not only view classic pieces of art but also access information from experts who discuss the artist and the history of the particular piece, get a critique about the piece, learn the monetary value of the piece of art, etc. In a social studies class, you can access original documents such the U.S. Constitution, Bill of Rights, or Declaration of Independence. You can find original newspaper articles that describe major historical events, such as man's first walk on the moon. You can engage interactive science sites that help students understand the basic principles of electricity.

The point is technology has put more information, more accurate data, and more interesting concepts at your fingertips. History no longer needs to be boring, science can be exciting and exploratory, art can be awesome, mathematics can be understandable, music can be inspiring, and literature can be engaging. The technology is available to make all of this happen. It can make learning more realistic and more authentic.

According to many writers in the field of computer literacy, "the WWW [used] in a learner-centered, authentic, problem-based, and collaborative environment can lead to the development of complex thinking skills" (Bradshaw, Bishop, Gens, Miller, & Rogers, 2002, p. 280). Technology—specifically, the computer and the Internet—can help students to connect the different kinds of knowledge they are exposed to into a coherent whole much easier than their teachers can. With a click of the mouse, students can find answers to complex questions, solutions to problems, questions to ponder, ideas to explore, projects to do, and, yes, games to play. The point is that students have access to a lot of information that changes on a daily basis. They need to be able to harness that information in positive ways through the use of complex thinking skills, such as finding, retrieving, categorizing, analyzing, evaluating, and synthesizing information.

What does this mean to you? You need to become familiar with what is available on the Web that is appropriate for your subject area. Not only are you looking for sites within your subject area, but you might also want to explore sites that will help you to design activities for your classroom. One such site is the WebQuest Page (http://webquest.org). On this website, Bernie Dodge of San Diego State University defines a WebQuest as an inquiry activity in which the information the students use is derived partly or totally from the Internet. Short-term WebQuests (two or three days) are designed for knowledge acquisition and integration, and long-term WebQuests (one week to one month) are designed to extend and refine knowledge. Together, these two activities engage learners in all levels of higher-order thinking. The website provides you with guidelines to set up an effective WebQuest.

You need to know whether the textbooks you use have accompanying CDs with appropriate lessons that focus on higher-order thinking skills. Most textbooks include CDs that not only include material for remediation and review, but also activities and projects that enrich students' learning by providing them more depth or breadth to their understanding of the content. The CDs may also provide self-check activities that can help students monitor their own learning.

You need to become comfortable using technology in your classroom. If you are a current student in a teacher-preparation program, chances are you are getting much instruction in using and incorporating technology into your classroom teaching. If, on the other hand, you graduated a while ago and are now finding yourself in a teaching situation, you may not have had much experience using technology as a learning tool and certainly not as a teaching tool. Therefore, you might want to access any and every opportunity provided to you through your school or district to become knowledgeable about using technology. You can also become an explorer of the Internet and find your own sites for use in knowledge acquisition. Most college and university libraries have access to a variety of databases that can provide you with information about how to integrate technology into your classroom. You can find specific lessons on how to teach each of the thinking strategies described in this chapter. The information is endless.

You need to communicate with your colleagues. Most good ideas that teachers use in their classrooms come from their colleagues. Start talking to your peers. Find out whether they are using technology and how. Ask them for resources. Ask them what works and does not work. Ask them how you can use technology effectively if you only have one or two computers in your room and your class size or smallest class is 25 students. Go to the curriculum resource person in your school (sometimes that person is your librarian or media specialist) and ask him or her for help. These individuals are trained to be a resource for you.

Be a risk taker. Don't be afraid to use the technology available to you. You might start simply. For example, start using the overhead projector instead of the chalkboard. It is much easier to list ideas in a brainstorming situation if you can keep your eyes on your students rather than your back to them while you write on the board. Introduce films, videos, or CDs in your classroom and structure your debriefing of these around higher-order questions. Give students an assignment that asks them to find a specific site on the Internet and give them a learner's guide (a series of questions they need to answer) to use as they work through the site, asking questions at all levels of Bloom's revised taxonomy. Many students may have computers at home; others will not. So be certain that if you use such an activity, you provide ample time for those students who must use school computers to get the assignment done.

Learning Tenets
That Support Thinking Patterns

All of the Learning Tenets that we believe in are appropriate as you incorporate higher-order thinking skills into your classroom teaching.

The brain seeks to classify information and the things to be learned.

As you think back to what you have learned about higher-order thinking, you will realize that this type of thinking asks students to classify and categorize information. You cannot get far in higher-order thinking if you cannot bring sense to the information you are receiving, and bringing sense means placing information into categories already in existence or creating new categories.

The emotional system drives attention, and attention drives meaning and memory.

When you are engaged in higher-order thinking, you become emotional about what you are saying, doing, and thinking. One of the reasons that de Bono's six thinking hats are so popular is that he recognizes the role of emotion in the thinking process and specifically calls attention to the fact that as you engage in complex thinking, you cannot remove emotion from your actions. You may get angry, frustrated, tired, intolerant, excited, perplexed, or satisfied during your activities. Each of these emotions creates a different action and a different memory of what happened. Most of you can remember an "aha!" moment when you finally caught on to something that had been perplexing you, and you never forgot what you learned. You can also remember when you were so frustrated that no clear thinking could occur, and you clearly remember what you did not learn. Sometimes that experience creates interference in your thinking when you confront that content again. Interference can eventually translate into a fear of learning something.

Learning occurs in both conscious and unconscious states.

Although the intent of higher-order thinking is to engage students consciously in their learning, the nature of the problems or situations that you ask students to engage in can have a residual effect. Have you ever worked on a problem for awhile, did not find a satisfactory solution, put it aside, and did something totally different? Then, maybe even a day or two later, out of the clear blue sky, the solution hits you. What this suggests is that you never put the problem out of your mind. You simply did not pursue direct thinking about it, yet your mind kept playing with the idea and then, bingo—solution! What this tells you as a teacher is that you need to provide adequate time for students to engage in higher-order thinking skills. Problem solving, critical thinking, creative thinking, and decision making do not always work on a specified time schedule. Granted, you cannot always give as much time to the activity as it needs, but do not assume that if students do not find an effective or plausible answer, they can not think—they may need more time.

The brain is designed for ups and down, not constant attention.

Higher-order thinking is a very complex and intensive activity. Sometimes you can think creatively or critically for long periods of time and then simply shut down. In this circumstance, your brain is saying, "I can't process any more." The best thing to do under this condition is to find an alternative activity to engage in, one that is not so intense. Give your brain a rest. Once you are refreshed, your thinking may easily get back on target.

Learning occurs through processing and active engagement with visual, auditory, and kinesthetic modalities.

As you think back to the various strategies discussed in this chapter, you will realize that higher-order thinking is precisely what this tenet is all about. You cannot think at higher cognitive levels without being actively engaged with your visual, auditory and kinesthetic modalities.

Good teaching is about recognizing and selecting instructional patterns that match the context for learning and the students we are teaching.

Good teaching includes teaching students to think, and to get students to think critically and creatively and to positively engage in problem-solving skills and systematic decision making, you must help them learn these skills and apply them appropriately to their life situations. Strong thinking skills will help any student succeed in life. Every student can learn how to think. Some will do it better than others, but all students need to have the opportunity to develop their potential for thinking, just as they need to maximize their potential for learning—the two go hand in hand.

Summary

Thinking skills are best suited to Part VI, "Thinking and Organizing the Content." In this chapter, we reviewed the research on why it is necessary to learn thinking skills. The primary reason for doing so is the diverse society in which we live, where simple solutions are no longer viable responses to the complex problems we face. In defining thinking skills, we revealed how many different definitions exist and how they are all intertwined and intermingled. We specifically addressed teaching for, of, and about thinking skills and focused on four categories of thinking that seem to encompass the multiple definitions of thinking skills: problem solving, decision making, critical thinking, and creative thinking. We provided suggestions on how today's technology can enhance the learning of thinking skills and provided information on how assessment of thinking skills is an integral part of the development of the skills themselves.

Thought to Action

1. Make a list of the kinds of questions you would like to ask your students as they engage in each of the four categories of thinking skills: problem solving, decision making, critical thinking, and creative thinking. Once you have these lists developed, look to see whether you listed similar questions for each category. How can you use this knowledge as you think about incorporating thinking skills into your content area?

2. Examine the curriculum materials you will be using in your classroom. Pay specific attention to the end-of-the-chapter activities. How are these activities related to the teaching of thinking skills in your content area?

3. Design a unit that you are going to teach. In that unit, specifically plan to incorporate higher-order thinking skills. Which skills will you incorporate? Why? How do they relate specifically to the content you are planning to teach? How will you assess the students' use of those skills?

4. Using the Internet, find examples of assessments for student thinking in your content area. What strategies are suggested? Confer with a colleague in a different subject field. What similarities do you find? If you work together as a team, how could you help each other to teach these skills?

5. Form a small discussion group. Talk to each other about the impact of the No Child Left Behind legislation and how it is enhancing or inhibiting the teachers' ability to teach higher-order thinking skills in the classroom.

ON YOUR OWN

Log on to the web-based student study site at http://www.sagepub.com/holt for access to a Standards-Based Student Project that will help you connect what you have learned in this chapter to your state's standards; study aids, such as electronic flashcards; and research recommendations, including journal article links and other Web resources.

13

Memorization

MEMORIZATION HAS A LONG HISTORY AS A WAY OF LEARNING. BECAUSE MEMORIZATION HAS been a dominant way to learn, memory systems date back to antiquity. During ancient times, a trained memory was a valuable commodity. There were no note-taking devices. Epic poems were kept alive by bards and storytellers who would deliver lengthy speeches without fail. The *Iliad* and *Odyssey* of Homer date back to around 800 BC. Orators would memorize these long passages and repeat them from one generation to the next. For the past 2,000 years, the *Ramayana* has been among the most important literary and oral texts of South Asia. This epic poem provides insights into many aspects of Indian culture and continues to influence the politics, religion, and art of modern India today. Priests called bhagvatars chanted the *Ramayana,* a 24,000-verse epic poem recited in 24 performances of four hours each. These amazing memorization feats were accomplished using rhyme, rhythm, and a monotonous hypnotic inflection (Gardner-Gordon, 1993)

Memorization has been given a bad reputation, yet memory and the ability to recall information are essential components of learning. The bad reputation is rooted in the various levels of thinking. The lowest level of Bloom's taxonomy is knowledge, defined as rote rehearsal or memorization. We want our students to be able to think beyond the lowest level of the taxonomy. We want them to develop critical and creative thinking, which means going beyond memorizing facts, concepts, and information. Mental discipline theories, which became popular during the 19th century, contend that learning consists of disciplining or training the mind. In a typical classroom, a teacher who believes in the mental discipline concept of learning would use activities that require students to practice specific learning tasks until those tasks become automatic. Teachers would use a lot of recitation, having students memorize and repeat passages. Drill-like question-and-answer sessions are a common strategy for those who subscribe to mental discipline theories of learning.

You probably have had exposure to memorization since childhood. If your parents sang to you, you inevitably learned some nursery rhymes by heart. You might be able to recall some advertising slogans or jingles from television, and chances are, you can recall the alphabet song.

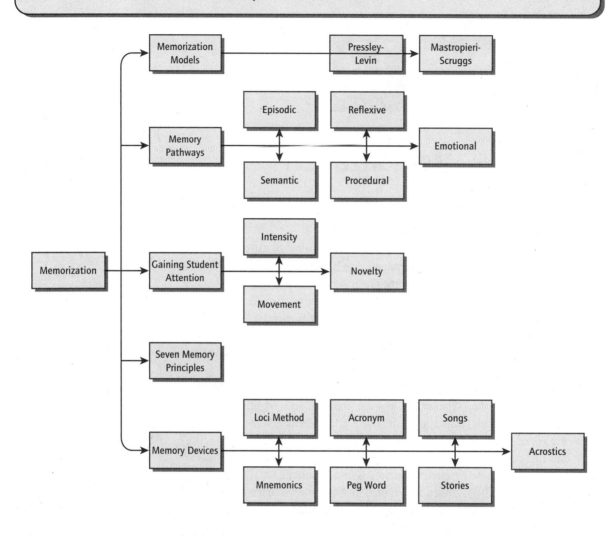

As easy as it seems that you can learn slogans and songs, why is it that students find it difficult to recall things learned in school? In this chapter, we will explore this question and what you can do to improve your students' memories and ways of memorizing.

As a teacher, you will spend much of your time providing content information to your students. Whether you are teaching auto mechanics, English, mathematics, or biology, during the course of a day, you will ask students to follow directions, listen, write, read, and most important, remember. Remembering in the context of a school environment is about being able to recall what was learned and repeat that information on a multiple-choice or short-answer test or in a classroom discussion. The emphasis placed on students remembering what they learned is heightened by the current accountability measures for teachers and schools. Various states have implemented high-stakes testing tied to assessing the quality of the schools. The success of students on these tests is dependent on their ability to memorize not only specific content but also processes. So much rides on the students' ability to remember. If the students do well

Developing connections with the material to be learned is Phase 2 of the Pressley–Levin memorization model.

on the tests, the school gets a good grade and additional resources. If the students do not perform well on the tests, the schools get a bad grade and experiences the consequences of continued poor performance, such as prescribed curriculum, student transfers, and teacher and administrator reassignment.

A student's ability to remember is influenced by how information is received, stored, and retained. Memory is the biological process whereby information is coded and retrieved. "Memory is a collection of complex electrochemical responses activated through multiple sensory channels and stored in unique and elaborate neuronal networks" (Markowitz & Jensen, 1999, p. 7). From an instructional perspective, knowing how information is received, stored, and retained can help you to increase the potential of all students to learn.

RESEARCH ANCHOR

Pressley–Levin Memorization Model

The first model for memorization was developed in 1982 by Pressley, Levin, and Delaney. There are four phases in this model

- Phase 1: Attending to the material
- Phase 2: Developing connections with the material

- Phase 3: Expanding sensory images

- Phase 4: Practice the recall

Phase 1, attending to the material, uses techniques such as highlighting, underlining, listing, and reflecting to help you to recall the information. In Phase 2, developing connections with the material, you develop a connection with the material by using link words, keywords, or other mnemonic techniques to help you remember. In Phase 3, expanding sensory images, you develop further associations with the material and sometimes exaggerate the material to a ridiculous degree to remember it. In Phase 4, practice the recall, you practice the recall until it is completely learned (Joyce, Weil, & Calhoun, 2000).

Mastropieri–Scruggs Memorization Model

A second memorization model developed by Mastropieri and Scruggs (1994) is applicable to all curriculum areas in which material needs to be memorized. The students memorize the information to be learned and become more independent of the teacher as they develop their own system for recalling the material. The steps in the model are as follows:

- Step 1: Organizing information to be learned

- Step 2: Ordering information to be learned

- Step 3: Linking information to familiar material through sounds and meanings

- Step 4: Linking information to visual representations

Step 1: Organizing Information to be Learned

Information that is organized is easier to remember. Consider, for example, the following list of words:

List 1

Kev

Ret

Mig

Stee

Gox

Saz

Jex

If you were shown the seven nonsense words in List 1 and given just 10 seconds to recall the items in the list without writing down the words, how successful would you be? Could you remember four out of seven? Or would you do worse? Now, let's examine a second list of seven words to remember. Give yourself 10 seconds to memorize the list without writing the words down.

List 2

Box

Run

Bat

Top

Move

Jet

Hat

How successful were you with this set of words? Did you remember more words than in the first list? If so, why do you think that this list worked better? Perhaps you did better because you could identify these words—they were not nonsense words. Now let's look at a third list. Give yourself 10 seconds to memorize the list.

List 3

Mary

Smith

Went

To

The

Store

Today

How successful were you? The reality is that most everyone will remember the third list because the order of the words makes a complete thought. This illustration supports the notion that information that is organized is easier to remember. It also supports the second step in this model.

Step 2: Ordering Information to be Learned

Information learned in a series is easier to assimilate and retain, especially if there is meaning to the series. In the previous example, when the words in List 3 were put together in a sentence (a series), you were able to say the words and remember them. The combination of the words also represented something meaningful. It made sense. Order is simply another way of organizing information.

Step 3: Linking Information to Familiar Material Through Sounds or Meaning

Often, if we can relate certain sounds of words to the things we are trying to remember, it is easier to recall them. For example, if we are trying to remember the names of the states, we could remember the name George for the state Georgia. Or we could remember the continents in order if we arranged them by size: Asia, Africa, North America, South America, Antarctica, Europe, and Australia. Other examples may include the following:

Apple = Washington

Peach = Georgia

Shuttle, Orange = Florida

Golden Gate = California

Longhorn = Texas

Step Four: Linking Information to Visual Representations

It is true that a picture is worth a thousand words. Going back to the example of remembering the states, Florida can be remembered with a picture of an orange. Why? Because Florida is one of the largest producers of oranges. Allow students to make visual associations to remember key terms.

As we mentioned in the introduction to this chapter, the study of memory has a long history, and memorizing can be considered one of the first teaching strategies. For example, early Greek and Roman orators would associate each thought in a speech to a part of their home. These were called *loci* or *places* (Lorayne & Lucas, 1974). The opening of the speech might be associated with the front door. The next thought in the speech could be the entry way, and so forth. To recall each part or thought in a speech, the orator would actually go on a mental tour of his home. The English expression "in the first place" is derived from this memory technique.

GAINING STUDENT ATTENTION THROUGH NOVELTY, INTENSITY, AND MOVEMENT

The body must organize sensory data into useful, meaningful patterns. Individuals may vary as to how well they remember and by how well they reuse and organize information. Most of us have a mixture of strengths and weaknesses when it comes to memory. If you want to develop your students' capacities for learning, it is vital that you understand what memory is and how memory works. As you develop a plan for instruction, it is sometimes helpful to use a memory technique to increase your students' chances of remembering the content. But before students can use a memory technique, they must attend to the information to be learned.

Attending to information is the first step in learning. Our attentional system has natural highs and lows that occur in alternating rhythms lasting about 90–110 minutes. This means that we have about 16 cycles in a 24-hour period. Consider these attentional cycles as you observe students who may be asleep in your class or who are consistently drowsy. Getting students to move, play "Simon Says," or stretch can help focus their attention.

When the attentional system experiences highs and lows, there is a change in blood flow. These periods of alternating efficiency seem to correlate with a known rhythm called the *basic rest activity cycle,* discovered by sleep-deprivation researchers. Researchers suggest taking 20-minute breaks several times during the day. Pierce J. Howard (1994) said that in general, workers need 5- to 10-minute breaks every hour and a half. This information has direct implications for students and teachers in schools. The time between classes should not be considered a break because in a high school setting, this is not truly downtime (Jensen, 1998). Some schools that have considered this research have converted to block schedules that allow teachers and students to take breaks without feeling pressured to teach content every minute.

Harry Lorayne began as a professional magician and now works as a memory-training expert. He is the founder and president of the Harry Lorayne School of Memory in New York City. He presents executive programs in memory training for industrial firms and has appeared frequently on national television talk shows and special programs.

His writings include *How to Develop a Super-Power Memory* (1956), *Secrets of Mind Power* (1961), *Miracle Math* (1966), *Instant Mind Power* (1967), *Memory Isometrics Course* (1968), *Mental Magnetism Course* (1969), *Good Memory—Good Student! (Grades 5–9)* (1972), *Good Memory—Successful Student! (Grades 9–12)* (1973), *The Memory Book* (with Jerry Lucas, 1974), *Remembering People* (1975), *The Magic Book* (1977), *Harry Lorayne's The Card Classics of Ken Krenzel* (1978), *Introductory Psychology* (contributor, 1978), *Harry Lorayne's Quantum Leaps* (1979), *Harry Lorayne's Best of Friends* (1982), *Harry Lorayne's Page-a-Minute Memory Book* (1985), *Star Quality: The Magic of David Regal* (1987), *Memory Makes Money* (1988), *Super Memory, Super Student: How to Raise Your Grades in 30 Days* (1990), *Trend Setters* (1990), *The Complete Guide to Memory Mastery* (1998), *The Himber Wallet Book: All You Ever Wanted to Know About the Himber Wallet—and More* (1998), *The Official Know-It-All's Guide to Memory Mastery* (1999), and *Super Power Memory: Your Absolute, Quintessential, All You Wanted to Know Complete Guide* (2000). He is the author of 13 books on card magic and a contributor to magazines and newspapers.

Source: Contemporary Authors Online; reproduced in the Biography Resource Center (Farmington Hills, MI: Thomson Gale, 2005).

Jerry Lucas, following his basketball career, began to devote increasing amounts of time to developing and teaching his system of memorizing and organizing information. He developed this ability as a youngster when he began playing a game he has pursued throughout his life—organizing the letters of words alphabetically. Lucas has perfected this ability to the point that he can instantly recite the alphabetic arrangement of any word on request. In addition, he terms himself a "compulsive counter," telling *Sports Illustrated* that even on the basketball court, he constantly counted such things as the steps in an aisle, the cracks in a floor, or the people in the stands wearing red.

Over the years, these abilities have led Lucas to develop a unique mental cataloging system for storing information. Based largely on the use of counting and mnemonics (word association), Lucas's system allows him to memorize huge volumes of material in minutes. In college, he amazed his roommate, fellow basketball player John Havlicek, with his ability to memorize the contents of a book in 15 minutes. "John was the first person I revealed my system to," Lucas told *Sports Illustrated.*

His writings include *Championship Card Tricks* (1973), *The Memory Book* (with Harry Lorayne, 1974), *Remember the Word, Theomatics: God's Best-Kept Secret Revealed* (with Del Washburn, 1977), and *Ready, Set, Remember* (1978).

Source: Contemporary Authors Online; reproduced in the Biography Resource Center (Farmington Hills, MI: Thomson Gale, 2005).

Martin and Juan are two students in Mr. Amiglio's class. On the windowsill of Mr. Amiglio's classroom sits a squirrel. Martin, who is seated closest to the window, is watching the squirrel. He reaches over to Juan and taps him on the leg. Then he nods in the direction of the window so that Juan can see the squirrel. The squirrel's head bobs up and down as it listens and watches for any sounds or dangers. The squirrel's tail is arched above its back, and as it listens to the surroundings, it makes quick movements back and forth on the windowsill.

Mr. Amiglio is standing at the front of the classroom talking about social studies; he is not aware of the squirrel. Juan and Martin are not listening and begin to mimic the squirrel's actions. Finally, Mr. Amiglio sees Martin and Juan watching the squirrel and says, "Martin, please pay attention. Juan, that goes for you, too."

Like Martin and Juan in Mr. Amiglio's classroom, students are often criticized for not paying attention. Technically, there is no such thing as not paying attention because the brain is always paying attention to something. What we really mean is that Martin and Juan are not paying attention to us or to what is being said in the classroom.

We know that attention is selective. The brain is constantly scanning the environment, and it is not always possible to focus and sustain attention on a specific stimulus. It would be inefficient and perhaps impossible in everyday life to consciously determine what we are going to focus on at every given moment. Getting our students to focus their attention on us is the first step in the memorization process. We can't expect students to memorize or be able to recall when they are not paying attention. This may sound obvious, but much of the time in school, students are paying attention, it's just that they are not paying attention to the right things.

Elements of novelty, intensity, and movement all affect how information is received and attended to by a learner. Let's explore these in relation to the instructional process.

Things that are novel get our attention. As the brain sees something for the first time, it scans to see familiar patterns. If something that we see or hear is not familiar, then it gets our attention because it is novel. Television advertisements employ this technique quite well. A favorite commercial about identity theft depicts an elderly woman who looks like she would have a sweet, quiet disposition. The advertisement gets the viewer's attention by giving this woman a man's husky, deep voice. This is not only funny but also grabs your attention as she begins to dance and sing on screen.

In the context of the classroom, teachers have used various techniques to get students' attention. Turning the lights on and off to get students to settle down is a common technique. Another technique explained in the direct teaching model is the anticipatory set. Good teachers understand the importance of getting students' attention by setting the tone for the lesson. This can be accomplished using creative sets for the lesson (humor, prose, changing your voice, wearing a costume) or other means for capturing students' attention. Often, these techniques lose their novelty if they are overused because the brain has a tendency toward habituation. If a sight or sound is new and unusual, we will initially pay close attention. But if this same sight or sound occurs over and over, the brain normally becomes so accustomed to the stimulus that it is ignored. If you have ever lived near a railroad track, then you have experienced this phenomenon. You hear the same train every day, and, chances are, your brain filters out this sound because it becomes a habit and is no longer important to the sensory system.

A first important step in the classroom environment is to maintain a safe and orderly classroom, but because of the brain's tendency toward habituation, change is important to keep students' attention. Effective teachers will tweak classroom routines to maintain the novelty needed for keeping students' interest and attention.

A second factor that influences our attention is the intensity of the sound or sight. The louder the sound or the brighter the light, the more it will draw our attention. This explains why emergency vehicles have bright flashing lights and loud sirens. Additionally, the volume of television commercials is louder to get the viewer's attention. Applying sound or lighting techniques to mark transitions in classroom routines can effectively set the tone and intensity of the classroom.

The third factor that draws our attention is movement. Movement can be used as an attention-getting device. We can site several examples from everyday life when we see movement that draws our attention. A person waving his or her hands or a billboard with bright flashing neon lights draws our attention. Incorporating movement into the classroom will help students focus their attention. It will keep the blood flowing and help keep students more active in the learning process.

Through advances in technology, scientists can now see what is going on in our heads. The brain sorts information as it is received, discarding what is irrelevant, and stores other bits of information we have seen, heard, or thought. Biologically speaking, the brain is programmed to attend first to information that has strong emotional content. Our brains and our students' brains are designed to pay attention not only to physical dangers but also to facial expressions, body language, and other verbal and nonverbal communications.

The *thalamus* is a sort of relay station that passes information to the brain's cortex for further processing. At the same time, information is sent to the *amygdala*. Our brains are equipped with this type of parallel processing. When information is sent to the amygdala, the brain determines the emotional relevance of the incoming stimuli. Should I run? Is this going to hurt me? At the same time, the cortex is processing the incoming stimuli rationally, placing it in context to make sense of it and to decide on a course of action (Wolfe, 2001). In his book *The Emotional Brain* (1996), Joseph LeDoux called the thalamus–amygdala pathway the "quick and dirty route."

At times when an experience happens to us, as humans, we may respond with a less-than-rational approach. As teachers, we may have observed this reaction in our students as they are confronted with unconscious emotional responses. Maintaining and sustaining attention are the first requirements for storing information in the brain and are needed for memorization. We know that in the initial processing of stimuli in the brain, there are three factors that influence our immediate attention: novelty, intensity, and movement. We know that each of these factors is largely regulated and unconscious.

MEMORY PRINCIPLES

Memory principles can be used in at least two ways. One way is to check whether your presentation to the students contains the memory principles. For example, as a teacher, ask yourself the following questions: Did I establish the lesson's relevance? Did I help the students to focus on the most important parts? Did I use a multisensory approach when I presented the material?

When you teach your students the concepts, facts, and information from your content area, it is important to provide them with the skills to increase their memory potential. Examine the principles that are important for memorization and check whether you have incorporated these principles of memory into your lesson.

The second way to use memory principles is to refer students to the questions after each principle to assist them with their memory potential. If you are working with high school students, give them the memory principles and have them complete a self-check on each in relation to the things that they must learn. The following principles, identified by Markowitz and Jensen (1999), can be an important planning tool when considering the tasks that you want your students to memorize or learn:

- Personal relevance: Is what you want to remember meaningful? If not, can you make it so?

- Concentration: Have you clearly focused on the information you want to remember? The more attention you prescribe it, the stronger the memory trace.

- Multisensory perception: Have you imagined or visualized what you want to remember? Have you talked about it, manipulated it, or associated a feeling to encode it?

- State dependence: Is it possible for you to match your state of learning when you need to recall the information? For example, if you study for an exam under the mild influence of caffeine, you will remember it best when you are in the same state.

- Mnemonics: Have you applied a memory strategy to the information you want to remember? There are countless possibilities listed in this chapter.

- Mood or attitude: Are you in a conducive state of mind for learning, free of intense stress, depression, anxiety, or fear? Do you have a "can do" attitude?

- Mental organization: Are you aware of your natural inclinations or preferred modalities for processing, organizing, storing, and retrieving information? Do you consciously encode the information you want to recall?

These seven principles of memory are important considerations as you plan activities that will assist learners with the content and the things to be learned. Developing these skills in your lesson planning or allowing students to check themselves on each will assist them with their learning. In this way, the responsibility for learning is shared between you and your students.

In school, you probably were asked to memorize the pledge of alliance to the flag, the alphabet, the states and their capitals, and the elements on the periodic table. As you examine concepts that are appropriate for your subject area, you will find rules, principles, and concepts that, if remembered, will make learning additional information easier and more efficient. For example, knowing the rules of spelling, such as "I before e, except after c or when followed by g," makes it easier to form words. Knowing addition and multiplication tables makes calculations in mathematics easier. Remembering specific events in history, such as the bombing of Pearl Harbor or Neil Armstrong walking on the moon, helps you to conceptualize other events in history. Recognizing major geographic landforms can help you to understand weather concepts, transportation routes, or agricultural productions. The more we provide students with memory devices, the greater the chance that their learning will be remembered.

MEMORY LEARNING TECHNIQUES

Memory devices are techniques that learners can use to connect the material to be learned. *Mnemonics* are techniques that you can learn to use that will help you retain information. Basically, the brain remembers because it has another stimulus associated with the information you are trying to remember. Some techniques are more useful than others; it depends on your learning style and what stimuli you respond to. In music, "every good boy does fine" provides the key to each line of the musical staff, and "good boys do fine always" provides a way to remember the lines in another staff. Another example, "my dear Aunt Sally" (multiply, divide, add, subtract), is a mnemonic aide to remember how to perform math.

The *loci method* associates what you need to remember with a set of objects in a familiar location. You move from one object to another in your mind's eye to trigger a memory of each item. You can also use this method by remembering different rooms in a building and associating each room with an item to be remembered. This method was used in ancient times before the printing press and other note-taking devices were invented.

Suppose, for example, that I need to give a presentation about Gardner's multiple intelligences. I need to remember the eight intelligences, and because I know I will be under pressure, I use the loci method to make sure that I remember them in the correct order. So, I think of my office. The *window* represents visual intelligence, the *telephone* represents verbal intelligence, the *computer* represents logical intelligence, the *chair* represents bodily intelligence, the *stereo* represents musical intelligence, the *meeting table* represents interpersonal intelligence, and the *armchair* represents intrapersonal or reflective intelligence. The *bookcase* is my cue for the recognition and classification of naturalist intelligence. It doesn't matter if the objects do not remind you directly of the item to be remembered, but it can be an added stimulus if they do.

The *peg-word technique* is similar to the loci method, but instead of using a location, it uses concrete items. The peg-word system is good for remembering numbers. To use this technique, think of objects that can be associated with each number and then think of a scenario that puts the objects in order. It is helpful if you describe the scenario out loud and visualize it in your head. For example, suppose that I have to remember the office phone number **845-086-4068**. My peg words are as follows:

0—sky, for openness and nothingness

4—door, because it rhymes

5—dive, because it rhymes

6—guitar, because the number looks like it

8—a jelly donut, because the number looks like it

My scenario, then, could be something like this: "A jelly donut (8) went through the door (4) and took a dive (5). The room had no roof except for the sky (0). The jelly donut (8) reached for a guitar (6). He began to sing, "The door (4) opened to the sky (0) is like a guitar (6) playing a song about jelly donuts (8)."

An *acronym* is a word made from the first letter of each item you need to remember. This technique is very useful for remembering secure computer passwords or complicated concepts. Acronyms that are used frequently enter our everyday vocabulary, and the original meaning attached to the acronym may be lost—for example, SWOT, a technique used to analyze a program, is made up of the first letters of the words strengths, weaknesses, opportunities, and threats. In education, we like to use acronyms all the time to reflect names of organizations (e.g., NAME = National Association of Multicultural Education), programs (LEAP = Learning Enhancement for Academic Progress), or companies (IBM = International Business Machines).

Acrostics create a link between a letter in the word to be remembered and a phrase. For example, "Richard of York Gave Battle in Vain" corresponds to red, orange, yellow, green, blue, indigo, and violet, the colors of the rainbow. You can make up your own acrostic when you need to remember to take your belongings—Palm Pilot, purse, phone, and keys—by remembering a nonsense phrase such as "Plenty of People Pick Kevin."

When you have a number of things to remember, you might make up a *story* that relates each idea or object to one another. The story can be as silly as you like, but it needs a single story line to work well. For example, suppose I have to remember to complete the following tasks:

- Clean the condo

- Pick up rental car

- Go to hardware store to have duplicate keys made

- Buy steaks for dinner

- Do a load of wash

My story could be, "With a dust mop in one hand, I am driving down the road as I "steak out" what I am doing. I now have the key to solving the load of pressure I feel from the tasks at hand."

Making up a *song or rhyme* to remember things can work well, particularly in a small group of people who enjoy being a bit silly. For example, the tune "Twinkle, Twinkle Little Star" is used to teach children the alphabet, and in fact I still sing it while alphabetizing material to remind me of the order.

Sometimes, the physical act of *writing* something down will help you to remember an idea, book, activity, or whatever. This is a common technique when we need to remember things to be purchased at a store. You also might draw pictures to remind you of certain things. This technique is great for people who have a more visual learning style. The pictures can be purely symbols, and no drawing skill is required—they just provide stimulation for your mind to fasten onto.

Use particular *movements* associated with different words to remember them. This works well with a chain of movements that are linked together. An example is the song *YMCA*. As you sing the song, form each letter with your hands.

Each of these techniques is a way that students can encode the content to be learned into their memories. Using memory devices will increase students' chances for remembering. When this occurs, it is called *positive transfer*. As the brain takes in information, it checks an existing schema; if the fit is good, what was learned or stored previously gives meaning to the new information, and there is positive transfer. If the new information is similar in some aspect but not a complete fit, *negative transfer* may occur (Wolfe, 2001, p. 72).

When students are engaged with each other and with the material, they are more likely to recall the things to be learned.

CLASSROOM SCENARIO

The ninth-grade class is practicing terms for science. The teacher, Ms. Morgan, knows that if the students can create a phrase that contains the first letter of each step in the mitosis of the onion root, then they will be more likely to recall this information for their test. As the class begins, the various steps are written on the board. Ms. Morgan asks the students to look at the first letter of each step in the cell-division process.

Ms. Morgan asks the students, "How can we remember the steps involved in the mitosis of the onion root?" Ms. Morgan directs the students' attention to the first letter of each of the stages involved: I, P, M, A, and T. Then she asks, "What could we do with these letters to help us remember the steps?" Gerard suggests, "We could create a phrase or a saying." Ms. Morgan says, "Okay, good. As long as the phrase is not derogatory or hurtful to anyone, let's think of a way we can

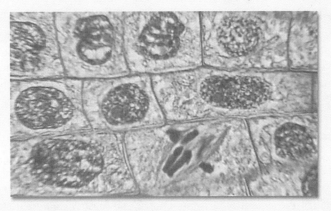

Onion Root Tip Mitosis

(Continued)

remember." The students come up with, "I Put Mary's Apple Together."

This is an example of the keyword system, which is designed to assist students with their recall of certain processes. The idea is that a single word is used to represent a longer thought or subordinate thoughts. During an exam, when asked to name the steps of mitosis, the students will be able to recall the order by remembering the phrase, "I Put Mary's Apple Together." The key-word system explained is just one idea that can help learners to enhance their memory of content material.

MEMORY PATHWAYS

At any given moment, our sensory receptors are receiving vast amounts of information and giving us more input than we can possibly attend to. If we were aware of all the images, sounds, smells, and tastes that are simultaneously impinging on our bodies, we would experience sensory overload (Wolfe, 2001). As new information is received by our brain, the *reticular activating system* plays an important role in filtering the thousands of stimuli that our body takes in. Without the body's reticular activating system, which helps to sort, filter, and process sensory information, we would not be able to function. Many of these functions occur automatically and unconsciously. As stimuli are received from the world around us, the information is assembled, sorted, and discarded, directing only some of it to our conscious attention.

We know where memory processes begin, but scientists are still learning how memory works. In circuits or networks of neurons, the brain stores memory in various locations—in the visual, auditory, and motor cortices. Memory does not exist in just one location. The memory pathways begin in specific areas of the brain. Each memory area contains the files in which memory is stored. The memories themselves are not stored in these areas; rather these areas are where each memory is labeled. The labeling process makes the difference in how quickly we store and retrieve information (Sprenger, 1999, p. 47).

Memory can be classified by the manner in which it is encoded and retrieved. This means that memory can be consciously or instinctually formed. When memories are consciously formed, this is called *explicit* or *declarative* memory. This is the type of memory that, as learners, we can explain, write about, or describe. When memory is formed organically or automatically, it is said to be *implicit* or *nondeclarative*. This is the type of memory that may be stored in the brain, but we don't know it or can't describe it. Skill learning, priming, and classical conditioning are all examples of implicit memories. Another way that memory can be classified is by the element of time. For example, we have immediate perceptual memory, as well as short-term, working, and long-term memories. For each of these memory types, the duration of time is the critical attribute for classification. For an explanation of these differences, refer to Table 13.1 and Figure 13.1.

Discoveries about the brain and its function are ongoing, but the information generated so far can inform educators about the learning and memory process. There are two memory pathways that are explicit: semantic and episodic. There are four memory pathways that are implicit: procedural, reflexive, emotional, and sensory conditioning. Flashbulb memory is a type of memory obtained as a result of extreme emotion, and it is unique to each individual (Markowitz & Jensen, 1999). Each of these types can be used for storing information.

TABLE 13.1	Memory Storage
Immediate perceptual memory	One-second memory (such as that used when typing) or a visual circumstance (pictures moving in the mind)
Short-term memory	Lasts 15–20 seconds unless it is consciously rehearsed. On average, a person 15 years or older can hold up to seven items in short-term memory (such as a telephone number).
Short-term memory buffers	These are temporary storage areas located in each of the auditory, visual, and kinesthetic areas that hold information before it goes to working memory or long-term memory.
Working memory	Memory located in the prefrontal cortex that can be used for hours (such as cramming for a test). This method of study allows us to hold onto information for hours if it is repeated enough. Students will use working memory to get the facts straight just before an exam. They may do well on the exam, but the information does not make it to long-term memory.
Long-term memory	Memory stored for an indefinite period

Explicit Memory Pathways

Semantic memory operates word by word, and it uses working memory (Sprenger, 1999). Most academic and professional knowledge—ideas, facts, figures, and typical exam questions, as well as names, dates, identification numbers, movies, books, pictures, videos, technical information, and written stories—are all examples of the kind of information that is processed semantically. Most classrooms situations rely on semantic memory. Semantic memory is the weakest of our retrieval systems (Markowitz & Jensen, 1999). To successfully encode this information into long-term memory, students and teachers need to interact with the concepts to be learned by using various strategies. Semantic teaching strategies allow word information to be processed and used in semantic and other memory lanes when the information is successfully encoded.

Episodic memory deals with locations; it is also known as our autobiographical memory. By using the context in which you experienced an event, you can easily reactivate the memory. The hippocampus, which stores all factual information, is the gateway to the episodic memory lane.

Implicit Memory Pathways

Procedural memory is also known as motor memory. It is used when we ride a bike, drive a car, skip, skate, or tie our shoelaces. It represents the "how" of our memory bank. Procedural memory is embedded through practice and skills that become automatic over time.

Reflexive memory or automatic memory is conditioned-response memory. Certain stimuli automatically trigger this memory. For example, after hearing the first few notes or

FIGURE 13.1   Memory Pathways

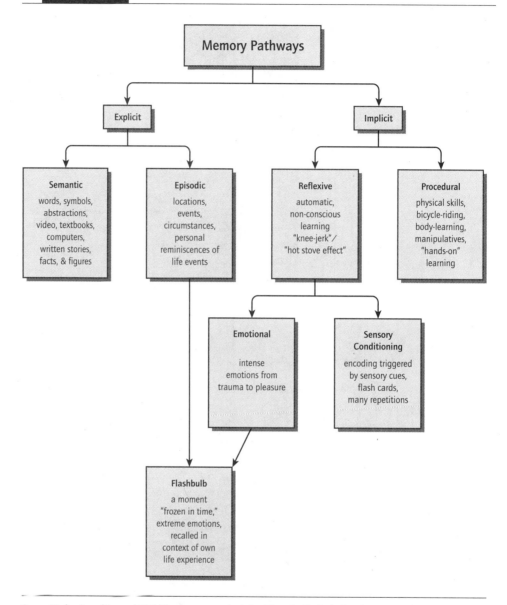

Source: Markowitz and Jensen (1999). *The great memory book*. San Diego: Ca. The Brain Store Inc.

words of a song, your memory is triggered and you begin to sing along. Automatic memory is located in the cerebellum (Sprenger, 1999). Other memory may be opened as you access your automatic memory. For example, you may remember that the last time you thought about this song was when you were in high school or at your school prom. Once the automatic memory is activated, it is possible to access your procedural, emotional, and semantic memories.

Emotional memory takes precedence over all other kinds of memory (Sprenger, 1999). Emotional memory is opened by the amygdala (the emotional center), located in the forebrain next to the hippocampus. Emotion strongly influences whether the brain initially attends to arriving information and whether this information is sustained. "We know emotion is very important to the educative process because it drives attention, which drives learning and memory" (Sylwester, 1995, p. 72). Information that is emotionally laden is easier to remember. However, if information calls for a strong emotion, such as fear, then the amygdala takes over to prepare the body. Daniel Goleman (1995) calls this response a "neural hijacking."

If we rehearse material over and over and it is successfully encoded using our senses, then *sensory conditioning* results. Sensory conditioning is triggered by sights, sounds, smells, and the environment around us. An example of sensory conditioning might be flash cards or certain forms of oral rehearsal.

Flashbulb memory, which is unique to each individual, is usually a vivid recollection of an extremely emotional or shocking event. More than one person may have the same recollection of a historical event, such as the September 11 terrorist attacks, man's first walk on the moon, or President Kennedy's assassination. However, each person's memory is stored in the context of one's own life experience. The details of these memories may fade over time even though they are stored with vivid memories because of their emotional content.

Emotional memory takes precedence over all other kinds of memory.

ASSESSMENT

First, you need to determine how important it is for you to asses how well a student's memory is working. Do you need to directly measure what the students have memorized, or can you do that indirectly? An example of direct memory would be having students match words to a list of definitions or state capitals to names of states. If you plan to assess this type of knowledge, then you need to be sure your lessons are focused on this need to memorize facts and their relationships to each other.

If your lesson outcome is about the process or concepts, then you can construct application-type questions. For example, a question might be, "Find the solution to 3 + 4 (2+6)/2–5." To solve this problem, students need to remember that operations in parentheses come first, so you have

$$3 + \frac{4(8)}{2} - 5$$

then you multiply

$$3 + \frac{32}{2} - 5$$

divide 3 + 16–5, add 19–5, and subtract 14. If we understand the concept, we may shorten our thinking process to 3 + 2 (2 + 6)–5 = 3 + 16–5 = 19–5 = 14. Because we remember, we can simplify fractions first before doing other operations.

TECHNOLOGY

Electronic technology has produced some memory games that children can use to help them acquire basic knowledge and facts. For example, place flash cards face down in a pattern on the desk or floor. The object of the game is to find a match to the card you pick up. When a match is found, you get a point. Teachers have always found flash cards useful in helping students to memorize math and reading tasks. But rather than just holding up a flash card in front of the class, teachers can engage students in activity by creating a "flash card game." Like the popular television program *Concentration*, players rotate turns to uncover matching items. Once the items are matched, a panel is revealed with clues to a phrase or riddle. Electronic versions of this game are now available using a split computer screen. Students are provided a choice to find the matched card or pair.

Simon is a toy that was produced to enhance a player's memory. *Simon* is circular in shape and has buttons (panels) that can be pushed. Once the game is turned on, the lighted panels produce a light pattern with a sound. The object is to push the panels to produce the same sounds in the same sequence. As the player replicates the same sounds and sequences, the sequence becomes more difficult.

These manufactured games are just a few examples of how memory and technology can be combined to assist learners.

Learning Tenets
That Support Memorization

The brain seeks to classify information and the things to be learned.

As you examine the concepts within your subject area that you want your students to recall for quizzes or exams, consider the information that was presented in this chapter about increasing your students' ability to remember. The brain takes in information and checks to see whether existing schema or information is present. If information already exists, the brain will classify and align the new information with the old. However, if the concepts from your subject are new and unfamiliar to the students, then you may need to help them make the connection. Use instructional techniques that cue the memory. The memory techniques you select can help learners to recall the information and recognize patterns within the content to be learned.

Review the seven principles of memory with your students: personal relevance, concentration, multisensory perception, state dependence, mnemonics, mood or attitude, and mental organization. Ask them to develop a memory system that supports the seven principles.

**The emotional system drives attention,
and attention drives meaning and memory.**

We know that as students attend to information, the brain will seek emotional elements to decide whether to maintain that attention. This means that emotional considerations for learning something and the ability to remember it are important. Emotions can be evoked through music or through nonverbal and verbal communications. Tone is important when emphasizing important concepts. Start each lesson with an emotional element to keep students' interest in the things to be learned.

A creative anticipatory set can be used to incorporate emotion. For example, music, voice tone, analogy, and humor are all excellent devices for creating an emotional element in the instructional lesson.

Learning occurs in both conscious and unconscious states.

When you examine the memory pathways described in this chapter (see Figure 13.1), you can see that we use explicit and implicit types of memory. Explicit memories are things that are learned semantically in school and remembered from our life experience. Content knowledge is explicit and semantic (concepts, skills, symbols, and textbook information). For students to transfer this information to their long-term memories, we must use the mnemonic devices and processing strategies described in this chapter. Implicit memory is reflexive, procedural, emotional; it is about sensory conditioning. Memories that are implicit may be automatic and unconscious. For example, have you ever driven home and then wondered which route you took to get there? Or have you ever walked into your kitchen to get something, only to find that by the time you arrived, you had forgotten what you were after? If students become programmed to remember basic facts, then these skills become automatic. Understanding explicit and implicit types of memory pathways and how students learn these conscious and unconscious forms of learning is important to memorization.

The brain is designed for ups and downs, not constant attention.

After reading this chapter, you now understand the importance of novelty, intensity, and movement. When incorporated into lessons, these elements will help students to remember because they invoke curiosity and stimulate attention. Taking periodic stretches between focused tasks will help students to maintain attention. In addition, teachers who plan an effective, creative opening to the lesson (anticipatory set) will establish a routine in the classroom that students will come to enjoy. Dressing up as a historical figure or using puns, analogy, humor, or daily quotes are all ways that can keep boredom out of the classroom and help to maintain student attention.

Learning occurs through processing and active engagement with visual, auditory, and kinesthetic modalities.

Life experience is incidental. There is no guarantee that everything we experience in life will be encoded and later retrieved. Our preferences, interests, and survival needs direct our attention and determine how well information is encoded. It takes effort to be able to encode something and later retrieve it. No one knows this better than teachers. Student may memorize information for a test, but later they may not be able to retrieve it. This happens a lot because students may study for 10 to 12 hours to cram, or they may memorize their notes for an exam using their working memory. The next day, after they have taken the test, students may or may not remember the information. The information stayed in their working memory but was not truly learned. Strategies for processing information are helpful ways to successfully encode information into long-term memory. One processing strategy, elaborative rehearsal, is used to practice information that will need to be recalled later. When we process information using our senses and consolidate information, our memory will be better.

Good teaching is about recognizing and selecting instructional patterns that match the context for learning and the students we are teaching.

So much of what was presented in this chapter is about how students attend to the information that we want them to learn. Attending to the things to be learned is the first important step. We have informed you about the ways that the brain receives, stores, and processes information. It matters most whether students are paying attention. So good teaching is about recognizing whether your students are "with you" in what you are trying to present because there is no hope that any instructional pattern will be successful without students first attending to the things to be learned.

Summary

This chapter is best suited to Part VI, "Thinking and Organizing the Content," because when we memorize, we manipulate and organize the things to be learned. This chapter has introduced several memory strategies or mnemonic devices that can help students to recall information. To be an effective teacher who is focused on your students' learning, you may want to become familiar with these techniques. Additionally, with an understanding of the memory pathways presented here, you can identify the different memory types. Memorization was once thought of as bad for students, but as we understand more about how the brain stores memory, we can enhance in our students' memories by using appropriate learning techniques.

Thought to Action

1. What is your earliest memory? What age were you? Why do you suppose some individuals can remember things at a very young age and others cannot?

2. Visit a classroom to examine the amount of memory work that students are required to complete. Develop a memory strategy (mnemonic device) for the information to be learned. How would you implement your idea? Which memory device would you use and why?

3. Purchase the memory toy *Simon*. How might this toy help your students with their memory and pattern recognition? Develop a strategy for using this game in your classroom. How might this toy assist a developmentally challenged student?

4. Write a story using the peg-word technique for something that you want to remember. How might this technique be useful for your students?

ON YOUR OWN

Log on to the web-based student study site at http://www.sagepub.com/holt for access to a Standards-Based Student Project that will help you connect what you have learned in this chapter to your state's standards; study aids, such as electronic flashcards; and research recommendations, including journal article links and other Web resources.

14

Attaining Concepts

THE SUBJECTS THAT YOU TEACH REPRESENT YOUR CONTENT. CONTENT CONSISTS OF IDEAS, concepts, descriptive information, and facts. Content can be modified, accelerated, and paced through your delivery of instruction. A concept is defined as a set of specific objects, symbols, or events that are grouped together or categorized on the basis of shared characteristics, called *attributes* (Merrill, Tennyson, & Posey, 1992). When you are presenting concepts from the subjects that you teach, it is imperative to understand the relationship between and among ideas so that you can enlighten your students as to these relationships.

One method for helping students to see and understand the relationship between concepts is the instructional pattern called *concept attainment*. Concept sets containing attributes have shared characteristics that can be grouped together. Critical attributes are essential; they are necessary for membership in a class. The concept-attainment pattern of instruction requires students to learn to distinguish the essential from the nonessential attributes of a category or concept by comparing examples and nonexamples (Bruner, Goodnow, & Austin, 1956).

When you teach inductively through the use of examples and nonexamples, you promote learning because this strategy actively involves the students in constructing a personal understanding of a new concept.

RESEARCH ANCHOR

Concepts and categories, in the broadest sense of the words, can be any ideas that we have in our heads. Some people use the word *idea* synonymously with *concept*. Others may view concepts as *themes*. For example, we will study the *Industrial Revolution*. Another way to use concepts is through broad general statements such as, "All men are human." When we approach concepts in a teaching environment, it is likely that they will be defined by their attributes. We have a

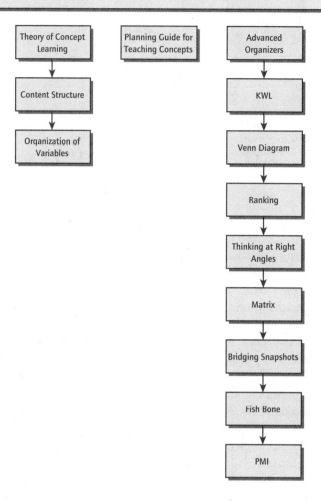

concept of a car, and we have concepts of various models—four-wheel drive, front-wheel drive, three- or four-wheel designs—that have the attributes or features of being a car. Similarly, we have the concept of cat, and we have the attributes or features of mammal, various colors, superstitions, and cats with nine lives.

When you begin to examine the content that you are teaching, you will realize that information is grouped or clustered together. Concepts can be grouped as abstract ideas, names or labels, examples, nonexamples, or critical attributes. Concepts can be categorized and defined in a systems approach. The terms *superordinate*, *subordinate*, and *coordinate* are important to understand in relation to the concept that you might be teaching. If you want to systematically present your subject area, it is imperative that you know the relationship between the ideas (concepts) so that you can broaden your students' knowledge base.

The term *superordinate* is defined as a concept that can be divided into smaller or component concepts. When a concept in a hierarchical system is grouped together with at least one

TABLE 14.1	Hierarchical System of Concepts

Universe (**Superordinate**)	
Earth (**Concept**)	Saturn (**Coordinate**)
People	
Cultures	
Oceans	
Continents (**Subordinate**)	

or more concepts of the same level, they form *coordinate concepts*. The various subcategories or relational parts of the concept are *subordinate* (see Table 14.1). For example, if the concept you are teaching is Earth, the superordinate concept would be the universe. The subordinate concepts would be people, culture, oceans, etc. The coordinate concept would be a different planet in the universe, such as Saturn.

Peter Martorella (1999) suggests a planning guide for teaching concepts. He states the following:

> To initiate the process of teaching a concept, you need to ask yourself several basic questions: Do educators and subject matter specialists suggest the concept be taught? Should a student receive systematic instruction in the concept, or is it more appropriately acquired through informal means? Is there a sufficient agreement on the criterial attributes and the concept rule to have a basis for designing instructions? Assuming the answers are yes to these questions, you are ready to move on to the next phase of instructional planning using the following inventory:
>
> 1. What name is most commonly applied to the concept? (Example: Lake)
>
> 2. What is a statement of the concept's rule or definition (the arrangement of its critical attributes)? (Example: body of water surrounded by land on all sides)
>
> 3. What are the essential characteristics of criterial attributes of the concept based on your readings and reference sources? (Example: land, water, surroundings)
>
> 4. What are some noncriterial attributes typically associated with the concept? (size, location, depth)
>
> 5. What is an example that best or most clearly represents the most typical case of the concept? (Example: aerial photo clearly showing all the features of a lake)
>
> 6. What are some other interesting and learner-relevant examples or cases of the concept that you can use in its explanation? (Example: local lakes, mountain lakes, desert lakes)
>
> 7. What are some contrasting nonexamples of the concept that will help clarify and illustrate the concept? (Example: ocean, stream)
>
> 8. What are some cues, questions, or directions that you can employ to call attention to criterial attributes and noncriterial attributes in the concept examples? (Example: "Look at all the points where the water meets the land.")

Jerome S. Bruner is a psychologist who has made exceptional contributions to the study of cognition, perception, and education. After earning a Ph.D. from Harvard University, he joined the faculty there and began to develop a new theory of perception, which would come to be known as the "New Look." This theory contends that perception is not simply what happens immediately when one "sees" something, but a way of processing information that involves selection and interpretation. Bruner's area of study then moved into cognition through his studies with George Miller. In 1960, the two men opened the Center for Cognitive Studies at Harvard, convinced that psychology should be part of the cognitive process.

Bruner's writings include *Public Thinking on Post-War Problems* (1943), *Mandate From the People* (1944), *Perception and Personality: A Symposium* (editor, 1950; reprinted 1968), *A Study of Thinking* (with Jacqueline J. Goodnow and George A. Austin, 1956; reprinted 1977), *Opinions and Personality* (with Mortimer B. Smith and R. W. White, 1956), *The Process of Education* (1960; reprinted 1977), *On Knowing: Essays for the Left Hand* (1962; reprinted 1979), *Man: A Course of Study* (1965), *Learning About Learning: A Conference Report* (editor, 1966), *Toward a Theory of Instruction* (1966), *Process of Cognitive Growth: Infancy* (Heinz Werner lectures, 1968), *The Relevance of Education* (edited by Anita Gil, 1971; new edition, 1973), *Beyond the Information Given: Studies in the Psychology of Knowing* (edited by Jeremy M. Anglin, 1973), *The Growth of Competence* (edited with Kevin Connolly, 1974), *Play: Its Role in Development and Evolution* (edited with Alison Jolly and Kathy Sylva, 1976), *Human Growth and Development: The Wolfson College Lectures, 1976* (edited with Alison Garton, 1978), *Under Five in Britain* (1980), *The Social Foundations of Language and Thought: Essays in Honor of Jerome S. Bruner* (afterword, 1980). *Child's Talk: Learning to Use Language* (with Rita Watson, 1983), *In Search of Mind: Essays in Autobiography* (1983), *Actual Minds, Possible Worlds* (1986), *Making Sense: The Child's Construction of the World* (edited with Helen Haste, 1987), *Interaction in Human Development* (edited with Marc H. Bornstein, 1989), *Acts of Meaning* (1990), *Constructing Panic: The Discourse of Agoraphobia* (foreword, 1999), *The Culture of Education* (1996), *Minding the Law: How Courts Rely on Storytelling, and How Their Stories Change the Way We Understand Law and Ourselves* (with Anthony G. Amsterdam, 2000), and *Making Stories: Law, Literature, Life* (2002).

Source: Contemporary Authors Online; reproduced in the Biography Resource Center (Farmington Hills, MI: Thomson Gale, 2005).

Jacqueline J. Goodnow attended University of Sydney. She is a member of the Australian Psychological Society, Academy of Social Sciences in Australia, American Psychological Association, and Phi Beta Kappa. Her writings include *A Study of Thinking* (with Jerome S. Bruner and others, 1956), *Children Drawing* (edited with Jerome S. Bruner and others, 1977), *Children and Families in Australia* (with A. Burns, 1979), and *Men, Women, and Household Work* (coauthor, 1994).

Source: Wilson Web.

9. What is the most efficient, interesting, and thought provoking medium (or media) by which to present examples and nonexamples? (Example: power point slide show, aerial photos)

10. What level of concept mastery do you expect of students, and how will you assess it? (Example: Be able to define *lake* and state the similarities and differences this body of water has with other major bodies through a project.)

Organizing instruction around concepts helps to reduce the complexity of the content, provides direction for the activity, and helps students to think about ordering and relating classes of events. The principles of concept attainment are as follows:

- Conceptual clarity: Begin by developing with the students a definition of the concept, stating it clearly in a manner that is appropriate to the learners. Review each of the attributes of the concept provided in the definition to make sure students are familiar with these terms. Although presenting the definition facilitates concept learning, it is not sufficient to provide a definition alone; memorizing a definition can lead to mere verbalization of a series of words with no underlying grasp of meaning.

- Multiple examples: Provide students with a clear example of the concept in whatever format is useful and appropriate, such as a picture or a short prose passage. Try to present an example that is vivid, has imagery, and calls up familiar associations. Elaborate how the example fits the concept and its attributes.

- Multiple discrimination: Engage students in a period of practice during which they are presented with a series of additional cases. Using the initial example as a model, students must decide whether each new case is an example of the concept. Provide feedback so that students know whether they are discriminating accurately.

- Conceptual competence: Students can successfully identify the concepts.

It appears that during the process of discriminating between examples and nonexamples, students elaborate and complete the conceptual knowledge that becomes embedded in their memory. The number of examples and nonexamples that need to be presented to complete this process varies according to the nature of the learners. Generally, the more practice, the better. In this regard, the important process of elaboration through multiple examples is exactly what is missing from most textbook presentations of concepts, and this is why students often have a difficult time learning key concepts in a meaningful way from textbook sources alone (Georgia Department of Education, 2003).

CONCEPTS VERSUS GENERALIZATIONS

According to Taba (1971), there is a difference between naming concepts and naming generalizations. Taba believed that students make generalizations only after data are organized. She believed that students can be led toward making generalizations through concept development and concept-attainment strategies. In her book *A Teacher's Handbook to Elementary School Social Studies,* Taba defined the difference between a concept and a generalization in the following way:

Generalizations, like concepts, are the end products of a process of an individual's abstracting from a group of items of his experience those elements or characteristics the items share, and expressing his recognition of this commonality in a way that is convincing to others. The two major differences between concepts and generalizations are first of all, that in generalizations the verbal form of the process is expressed as a sentence rather than a word or phrase as in the case of concepts, and second, that generalizations are here taken as representing a higher level of thinking than concepts in that they are a statement of relationships among two or more of these concepts. (1971, p. 72)

According to Tennyson and Cocchiarella (1986), concept learning is a two-phase process. In the first phase, the students learn the formation of conceptual knowledge. In the second phase, the students are involved with the development of procedural knowledge. Conceptual knowledge is formed in memory by the integrated storage of meaningful dimensions selected from known examples and the connection of this entity in a given domain of information—that is, conceptual knowledge is more than just the storage of declarative knowledge or verbal information (Anderson, 1980). Conceptual knowledge is also an understanding of a concept's operational structure within itself and between associated concepts. Procedural knowledge, on the other hand, is developed by using conceptual knowledge to solve domain-specific problems. Therefore, conceptual knowledge in terms of cognitive science is the storage and integration of information, whereas procedural knowledge is the retrieval of knowledge in the service of solving problems. Although these two processes seem sequential, they do interact such that the use of procedural knowledge in problem solving elaborates conceptual knowledge.

THEORY OF CONCEPT LEARNING

The two-phase theory of concept learning is composed of two fundamental components of design. The first is the content structure in relation to domain-specific information. The second is the organization of instructional design variables related to the use of specific content structures. The two basic components of the Tennyson–Cocchiarella model show the relationship between the concept-teaching variable and the associated cognitive processes that affect concept learning.

Studies conducted by Homa, Sterling, and Trepel (1981) seem to confirm the findings of Tennyson and Cocchiarella, indicating that the formation of conceptual knowledge seems to be an initial phase in concept learning. An instructional strategy that presents clear cases of the concept, along with directions to compare a best example with additional expository examples and information on the critical attributes, is the most effective means for abstracting information to form conceptual knowledge.

In an instructional context, the phases of the concept-attainment model are as follows:

- **Phase 1: Presentation of data and identification of the concept**

    Teacher presents labeled examples in pairs (yes or no)

    Students compare attributes in positive and negative examples

    Students generate and test hypotheses

    Students state a definition according to the essential attributes

- **Phase 2: Testing attainment of the concept**

  Students identify additional unlabeled examples as yes or no

  Teacher confirms hypotheses, names the concept, and restates definitions according to essential attributes

  Students generate examples

- **Phase 3: Analysis of thinking strategies**

  Students describe thoughts

  Students discuss the role of hypotheses and attributes

  Students discuss the type and number of hypotheses

Prior to teaching the concept-attainment model, it is recommended that you select the concepts to be taught. Additionally, you must organize the material into positive and negative examples and sequence the examples (Joyce, Weil, & Calhoun, 2004).

ADVANCE ORGANIZERS

To reinforce the concepts that you want your students to remember and to help them see the relationship between concepts, it is important to use *advance organizers*. An advance organizer helps students see a conceptual view of what is to come and prepares them to store, label, and package the content for later retention (Ausubel, 1968). There are many types of advance

Here, the teacher is presenting the concepts to be learned to the students, Phase 1 of the concept-attainment model.

organizers. Advance organizers can be verbal or visual. According to Jensen (1997), an advance organizer that is visual is more easily encoded and retrieved than text material:

> The eyes are designed to take in 30 million bits of information per second. In the learning context, it makes sense to take advantage of this amazing organ that is hungry for pictures, movies, and images. But, most of what the brain learns is nonconscious. In fact, studies done on the impact of peripherals (posters, pictures, drawings, symbols) suggest they are much more powerful influences on the brain than previously thought. After two weeks, the effects of direct instruction have diminished. But the effects of peripherals often go up. (p. 19)

This substantiates the importance of providing learners with the mental scaffolding (advance organizer) needed to see the concepts to be learned. It also recognizes that visual organizers enable some learners to encode content more easily than text.

When Ausubel introduced the idea of the advance organizer during the 1960s, he had no idea that his theory was compatible with how the brain works. Ausubel felt that advance organizers are best used to aide learning by assimilating new information, and that when used effectively, they can bridge the gap between what is already known and what can and will be learned.

Ivie (1998) contended that Ausubel's ideas all fit together in a logically consistent system. The basic premise is logical but simple: Thinking is an orderly activity; knowledge is arranged in a hierarchical pattern; higher-level concepts subsume lower-level ones; learning is essentially a matter of fitting new information into an already existing cognitive structure; retention and forgetting are two different aspects of the same process, called *subsumption*. Ivie also concluded that the logic employed by Ausubel allows for a five-step process of instruction:

- Step 1: The teacher determines whether the learners already possess the relevant concepts in their cognitive structure.

- Step 2: The teacher provides appropriate advance organizers, which, when used correctly, can cement or anchor the new material within the existing cognitive structure.

- Step 3: The teacher presents the new material in an organized manner, making certain that the students are subsuming the new information under appropriate organizers.

- Step 4: The teacher provides the students with sufficient practice (drills) so that the material is learned thoroughly and becomes an integrated part of the student's cognitive structure.

- Step 5: The teacher guides the student through a problem-solving situation that uses higher-order thinking skills and helps to anchor the new information.

Ausubel maintains that a person's existing cognitive structure is the foremost factor governing whether new material will be meaningful and how well it can be acquired and retained. This can be done by giving to the students the concepts that govern the information to be presented to them.

Diagrams that allow students to process thinking skills may include webs, matrices, or other visual diagrams. These visual tools are also referred to as cognitive maps, visual displays, or graphic organizers. There is a saying that "thinking is invisible talk." To see what students are thinking and how they are thinking, these cognitive tools can be used (Bellanca & Fogarty, 1990). These tools can help students organize, reorganize, and modify connections

The students in Mr. Evans's language arts class are filing into the room following lunch. Mr. Evans greets them at the door and welcomes each student with a smile. As the students enter the room, they notice a laptop computer on a utility cart between the rows of desks. Connected to the laptop is an LCD panel projecting a two-column image with the word *Yes* on one side of the screen and *No* on the other side. As the students examine the screen and take their seats, they wonder what they will be doing today.

Once everyone has entered the room, Mr. Evans closes the door and begins, "Today, we are going to examine the relationships between sentences. As I reveal sample sentences on the screen, you are to examine the sentences in the *Yes* column and the sentences in the *No* column to determine the idea I have in mind."

"Are you ready?" Everyone gives a nod as they face the screen to wait for the first sentence.

As Mr. Evans clicks the mouse, two sets of sentences appear on opposite sides of the screen.

Yes	No
The boat flowed effortlessly through the canal.	The car sped around the corner.

"I know," says Elba. "The sentence on the left has to do with water and the sentence on the right has to do with land."

Phil speaks up and says, "Well that would make sense if this was science class. But since this is English class, it must have to do with the words in the sentence."

Two more sentences appear on the screen.

Yes	No
The boat flowed effortlessly through the canal.	The car sped around the corner.
I immediately gulped the water.	I drank the Coke in one long swallow.

Betty says, "Does it have to do with movement? Everything in the sentences moves: boats, cars, Coke, or water moving down your throat."

Mr. Evans says, "Well, no, but I like the way you are thinking and participating. Let's examine some more sentences."

Yes	No
The boat flowed effortlessly through the canal.	The car sped around the corner.
I immediately gulped the water.	I drank the Coke in one long swallow.
With sneakers on, she could move more quickly among the patients.	The man with the brown hat is my uncle.
The flowers were the most creatively arranged creations that I have ever seen.	I learned a lot from my fourth-period science class.

Mr. Evans says, "Now that you have seen other examples, what can you tell me about these sentences?"

(Continued)

This time several hands go up. Mr. Evans scans the room and then calls on Clarissa.

Clarissa says, "All the ones in the *Yes* column have a word that ends with *-ly*."

"Okay," says Mr. Evans. "That is a part of it. What can we say about the *-ly* words?"

Alfred responds, "They tell how something is done."

"Okay, good, Alfred. What else can we summarize about the *-ly* words?"

Pause . . .

"What is the name for words that describe how things are done?"

No one responds.

Mr. Evans then says, "The name for words that tell how something is done and that sometimes ends in *-ly* is *adverb*. Do you think all words that end in *-ly* are adverbs?"

Mr. Evans continues, "As we will see, adverbs often tell when, where, why, or under what conditions something happens or happened. Adverbs frequently end in *-ly*; however, many words and phrases that do not end in *-ly* serve an adverbial function, and an *-ly* ending is not a guarantee that a word is an adverb. The words *lovely, lonely, motherly, friendly, neighborly*, for example, are adjectives: 'That *lovely* woman lives in a *friendly* neighborhood.'"

Mr. Evans says, "Both lovely and friendly are adjectives."

Mr. Evans asks the students to form groups of three. Then, using chart paper with yes and no columns, the students generate sample sentences with adverbs, trying very hard to distinguish between adverbs and adjectives. At the end of the class, Mr. Evans asks the students to present their examples and write a definition of an adverb.

Teaching aides help to organize students' thinking and serve as an advance organizer to increase student learning.

TABLE 14.2	Quick Reference: Thinking Lesson Planner
Thinking Microskill	*Cognitive Organizers*
Comparing and contrasting	Venn diagram
Brainstorming	Mind map
Associating ideas	Thinking at right angles
Classifying	Matrix
Analyzing attributes	Web
Prioritizing	Ranking
Evaluating	PMI (plus, minus, most interesting)
Sequencing	Bridging snapshots
Analyzing	Fishbone
Predicting and evaluating	KWL (know, want to know, learned)

as they process information. Certain organizers are used for specific purposes. For example, attribute webs are useful for analyzing traits; a list is best for ranking ideas; and a Venn diagram can display the similarities and differences for comparing and contrasting (Bellanca & Fogarty, 1990).

Bellanca and Fogarty have organized thinking microskills matched to a cognitive map that can be mixed and matched to fit the specific instructional target for your lessons.

ASSESSMENT

Assessing whether students understand a concept may mean allowing them to practice generating their own ideas following the steps of the lesson. Students could conduct a "turn to your neighbor" exercise and explain the concept learned to one another in their own words. Students should be provided time to list other related ideas to ensure that they understand them. Asking them to draw a web or to illustrate the relationship between ideas is excellent. Forming groups to allow students to practice the process of attaining concepts will assist students with thinking and problem solving.

TECHNOLOGY

When presenting the attributes that support your concepts, identify the best means for displaying the examples and nonexamples. Often, using some form of technology can assist you with this process (i.e., an LCD panel with PowerPoint). For cognitive organizers, using *Kids-piration* or *Inspiration* software is best.

FIGURE 14.1 Cognitive Organizers

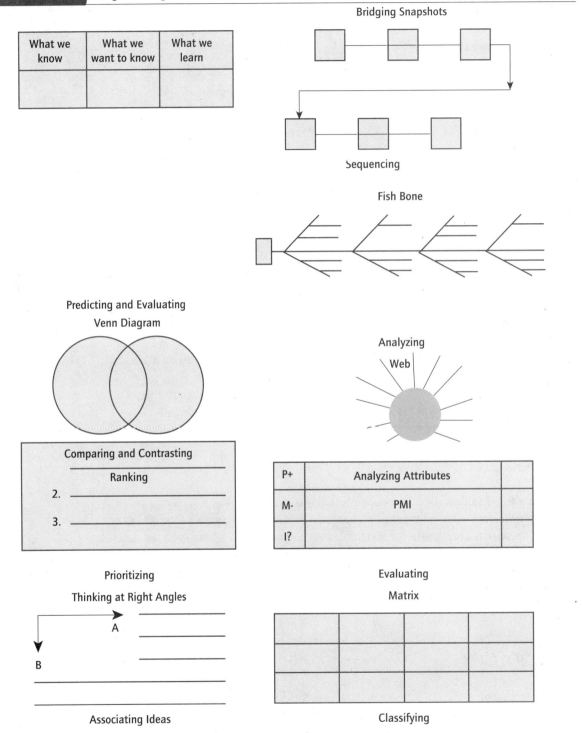

Source: Bellanca and Fogarty (1990).

The brain seeks to classify information and the things to be learned.

Students' ability to understand the relationship between ideas presented by the teacher and the concept is supported by the way the brain classifies information. The brain will check the information stored against the new information being presented. Objects or events are sorted into concept categories through a check of their basic characteristics. The brain checks these events and memories against our past mental models or prototypes, which represent our notion of a typical case of the concept. If an item meets the criteria for an item we hold in our brain, we connect the concept name with the phenomenon. This process of checking the old with the new describes the concept-attainment process. Our world is composed of millions of bits and pieces of information. If each of these pieces of knowledge required a separate classification, the brain would be overloaded and the information would be unwieldy. Concepts allow us to organize and store similar pieces of information efficiently. When students engage in this activity, they increase their ability to think.

The emotional system drives attention, and attention drives meaning and memory.

When the teacher begins with a question that asks students to help find a concept, this arouses students' curiosity. When students are curious about what they are learning, they are likely to attend to what is being said. Presenting information in this manner engages the students more than telling them what they will learn. Most patterns of instruction are taught deductively. Concept attainment is an inductive process. This format grabs the students' attention because it is a novel way for them to be taught. Arousing students' emotions through this process helps them to encode the new content.

For young students, varying your tone of voice as you begin the lesson will help to arouse an emotional response. You could say, "I have a secret . . . " or, "I have an idea that you must guess . . . " Evoking emotion when you present the lesson sets the tone and excitement for what is to be learned.

Learning occurs in both conscious and unconscious states.

It may not be obvious to all students how the class arrived at a concept during its presentation. In other words, you may receive answers to your questions from only your brightest students. Adapting to this form of thinking may take time for some learners. Scan the entire class for students' expressions to learn whether they are following the inductive thinking process. If some students look confused, you may have to provide extra assistance and practice, or the idea may not have sunk in yet. For example, when you were little, you may have been told a joke. Everyone in the room laughed after the punch line, so you laughed. But you really did not understand the punch line, nor did you get the joke. After the pressure to laugh was off, you began to think about it, and then you got it. As we learn new things, we draw on our conceptual banks. We are constantly replacing old concepts with new ones as our learning experiences are shaped. Remember, learning is both conscious and unconscious.

Learning occurs through processing and active engagement with visual, auditory, and kinesthetic modalities.

When you use a visual organizer, it assists learners with their thinking and helps to illustrate the relationship between concepts. A picture is worth a thousand words. The brain can encode pictures more easily than text. So using visual organizers to assist students with their understanding of concepts can reinforce the content to be learned. The organizational chart with the class agenda is a sample advance organizer.

Good teaching is about recognizing and selecting instructional patterns that match the context for learning and the students we are teaching.

Varying your delivery techniques will keep your classroom alive and help motivate your students to learn. The concept-attainment model evokes students' curiosity. When used, the concept-attainment pattern of instruction will vary your classroom-delivery repertoire.

Summary

The concept-attainment pattern of instruction can assist students with their analytical thinking process. The concept-attainment pattern is best suited to Part VI, "Thinking and Organizing the Content," because when examining the best approach to teach concepts, you are manipulating and organizing the concepts within the subjects to be learned. In our human experience, we may share concepts from life events. For concepts to function as a shared experience, they must exist in some public domain that each person holds in common. These shared experiences are the basis of communication and must be understood by anyone claiming to have learned the concept. Two individuals who find that they have a lot in common have discovered the personal side of concepts and may discover that each has had similar experiences. Broadening students' opportunities through the exploration of concepts in the content that we teach helps them to think outside of the box. It helps students realize how information is clustered and often can motivate them to learn.

Thought to Action

1. Examine a textbook that you use or will be using. Open the book to a chapter that lists possible concepts that can be taught. List these concepts and the positive and negative attributes or examples and nonexamples. Formulate a series of questions that can be asked. Visualize yourself teaching this way in front of your class. Practice with a friend the inductive thinking process to see whether you can guide him or her to the concept that you have in mind.

2. Think of a way that you can create a bulletin board that incorporates the concept-attainment idea. Have students pull off pieces of paper that reveal clues from a board about a concept that you want them to learn.

3. Pair up with a friend and take a moment to examine this list of concepts. What are the common attributes? What are noncritical attributes that might be present in examples of these concepts?

Mammal	Road sign
State	Death
River	Autumn
Triangle	Square
Comb	Tree

4. Interview a teacher to see whether he or she uses this pattern of instruction. If so, what was the reaction to the concept-attainment pattern of instruction?

ON YOUR OWN

Log on to the web-based student study site at http://www.sagepub.com/holt for access to a Standards-Based Student Project that will help you connect what you have learned in this chapter to your state's standards; study aids, such as electronic flashcards; and research recommendations, including journal article links and other Web resources.

15

Inquiry

INQUIRY IS A POPULAR PATTERN OF INSTRUCTION THAT HAS GAINED MORE ATTENTION AS NEW IDEAS have been developed that support educational reform. Inquiry has many definitions and variations based on the content and context of the instructional setting. However, questions are at the heart of inquiry. You provide students with an opportunity to examine and explore new ideas, which can lead them to formulate meaningful questions for further examination. Inquiry encourages critical-thinking skills, which assist with independent learning (Duckworth, 1987; van Zee, 2000).

Questions can be generated by the teacher or by the students. You can initiate the questions, and the questions can be further broadened by the students. To expand students' thoughts and ideas, you must be able to interpret and extract their thinking to assist them with the understanding and ideas. Extracting from student understanding means making use of various types of questions such as probing, prompts, eliciting, and closure-seeking questions. These types of questions will be defined in this chapter and examples will be provided. Through the use of questions, you can ascertain students' knowledge of the content and structure lessons to meet the learning demands of the class.

An inquiry-based model of teaching is not a "lock-step" instructional strategy. Just as you modify and adjust the curriculum to meet the learning needs of your specific population, inquiry can grow and change. Defined in this way, inquiry is a process; when opportunities are provided to extract meaning from the process, then thinking patterns are enhanced. We have classified inquiry in "Thinking and Organizing the Content," Part VI of this book. As a framework for thinking about content, inquiry is not lacking in interaction between the teacher, the student, and the content. In fact, successful classroom interactions can lead students to develop problem-solving, critical-thinking, and creative-thinking skills.

Although the content area of science has paid special attention to inquiry-based instruction, other content areas have also developed inquiry techniques. The National Science Education Standards (NRC, 1996) define inquiry as various approaches to studying and learning in the natural world. Inquiry is described as a way for students to plan and investigate their

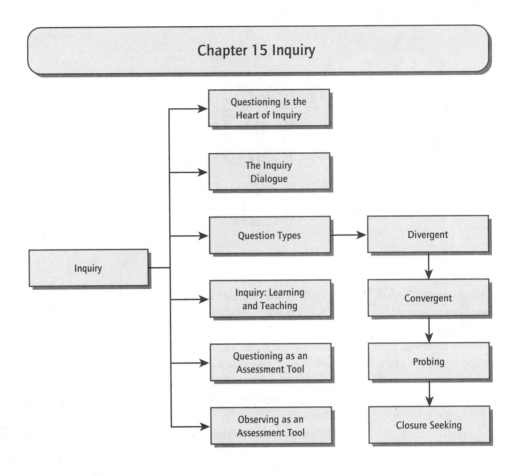

Chapter 15 Inquiry

Inquiry
- Questioning Is the Heart of Inquiry
- The Inquiry Dialogue
- Question Types → Divergent → Convergent → Probing → Closure Seeking
- Inquiry: Learning and Teaching
- Questioning as an Assessment Tool
- Observing as an Assessment Tool

understanding of ideas. Students learn how to solve problems and create solutions by experiencing them in real and meaningful encounters.

RESEARCH ANCHOR

J. Richard Suchman (1966) conceptualized the theory of inquiry as an instructional strategy. Suchman believed that the more active students are in the decision-making process of collecting and interpreting information, the more meaningful the learning will be. Inquiry involves the students more extensively in their learning compared to other instructional patterns. Inquiry allows students to explore their inquisitiveness, develops thinking skills, and builds on students' natural curiosity and need to explore. Additionally, other purposes for inquiry include teaching problem solving, decision making, and conceptualization (Hunkins, 1989).

Inquiry as a process has been aligned with thinking strategies. The key characteristics of all forms of inquiry are student involvement and the ability to process information in particular ways to arrive as some insight or conclusion. The role of the teacher may vary with different forms of inquiry. *Guided inquiry* uses teacher involvement, *open inquiry* uses slight teacher involvement, and *individualized inquiry* uses no teacher involvement. Ideally, individualized inquiry is the ultimate goal—having students so competent in thinking and asking questions that they motivate themselves to seek answers to problems.

The students pictured here are forming their thinking through inquiry by answering the teacher's questions about what they observed.

GUIDED INQUIRY

The amount of teacher intervention in the inquiry process distinguishes guided from open inquiry. In guided inquiry, the teacher generally begins with an open-ended question or some form of data. The students make observations and inductively arrive at some conclusion, generalization, or solution that is generally a predetermined goal from the teacher's perspective.

The steps in the guided inquiry are as follows:

1. Teacher: Present example.

2. Students: Describe example.

3. Teacher: Present additional example.

4. Students: Describe second example and compare to the first example.

5. Teacher: Present additional examples and nonexamples.

6. Students: Compare and contrast examples.

7. Teacher: Prompt students to identify characteristics or relationships.

8. Students: Ask students to state the definition or relationship.

9. Teacher: Ask for additional examples.

J. Richard Suchman, the originator of an inquiry teaching program that has been widely used throughout the United States, once said that "inquiry is the way people learn when they're left alone." To Suchman, inquiry is a natural way for human beings to learn about their environment. Think for moment about a very young child left in a yard with objects that he or she is free to explore. The child, without any coaxing, will begin to explore the objects by throwing, touching, pulling, and banging them and trying to take them apart. The child learns about the objects and how they interact by exploring them, by developing his or her own ideas about them—in short, he or she learns about them by inquiry. Many authors have discussed the nature of inquiry using terms such as *inductive thinking*, *creative thinking*, *discovery learning*, the *scientific method*, and the like.

Perhaps the best example of inductive inquiry is the Inquiry Development Program, developed a number of years ago by J. Richard Suchman. Suchman produced a number of inquiry programs designed to help students find out about science phenomena through inquiry. Suchman's views on inquiry are quite applicable today, and this statement is worth pondering:

> Inquiry is the active pursuit of meaning involving thought processes that change experience to bits of knowledge. When we see a strange object, for example, we may be puzzled about what it is, what it is made of, what it is used for, how it came into being, and so forth. *To find answers to questions* (emphasis mine) such as these we might examine the object closely, subject it to certain tests, compare it with other, more familiar objects, or ask people about it, and for a time our searching would be aimed at finding out whether any of these theories made sense. Or we might simply cast about for information that would suggest new theories for us to test. All these activities—observing, theorizing, experimenting, theory testing—are part of inquiry. The purpose of the activity is to gather enough information to put together theories that will make new experiences less strange and more meaningful. (Suchman, 1968, p.1)

The key to the inquiry model proposed by Suchman is providing "problem-focused events." Suchman's program provided films of such events, but he also advocated demonstrations and developed a series of idea books for the purpose of helping students organize concepts. It is the inquiry demonstrations that we use to help you develop inquiry lessons.

Source: 7.4 Inquiry Models of Teaching, retrieved July 21, 2004, from http://scied.gsu.edu/hassard/mos/7.4.html.

Because the teacher is involved in guiding the process, there is less freedom for student-initiated learning outcomes. The degree of focus is guided by the teacher and may ask students to create categories, or it may be more structured to ascertain certain conceptual understandings. This inductive process closely resembles the thinking strategy for attaining concepts.

THE ROLE OF QUESTIONS IN THE GUIDED-INQUIRY PROCESS

As students make inferences about their observations from the data, the teacher must be skillful in asking questions to lead students to the appropriate solution. Your ability to pace student

Here, a teacher is reflecting on the type of inquiry questions to be developed for her next lesson.

interaction during the guided-inquiry process is dependent on understanding question types. Certain questions can expand student participation, and other questions can limit student participation. For example, in your classroom, the initial question (opening question) should usually be open ended or divergent. A *divergent question* is a question that has many possible responses. For example, while holding an item in your hand, you might ask, "What can you tell me about this object?" This question is divergent and asks for an initial student response.

The action of *eliciting* takes place any time that you are trying to extract responses from students who are not responding. Eliciting questions encourage an initial response from the class, expand participation to include a larger percentage of the class, and rekindle a discussion that is losing momentum. Table 15.1, adapted from Esler and Sciortino (1991), explains the purposes and examples of eliciting questions.

Regarding the pace of the inquiry dialogue, you may want to consider another type of question that is the opposite of divergent. A *convergent question* limits participation and normally has a single correct response—for example, "What is today's date?" Convergent questions are considered low-level types of questions. As you examine the purpose and the direction of the guided inquiry, keep in mind that divergent questions expand participation and convergent questions limit participation.

TABLE 15.1	Purposes and Examples of Eliciting Questions

Purposes

- Encourage initial response
- Expand participation
- Elicit responses from reluctant students
- Regain momentum

Examples

- "Can someone put the following data into sequence?" (Convergent)
- "How many different ways do you think?" (Divergent)
- "Can anyone else. . . "
- "John, you have good ideas. What do you think?"
- "In your opinion, which is the best ice cream?"
- "How would you feel if . . . ?"
- "Can we summarize the arguments for both sides?"
- "If I told you that . . . would you say?"

Probing questions are often open-ended questions designed to get students to examine what they know about a topic and what they want to investigate. Probing questions are asked to get students to examine the depth of the content. The utilitarian open-ended stem questions can be used in wide-ranging settings. Questions such as, "What can you tell me about birds?" can work just as well with areas such as the laws of motion or plant cells. Probing questions can be used to extend, redirect, justify, and clarify ideas (see Table 15.2).

If the probing questions that you pose are not framed in a consistent manner to help students make connections to the concept, students will not have enough information or prior knowledge to participate in the classroom dialogue. Open-ended probing stem questions are best to foster inquiry.

Rowe (1987) researched the effect of *wait time* in teacher questioning. She defined two types of wait time: (1) the time after the teacher finishes the question until the student begins the answer, and (2) the time after a student gives an answer and before the teacher talks again. Rowe found that the quality and quantity of students' responses increased with longer wait time. Ideally, teachers should wait three to five seconds after asking a question before expecting a response. Rowe (1978) describes several benefits of increased wait time: The length of responses from students increases. Students are more likely to support inferences with evidence. Students speculate more about other explanations or ways to think about the topic. The number of questions from students increases. There are more responses, and they are richer when wait time increases. The need for disciplinary action also decreases. Student-to-student interaction and cooperation increase. More students voluntarily participate. Students gain confidence in their ability to explain and challenge situations. Finally, achievement on written tests improves.

Another type of question that is used to pace the inquiry dialogue is *closure-seeking questions*. These questions invite students to begin to seek conclusions, help students to clarify issues or ideas, solicit procedures, and direct students to interpret research data (see Table 15.3).

TABLE 15.2	Purposes and Examples of Probing Questions

Purposes
- Extend ideas
- Redirect ideas
- Justify ideas
- Clarify ideas

Examples
- "Can we add anything to this?"
- "Have we mentioned all points of view?"
- "Is there a better way?"
- "Dose anyone have another idea?"
- "What is some information we need?"
- "Why do you think this way?"
- "How did you arrive at that conclusion?"
- "That's good—would you restate that so everyone will understand?"
- "I don't understand. Could you . . . ?"

TABLE 15.3	Purposes and Examples of Closure-Seeking Questions

Purpose	Examples
Invite students to begin to see conclusions	"What can be concluded from this?" "What can we say about . . . ?"
Seek clarification of issues	"What information is important when solving this problem?" "What other consideration can be made given this issue?"
Solicit procedures	"How can we find the information necessary to solve the problem?" "How can we test our best guess?"
Direct students to interpret research data	"Based on our research data, what can be concluded?" "What does our information show about the relationship between . . . and the . . . ?"

Source: Esler and Sciortino (1991).

The *open-inquiry* format is different from the guided-inquiry format. In the data-collection phase of the process, students are free to explore additional resources and gather data to seek solutions to their questions. Students' freedom to initiate and think is expanded in open inquiry, and students are permitted to ask questions. The students assume more responsibility for their learning with open inquiry. The teacher's role is to facilitate and oversee the students as they gather additional information to solve the inquiry. The teacher may act as a resource or suggest other people from the community. The process remains inductive but allows students to access the Internet and other resource materials.

Fenton (1968), a leading social studies educator, proposed the following steps for the inquiry process as it applies to social studies:

1. Recognizing a problem from data

2. Formulating hypotheses

3. Recognizing the logical implications of hypotheses

4. Gathering data on the basis of logical implications

5. Interpreting, analyzing, and evaluating the data

6. Evaluating the hypotheses in light of the data

The following is an illustration of these six steps of open inquiry. Let's say that as part of a social studies class, a group of students becomes concerned about the environment and about a lake in their community that has become polluted. In open inquiry, they would follow these steps:

- Step 1: The students identify the problem and then ascertain the extent of community support for cleaning the lake.

- Step 2: The teacher guides the students as they propose ideas about how they could obtain support. The students' ideas include surveying the citizens, interviewing city officials, attending a city council meeting, and or writing state and federal governments to see what guidelines might exist.

- Step 3: After discussion and clarification, the students decide they can do two things on their list. The students decide to write city officials and attend a city council meeting.

- Step 4: In this step, the students gather data (open inquiry) regarding the two approaches on their list. This may occur over time and could take one week or several weeks. This may involve time outside class.

- Step 5: The students interpret and analyze the results of their letter writing and their attendance at a city council meeting.

- Step 6: The students evaluate the action of the city council in light of their concerns about the polluted lake.

Another form of inquiry is called *individualized inquiry*. This form of inquiry is closely aligned with open inquiry but occurs when students want to pursue other questions or data based on a topic that has personal meaning for them. Students operate independently of the teacher's directions. Examples may include an art student who wants to pursue more information about impressionistic paintings after learning about Monet; a U.S. history student who wants to learn about the Congress after studying the three branches of government; or a physical education student who wants to travel to the National Baseball Hall of Fame in Cooperstown, New York.

THE SOCRATIC METHOD OF QUESTIONING

We have mentioned that questioning is at the heart of the inquiry process. As an instructional strategy, questioning dates back to the time of Plato and Socrates in 335 BC (Clegg, 1987). The book *Meno* documents what has become known as Socratic dialogue or the *Socratic method* of teaching (Clegg, 1987). In this method, the teacher uses questions to lead students to inferences (Hunkins, 1976). Used in universities throughout the middle ages and in law schools today, this method of teaching is the foundation of current methods that use questioning (Clegg, 1987).

Inquiry can be deductive when students process questions and then formulate a logical conclusion based on the information presented. As a deductive method, inquiry is a variation of the Socratic method. This method is often used by lawyers in the courtroom to deduce information. When used as an instructional pattern, the teacher controls the data, guides the inquiry, and raises questions to elicit propositions that most likely will lead to logical outcomes.

The following sample dialogue illustrates the Socratic method:

Teacher: A company wants to begin offshore drilling for oil. How might this affect people?

Student: It would cause pollution.

Teacher: Is it ever worth it to risk pollution?

Student: Yes, if people need jobs.

Teacher: Are there other benefits to offshore drilling?

Student: The company would pay taxes.

Teacher: Are there other benefits?

Student: The oil may be needed for our cars.

Teacher: Under what conditions should the decision be made to permit the offshore drilling?

Student: When the need is greater than the risk of pollution.

By leading students through a discussion using questions, the Socratic technique can help students develop logical thinking. Practice with problem-solving procedures in a variety of situations enables learners to begin to assimilate both the information and the process (Esler & Sciortino, 1991).

THE INQUIRY DIALOGUE

Clarifying student understanding through your questioning is a technique that students may find interesting. Students may not have been encouraged to expand their thinking through questioning; therefore, questioning needs to be fostered in an uncritical manner. For students to share their thoughts, they must know that they will not be chastised or ridiculed for their answers. Forming questions and learning must be personally driven for the student to develop a sense of inquisitiveness. The search for answers grows from questions.

Constructivism does play a significant role in connecting theoretical learning to inquiry-based instruction (Lorsbach & Tobin, 1992). *Constructivism* is defined as actively engaging the student in the process of learning or the human construction of knowledge. Social constructionists believe that the role of the student is to participate in the learning environment. The student actively constructs knowledge that connects to his or her existing knowledge (Gredler, 2001). Influenced by Dewey's educational philosophy, inquiry-based instruction is a hybrid of teaching and learning. Dewey held that a community of students participates in the creation of new knowledge (Gredler, 2001).

"Watching, listening, writing, reading, talking, replaying, and wondering about what is happening prepares the way for inquiry" (Saul, Reardon, Pearce, Dieckman, & Neutze, 2002, p. 18). Dewey's position was that learning occurs through social construction and varied experiences—in other words, when the learning is focused on the student. Social constructs, in Dewey's opinion, are the cornerstone of humanity. Social construction is produced through interacting with the learning environment, forming thoughts, elaborating ideas, and testing ideas. Without society, there would be no communication or interaction of ideas, hopes, or opinions; thus, education would be ineffective. The connection between education and communication is essential (Dewey, 1916; Lemke, 1990). In addition, experiences are the foundation for furthering learning and knowledge creation (Ornstein & Hunkins, 1998).

Making a case for social interaction, Dewey (1916) suggested that teachers ground their educational practices in students' needs and capabilities, not just the subject matter. Students need an atmosphere that provides a foundation; this foundation can identify their needs and capabilities. Dewey (1916) said,

> Curiosity is but the tendency to make these conditions perceptible. It is the business of educators to supply an environment so that this reaching out of an experience may be fruitfully rewarded and kept continuously active. (p. 209)

Once the teacher identifies the requirements of the student, he or she can create an atmosphere of reflection and critical thinking that promotes dialogue and exploration for the students. Dewey (1910) described two essential elements of reflective thinking: the need to create uncertainty or doubt and the conscious effort to investigate. Solitary reflective thinking does not support the social construction of new knowledge. The social environment in which the reflective dialogue and exploration takes place is imperative for verification of thought, and it is the next step toward making meaning of the experience.

Dewey (1916) supported inquiry-based instruction. Through the application of social construction of knowledge and experience, students can stretch beyond their present learning stage and can foster the desire to learn in a social setting to make meaning in situations. These are all characteristics of inquiry-based instruction.

INQUIRY: LEARNING AND TEACHING

Students who examine and explore new ideas can formulate meaningful questions and devise methods to answer questions, provided that there is an atmosphere that fosters learning. Inquiry also encourages critical-thinking skills, which assist with independent learning (Duckworth, 1987; van Zee, 2000). The National Science Education Standards address the issue of giving

John Dewey's philosophical interest throughout his career has been called *epistemology* or the *theory of knowledge*. It is indicative of Dewey's critical stance toward past efforts in this area that he expressly rejected the term "epistemology," preferring the *theory of inquiry* or *experimental logic* as more representative of his own approach.

His writings include *My Pedagogic Creed* (1897), *The School and Society; Being Three Lectures by John Dewey Supplemented by a Statement of the University Elementary School* (1899; published as *The School and Society*, edited by Jo Ann Boydston, with a preface by Joe R. Burnett, 1980), *The Elementary School Record* (1900), *The Educational Situation* (1902), *The Child and the Curriculum,* (1902), *The School and the Child; Being Selections from the Educational Essays of John Dewey* (1907), *Ethical Principles Underlying Education* (1908), *Moral Principles in Education* (1909), *Educational Essays by John Dewey* (1910), *Interest and Effort in Education* (1913), *Schools of To-morrow* (with Evelyn Dewey, 1915; published as *Schools of Tomorrow*, 1962), *Democracy and Education: An Introduction to the Philosophy of Education* (1916), *Progressive Education and the Science of Education* (1928), *The Sources of a Science of Education* (1929), *American Education Past and Future* (1931), *The Way Out of Educational Confusion* (1931), *Education and the Social Order* (1934), *Experience and Education* (1938; 60th anniversary edition, 1998), *Education Today* (edited and with a foreword by Joseph Ratner, 1940, 1969), *Philosophy of Education* (also published as *Problems of Men,* 1946), *The Child and the Curriculum, and The School and Society* (introduction by Leonard Carmichael, 1956, introduction by Philip W. Jackson, 1990), *Dewey on Education* (introduction and notes by Martin S. Dworkin, 1959), *Dictionary of Education* (1959; edited by Ralph B. Winn and with a foreword by John Herman Randall, Jr., 1972), *The Relation of Theory to Practice in Education* (1962), *John Dewey on Education: Selected Writings* (edited and with an introduction by Reginald D. Archambault, 1964), *Lectures in the Philosophy of Education, 1899* (1966), *Selected Educational Writings* (with an introduction and commentary by F. W. Garforth, 1966), and *Philosophy and Education in Their Historic Relations* (compiled by Elsie Ripley Clapp, edited and with an introduction by J. J. Chambliss, 1993).

Source: "John Dewey," Dictionary of American Biography, Supplement 5: 1951–1955. American Council of Learned Societies, 1977.

students a voice in decisions about the content of the work. Requiring responsibility for all members in the group or classroom is important. By developing a sense of purpose or relevance in a task, the student will probe topics that relate to the content (NRC, 1996).

Students should perceive themselves as a community of science students (Duckworth, 1987; NRC, 1996). The development of science, both process and content, is reliant on sharing and discussing ideas. Inquiry should be viewed as a social learning process whereby communication leads to the development of understanding and learning science. Students must see science as a collaborative endeavor that is dependent on the sharing and debating of issues and ideas (NRC, 2000).

Providing opportunities for collaboration with other students is an important component of inquiry-based instruction. Collaboration with others allows students to make meaning of their investigations and prior experiences. It gives all students an opportunity to check for self-understanding. The struggle to make meaning gives students and their peers openings that may lead to further questions or challenges. Teachers who facilitate collaboration support students' ability to build and share ideas and new knowledge (Hogan & Corey, 2001; Wallace, Krajcik & Soloway, 1996).

When teachers narrow classroom discussions from broad generalizations, this helps students to think and formulate their own questions. From broad generalizations, students draw on their past experiences to connect with the new information. During this process, students may request tools or resources based on their past knowledge or experiences (Barclay, 1987; Duckworth, 2001).

A case study examining student-generated inquiry discussions found that using the process of inquiry to learn allows students' background knowledge, experiences, and skills to influence how the student thinks and makes sense of new knowledge (van Zee, Iwasyk, Kurose, Simpson, & Wild, 2001). New meaning is built when previous knowledge, experiences, and skills meet with new knowledge, experiences, and skills. The new meaning may cause dissonance in the students' thinking and learning, or students may see the connection between the old ways and the new ways. Students create conceptual barriers because they are reluctant to let go of their old beliefs about concepts. Students can find new ways to make the old beliefs fit into the current understanding. Teachers can facilitate learning situations so that the students explore and test their misconceptions. Students need opportunities to test the limits of their beliefs; through questions that lead to meaningful answers, students can confirm or rethink their beliefs (van Zee et al., 2001).

Pearce (1999) asserted that students are naturally full of questions but have been stifled in the current educational system. Students have been conditioned through their schooling to wait for the teacher to give them questions, which, in turn, will lead them to the "right" answer. By modifying and enhancing student learning, you can slowly transition from teacher-directed activities to guided-inquiry-based learning experiences. Starting with given problems, procedures and answers may need to be established for the teacher to ascertain the students' prior knowledge. Clarifying what the students know by replacing it with new knowledge or information is a difficult transition for students. Accepting that learning is about the journey, not the destination, is troublesome for the student and teacher (Duckworth, 1987). Students can be easily upset by "wrong" questions. They may not have been encouraged to question their thinking; therefore, they do not have questions to further the dialogue or investigation. Inquiry learning must be personally driven. The concern for content and process must be linked with good questions and previous knowledge (van Zee et al., 2001).

When appropriate, the learning can move to an open problem, procedure, or solution or student-centered, inquiry-based learning experience. Students need to be allowed to figure out procedures on their own if they are to create new experiences and learning events. Palincsar, Collins, and Marano (2000) conducted a study on engaging students with learning disabilities in guided-inquiry-based instruction. They found that if guidelines and strategies are not established at the beginning, students will be confused and will not know what data to collect or what is relevant to the problem they are investigating. A series of events leading from teacher-directed to student-directed events is essential for successful inquiry-based learning and teaching (NRC, 1996).

Bianchini and Colburn (2000) investigated Colburn's use of inquiry to teach the nature of science with prospective elementary school teachers. The study suggested that the nature of science be used as the content for the context of teaching inquiry-based science instruction. During their study with prospective elementary school teachers, the researchers asked the question, "How can teachers use inquiry to teach the nature of science?" (Bianchini & Colburn, 2000, p. 180). Colburn, the teacher-researcher in the group, focused on a conceptual framework relating the nature of science. The six main concepts were as follows:

1. There is no right way to solve a problem.

2. Similar science experiences can be perceived differently.

3. Evidence of understanding should be provided rather than assumed.

4. The existence of evidence does not mean that a conclusion is true.

5. A community of scientists should communicate with each other.

6. A community of scientists should share their results as a valued process.

Neglecting certain aspects of the nature of science in the process of inquiry-based instruction can reinforce misconceptions. The benefits as well as the limits of the study were influenced by the teacher-researcher's approach and prior experiences with inquiry-based instruction (Bianchini & Colburn, 2000).

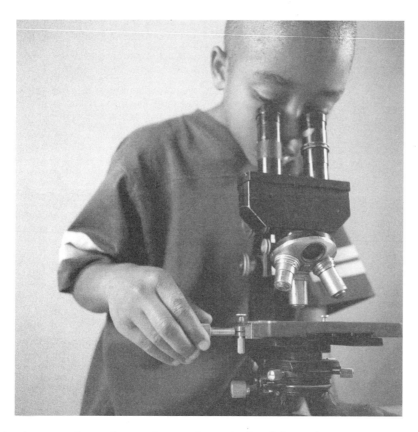

Open inquiry occurs when students are free to explore and collect their own data.

Magnets: Teacher Questions

Ms. Chen's third-grade students file into the classroom and sit down in their seats. The walls are filled with student essays and drawings. Each round table has three or four students. On each table there is a cup with a number on it to identify the table. The cup holds pencils and erasers for the students to use each day. In preparation for the day, there are tubs of materials on the desks. These tubs contain items that will be used during the lesson. Today's lesson will introduce the concept of magnets.

Ms. Chen: Today we are going to investigate magnets. Tell me about magnets. How about someone at Table 4?

Mario: They stick to things.

Ms. Chen: What do you mean by "stick to things?"

Mario: You know, attract.

Ms. Chen: Well, I think I know what you mean by attract. What does anyone else think they know about magnets and attracting?

Ginnie: Like when you have metal and a magnet, they always attract each other?

Ms. Chen: Always?

Hands fly into the air as students rattle off what they know about magnets, attracting, and metal. In the chaos, Ms. Chen asks the students to write down what they know or think they know to be true about magnets, attracting, and metals.

After several minutes and continued checking in with the tables about their progress on recording their thoughts, Ms. Chen asks the students to share what they wrote in their journals with the other students at their tables. After the small groups share their ideas, Ms. Chen asks them to come up with one list of student-generated information to share with the whole class.

Ms. Chen then posts all the student-generated information on the board.

Ms. Chen: Wow, Table 2, this looks like you know a lot. But how do you know whether it is true or not?

Joshua: Could we try it out? You know, like test it with the stuff in the baskets?

Ms. Chen: What kinds of questions do you have about Joshua's statement?

Maggie: I still don't get it. Ginnie said that magnets attract metals. I think magnets attract metals, but I am not sure if they will attract all metals.

Ms. Chen: How could you put that statement into the form of a question?

Maggie makes a face as she concentrates. Other students in class wave their hands in the air, some offering their ideas and suggestions.

Maggie: [Speaking slowly and thoughtfully] I think that my question would be, do all metals attract magnets?

Ms. Chen: How would you test your question?

Maggie: I would line up all the different metals and test each one with the magnet.

Ms. Chen: How would you share this information with others?

Joshua: We could make a chart with the names of the different metals and whether they attracted or not.

By accessing the students' prior knowledge with open-ended questions, Ms. Chen was able to determine what her students knew and where she could direct the next activity. Because the students had a fundamental understanding of attraction, she did not have to discuss this at length with the students.

Ms. Chen provided a topic, question, and materials, yet the students initiated the design of their procedure, came up with their own results, and reported what they learned about the relationship between metals and magnets to the whole class. This activity is similar to activities in textbooks, but it was "opened up" to make room for student discovery and investigation. By opening up an activity, students are able to explore what they know and see how it aligns with what they experience. Some students—and adults—are put off by not following a concrete set of directions, fearing that they may get the "wrong" answer. That is why processing the activity at the end of the lesson provides closure and a check of understanding.

Magnets: Student Questions

Armando does not follow Ms. Chen's directions to create a question. He looks around and then starts to play with the magnets in the tray. The girls at his table go right to work, following the directions. Armando continues to play with the magnets.

Anita: Come on, Armando. We have stuff we need to do, please.

Armando: I know how it works, so I don't need to do it.

Hearing the plea from the girls at the table, Ms. Chen takes a chair from the corner, walks over to the table with the chair and sits down.

Ms. Chen: What do you think you are supposed to do?

Anita: Show how a magnet works.

Ms. Chen: What do you think Anita means by "how it works?"

Armando: I know how it works, but I just can't explain it.

Ms. Chen: What have you noticed about the magnets and the different metals you have in the basket?

Armando gives Ms. Chen a blank look. He does not want to be wrong. Ms. Chen senses that Armando feels uncomfortable, but she waits, not wanting to rush him into an answer. After an appropriate amount of wait time, she continues.

Ms. Chen: How do you know they are different?

Armando: Because they look different.

Ms. Chen: Do you think that each metal will attract the magnet?

Armando and the girls at the table all shake their heads no.

Anita: I know nails attract to magnets, and I think the paperclips will attract, too.

Ms. Chen: OK, do you think you can predict which metals will attract to the magnet and which ones won't?

The students all nod in agreement.

Ms. Chen: I would like you to consider two questions before I leave your group. First, how will you show the rest of the class your predictions? And second, how will you show that you know which metals were attracted to the magnets and which ones did not attract?"

The groups at the table quickly huddle together, scribble on their papers, and examine the metallic items. The students spentd the next five minutes predicting and testing the magnet on all the items in the tray and some items not in the tray. They start to write down answers on their worksheet.

(Continued)

Armando continues to test the magnet, and then he puts two magnets together. The magnets do not stick together but instead jump. Armando recoils.

Armando: What's that about?

Anita: That was cool. Do it again.

Armando: Why did it do that?

Diana: Maybe one side works and the other doesn't?

Armando: Why do you say that?

Diana: Because one side attracts and the other side doesn't.

Anita: I think the magnet has two sides.

Quickly, he repeats the "trick," as he is now calling it, for the girls. The girls, now fascinated by the trick, want to know how Armando knew how to do it. He said he wanted to know more.

Giving students an initial focus for an activity requires time for students to play with an objective. If students are given an opportunity within a structured period of time to play and experiment, it can substantially intensify the learning experiences. When the students were given five or six minutes to purposefully play with the magnets, they were able to develop some questions of their own to investigate.

By providing an opportunity to uncover answers, student-directed inquiry can begin to emerge. Armando's persistent play provided a platform for further questions and investigations, moving away from teacher-guided inquiry and toward student-directed inquiry.

ASSESSMENT

Assessment and *evaluation* are two terms that are often interchanged (Krajcik, Czerniak, & Berger, 2003). Assessment focuses on the learning, whereas evaluation focuses on the teaching. Assessment is based on learning for understanding, and evaluation is based on judging the teaching. There are two general forms of assessment: *formative* and *summative*. Formative assessment is an ongoing process that can occur at any time during the lesson and is used as feedback. A formative assessment may influence how or what you plan for an upcoming lesson. Summative assessment is used to condense the main points learned in a lesson. A summative assessment is frequently used at the end of a lesson.

A primary thought about assessment: Assess early and often. Assessment is used as a tool to gauge the progress of student learning. If you assess regularly, you will have a better working idea of students' abilities and misconceptions about concepts. Assessment that is informal and ongoing allows you and the student to develop connections between what the students know and what you anticipate that the students will learn. Feedback on student work, a form of assessment, can be either positive or negative. It allows you to examine the product closely and provide solid evidence of student understanding (Harlen, 1999). The implementation of an assessment procedure requires thought and planning.

Cody (2003) suggests giving a preassessment before the inquiry is started. Preassessment gives the students an opportunity to share what they already know about the topic and a chance

Francis P. Hunkins was an elementary school teacher in Gloucester, Massachusetts and later a professor of education at the University of Washington–Seattle. He was a field reader for the U.S. Office of Education and a field evaluator for the Educational Media Selection Centers project. He was a member of the National Council for the Social Studies task force for the study of international education, 1970–72 and a consultant to the Bureau of Indian Affairs and Coronet Films.

His writings include *The Influence of Analysis and Evaluation Questions on Achievement and Critical Thinking in Sixth-Grade Social Studies* (1968), *Asking About the U.S.A. and Its Neighbors* (with O. L. Davis, Jr., 1971, 1975), *Seeing Near and Far* (1971, 1975), *Observing People and Places* (1971, 1975). *Comparing Ways and Means* (1971, 1975), *Investigating Communities and Cultures* (1971, 1975), *Learning About Countries and Societies* (1971, 1975), *Questioning Strategies and Techniques* (1972), *Social Studies for the Evolving Individual* (with Patricia F. Spears, 1973), *Involving Students in Questioning* (1976), *Review of Research in Social Studies Education, 1970–1975* (1977), *Curriculum Development: Program Improvement* (1980), *Social Studies in the Elementary School* (with Jan Jeter and Phyllis F. Maxey, 1982), and *Curriculum: Foundations, Principles, and Issues* (with Allan C. Ornstein, 1988).

Source: *Contemporary Authors Online*; reproduced in the *Biography Resource Center* (Farmington Hills, MI: Thomson Gale, 2005).

for you to build on that prior knowledge. Cody (2003) states, "I am using assessment not only as a measurement of achievement following instruction, but as a tool of instruction as it unfolds, informing me and the students so that we can work together to learn from each other."

Assessing student learning through multiple sources is another way to verify and confirm student progress. Using only one source or one type of assessment can lead to an imbalance in truly understanding student learning. Processing student learning by questioning and observing makes the inquiry instructional pattern relevant for most classrooms. By processing the learning, you can clearly understand whether the objectives of the lesson have been met.

Questioning as an Assessment Tool

Asking questions is a suitable method to elicit student understanding, but it can also lead students astray from the original intent or focus of the lesson. Duckworth (1987) discusses posing questions without preconceived ideas about the right answer. Offering openness to multiple answers, not just open-endedness, gives students a chance to think things through and share how they came to know that idea. If you question too much, you can lead the student astray from the focus of the lesson or topic.

The National Science Education Standards state, "In the science classroom envisioned by the Standards, effective teachers continually create opportunities that challenge students and promote inquiry by asking questions" (NRC, 1996, p. 33). Attaining prior knowledge about a concept and eliciting answers from students guides the learning. Using the insight from the answers provided by the students, you can adjust the line of questioning and glean the intended direction of the lesson and its goals.

Curiosity drives questioning. With an inquiry-based instructional approach, you may first ask guiding questions. Once the students are curious about a concept or topic, they create their questions on a pathway to learning. Inquiry can be an evolving process. Your questions or teacher-structured questions may be the focus of the beginning portion of a unit, and this may lead to student-directed questions toward the end of the unit.

Observing as an Assessment Tool

Checking in on student understanding and individual progress provides the teacher with feedback that can be used to make choices about the next step in the instruction. Observable behaviors can be indicators of student progress. This feedback is constructive and valuable because it identifies student misconceptions. By watching and listening, you will have a better understanding of the students' ability than can be obtained by relying solely on paper-pencil work.

TECHNOLOGY

The National Science Foundation supports several inquiry-based curriculum projects. Most, such as WISE (Web-based Inquiry Science Environment), Hi-CE (Center for Highly Interactive Computing Education), and LeTUS (Learning Technologies in Urban Schools), are designed for middle and high school students exploring a variety of topics related to science.

Although inquiry is focused on science, other websites support this model. The Exploratorium Institute for Inquiry (http://www.exploratorium.edu) is a museum-based website designed to give students an opportunity to investigate online or recreate activities.

Colburn (1998) a teacher-researcher, used the Internet as a vehicle for his students. When students in the classroom are given choice and opportunity, this supports the notion that students are capable of learning. Experience with the Internet provided another way for students to contribute to their learning. Empowering students to examine their own questions by designing learning experiences allowed them to follow through on their own ideas using the Internet.

Learning Tenets
That Support Inquiry

The brain seeks to classify information and the things to be learned.

A distinctive feature of inquiry is the ability to draw on all of the senses to engage the brain. Questions may be evoked by seeing, hearing, smelling, tasting, or touching. By combining the senses, the questions can become complex and overwhelming. This is why the questions you initially present to students must be focused. As the students become more familiar with the process of inquiry, they can accept more responsibility for their learning. As they develop a direction for their learning, you can engage more and more of their senses and expand their cognitive growth.

**The emotional system drives attention,
and attention drives meaning and memory.**

Dewey (1916) suggested that learning is a social experience. In a social setting, the feeling of being safe is critical to inquiry. Students may not ask questions or provide answers if they know they might be teased or ridiculed. So a feeling of community plays a significant role in nurturing an atmosphere in which students can ask questions without fear of reprisal.

Community building is an inclusive strategy that is fashioned around the idea of establishing a feeling of unity and involvement with a group. It supports an atmosphere that provides trust, a feeling of belonging to a group that cares, and a chance to model affirming and diverse thinking through cooperation and collaboration (Kagan, 1994). If your students know more about the other students in the classroom, they will be more open to asking questions and listening to responses.

Learning occurs in both conscious and unconscious states.

When students are engaged in a lesson with a teacher who is using the Socratic method of questioning, the students' curiosity is aroused. They are consciously listening and participating as the lesson unfolds. This type of thinking is both conscious and unconscious. The students may be very familiar with the teachers' intended outcome, but for the moment, they are confused about the direction of the lesson. As more information is revealed about the topic under investigation, the students will check their perceived hypothesis against what is being revealed. Inquiry supports a way of thinking, and the evidence revealed during the inquiry reveals a way of knowing. This thinking can be conscious and unconscious as the outcomes are gradually discovered within the lesson.

The brain is designed for ups and downs, not constant attention.

Wait time is an aspect of inquiry. Giving students time to think about a concept, cultivate an idea, and then ask a question or give an answer requires more than rapid-fire dialogue. There may be moments in an inquiry-based classroom of raucous conversation and deadening silence.

When students feel comfortable asking questions, the questions may be a stream of self-organizing thoughts. This type of discourse may stop for no apparent reason because the student has self-talked himself or herself through a concept. Once students have achieved an answer to their question, they may mentally move on without explaining.

**Learning occurs through processing and active
engagement with visual, auditory, and kinesthetic modalities.**

All of the senses may be involved in inquiry. The more exposure students have to different perspectives on a similar concept, the more likely they are to remember and apply the concept. Reading, writing, telling, drawing, and acting are all ways of displaying knowledge. These actions will lead you to see the reflective practices of students: how they came to know the concept. They can provide a platform for demonstrating knowledge as well as a springboard for multi-layered learning experiences.

**Good teaching is about recognizing and selecting instructional patterns
that match the context for learning and the students we are teaching.**

Defining what students should know and be able to do with a concept will help you decide how to incorporate inquiry into your practice. Because student responsibility becomes greater as inquiry moves from the traditional hands-on approach to the student-centered approach, you may have to step back and examine your role in the classroom. You may want to take some time to reflect on the following questions:

Are you willing to take time to develop inquiry?

- Are you willing to ease students into accepting responsibility?

- Are you willing to let them learn without giving them the answers?

Summary

In this chapter, we presented various forms of inquiry, including guided, open, and individualized inquiry. Inquiry as a pattern of instruction is best suited to Part VI, "Thinking and Organizing the Content," because teachers guide the students through an inductive thinking process by manipulating data. We have cited research that indicates inquiry has several advantages because it helps students solve problems, raises students' motivation for learning, and develops higher-level cognitive skills.

Leading students to question their own thinking or promoting new thinking patterns can cause students to want to discover more. By focusing on their predictions, teachers are able to determine what students are thinking as it relates to the content or process. The students can concentrate on the predictions they thought would happen, not on what was supposed to happen. The ability to question gives the student a scaffold to examine more than just the surface (van Zee et al., 2001).

Teachers working with students can gradually modify the activities and investigations toward the inquiry-based process. The teacher can target learning toward an inquiry-based process by allowing the students to understand procedures for themselves, design the data table to display results, or revise or repeat the procedures. Inquiry-based instruction leads to more independent thinking, higher-level thinking, and greater expectations on the students' part (NRC, 1996).

Thought to Action

1. Select a lesson that you have presented in the past and create a series of open-ended questions that could accompany the lesson. Also provide probing and prompting questions that you could use to examine students' understanding of the lesson.

2. What might a classroom that uses inquiry look and sound like? Be sure to describe the teacher, students, physical layout, atmosphere, and other details.

3. Identify a key concept, search for an activity, and reshape the activity so that it progresses from a teacher-guided to a student-directed activity.

4. If you have students who are reluctant to share aloud in the classroom, what strategies could you use to provide a platform for students to ask questions?

5. Some educators believe that inquiry is too wishy-washy. Outline several points that support the use of inquiry-based instruction.

6. At the end of a unit, ask your students to write two questions they still have about the topic. Use those questions to develop an extension unit or learning center for additional activities.

ON YOUR OWN

Log on to the web-based student study site at http://www.sagepub.com/holt
for access to a Standards-Based Student Project that will help you connect what
you have learned in this chapter to your state's standards; study aids, such as
electronic flashcards; and research recommendations, including journal article
links and other Web resources.

Glossary

Acronym: A word made from the first letter of each item you need to remember.

Acrostic: A link between a letter in a word to be remembered and a phrase. For example, "every good boy does fine" (EGBDF) can be used to remember the notes in a staff.

Advance organizer: Verbal phrases (e.g., "The paragraph you are about to read is about cells") or graphics that provide what cognitive psychologists call the "mental scaffolding" to learn new information. David Ausubel developed the theory of advance organizers.

Affective domain: One of the three domains of learning defined by Benjamin Bloom and associates. The affective domain deals with attitudes and feelings.

Afferents: The electrical and chemical inputs that arrive at the neuron through the dendrites.

Alternative assessment: Assessment strategies that are different from traditional assessment strategies, such as portfolios or performance assessments.

Anticipatory set: An opening or attention grabber that is stated at the beginning of instruction. Anticipatory sets can be a famous quote, riddle, song, phrase, or a specific action. The term comes from Madeline Hunter's research on direct instruction.

Artistic creation: A form of synthesis; a deliberate search for goals that can be reproduced in a painting, poem, or musical composition (Glatthorn & Baron, 1991).

Assertive discipline: A classroom management model developed by Lee Canter that uses positive reinforcement as a form of behavior modification.

Assessment: A term used to determine learner outcomes.

Attaining concepts: The name given to one of the instructional strategies found in Part VI, "Thinking and Organizing the Content."

Authentic assessment: A form of assessment that reflects a real-life situation

Axon: A primary output pathway by which the neuron sends information to other neurons.

Behavior modification: A systematic application of behavior techniques used to increase desirable behavior and decrease undesirable behavior.

Behaviorism: Psychology from the behaviorist view is a purely objective, experimental view of natural science. Its theoretical goal is the prediction and control of behavior.

Bilingual Education Act: Title VII of the Elementary and Secondary Education Act, the Bilingual Education Act of 1972, transformed the way language-minority children are taught in the United States and promoted equal access to the curriculum. The act expired January 8, 2002, and was replaced with the English Language Acquisition Act, a part of the No Child Left Behind legislation.

Blue-Backed Speller: The first volume of Noah Webster's book *A Grammatical Institute of the English Language,* so named for its blue cover. This school book is so popular that it has never been out of print. The book has helped teach students to read for nearly 100 years and is an important part of the history of American education.

Boston School Committee: The first school board to be approached to end segregation in 1846. The request was denied by the board.

Brain-based learning theories: Theories of learning based on new technology from the medical fields, cognitive science, and neuroscience that inform us about the biological operations of the brain.

Brown v. Board of Education of Topeka: The 1954 U.S. Supreme Court decision that ruled separate but equal schools were unconstitutional.

Channel One Television: A service provided to more than 25% of American schools in exchange for free media equipment. Schools must guarantee that students will watch commercials and news geared toward young people for a minimum of 12 minutes each day.

Charter schools: Alternative schools that are publicly financed to meet the needs of unique populations of students.

Checker: In cooperative learning, an assigned role given to a student working in a group on an academic task. The purpose of assigning roles to students in a group is to ensure individual accountability. The checker's role is to check the work of the group.

Choice theory: A theory of behavior developed by William Glasser that says all people are driven by six basic needs: survival, power, love, belonging, freedom, and fun.

Chunking: Isolation of bits of information in the content to be taught in a skill sequence.

Civil Rights Act: Dramatic 1964 federal legislation passed that guaranteed equal access to public facilities regardless of race, color, religion, or national origin. Based on the ideas of President John F. Kennedy and signed by President Lyndon B. Johnson.

Classroom academic rules: Rules related to students' academic work, such as rules for makeup work, extra credit, neatness in completing work, taking notes, etc.

Classroom communication: The interactive pattern of verbal and nonverbal behavior between the students and teacher in a classroom.

Classroom conduct rules: Rules that assist the teacher and students with the daily routine of the classroom. For example, rules that define how students speak in the classroom, washroom rules, gum chewing, tardiness policy, etc.

Classroom management: All of the things that teachers do to manage students' time, materials, and space in the classroom.

Classroom organization: Teachers have an option of three types of classroom organization structures: competitive, individual, or cooperative.

Client-centered teaching: Term coined by Carl Rogers, a psychologist who based his principles of interaction on the needs of individual clients or learners.

Closure-seeking questions: Questions that allow the lesson to come to its end—for example, "Can anyone summarize what we have learned?"

Coercive power: A type of power that is used to force students to conform to the demands of the teacher or to school policy. It is not effective and can lead to disrespect or a lack of trust.

Cognitive domain: One of the three domains of learning defined by Benjamin Bloom and associates. It describes the hierarchical nature of cognitive processing: knowledge, comprehension, application, analysis, synthesis, and evaluation.

Computerized axial tomography (CAT): A scanning procedure developed during the 1970s to enhance x-ray images.

Concept: A set of specific ideas, objects, symbols, or events that are characterized on the basis of shared characteristics.

Conceptual knowledge: In cognitive science, the storage and integration of information.

Conceptual systems theory: Theory developed by O. J. Harvey, David Hunt, and Harry Schroeder to describe the relationship that individuals have with concepts, information, organization, and their world.

Conceptualization: Generalizing from specifics; developing a framework for thoughts and ideas.

Constructivism: The construction of new ideas or concepts based on a learner's current or past knowledge.

Contracts: An agreed-upon action plan between a student and teacher for improving a student's behavior.

Convergent questions: Questions categorized as low-level thinking that have only one correct response. Convergent questions limit classroom interaction.

Cooperative discipline: A discipline model developed by Linda Albert that focuses on strategies for improving student behavior.

Cooperative learning: When two to five students are grouped together to work on academic tasks.

Coordinate concept: A concept in a hierarchical system that can be grouped with at least one or more concepts of the same level.

Creative learner: A person who develops new or original ideas or products.

Creative thinking: The process for developing new ideas or original products.

Critical thinking: Understanding particular meanings, relationships, theories, or proofs.

Curriculum standards: A set of learning outcomes, often authored by educators within discipline-specific content areas.

Daily review: The practice of going over material taught in a previous lesson.

Decision making: The ability to seek a solution or answer to a problem.

Deductive thinking: Reasoning from the general to the specific according to the rules of logic.

Dendrites: Tree-like branches found in the brain that collect and send information to the neurons.

Diagnosis: A critical analysis of the nature of something.

Direct instruction: The most popular form of instruction, in which the teacher is the purveyor of knowledge; lecture.

Discipline: A state of order based on a rule or the authority of the teacher and punishment that is meant to train.

DISTAR: Trade name given to a set of materials developed during the 1970s by Science Research and Associates; often used for teaching reading and arithmetic.

Divergent questions: Open-ended questions that allow for multiple responses.

Education of All Handicapped Children Act: Legislation passed in 1975 that assured all handicapped children access to free public education designed to meet their special needs, emphasizing education in the least restrictive environment.

Electroencephalogram (EEG): A medical device that produces readings about the electrical output of the brain.

Elementary and Secondary Education Act of 1965: A legislative act signed by President Lyndon B. Johnson to assist with the War on Poverty. This act allocated resources and funding (Title I) for educationally deprived children.

Emotional intelligence theory: A term coined by John Mayer and Peter Salovey in the early 1990s to describe a person's ability to understand his or her emotions and those of others. The theory was popularized by Daniel Goleman (1995) in his book *Emotional Intelligence: Why It Can Matter More Than IQ*.

Emotional memory: The brain's emotional center, called the amygdala, interacts with memory-related brain regions during the formation of emotional memories, perhaps to give such memories their indelible emotional resonance.

Enactment: The name given to a role-play situation with a group of students.

Encourager: In cooperative learning, an assigned role given to a student working in a group on an academic task. The purpose of assigning roles to students in a group is to ensure individual accountability. The role of the encourager is to encourage all members of the group to participate in the academic task.

Energizer: In cooperative learning, an assigned role given to a student working in a group on an academic task. The purpose of assigning roles to students in a group is to ensure individual accountability. The job of the energizer is to energize the work of the group.

ESOL: English for speakers of other languages.

Episodic memory: A type of declarative memory formed from episodes in one's life.

Essay item: A subjective examination item that requires students to construct a free-response answer.

Evaluation: To examine or judge carefully (appraise).

Existential learner: A learner who sees the world and his or her place in it in the context of the "big picture." Existential learners learn through meditation, historical context, philosophy, spirituality, and knowing the value of things.

Expert power: Individuals who are perceived as leaders; a type of power that is derived from being successful.

Explicit memory pathway: Memory that is consciously formed (declarative and explicit). As learners, we can explain, write about, or describe this type of memory.

Explicit teaching: A form of direct instruction with the objective to teach students to master a body of knowledge.

Extinction: A part of behavior modification that purports that if behavior is ignored, it will become extinct.

Face-to-face interaction: One of the five basic elements of cooperative learning in which students work in groups seated across from one another.

Feedback correctives: Clarifying students' work during guided practice; a step in direct instruction.

Flashbulb memory: Memory that is unique to each individual; usually a vivid recollection of an extremely emotional or shocking event.

Flexibility: In thinking, the ability to provide a variety of different ideas in a given situation.

Florida Comprehensive Achievement Test (FCAT): A norm-referenced test given in the state of Florida to assess student knowledge in various subject areas.

Fluency: In thinking, the ability to provide numerous responses in a given situation.

Formal cooperative learning groups: Cooperative learning groups that practice all five basic elements of cooperative learning and stay together for a specified period of time.

Formative evaluation: Ongoing evaluation; used to monitor student or program progress.

Functional magnetic resonance imaging (fMRI): A medical instrument that shows not only structures of the brain but also neural activity.

Game: An activity providing entertainment or amusement.

Generalization: A principle, statement, or idea having general application.

Glial cells: The most common cell in the brain; assists with the migration of neurons during fetal brain development. *Glial* means "glue."

Goal: The purpose for which an activity or endeavor is directed.

Goals 2000: Educate America Act: Legislation passed in 1994 that provided a framework identifying world-class academic standards for schools to meet by 2000.

Grading standards: Criteria for the assignment of students' grades.

Group processing: A term associated with cooperative learning; the action of the group to reflect on how well it managed an academic task and the action of the teacher to stop and change the state of the classroom.

Guided inquiry: A process whereby the teacher leads students to discover the objective of the lesson through a series of well-constructed questions.

Guided practice: A step in the direct teaching lesson format proposed by Madeline Hunter. Following an explanation of the content material, the teacher allows the students to practice the skill learned during class, monitoring the progress of the class and answering any questions about what was learned.

Homeschooling: An educational alternative in which parents assume the responsibility of educating their children.

Humanistic psychology: A form of psychology in which priority is given to the human condition. Emphasis is placed on the individual.

Hypothesis testing: Testing of an educated guess; predicting or judging an outcome.

Implicit memory pathway: A type of memory that is organically formed (automatic) and nondeclarative.

Independent practice: A step in the direct teaching lesson format introduced by Madeline Hunter; practice on material learned independent of the teacher.

Individual accountability: One of the five basic elements of cooperative learning, often achieved by members in a group when individual roles are assigned. While working in a group, each group member needs to contribute to the success of the group by serving in a role or by contributing to the overall work of the group.

Individualized education plan (IEP): An educational plan designed by a teacher or group of educational specialists to provide individual students with goals, objectives, strategies, and assessments to meet their unique learning needs; initially used in special needs classes.

Individualized inquiry: A form of inquiry that is closely aligned with open inquiry but occurs when students want to pursue other questions or data related to a topic that has personal meaning for a student.

Inductive thinking: The examination of specific information to form a generalization according to the rules of logic.

Informal cooperative learning groups: A group formed for a specific academic task during one lesson. The students work together but do not stay together for a extended period of time.

Input: One of the steps in Madeline Hunter's lesson-effectiveness design.

Inquiry: A type of instructional strategy that uses inductive thinking; the teacher forms questions to help students reach the lesson outcome. Awareness of problem-solving and critical-thinking skills and the ability to apply them to a given situation.

Insight: The "eureka" phenomenon or, as others have defined it, the light bulb going on; solutions come suddenly and with certainty.

Instructional objectives: Objectives designed to guide instructional activities.

Intensity: An action, sound, or movement that gets our attention is considered intense. Our level of attention is sometimes influenced by the intensity of the sounds in our environment.

Interpersonal small group skills: One of the five basic elements of cooperative learning and a necessary skill for the development of students' social skills.

Jigsaw II: A cooperative learning activity in which students are divided into groups based on a division of content or chapter material. Each group meets with other groups and becomes an expert on a section of material. The students then return to their home base team and teach each other the material.

Keyword system: A memorization strategy that helps students recall the steps to be learned. For each beginning letter of a process, the students think of a phrase to assist their memory.

Learning modalities: Visual, auditory, and kinesthetic forms of learning.

Learning theories: A set of statements used to explain a certain learning phenomena; characteristics about learning.

Legitimate power: The role, influence, or authority carried by a teacher or a person in charge of others.

Lesson plan: A description of how learning will occur for individuals or for a classroom of students; guide created by a teacher to instruct students' learning.

Loci method: Assignment of a location for things that must be remembered.

Loco parentis: When the power of the parents is transferred to school officials or teachers.

Magnetic resonance imaging (MRI): A medical device that measures the emissions given off by oxygen and glucose, indicating how the brain consumes these substances.

Magnetoencephalography (MEG): A medical device that that uses high-tech sensors and liquid cooled helium to locate faint magnetic fields generated by the brain's neural network.

Mastery learning: A teaching strategy based on the premise that all students can master the content.

Matching item: A form of objective testing item.

Material handler: In cooperative learning, an assigned role given to a student working in a group on an academic task. The purpose of assigning roles to students in a group is to ensure individual accountability. The job of the material handler is to handle the materials for the group (books, pens, art supplies, or lab materials).

Measurement: A term used to describe how a student is assessed.

Memorization: The recall of information stored in one's mind; learning by heart.

Metacognition: Thinking about thinking.

Mnemonics: A system to improve or develop memory.

Modeling: When teachers demonstrate appropriate behaviors or skills that they want their students to learn.

Multiple-choice item: A form of objective testing item.

Multiple intelligences: A theory proposed by Howard Gardner that identifies eight intelligences: linguistic, logical-mathematical, spatial, bodily-kinesthetic, musical, interpersonal, intrapersonal, and naturalistic.

Nation at Risk: A 1983 report published by the National Commission on Excellence in Education that decried the mediocrity of American public education and called for reform.

National Council for Accreditation for Teacher Education (NCATE): The accrediting body for colleges of education.

National Science Foundation: An independent federal agency founded in the 1950s to promote the sciences and advance national health, prosperity, and welfare. This agency provides grants to colleges, universities, and K–12 schools to support research in the sciences, mathematics, and engineering.

Near-infrared spectroscopy (NIRS): A medical device that combines multimodal imaging.

Negative reinforcement: The strengthening of a particular behavior by the consequence of stopping or avoiding a negative condition; a component of behavior modification.

Neurotransmitter: A chemical substance such as acetylcholine or dopamine that transmits nerve impulses across a synapse.

No Child Left Behind Act (NCLB): The 2002 reauthorization of the Elementary and Secondary Education Act. The NCLB is broad-based legislation that established criteria for the distribution of federal dollars based on student achievement on high-stakes testing. The legislation dictates how data are to be reported to the federal government and identifies the type of research the federal government will support.

Noise monitor: In cooperative learning, an assigned role given to a student working in a group on an academic task. The purpose of assigning roles to students in a group is to ensure individual accountability. The noise monitor's role is keep the noise down.

Nondirective learning: A student-centered strategy of instruction. Major personal learning decisions are made by the student, and the teacher serves as a facilitator, providing resources, emotional support, and feedback.

Northwest Ordinance: Legislation enacted in 1787 that allowed westward expansion and provided guidelines for the establishment of states west of the Ohio River.

Novelty: Something new or unusual; an innovation. An unexpected behavior exhibited by a teacher to retain students' attention.

Open inquiry: A type of instructional strategy that has little teacher involvement.

Operant conditioning: A part of behavior modification in which the likelihood of behavior is increased or decreased based on positive or negative reinforcement.

Opinionated learner: A type of learner that composes half of the K–12 population and prefers the teacher to assume the role of lecturer, discussion leader, and assignment creator. The student's emphasis is the collection of knowledge, but he or she does not choose to analyze, synthesize, or evaluate information.

PMI: An acronym for plus, minus, and most interesting; a tool for assisting learners with their ability to judge or critique.

Paraphraser: In cooperative learning, an assigned role given to a student working in a group on an academic task. The purpose of assigning roles to students in a group is to ensure individual accountability. The paraphraser's role is to summarize the work of the group by stating in his or her own words what occurred.

Parent conferencing: A parent or guardian meeting with a teacher in which a student's progress in school is discussed.

Peg-word technique: A technique used in memorization in which a word is assigned or associated with another word to assist with recall.

Performance assessment: A form of assessment that evaluates students' demonstration of skills or products they created.

Performance standards: A predetermined, measurable level of achievement that is demonstrated by the action of a student.

Personalized system of instruction (Keller Plan): A personalized system of instruction used in mastery learning.

Portfolio assessment: An alternative assessment made up of student work samples.

Portfolio: A collection of student work samples.

Positive classroom atmosphere: An academic climate in which students are not threatened by the teacher, other students, or the rules of the classroom.

Positive interdependence: One of the five basic elements of cooperative learning in which a group of students develop mutual trust in one another, share materials, and follow the rules for operating efficiently within a group.

Positive reinforcement: A component of behavior modification in which an external reward is provided for correct behavior.

Positive transfer: The successful application of something learned.

Positron emission tomography (PET): A medical device that measures the emissions given off by oxygen and glucose, indicating how the brain consumes these substances.

Post-active phase of teaching: The phase that follows the teaching and learning; the assessment or evaluation phase of teaching.

Praiser: In cooperative learning, an assigned role given to a student working in a group on an academic task. The purpose of assigning roles to students in a group is to ensure individual accountability. The praiser's role is to provide positive feedback to the group members.

Pre-active phase of teaching: The planning phase of teaching and learning in which both short-term and long-term goals are established.

Privatization: The action or conversion of a school from a public to a private school.

Prober: In cooperative learning, an assigned role given to a student working in a group on an academic task. The purpose of assigning roles to students in a group is to ensure individual accountability. The prober's job is to ask questions of group members to get them to elaborate on what they have said.

Probing questions: Questions that ask for more detail regarding what is being discussed.

Problem solving: The ability to find a solution to a problem

Procedural knowledge: Knowledge that explains how to do something and the steps to follow.

Procedural memory: Often called motor memory, this is our embedded memory that is practiced through skill development and becomes automatic over time.

Process-product research: Research developed in the 1970s and 1980s that examined learner outcomes based on the action of the teacher.

Programmed instruction: Self-paced, structured learning based on the mastery of small chunks of information with immediate feedback and positive reinforcement.

Progressive education movement: Popular between 1890 and 1920, the movement, led by John Dewey, opposed the separation of academic education for the few and narrow vocational education for the masses; it promoted child-centered education, social reconstruction, democratization of all public institutions, independent thinking, and creativity.

Project Follow Through: A large research study conducted to assess the effectiveness of direct instruction.

Psychomotor domain: One of the three domains of learning defined by Benjamin Bloom. The psychomotor domain is about reflex movement, fundamental movement, and physical abilities of the learning.

Reader: In cooperative learning, an assigned role given to a student working in a group on an academic task. The purpose of assigning roles to students in a group is to ensure individual accountability. The reader's role is to read the activity or task assigned to the group.

Reasoning: Systematic inferring of information according to the rules of logic.

Recorder: In cooperative learning, an assigned role given to a student working in a group on an academic task. The purpose of assigning roles to students in a group is to ensure individual accountability. The recorder's job is to record in writing the work of the group.

Referent power: A power bestowed on a teacher because students refer to him or her. The teachers is liked, fair, trustworthy, and students know the teacher cares about them.

Reflection: A person thinking about an event and pondering its significance.

Reflexive memory: A person's automatic or conditioned-response memory. Certain stimuli automatically trigger this memory, such as remembering where you were when a certain song played.

Relater/elaboration seeker: In cooperative learning, an assigned role given to a student working in a group on an academic task. The purpose of assigning roles to students in a group is to ensure individual accountability. The relater/elaboration seeker's job is to explain the relevance of today's lesson to the larger unit of study or to what was previously taught about the topic.

Reward power: A teacher's use of rewards, privileges, approval, or compensation with students.

Role play: An instructional model that allows students to imagine that they are themselves or another person in a particular situation.

Roundtable: A cooperative learning discussion or conversation.

Satiation: To satisfy to excess; a component of behavior modification.

School action plan: A document that addresses and outlines a plan for improvement at a school.

Science Research Associates (SRA): A company that designed highly popular mastery learning materials.

Self-actualization: Obtaining the peak of human performance; to be fully whole and satisfied as an adult.

Self-concept: A person's mental image of the self.

Self-concept theory: Abraham Maslow's theory, which is based on a hierarchy of needs that includes five sets of goals: physiological needs, safety, love, esteem, and self-actualization.

Self-taught instruction: An approach in which motivated learners instruct themselves

Semantics: The interpretation of a word, sentence, or phrase.

Sensory memory: A type of memory that is triggered by sights sounds, smells, and the environment around us; a type of memory processed through our senses.

Simulation: A replication of a real-life event or action.

Single-photon emission computerized tomography (SPECT): A medical device that combines multi-modal imaging.

Social skills: The skills related to being able to get along with others.

Socratic method: A line of questioning developed by Socrates that leads students to follow logical thinking.

States of growth: The relationship that individuals have with concepts, generalizations, and the organization of information to be learned.

Stimulus-response (S-R): A component of classical conditioning; a voluntary or involuntary reaction to a stimulus.

Student awareness theory: Teacher and student recognition of the states of growth accomplished by learners in their environment.

Student rights: The constitutional rights of students.

Student teams achievement division (STAD): A type of cooperative learning group developed by Robert Slavin.

Subordinate concept: Content that is divided into certain facts or concepts to be learned; a subcomponent or part of a larger concept is subordinate; a fact or characteristic of a larger concept.

Summative assessment: Assessment strategy that measures cumulative learning.

Superordinate concept: The overall category from which concepts are formed. For example, a butte is a type of landform; therefore, the word *landform* is superordinate to the concept of *butte*.

Synapse: The small gap that separates neurons.

Teacher as individual facilitator: When a teacher's role as a nondirective educator is to engage in positive interaction with a single student.

Teacher attributes: The personal or social characteristics of a teacher.

Teacher as classroom facilitator: When a teacher's role as a nondirective educator is to engage in positive interaction with a classroom of students.

Teacher power: There are five types of teacher power: expert, referent, legitimate, reward, and coercive.

Teaching-effectiveness training: A six-step model of classroom management that uses "I" messages from the teacher (e.g., "I am angry" or "I am pleased with your performance.").

Think-pair-share: A type of cooperative learning strategy developed by Spencer Kagan in which two persons are grouped informally to think about the content or question under investigation, then pair with another group and report or share their findings.

Three-step interview: A cooperative learning strategy developed by Spencer Kagan that involves three steps: (1) one-way interviews in pairs; (2) reversal of roles in each pair; and (3) joining pairs to report to the group what the partners shared during the interview.

Timekeeper: In cooperative learning, an assigned role given to a student working in a group on an academic task. The purpose of assigning roles to students in a group is to ensure individual accountability. The timekeeper's job is track the amount of time students spend working in the groups. If the teacher has directed the students to work for 10 minutes, the timekeeper's job is to honor the time given and help the group finish in the allotted time frame.

Title IX: Federal legislation passed in 1972 prohibiting the exclusion of any person from participation in school programs or activities receiving federal funds on the basis of gender.

Token-economy system: A system that rewards tokens, points, chips, or other external rewards to students who behave or achieve certain goals in the classroom. This is a component of behavior modification.

Two-choice response items: An objective form of assessment, such as true-false or yes-no.

Unit plan: An overall plan or conceptual framework for the teaching of a topic or concept that can be broken down into daily lesson plans.

Vouchers: A system that redirects the flow of education funding by allowing the dollars allocated per pupil to follow the student's enrollment in a school, whether it is public, private, or religious.

Wait time: A term coined by Mary Rowe to describe the amount of time a teacher waits for a student to respond following a question

Weekly, monthly reviews: A systematic plan for reviewing material that has been covered by the teacher.

Withitness: A term coined by Jacob Kounin to describe the perception that students have of teachers.

References

Adams, M. J. (1991). Balancing process and content. In A. Costa (Ed.), *Developing minds: Programs for teaching thinking* (rev. ed., pp. 1–2). Alexandria, VA: Association for Supervision and Curriculum Development.

Adams, G. L., & Engelmann, S. (1996). *Research on direct instruction: 25 years beyond DISTAR.* Englewood Cliffs, NJ: Ed Tech.

Albert, L. (1990). *Cooperative discipline: Classroom management that promotes self-esteem—A leader's guide.* Circle Pines, MN: American Guidance Service.

Alberto, P., & Troutman, A. (1986). *Applied behavior analysis for teachers: Influencing student performance* (2nd ed.). Upper Saddle, NJ: Merrill/Prentice Hall.

American Association of University Women (AAUW). (1992). *How schools shortchange girls: The AAUW report.* Annapolis Junction, MD: AAUW Educational Foundation.

Ames, N. L., & Miller, E. (2001). Personalizing middle schools. In *The Jossey-Bass reader on school reform.* San Francisco: Jossey-Bass.

Anderson, J. R. (1980). *Cognitive psychology and its implications.* San Francisco: W. H. Freeman.

Anderson, L. W. (1976). An empirical investigation of individual differences in time to learn. *Journal of Educational Psychology, 68*(2), 226–233.

Anderson, S., Barrett, C., Huston, M., Lay, L., Myr, G., Sexton, D., & Watson, B. (1992). *A mastery learning experiment* (Tech. Rep.). Yale, MI: Yale Public Schools.

Anderson, L. W., & Krathwohl, D. R. (Eds.). (2001). *A taxonomy for learning, teaching, and assessing: A revision of Bloom's taxonomy of educational objectives.* New York: Addison-Wesley/Longman.

Applebee, A., Langer, J., Mullis, I., & Jenkins, L. (1990). *The writing report card, 1984–1988.* Princeton, NJ: National Assessment of Educational Progress.

Armstrong, T. (1998). *David Hunt: Coordinating teaching methods with levels of student awareness.* Retrieved February 19, 2003, from http://ivcourses.ed.uidaho.edu.

Arnand, P., & Ross, S. (1987). Using computer-assisted instruction to personalize arithmetic materials for elementary school children. *Journal of Educational Psychology, 79,* 72–78.

Aronson, E., Blaney, N., Stephan, C., Sikes, J., & Snapp, M. (1978). *The jigsaw classroom.* Beverly Hills, CA: Sage.

Ausubel, D. (1968). *Educational psychology: A cognitive view.* New York: Holt, Rinehart & Winston.

Barbe, W., & Swassing, S. (1979). *Swassing-Barbe Modality Index.* Columbus, OH: Zaner-Bloser.

Barclay, C. S. (1987). Coping with inquiry. *Hands On, Winter.* Retrieved August 23, 2005, from www.terc.edu/handson/spring_95/copinquiry.html.

Bear, G. G., Minke, K. M., & Manning, M. A. (2002). Self-concept of students with learning disabilities: A meta-analysis. *School Psychology Review, 31*(3), 405–428.

Becker, W., & Engelmann, S. (1978). *Analysis of achievement data on six cohorts of low income children from 20 school districts in the University of Oregon Direct Instruction Follow Through model* (Tech. Rep. No. 78-1). Eugene, OR: University of Oregon, Office of Education, Project Follow Through.

Bellanca, J., & Fogarty, R. (1990). *Blueprints for thinking in the cooperative classroom.* Palatine, IL: Skylight.

Bernard, S., & Mondale, S. (Eds.). (2001). *School: The story of American public education.* Boston: Beacon Press.

Bereiter, C. (1967). *Acceleration of intellectual development in early childhood* (Final Rep. Project No. 2129, Contract No. OE 4-10-008). Urbana, IL: University of Illinois, College of Education.

Beyer, B. (1987). *Practical strategies for the teaching of thinking.* Newton, MA: Allyn & Bacon.

Bianchini, J., & Colburn, A. (2000). Teaching the nature of science through inquiry to prospective elementary teachers: A tale of two researchers. *Journal of Research in Science Teaching, 37*(2), 177–209.

Bigge, M., & Shermis, S. (1992). *Learning theories for teachers* (5th ed.). New York: HarperCollins.

Block, J. H. (1971). *Mastery learning: Theory and practice.* New York: Holt, Rinehart & Winston.

Block, J. H. (1973). Teachers, teaching, and mastery learning. *Today's Education, 63*(7), 30–37.

Block, J. H. (1988). Responses to Slavin: Mastery learning works. *Educational Leadership, 46*(2), 25.

Block, J. H., & Burns, R. B. (1976). Mastery learning. In L. S. Shulman (Ed.), *Review of research in education* (vol. 4, pp. 3–49). Itasca, IL: F. E. Peacock.

Bloom, B. S. (1968). Learning for mastery. *Evaluation Comment, 1*(2), 1–5.

Bloom, B. S. (1976). *Human characteristics and school learning.* New York: McGraw-Hill.

Bloom, B. S., Englehart, M. D., Furst, E. J., Hill, W. H., & Krathwohl, D. R. (Eds.). (1956). *Taxonomy of educational objectives; Handbook I: Cognitive domain.* New York: David McKay.

Bloom, B. S., Hastings, J. T., & Madaus, G. F. (1971). *Handbook on formative and summative evaluation of student learning.* New York: McGraw-Hill.

Bocchino, R. (1999). *Emotional literacy: To be a different kind of smart.* Thousand Oaks, CA: Corwin.

Boeree, C. G. (1998). *Carl Rogers 1902–1987.* Retrieved October 27, 2002, from www.ship.edu/~cgboeree/rogers.html.

Borich, G. D. (2004). *Effective teaching methods.* Upper Saddle River, NJ: Pearson Education.

Bradshaw, A., Bishop, J., Gens, L., Miller, S., & Rogers, M. (2002, September). The relationship of the World Wide Web to thinking skills. *Educational Media International, 39,* 3–4, 275–284.

Bruner, J. (1960). *The process of education.* Cambridge, MA: Harvard University Press.

Bruner, J. (1986). *Actual minds, possible worlds.* Cambridge, MA: Harvard University Press.

Bruner, J., Goodnow, J., & Austin, G. (1956). *A study of thinking.* New York: Wiley.

Burden, P., & Byrd, D. (2003). *Methods for effective teaching* (3rd ed.). Boston: Pearson Education.

Cangelosi, J. (2004). *Classroom management strategies: Gaining and maintaining students' cooperation.* Danvers, MA: Wiley.

Canter, L. (1989). Assertive discipline—More than names on the board and marbles in a jar. *Phi Delta Kappan, 71*(1), 57–61.

Canter, L., & Canter, M. (1976). *Assertive discipline: A take-charge approach for today's educator.* Seal Beach, CA: Lee Canter & Assoc.

Carlson, R. (1989). Malcolm Knowles: Apostle of andragogy. *Vitae Scholasticae, 8*(1), 217–233.

Carroll, J. B. (1963). A model of school learning. *Teachers College Record, 64*(8), 723–733.

Caruso, D. R., Mayer, J. D., & Salovey, P. (2002). Relation of an ability measure of emotional intelligence to personality. *Journal of Personality Assessment, 79*(2), 306–320.

Christopher, E. M., & Smith, L. E. (1990). Shaping the content of simulation/games. In D. Crookall & R. L. Oxford (Eds.), *Simulation, gaming, and language learning* (pp. 47–54). New York: Newbury House.

Clark, D. (2000). *Carl Rogers.* Retrieved November 3, 2002, from www.nwlink.com/~donclark/hrd/history/history.html.

Clegg, A. A., Jr. (1987). Why questions? In W. W. Wilen (Ed.), *Questions, questioning techniques, and effective teaching* (pp. 11–22). Washington, DC: National Education Association.

Cody, A. (2003). *How can assessment serve our students?* Retrieved June 24, 2004, from http://tlc.ousd.k12.ca.us/~acody/assessment.html.

Colburn, A. (1998). *How to make a lab activity more open ended.* Retrieved June 24, 2004, from www.exploratorium.edu/IFI/resources/workshops/lab_activities.html.

Cole, N. (1990). Conceptions of educational achievement. *Educational Researcher, 19*(3), 2–7.

Costa, A. (Ed.). (1991). *Developing minds: A resource book for teachers* (rev. ed.). Alexandria, VA: Association for Supervision and Curriculum Development.

Coulson, W. R. (1989, April). Founder of "values-free" education "owes parents an apology." *American Family Association Journal,* 17–18.

Coulson, W. R. (1997). *The role of psychology in current educational reform.* New Paltz, NY: Empire State Task Force for Excellence in Educational Methods.

Coyner, M., & Wilson, D. (2002). *Research-based graduate education and professional development: Top 10 ways to turn on your superbrain.* Retrieved July 12, 2003, from www.brainsmart.com/superbr.asp.

Cunningham, L. A. (2002). *Happiness in half the time.* New York: Writers Club Press.

Curwin, R. L., & Mendler, A. N. (1999). *As tough as necessary: Countering violence, aggression, and hostility in our schools.* Alexandria, VA: Association for Supervision and Curriculum Development.

Daniels, D. (2002). *Carl Rogers summary.* Retrieved November 10, 2002, from www.sonoma.edu/users/d/daniels/Rogers.html.

Danielson, C. (2002). *Enhancing student achievement.* Alexandria, VA: Association for Supervision and Curriculum Development.

Davis, B., Sumara, D., & Luce- Kapler, R. (2000). *Engaging minds: Learning and teaching in a complex world.* Mahwah, NJ: Lawrence Erlbaum.

de Bono, E. (1985). *Six thinking hats.* New York: Little, Brown.

Deutsch, M. (1962). Cooperation and trust: Some theoretical notes. In M. R. Jones (Ed.), *Nebraska Symposium on Motivation* (pp. 275–319). Lincoln: University of Nebraska Press.

Dewey, J. (1910). *How we think.* Amherst, NY: Prometheus Books.

Dewey, J. (1916). *Democracy and education.* New York: Free Press.

Dodge, B. (1997). *Some thoughts about WebQuests.* Retrieved June 30, 2004, from http://webquest.sdsu.edu/about_webquests.html.

Dossey, J., Mullis, I., Lingquist, M., & Chambers, D. (1988). *The mathematics report card—Are we measuring up?* Princeton, NJ: National Assessment of Educational Progress.

Dover, K. H. (1999, December). Carl Rogers and experiential learning. *Lifelong Learning, 4,* 1–5.

Duckworth, E. (1987). *The having of wonderful ideas.* New York: Teachers College Press.

Duckworth, E. (2001). Inventing density. In E. Duckworth (Ed.), *Tell me more: Listening to learners explain.* (pp. 1–41). New York: Teachers College Press.

Duffrin, E. (1996). *Direct instruction making waves.* Retrieved September 22, 2005, from www.catalyst-chicago.org./09-96/096main.htm.

Eaker, R., DuFour, R., & Burnette, R. (2002). *Getting started: Reculturing schools to become professional learning communities.* Bloomington, IN: National Educational Service.

Education Commission of the States. (1982). *Report.* Denver, CO: Author.

Eggen, P. D., & Kauchak, D. P. (1996). *Strategies for teachers: Teaching content and thinking skills* (3rd ed.). Needham Heights, MA: Allyn & Bacon.

Elias, M. J. (2001). How socio-emotional learning is infused into academics in a social decision-making/social problem-solving program. *CEIC Review, 10*(2), 16–17.

Engelmann, S., & Bruner, E. (1974). *DISTAR reading* (2nd ed.). Chicago: Science Research Associates.

Ennis, R. (1991). Goals for a critical thinking curriculum. In A. Costa (Ed.), *Developing minds: A resource book for teachers* (rev. ed., pp. 68–71). Alexandria, VA: Association for Supervision and Curriculum Development.

Ennis, R. (2000a, October). *Teaching critical thinking: A few suggestions.* Retrieved July 21, 2004, from www.criticalthinking.net/teaching.html.

Ennis, R. (2000b, October 18). *An outline of goals for critical thinking curriculum and its assessments.* Retrieved July 21, 2004, from www.criticalthinking.net/goals.html.

Esler, B., & Sciortino, P. (1991). *Methods for teaching: An overview of current practices* (2nd ed.). Raleigh, NC: Contemporary Publishing.

Evans, R. I. (1975). *Carl Rogers: The man and his ideas.* New York: Dutton.

Facundo, B. (1984). *Freire-inspired programs in the United States and Puerto Rico: A critical evaluation.* Washington, DC: Latino Institute.

Fenton, E. (1968). Inquiry and structure. In R. Allen, J. Fleckenstein, & P. Lyons (Eds.), *Inquiry in social studies.* Washington, DC: National Council on Social Studies.

Feuerstein, R. (1980). *Instrumental enrichment.* Baltimore: University Park Press.

Fitzpatrick, S. (Speaker). (1996). *The brain, the mind, and the classroom* [cassette recording]. Alexandria, VA: Association for Supervision and Curriculum Development.

Florida Department of Education, Office of School Improvement. (2002). *Wave series No. 3.* Tallahassee, FL: Bureau of Education for Exceptional Students.

Fogarty, R., & Bellanca, J. (1990). *Blueprints for thinking in the cooperative classroom.* Palatino, IL: Skylight.

Freire, P. (1970). *The pedagogy of the oppressed.* New York: Continuum.

French, J. R. P., & Raven, B. (1959). The bases of social power. In D. Cartwright (Ed.), *Studies in social power* (pp. 150–167). Ann Arbor, MI: Institute of Social Research.

Frey, W. (2004, May). *The new great migration: Black Americans' return to the South.* Washington, DC: Brookings Institution, Center on Urban and Metropolitan Policy. Retrieved May 20, 2004, from www.brookings.org/metro/publications/20040524_frey.html.

Gall, M. D. (1987). Review of research on questioning techniques. In W. W. Wilen (Ed.), *Questions, questioning techniques, and effective teaching* (pp. 23–48). Washington, DC: National Education Association.

Gallagher, J., & Aschner, M. (1963). A preliminary report on analyses of classroom interaction. *Merrill-Palmer Quarterly, 3,* 183–194.

Gallagher, J. D. (1998). *Classroom assessment for teachers.* Columbus, OH: Merrill.

Gardner, H. (1982). *Art, mind, and brain: A cognitive approach to creativity.* New York: BasicBooks.

Gardner, H. (1993). *Frames of mind: The theory of multiple intelligences.* Philadelphia, PA: BasicBooks.

Gardner, H. (2003, April). *Multiple intelligences after twenty years.* Paper presented at the Annual Meeting of the American Educational Research Association, Chicago, IL.

Gardner-Gordon, J. (1993). *The healing voice.* Freedom, CA: Crossing Press.

Geier, M. (1998). Role-playing in educational environments. *Internet TESL Journal, 4*(8). Retrieved April 27, 2004, from http://iteslj.org.

Gendlin, E. T. (1988). Carl Rogers (1902–1987). *American Psychologist, 43*(2), 127–128.

Georgia Department of Education. (2003). *Critical thinking skills program, concept attainment.* Retrieved December 29, 2003, from www.glc.k12.ga.us/password/trc/ttools/attach/critthink/conceptattain/.

Gersten, R. (1985). Direct instruction with special education students: A review of evaluation research. *Journal of Special Education, 19,* 41–58.

Gersten, R., Woodward, J., & Darch, C. (1986). Direct instruction: A research-based approach to curriculum design and teaching. *Exceptional Children, 53,* 17–31.

Gilbert, S. (2003, March 18). Scientists explore the molding of children's morals. *New York Times,* p. F5.

Given, B. (2002). *Teaching to the brain's natural learning systems.* Alexandria, VA: Association for Supervision and Curriculum Development.

Glasser, W. (1986). *Choice theory in the classroom* (rev. ed.). New York: HarperCollins.

Glasser, W. (1990). *The quality school: Managing students without coercion.* New York: HarperCollins.

Glatthorn, A., & Baron, J. (1991). The good thinker. In A. Costa (Ed.), *Developing minds: A resource book for teachers* (Rev. ed., pp. 63–67). Alexandria, VA: Association for Supervision and Curriculum Development.

Gluck, M. A., & Myers, C. (2001). *Gateway to memory: An introduction to neural network modeling of the hippocampus and learning.* Cambridge: MIT Press.

Golden, B. J., & Lesh, K. (2002). *Building self-esteem: Strategies for success in school and beyond.* Upper Saddle River, NJ: Prentice Hall.

Goleman, D. (1995). *Emotional intelligence.* New York: Bantam Books.

Good, T., & Grouws, D. (1979). The Missouri Mathematics Effectiveness Project: An experimental study in fourth-grade classrooms. *Journal of Educational Psychology, 71*(3), 355–362.

Goodlad, J. (1984). *A place called school.* New York: McGraw-Hill.

Gordon, T. (1974). *T.E.T.: Teacher effectiveness training.* New York: P. H. Wyden.

Graves, J. (1999). *Emotional intelligence and cognitive ability: Predicting performance in job simulated activities.* Unpublished doctoral dissertation, California School of Professional Psychology, San Diego, CA.

Gredler, M. (2001). *Learning and instruction: Theory into practice.* Upper Saddle River, NJ: Prentice–Hall.

Greene, M. (1978). *Landscapes of learning.* New York: Teachers College Press.

Greene, M. (1995). *Releasing the imagination.* San Francisco: Jossey-Bass.

Gregory, R., & Clemen, R. (2004). *Beyond critical thinking: A framework for developing the decision making skills of secondary students.* Eugene, OR: Decision Research.

Guskey, T. R. (1988). Responses to Slavin: Who defines best? *Educational Leadership, 46*(2), 26–28.

Guskey, T. R., & Pigott, T. D. (1988). Research on group-based mastery learning programs: A meta-analysis. *Journal of Educational Research, 81*(4), 197–216.

Hanley, S. J., & Abell, S. C. (2002). Maslow and relatedness: Creating an interpersonal model of self-actualization. *Journal of Humanistic Psychology, 42*(4), 37–58.

Hannaford, C. (1995). *Smart moves.* Arlington, VA: Great Ocean Publishing.

Harlen, W. (1999). Assessment in the inquiry classroom. *Inquiry: Thoughts, Views, and Strategies for the K–5 Classroom, 2,* 87–97.

Harris, R. (1998, July 1). *Introduction to creative thinking.* Retrieved July 17, 2004, from www.virtual salt.com/crebook.htm.

Harrow, A. (1972). *A taxonomy of the psychomotor domain: A guide for developing behavioral objectives.* New York: David McKay.

Hart, L. (1975). *Human brain and human learning.* New York: Longman.

Healy, J. (1994). *Your child's growing mind.* New York: Doubleday.

Hein, S. (2002). *History and definition of emotional intelligence.* Retrieved September 22, 2002, from www.work911.com/cgi-bin/links/jump.cgi?ID=3654.

Hogan, K., & Corey, C. (2001). Viewing classrooms as cultural contexts for fostering scientific literacy. *Anthropology and Education Quarterly, 32*(2), 214–243.

Homa, D., Sterling, S., & Trepel, L. (1981). Limitations of exemplar-based generalizations and the abstraction of categorical information. *Journal of Experimental Psychology: Human Learning and Memory, 7,* 418–439.

Hoversten, C., Doda, N., & Lounsbury, J. (1997). *Treasure chest: A teacher advisory source book.* Columbus, OH: National Middle School Association.

Howard, P. J. (1994). *The owner's manual for the brain.* Austin, TX: Leornian Press.

Huitt, W. (2001). *Humanism and open education.* Retrieved November 10, 2002, from http://chiron.valdosta.edu/whuitt/col/affsys/humed.html.

Hunkins, F. P. (1976). *Involving students in questioning.* Boston: Allyn & Bacon.

Hunkins, F. P. (1989). *Teaching thinking through effective questioning.* Norwood, MA: Christopher-Gordon.

Hunter, M. (1984). *Reinforcement theory for teachers.* El Segundo, CA: TIP Publications.

Hunter, M. (1994). *Enhancing teaching.* New York: Macmillan College.

Hymel, G. M., & Dyck, W. E. (1993, April 12–16). *The internationalization of Bloom's learning for mastery: A 25-year retrospective-prospective view.* Paper presented at the Annual Meeting of the American Educational Research Association, Atlanta, GA.

Ivie, S. (1998). Ausubel's learning theory: An approach to teaching and higher-order thinking skills. *High School Journal, 82,* 35–42.

Jamieson, A., Curry, A., & Martinez, G. (2001, March). *Current population reports, October 1999.* Washington, DC: U.S. Department of Commerce, Economics and Statistics Administration, U.S. Census Bureau. Retrieved March 24, 2004, from www.census.gov.

Jenkins, J. R., Antil, L. R., Wayne, S. K., & Vadasy, P. F. (2003). How cooperative learning works for special education and remedial students. *Exceptional Children, 69*(3), 279–292.

Jensen, E. (1995). *Super teaching.* Del Mar, CA: Turning Points for Teachers.

Jensen, E. (1997). *Brain-compatible strategies.* San Diego, CA: The Brain Store.

Jensen, E. (1998). *Teaching with the brain in mind.* Alexandria, VA: Association for Supervision and Curriculum Development.

Johnson, D. W., & Johnson, F. P. (1987). *Joining together: Group theory and group skills* (3rd ed). Englewood Cliffs, NJ: Prentice Hall.

Johnson, D. W., & Johnson, R. T. (1994). *Leading the cooperative school* (2nd ed.) Edina, MN: Interaction Books.

Johnson, D. W., & Johnson, R. T. (1989). *Cooperation and competition: Theory and research.* Edina, MN: Interaction.

Johnson, D. W., & Johnson, R. T. (1991). *Learning together and alone: Cooperative, competitive, and individualistic learning* (3rd ed.). Boston: Allyn & Bacon.

Johnson, D. W., Johnson, R. T., & Holubec, E. (1988). *Cooperation in the classroom.* Edina, MN: Interaction.

Jones, F. C. (1987). *Positive classroom discipline.* New York: McGraw-Hill.

Jones, K. (1982). *Simulations in language teaching.* Cambridge, UK: Cambridge University Press.

Jones, S. (2003). *Blueprint for student success: A guide to research-based teaching practices K–12.* Alexandria, VA: Association for Supervision and Curriculum Development.

Joyce, B. R. (1984). Dynamic disequilibrium: The intelligence of growth. *Theory into Practice, 23*(1), 26–35.

Joyce, B. R., Weil, M., & Calhoun, E. (2000). *Models of teaching* (6th ed.). Needham Heights, MA: Allyn & Bacon.

Joyce, B. R., Weil, M., & Calhoun, E. (2004). *Models of teaching* (7th ed.). Boston: Allyn & Bacon.

Kagan, S. (1989/90). The structural approach to cooperative learning. *Educational Leadership, 11*(3), 24–27.

Kagan, S. (1994). *Cooperative learning.* San Clemente, CA: Resources for Teachers.

Kahn, L. (2002, July 24–28). *A way of teaching: Reflections on student-centered learning in the college classroom.* Paper presented at the Carl Rogers Symposium, La Jolla, CA. Retrieved October 23, 2002, from www.saybrook.edu/crr/papers/kahn.html.

Kaplan, M. A. (1997). Learning to converse in a foreign language: The reception game. *Simulation and Gaming, 28,* 149–163.

Kearsley, G. (1998). *Experiential learning (C. Rogers).* Retrieved November 1, 2002, from http://TIP.psychology.org/rogers.html.

Kearsley, G. (1999). *Andragogy (M. Knowles).* Retrieved November 1, 2002, from http://TIP.psychology.org/knowles.html.

Keating, D. P., & Miller, F. K. (2000). Commentary: The dynamics of emotional development; Models, metaphors, and methods. In M. D. Lewis & I. Granic (Eds.), *Emotion, Development, and Self-Organization* (pp. 373–393). New York: Cambridge University Press.

King, K. A., Vidourek, R. A., Davis, B., & McClellan, W. (2002). Increasing self-esteem and school connectedness through a multidimensional mentoring program. *Journal of School Health, 72*(7), 294–300.

Kirschenbaum, H. (1979). *On becoming Carl Rogers.* New York: Delacorte Press.

Klatzky, R. (1975). *Human memory: Structures and processes.* San Francisco: W. H. Freeman.

Kohn, A. (2003). Almost there, but not quite. *Educational Leadership, 60*(6), 26–29.

Kotulak, R. (1996). *Inside the brain.* Kansas City, MO: Andrews McMeel.

Kounin, J. S. (1970). *Discipline and group management in classrooms.* New York: Holt, Rinehart & Winston.

Kozloff, M. A., LaNunziata, L., & Cowardin, J. (2000). Direct instruction: Its contributions to high school achievement. *High School Journal, 84,* 54–71.

Krajcik, J., Czerniak, C., & Berger, C. (2003). *Teaching science in elementary and middle school classrooms* (2nd ed.). New York: McGraw-Hill.

Krathwohl, D. R., Bloom, B. S., & Masia, B. B. (1964). *Taxonomy of educational objectives, the classification of educational goals; Handbook II: The affective domain.* New York: David McKay.

Kridel, C. A. (1999). Some books of the century. *Education Week, 19*(16), 40–41, 60.

Kulik, C. L., Kulik, J. A., & Bangert-Drowns, J. (1990). Effectiveness of mastery learning programs: A meta-analysis. *Review of Educational Research, 60,* 265–299.

Kysilka, M. L., & Biraimah, K. (1992). *The thinking teacher: Ideas for effective learning.* New York: McGraw-Hill.

Kysilka, M. L. & Davis, O. L., Jr. (1988). Teaching as thinking in action. In A. Wood, M. L. Kysilka, K. Biraimah, & J. Miller (Eds.), *Reading, writing, and thinking in education* (pp. 106–116). Needham Heights, MA: Ginn Press.

Ladousse, G. P. (1987). *Role play.* Oxford, UK: Oxford University Press.

Lai, P., & Biggs, J. (1994). Who benefits from mastery learning? *Contemporary Educational Psychology, 19*(1), 13–23.

Landphair, T. (2004, May 4). *Census projections: U.S. population will swell to 420 million by 2050.* Retrieved May 10, 2004, from www.voanews.com/English/americanlife.

LeDoux, J. (1996). *The emotional brain: the mysterious underpinnings of emotional life.* New York: Touchtone.

Lemke, J. (1990). *Talking science: Language, learning, and values.* Norwood, NJ: Ablex.

Levin, J., & Nolan, J. (2004). *Principles of classroom management: A professional decision making model.* Boston: Pearson Education.

Levine, S. J. (2002). To begin or to end: That might be the question. *Extension Education Extra, Michigan State University.* Retrieved October 29, 2002, from http://www.anrecs.msu.edu/extension/e31ist.htm.

Lewis, M. D. (2000). Emotional self-organization at three time scales. In M. D. Lews & I. Granic (Eds.), *Emotion, Development, and Self-Organization* (pp. 37–69). New York: Cambridge University Press.

Lieberman, E. J. (2002). *Otto Rank, psychologist and philosopher.* Retrieved November 19, 2002, from www.ottorank.com.

Lindsay, Jeffrey. (n.d.). *What the data really show: Direct instruction really works!* Retrieved September 1, 2005, from www.jefflindsay.com/EducData.shtml.

Link, F. (1991). Instrumental enrichment. In A. Costa (Ed.), *Developing minds: Programs for teaching thinking* (rev. ed., pp. 9–11). Alexandria, VA: Association for Supervision and Curriculum Development.

Lipman, M. (1991). Philosophy for children. In A. Costa (Ed.), *Developing minds: Programs for teaching thinking* (vol. 2, rev. ed., pp. 35–38). Alexandria, VA: Association for Supervision and Curriculum Development.

Lopes, P., & Salovey, L. (2001). Emotional intelligence and socio-emotional learning. *CEIC Review, 10*(6), 12–13.

Lorayne, H., & Lucas, J. (1974). *The memory book.* Briercliff Manor, NY: Lucas Educational Systems.

Lorsbach, A., & Tobin, K. (1992). *Research matters . . . to the science teacher* (Monograph No. 5). Washington, DC: National Association for Research in Science Teaching.

Lowry, R. J. (Ed.). (1973). *Dominance, self-esteem, self-actualization: Germinal papers of A. H. Maslow.* Belmont, CA: Wadsworth.

Lyons, R. E., Kysilka, M. L., & Pawlas, G. E. (1999). *The adjunct professor's guide to success: Surviving and thriving in the college classroom.* Boston: Allyn & Bacon.

Lyons, R. E., McIntosh, M., & Kysilka, M. L. (2003). *Teaching college in an age of accountability.* Boston: Allyn & Bacon.

Mafune, P. (2002). *Teaching and learning models.* Retrieved October 29, 2002, from the University of Pretoria: http://hagar.up.ac.za/catts/learner/cooplrn/B3a.html#anchor282182.

Mager, R. F. (1962). *Preparing instructional objectives.* Belmont, CA: Fearon.

Markowitz, K., & Jensen, E. (1999). *The great memory book.* San Diego, CA: Brain Store.

Martorella, P. (1999). Concept learning and higher-level thinking. In J. M. Cooper (Ed.), *Classroom teaching skills* (6th ed., p. 160). New York: Houghton Mifflin.

Marzano, R. J. (2003). *What works in schools: Translating research into action.* Alexandria, VA: Association for Supervision and Curriculum Development.

Maslow, A. H. (1962). *Toward a psychology of being.* Princeton, NJ: Van Nostrand.

Mastropieri, M. A., & Scruggs, T. E. (1994). *A practical guide for teaching science to students with special needs in inclusive settings.* Austin, TX: Pro-Ed.

Mather, N., & Goldstein, S. (2001). *Learning disabilities and challenging behaviors: A guide to intervention and classroom management.* Retrieved May 4, 2004, from www.ldonline.org/ld_indepth/behavior/behavior_modification.html.

Mayer, J., Salovey, P., & Sluyter, D. (1997). *Emotional development and emotional intelligence: Educational implications.* New York: BasicBooks.

McCombs, B. L. (2001). Learner-centered psychological principles: A framework for balancing academic and socio-emotional learning. *CEIC Review, 10*(6), 8–11.

McMillan, J. (1997). *Classroom assessment: Principles and practices for effective instruction.* Boston: Allyn & Bacon.

Melchior, T. M. (1994). *Counterpoint thinking: Connecting learning and thinking in schools.* Paper presented at the Sixth International Conference on Thinking, Cambridge, MA. Retrieved March 29, 2003, from www.chss.montclair.edu/inquiry/spr95/melchior.html.

Merrill, M. D., Tennyson, R. D., & Posey, L. O. (1992). *Teaching concepts: An instructional design guide.* Englewood Cliffs, NJ: Educational Technology Publications.

Molnar, A. (1996). *Giving kids the business.* Bolder, CO: Westview Press.

Monticello, Research Department. (1989). *Education: Jefferson quotations.* Retrieved September 14, 2005, from www.monticello.org/reports/quotes/education.html.

Morrision, H. C. (1926). *The practice of teaching in the secondary school.* Chicago: University of Chicago Press.

Mosley, A. A. (1997). *The effectiveness of "direct instruction" on reading achievement.* (Tech. Rep. No. 143). Chicago, IL: Chicago Public Schools. (ERIC Document Reproduction Service No. ED396268)

Motamedi, V., & Sumrall, W. J. (2000). Mastery learning and contemporary issues in education. *Action in Teacher Education, 22*(1), 32–42.

Mullis, I., & Jenkins, L. (1988). *The science report card: Elements of risks and recovery.* Princeton, NJ: National Assessment of Educational Progress.

Murdock, T. B., Anderman, L. H., & Hodge, S. A. (2000). Middle-grade predictors of students' motivation and behavior in high school. *Journal of Adolescent Research, 15*(3), 327–352.

National Commission on Excellence in Education. (1983). *A nation at risk: The imperative for education reform.* Washington, DC: Government Printing Office.

National Research Council (NRC). (1996). *National science education standards.* Washington, DC: National Academy Press.

National Research Council (NRC). (2000). *Inquiry and the national science education standards: A guide for teaching and learning.* Washington, DC: National Academy Press.

Neill, A. S. (1960). *Summerhill: A radical approach to child rearing.* New York: Hart Publishing.

Nesbit, C. R., & Rogers, C. A. (1997). Using cooperative learning to improve reading and science. *Reading and Writing Quarterly, 13*(1), 53–70.

O'Connor, R. E., Jenkins, J. R., Cole, K. N., & Mills, P. E. (1993). Two approaches to reading instruction with children with disabilities: Does program design make a difference? *Exceptional Children, 59,* 312–323.

Orange County Public Schools. (n.d.). *Florida performance measurement system.* Retrieved January 2004 from www.ocps.k12.fl.us.

Ornstein, A., & Hunkins, F. (1998). *Curriculum: Foundations, principles, and issues* (3rd ed.). Boston: Allyn & Bacon.

Ornstein, R. (1980). *Institute brochure.* Los Altos, CA: Institute for the Study of Human Knowledge.

Palincsar, A., Collins, K., & Marano, N. (2000). Investigation of the engagement and learning of students with learning disabilities in guided inquiry science teaching. *Learning, Speech, and Hearing Services in Schools, 31*(3), 240–251.

Papert, S. (2002). Seymour Papert on project-based learning. *Edutopia.* Retrieved September 22, 2005, from www.edutopia.org./php/interview.php?id=Art 901.

Parkerson, J. A. (1999). *Knowledge base: The facilitative teacher.* Retrieved October 30, 2002, from http://www.methodist.edu/education/facilitative.htm.

Parnes, Sidney (Ed). (1992). *Source book for creative problem solving.* Buffalo, NY: Creative Education Foundation.

Paul, R., & Elder, L. (2003). *How to study and learn a discipline.* Dillon Beach, CA: Foundation for Critical Thinking.

Paul, R., & Elder, L. (2004). The elements of critical thinking. Dillard, CA: Foundation for Critical Thinking. Retrieved July 21, 2004, from www.criticalthinking.org.

Pearce, C. (1999). *Nurturing science: Real science for the elementary classroom.* Portsmouth, NH: Heinemann.

Perkins, D. (1991). Educating for insight. *Educational Leadership, 49*(2), 4–8.

Perkins, D. (1995). *Outsmarting IQ: The emerging science of learnable intelligence.* New York: Free Press.

Perko, F. M. (1984, April 23–27). *Mastery learning in historical perspective.* Paper presented at the Annual Meeting of the American Educational Research Association, New Orleans, LA.

Peters, T. (1994). *The pursuit of wow! Every person's guide to topsy-turvy times.* New York: Vantage Books.

Plucker, J. (2002). *History of influences in the development of intelligences theory and testing.* Retrieved September 22, 2005, from Indiana University: www.indiana.edu/%7Eintell/carroll.shtml.

Pogrow, S. (1988). Teaching thinking skills to at-risk elementary students. *Educational Leadership, 45*(7), 79–85.

Polya, G. (1957). *How to solve it* (2nd. ed.). Princeton NJ: Princeton University Press.

Pontius, J., Dilts, R., & Bartlett, A. (Eds.) (2000). *Farmer field schools to community IPM: Ten years of IPM training in Asia.* Jakarta, Indonesia: IPM Programme.

Popham, W. J. (1999). *Classroom assessment: What teachers need to know* (2nd ed.). Boston: Allyn & Bacon.

Presseisen, B. (1991). Thinking skills: Meanings and models revisited. In A. Costa (Ed.), *Developing minds: A resource book for teaching thinking* (rev. ed., pp. 56–62). Alexandria, VA: Association for Supervision and Curriculum Development.

Pressley, M., Levin, J. R., & Delaney, H. D. (1982). The mnemonic keyword method. *Review of Educational Research, 52*(1), 61–91.

Ravitch, D. (2001). As American as public school: Introduction. In S. Bernard & S. Mondale (Eds.), *School: The story of American public education.* (pp. 63–70). Boston: Beacon Press.

Reaves, G. (2001). A nation at risk? In S. Bernard & S. Mondale (Eds.), *School: The story of American public education.* (pp. 183–213). Boston: Beacon Press.

Reeder, E. (2002). Measuring what counts: Memory vs. understanding. *Edutopia.* Retrieved October 30, 2002, from www.edutopia.org/php/article.php?id=Art 940.

Reilly, R. R., & Lewis, E. L. (1983). *Educational psychology: Applications for classroom learning and instruction.* New York: Macmillan.

Riley, K. (2002). *Schools behind barbed wire: The untold story of wartime internment and the children of arrested enemy aliens.* Lanham, MD: Rowman & Littlefield.

Rink, E., & Tricker, R. (2003). Resiliency-based research and adolescent health behaviors. *Prevention Researcher, 10*(1), 1–4.

Rogers, C. (1945). Signifigant aspects of client-centered therapy. *American Psychologist, 1,* 415–422.

Rogers, C. R. (1961). *On becoming a person.* Boston: Houghton Mifflin.

Rogers, C. R. (1969). *Freedom to learn: A view of what education might become.* Columbus, OH: Merrill.

Rogers, C. R. (1980). *A way of being.* Boston: Houghton Mifflin.

Rogers, C. R, Stevens, B., Gendlin, E., Shlien, J. M., & Van Dusen, W. (1967). *Person to person: The problem of being human.* Lafayette, CA: Real People Press.

Rosenshine, B. (1983). Teaching functions in instructional programs. *Elementary School Journal, 83*(4), 335–351.

Rosenshine, B. (1987). Explicit teaching. In D. Berliner & B. Rosenshine (Eds.), *Talks to teachers* (pp. 75–92). New York: Random House.

Rosenshine, B., & Stevens, R. (1986). Teaching functions. In M. C. Wittrock (Ed.), *Handbook of research on teaching* (3rd ed , pp. 376–391). New York: Macmillan.

Ross, M. R., Powell, S. R., & Elias, M. J. (2002). New roles for school psychologists: Addressing the social and emotional learning needs of students. *School Psychology Review, 31*(1), 43–53.

Ross, S. (1983). Increasing meaningfulness of quantitative material by adapting context to student background. *Journal of Educational Psychology, 75,* 519–529.

Rowan, J. (2002). The person-centered approach. *Journal of Humanistic Psychology Online, November.* Retrieved November 13, 2002, from http://ahpweb.org/articles/rogers.html.

Rowe, M. B. (1978). *Teaching science as continuous inquiry: A basic.* New York: McGraw-Hill.

Rowe, M. B. (1987). Using wait time to stimulate inquiry. In W. W. Wilen (Ed.), *Questions, questioning techniques, and effective teaching* (pp. 95–106). Washington, DC: National Education Association.

Sapp, D. A. (2000). Problem-based learning in the first-year composition classroom: Two cases. *PBL Insight, 5*(1), 10–15.

Satterly, D. (1981). *Assessments in schools.* Oxford, UK: Basil Blackwell.

Saul, W., Reardon, J., Pearce, C., Dieckman, D., & Neutze, D. (2002). *Science workshop: reading, writing, and thinking like a scientist.* Portsmouth, NH: Heinemann.

Saylor, J. G. (1982). *Who planned the curriculum? A curriculum plans reservoir model with historical examples.* West Lafayette, IN: Kappa Delta Pi.

Scarcella, R., & Crookall, D. (1990). Simulation/gaming and language acquisition. In D. Crookall & R. L. Oxford (Eds.), *Simulation, gaming, and language learning* (pp. 223–230). New York: Newbury House.

Scarcella, R., & Oxford, R. L. (1992). *The tapestry of language learning.* Boston: Heinle & Heinle.

Schank, R. C., Fano, A., Bell, B., & Jona, M. (1994). The design of goal-based scenarios. *Journal of the Learning Sciences, 3*(4), 305–345.

Schlechty, P. C. (1997). *Inventing better schools.* San Francisco: Jossey-Bass.

Schlesinger, A. (1998). *The disuniting of America: Reflections on a multicultural society.* New York: WW Norton.

Scott, L. U., & Heller, P. (1991). Team work works. *Science Teacher, 58*(1), 24–28.

Shaftel, G., & Shaftel, F. (1967). *Role-playing for social values: Decision-making in the social studies.* Englewood Cliffs, NJ: Prentice Hall.

Shane, H. G. (1981). Significant writings that have influenced the curriculum: 1906–1981. *Phi Delta Kappan, 63,* 311–314.

Simpson, B. J. (1966). The classification of educational objectives: Psychomotor domain. *Illinois Journal of Home Economics, 10*(4), 110–144.

Skaalvik, E. M., & Skaalvik, S. (2002). Internal and external frames of reference for academic self-concept. *Educational Psychologist, 37*(4), 233–244.

Skehan, P. (1998). *A cognitive approach to language learning.* Oxford, UK: Oxford University Press.

Slavin, R. E. (1981). Synthesis of research on cooperative learning. *Educational Leadership, 38*(8), 655–658.

Slavin, R. E. (1986). *Using student team learning.* Baltimore: Johns Hopkins University.

Slavin, R. E. (1987). Mastery learning reconsidered. *Review of Educational Research, 57*(2), 175–213.

Slavin, R. E. (1990). *Cooperative learning: Theory, research, and practice.* Englewood Cliffs, NJ: Prentice Hall.

Slavin, R. E., Karweit, N. L., & Wasik, B. A. (Eds.). (1994). *Preventing early school failure: Research, policy, and practice.* Boston: Allyn & Bacon.

Smith, M. K. (2001). Paulo Freire. *Informal education encyclopedia.* Retrieved October 31, 2002, from www.infed.org/thinkers/et-freir.htm.

Smith, M. K. (2002). Carl Rogers, core conditions, and education. *Informal education encyclopedia.* Retrieved October 31, 2002, from http://www.infed.org/thinkers/et-rogers.htm.

Snyder, S. (2003, February 28). A blueprint for better schools. *Philadelphia Inquirer.* Retrieved March 2, 2003, from www.philly.com/mld/inquirer/living/education/5280754.htm.

Spandel, V., & Culham, R. (1995). *Writing from the inside out: Revising for quality.* Portland, OR: Northwest Regional Educational Laboratory.

Sprenger, M. (1999). *Learning and memory: The brain in action.* Alexandria, VA: Association for Supervision and Curriculum Development.

Sprinthall, R., & Sprinthall, N. (1987). *Educational psychology: A developmental approach.* Reading, MA: Addison-Wesley.

Sternberg, R. (1988). *The triarchic mind: A new theory of intelligence.* New York: Viking Press.

Suchman, J. R. (1966). *Developing inquiry.* Chicago: Science Research Associates.

Suchman, J. R. (1968). *Inquiry development program: Teacher's guide.* Chicago: Science Research Associates.

Sylwester, R. (1995). *A celebration of neurons.* Alexandria, VA: Association for Supervision and Curriculum Development.

Taba, H. (1971). *A teacher's handbook to elementary school social studies.* Reading, MA: Addison-Wesley.

Tang, J. (1991). Findings from observational studies of collaborative work. *International Journal of Man-Machine Studies, 34*(2), 143–160.

Tennyson, R. D., & Cocchiarella, M. (1986). An empirically based instructional design theory for teaching concepts. *Review of Educational Research, 56*(1), 40–71.

Thompson, A. (1998). The adult and the curriculum. *Philosophy of Education Society Yearbook, 1998.* Retrieved September 22, 2005, from http://www.ed.uiuc.edu/EPS/PES-Yearbook/1998/thompson.html.

Thornburg, D. (2002). *The new basics: Education and the future of work in the telematic age.* Alexandria, VA: ASCD.

Tomlinson, C. A. (2005). *How to differentiate instruction in mixed-ability classrooms* (2nd ed.). Upper Saddle River, NJ: Pearson Education.

Torrance, E. P. (1966). *Torrance tests of creative thinking.* Bensenville, IL: Scholastic Testing.

Townsend, B. (2003). Q and A: Interview with University of South Florida professor Brenda Townsend. *Curriculum Review, 42*(6), 14–16.

Treicher, D. G. (1967). Are you missing the boat in training aids? *Film and AV Communications, 1, 14–16.*

Tyler, R. (1949). *Basic principles of curriculum and instruction.* Chicago: University of Chicago Press.

U.S. Census Bureau. (2003). *Statistical abstract of the United States: 2003.* Washington, DC: U.S. Census Bureau. Retrieved April 20, 2004, from www.census.gov.

U.S. Department of Education. (1994). *Goals 2000: Educate America Act.* Retrieved from www.ed.gov/legislation/Goals 2000/TheAct.

U.S. Department of Education, National Center for Education Statistics. (2003). *The condition of education 2003* (NCES 2003–67). Washington, DC: Government Printing Office.

University of Central Florida, College of Education. (2004). *Personal attributes.* Retrieved January 2004, from http://pegasus.cc.ucf.edu/~curinst.

Ury, W. L. (2002). *Must we fight?* San Francisco: Jossey-Bass.

Van Ments, M. (1983). *The effective use of role-play: A handbook for teachers and trainers.* London: Kogan Page.

van Zee, E. (2000). Analysis of student-generated inquiry discussions. *International Journal of Science Education, 22*(2), 115–142.

van Zee, E., Iwasyk, M., Kurose, A., Simpson, D., & Wild, J. (2001). Student and teacher questioning during conversations about science. *Journal of Research in Science Teaching, 38*(2), 159–190.

Vavrus, M. (1999). *Teaching for freedom: Carl Rogers and Maxine Greene.* Retrieved October 31, 2002, from http://192.211.16.13/curricular/PE/Rogers.htm.

Walberg, H. J. (1985). Examining the theory, practice, and outcomes of mastery learning. In D. U. Levine (Ed.), *Improving student achievement through mastery learning program* (pp. 1–10). San Francisco: Jossey-Bass.

Walberg, H. J. (1988). Responses to Slavin: What's the best evidence? *Educational Leadership, 46*(2), 28.

Wallace, R., Krajcik, J., & Soloway, E. (1996). An opportunity for inquiry. *D-lib magazine.* Retrieved from http://www.dlib.org/dlib/september96/umdl/09wallace.html#Part1.

Warmoth, A. (2002). *Carl Rogers' values and the Native American M.A. program.* Retrieved October 23, 2002, from http://www.saybrook.edu/crr/papers/warmoth.html.

Washburne, C. W. (1922). Educational measurement as a key to individualizing instruction and promotions. *Journal of Educational Research, 5,* 195–206.

Wehmeyer, M. L., Agran, M., & Hughes, C. (1998). *Teaching self-determination to students with disabilities.* Baltimore: Paul H. Brookes.

Weissbourd, R. P. (2003). Moral teachers, moral students. *Educational Leadership, 60*(6), 6–11.

Weissburg, R. P., Resnik, H., Payton, J., & O'Brien, M. U. (2003). Evaluating social and emotional learning programs. *Educational Leadership, 60*(6), 46–50.

White, W. A. T. (1988). A meta-analysis of the effects of direct instruction in special education. *Education and Treatment of Children, 11*(4), 364–374.

Whiting, B., & Render, G. F. (1987). Cognitive and affective outcomes of mastery learning: A review of sixteen semesters. *The Clearing House, 60*(6), 276–280.

Wilen, W., Ishler, M., Hutchison, J., & Kindsvatter, R. (2000). *Dynamics of effective teaching* (4th ed.). New York: Addison-Wesley/Longman.

William Glasser Institute. (2005). *Choice theory.* Retrieved September 15, 2005, from www.wglasser.com/whatisct.htm.

Wolfe, P. S. (2001). *Brain matters: Translating research into classroom practice.* Alexandria, VA: Association for Supervision of Curriculum and Development.

Wolfe, P. S., & Hall, T. E. (2003). Making inclusion a reality for students with severe disabilities. *TEACHING Exceptional Children, 35*(4), 56–61.

Wong, H., & Wong, R. (1998). *The first days of school.* Mountainview, CA: Harry Wong Publications.

Wood, E., Woloshyn, V., & Willoughby, T. (1995). *Cognitive strategy instruction for middle and high schools.* Cambridge, MA: Brookline Books.

Wright, J., & Wright, C. (1985). Personalized verbal problems: An application of language experience approach. *Journal of Educational Research, 79,* 358–362.

Yager, S., Johnson, R., & Johnson, D. (1985). Oral discussion, group-to-group individual transfer, and achievement in cooperative learning groups. *Journal of Educational Psychology, 77,* 50–66.

Zehr, M. A. (2003, March 19). Finding a way out. *Education Week.* Retrieved March 18, 2003, from http://edweek.org/ew/ew_printstory.cfm?slug=27nativity.h22.

Zimmer, B., & Alexander, G. (2000, May). Using Carl Rogers' communication principles to facilitate mutually supported learning online. *Online Tutoring Skills,* May 2000, 41–46.

Zimring, F. (1994). Carl Rogers (1902–1987). *Prospects, 24*(3/4), 411–422.

Zins, J. E., Weissburg, R. P., Wang, M. C., & Walburg, H. J. (2001). Socio-emotional learning and school success. *CEIC Review, 10*(6), 1–5.

Index

About the Authors

Larry C. Holt is Associate Professor at the University of Central Florida in the Department of Educational Studies. He received a bachelor's degree from Warren Wilson College, master's degree from Ball State University, and holds a doctorate in education from the University of Cincinnati. His research interests include general methods, presentation techniques, and student learning, middle-level education, and technology. His first book, *Cooperative Learning in Action,* was published by the National Middle School Association. His second book, *Teach Me, I Dare You,* will be published in 2006. He was a Fulbright scholar to the country of Lithuania in 1997–98.

Marcella L. Kysilka is Professor Emerita in the College of Education at the University of Central Florida. She received a bachelor's degree from The Ohio State University, a master's degree from Kent State University, and a doctorate in curriculum and instruction from the University of Texas at Austin. Kysilka has held many leadership roles in professional organizations: She has served as president of Kappa Delta Pi; editor of *The Educational Forum;* member of the board of directors and Leadership Council of the Association for Supervision and Curriculum Development; associate editor of the *Journal for Curriculum and Supervision;* president of the Florida Association for Supervision and Curriculum Development; president of the International Study Association for Teachers and Teaching; and executive secretary of the American Association for Curriculum and Teaching. She currently serves as editor of the *Florida Educational Leadership* journal.

She has published more than 60 journal articles and eight books. While at the University of Central Florida, she served as a full professor in the Educational Studies Department, associate dean of academic affairs, director of educational research, assistant chair to the Educational Studies Department, and coordinator of the curriculum and instruction doctoral program. She is currently a consultant with P.A.C.E. High School in Cincinnati, Ohio, a school for underachieving inner-city students, and teaches part time at the College of Mount St. Joseph.